THE NATIONS OF BRITAIN

THE NATIONS OF BRITAIN

Christopher G. A. Bryant

OXFORD

UNIVERSITY PRESS

OXFORD
UNIVERSITY PRESS

Great Clarendon Street, Oxford OX2 6DP

Oxford University Press is a department of the University of Oxford.
It furthers the University's objective of excellence in research, scholarship,
and education by publishing worldwide in

Oxford New York

Auckland Cape Town Dar es Salaam Hong Kong Karachi
Kuala Lumpur Madrid Melbourne Mexico City Nairobi
New Delhi Shanghai Taipei Toronto

With offices in

Argentina Austria Brazil Chile Czech Republic France Greece
Guatemala Hungary Italy Japan Poland Portugal Singapore
South Korea Switzerland Thailand Turkey Ukraine Vietnam

Oxford is a registered trademark of Oxford University Press
in the UK and in certain other countries

Published in the United States
by Oxford University Press Inc., New York

British Library Cataloguing in Publication Data

Data available

Library of Congress Cataloging in Publication Data

Data available

ISBN 0-19-874287-8   978-0-19-874287-6

1 3 5 7 9 10 8 6 4 2

Typeset by Laserwords Private Limited, Chennai, India

Printed in Great Britain
on acid-free paper by
Ashford Colour Press Ltd, Gosport, Hampshire

For Oliver and Tom

PREFACE AND ACKNOWLEDGEMENTS

Anyone writing on the nations of Britain has to engage with literatures in more disciplines than his or her own. In my own case I have had to go beyond sociology to history, political science, anthropology, cultural studies, and law. No doubt I have got a lot of things wrong but I have pressed on in the hope that broad coverage of so topical a matter might be of value to concerned citizens as well as academic specialists and their students. I would like readers to consider all the chapters—Britain as a whole—but I know that sometimes they will have a special interest in one of the nations of Britain and have therefore chosen to give the references for each chapter at its end.

It is a pleasure to thank publicly Graham Day, Leo Hickey, Lynn Jamieson, David McCrone, Gareth Rees, Brian Roberts, and Jon Tonge for their written comments on papers and draft chapters. Whether I have responded wisely is another matter and responsibility for this book is mine alone. I am grateful for help of other kinds from Richard Knowles, Andy Mycock, and Gareth Williams. I must also thank the University of Salford for allowing me sabbatical leave to work on the book in 2003–4.

I have particular debts to undergraduate political sociology students at the University of Salford and postgraduate political sociology students at the Central European University in Warsaw who challenged my thinking about Britain in many ways, to John Scott who suggested that I write this book in the first place and who then waited patiently, as did Oxford University Press, when it took me so long to do it, and to my wife Lizzie who encouraged me to persist even when the scale of the undertaking made damaging inroads on our leisure time and social life.

Figure 1.1 (A hierarchy of Welsh identity), is reprinted from Richard Jenkins, *Rethinking Ethnicity* (1997), with the permission of Sage Publications. Table 5.2 (National identity in England: an alternative measure, 1997 and 1999), is reprinted from, and Table 5.3 (English political attitudes 1999), is derived from tables in, John Curtice and Anthony Heath, 'Is the English lion about to roar?' in Roger Jowell et al. (eds.), *British Social Attitudes: the 17th Report* (2000) with the permission of Sage Publications. Table 6.1

(Identification with the regional level in British regions), is reprinted from Neil Ward and John Tomaney, 'Regionalism in the East of England', in John Tomaney and John Mawson (eds.), *England: The State of the Regions* (2002), with the permission of The Policy Press, University of Bristol. There are instances where we have been unable to trace or contact the copyright holder. If notified the publisher will be pleased to rectify any errors or omissions at the earliest opportunity.

Chris Bryant
Salford
March 2005

CONTENTS

LIST OF TABLES   xi

LIST OF FIGURES   xi

LIST OF MAPS   xi

1   Introduction: Thinking about the Union and its Future   1

    Britain in question   1

    Nations, nation-states, and nationalisms   12

2   Great Britain: The Post-Imperial Dilemma   33

    Imperial Britain   33

    Post-imperial Britain: first thoughts   42

    National and regional differences   45

    Can Britain be reforged?   57

3   Claiming Scotland   62

    Introduction   62

    1   Independent Scotland   67

    2   Civil Scotland   80

    3   Scotland in the Empire   89

    4   Little Scotland   90

    5   Scotland: civic and self-governing   92

    6   Scotland in Europe   107

    Conclusions   109

4   Voicing Wales   117

    Introduction   117

    1   Y Fro Gymraeg   126

    2   Labour Wales   135

    3   Anglo-British Wales   138

    4   Cymru-Wales   140

5 Modern Wales   146

6 Conclusions   149

5 Speaking for England   **157**

Introduction   157

1 English England   161

2 Anglo-British England   182

3 Little England   188

4 Cosmopolitan England   191

Conclusions   200

6 The English Regions: Who Cares?   **209**

Introduction   209

Regions, regional development agencies, and regional
assemblies   211

The North-East: a region conscious of itself   217

London: world city, metropolis, and region   221

Cornwall: nation, region, or county?   226

Conclusions: our regions, your choice   230

6 Britain: Relating to Others   **239**

Introduction   239

Ireland   239

The Commonwealth   255

The European Union   258

British citizenship   274

8 Conclusions: Britain and the Future   **284**

Contemporary constructions of Britain   284

Devolution, federalism, and asymmetry   288

Britishness in the twenty-first century   293

Index   **299**

LIST OF TABLES

1.1	National identity by country: 1992, 1997, 1999, 2001, and 2003	5
1.2	National identity by country (%): GHS 2001	7
1.3	Contemporary constructions of nation	27
2.1	The UK population: Censuses of 1801–2001 (millions, and England, Wales, and Scotland as % of GB)	49
2.2	Economic trends by nation and English region	53
2.3	Total identifiable expenditure on services by nation and English region (index)	54
2.4	Distribution of UK parliamentary seats by country and average electorate in 2003	56
3.1	Contemporary constructions of Scotland by time and place	65
3.2	Types of Scot	97
4.1	Contemporary constructions of Wales by time and place	125
5.1	Contemporary constructions of England by time and place	159
5.2	National identity in England: an alternative measure, 1997 and 1999	161
5.3	English political attitudes, 1999	162
6.1	Identification with the regional level in British Regions	213
7.1	Turnout in elections to the European Parliament, 1979–2004 (%)	269
7.2	British and comparator attitudes to Europe, 2004 (%)	270
8.1	Contemporary constructions of Britain by time and place	285

LIST OF FIGURES

1.1	A hierarchy of Welsh identity	28
1.2	Hierarchies of British identity	29

LIST OF MAPS

1.1	Britain with borders and capitals	xii
1.2	The English regions	208

MAP 1.1   **Britain with borders and capitals**

SCOTLAND

Edinburgh

B   B: Berwick finally to
England 1482

ENGLAND

WALES

M/G

M/G: Monmouthshire/Gwent
returned to Wales 1974   Cardiff   London ●

1

Introduction: Thinking about the Union and its Future

Britain in question

Is Britain an old nation with more than a thousand years of history? Or is Britain 'an invented nation, not so much older than the United States' as Peter Scott (1990: 168) claims. After all, the union of England and Scotland dates only from 1707, just seven decades before the American declaration of independence in 1776. And is Britain a nation-state (one nation and one state) as many politicians and citizens routinely suppose, or is it a union-state (one state uniting four nations, England, Scotland, Wales, and (part of) Ireland), or is it both (one state but five nations with Britain itself the overarching fifth nation)? Then again, is Britain just the first expansion of England, and the British Empire the second? Or is the making of Britain better regarded as an imperial project in which Scotland, in particular, but also Ireland and Wales, played major parts in the creation of the biggest empire the world has ever seen, albeit one whose time has long passed? And given that it has passed, is Britain today a post-imperial country without a *raison d'être*? Should we now expect 'the break-up of Britain' which Tom Nairn (1977) heralded more than a quarter of a century ago? Indeed, is devolution to Scotland and Wales a step towards that outcome? Or does Britain, albeit a post-imperial Britain, still have a future, perhaps a multicultural future? Was Britain a unitary state before devolution, and what is it now after devolution? Is it becoming a federal state without declaring itself as such? And *is* Britain now multicultural, and, if it is, does that mean it was unicultural before or has it always been multicultural, albeit in different ways at different times? In short, what does being British today consist of? Are there alternative ways of being British? Is there one version of Britain—and of England, of Scotland and of Wales—with which citizens can engage or which they can rework, or are there several? If Britain, England, Scotland and Wales are 'imagined communities', as Benedict Anderson (1983) would suggest, are they each imaginable in one way only or in many? Are there alternative constructions of each, alternative ways in which we can represent them to ourselves and to others abroad? And how is Britain defined by its relation to Others? In particular, what bearing do relations with Ireland, the Commonwealth, and the European Union have on versions of Britain and its constituent parts? Finally, in trying to formulate answers to constitutional questions, might there not be lessons available from abroad—in particular from Canada and Quebec, and Spain and Catalonia? Directly and indirectly, this book offers answers to many of these questions and supplies information and argument relevant to all of them. It is addressed not only to social scientists and their students, but also to fellow citizens contemplating the future of Britain (who are asked to bear with the copious referencing professional social scientists require).

(Great) Britain refers to England, Scotland, and Wales as a whole. According to Gwyn Williams (1991: 1) the practice of naming the whole island Britain and the people who live on it Britons began with the Romans who called the island Britannia and the people Britanni, names in turn derived from those used by the Celtic inhabitants. (The Greeks had called the island Albion, a name derived, in the sixth century BC, from the Irish name for the neighbouring island.) The popular belief, in England at least, that Britain (the country not the island) has a thousand years of history is misleading. There were ancient Britons, there was Roman Britain (which did not include most of what was to be come Scotland), and there were Britons (people speaking Brittonic languages) after the Romans left, but the possibility of Britain as a single political community dates only from 1603 when James VI of Scotland succeeded to the English throne on the death of Elizabeth I. He preferred the title James I of Great Britain but his hope that the union of the crowns would be swiftly followed by a union of the parliaments was frustrated by opposition in both countries. James therefore reigned as James VI of Scotland and James I of England with a parliament in Edinburgh and another at Westminster. His own move to London, however, signalled to everyone, including ambitious Scots, where the greater power lay. Throughout the seventeenth century any sense of Britain as a political community was very weak, and as a nation was non-existent. Great Britain came into being only in 1707 with the union of the two states, the closure of the parliament in Edinburgh and the inclusion of Scottish lords and commoners in the parliament at Westminster. Great Britain is not much older than the United States of America.

Northern Ireland, the residue of the union of Great Britain and Ireland in 1801, is an extension of the British state beyond Britain itself. The Unionist majority in Northern Ireland considers itself British, but the nationalist minority does not. References to Britain, Britons, and British in this book only include (the Unionist community in) Northern Ireland where the context makes that explicit. It is anachronistic to refer to Britain and Ireland as the British Isles. Ireland (Ierne to the Greeks, derived again from the Irish, Hibernia to the Romans) was only British when it was a British possession, or from the proclamation of the United Kingdom of Great Britain and Ireland in 1801—the origin of the 'United Kingdom'—incorporated within the union itself. The separation of twenty-six of the thirty-two counties of Ireland from the United Kingdom began with the establishment of the Irish Free State in 1922 and ended in 1949 with the departure from the Commonwealth of what was from that year the Republic of Ireland.[1] There is no reference to Wales in the full name of the United Kingdom, or representation of Wales in the Royal Standard or the Union Flag (the 'Union Jack'), because Wales had been neither a kingdom nor a state before it was incorporated within the English system of government, public administration, and law between 1536 and 1542. (The preamble to the 1536 act, which acquired the name 'act of union' only in Victorian times, refers to 'annexation'.)

The 'Great' in Great Britain does not indicate some official claim to greatness but rather distinguishes Britain from Britanny (Grande Bretagne from Bretagne in French). Celts from Devon and Cornwall began an emigration to Armorica in north-west 'France' in 460 which continued for two centuries. The reasons for it are not entirely clear. Threats to their lands from Saxon (and Irish) invaders have been suggested, but the migration seems to have been underway well before the threat was great. Philip Payton (2004: 61) suggests that the pull factor of underpopulated lands in Armorica may have been more important. Whatever the reason Britons from Cornwall were, by the middle of the sixth century, calling their new homeland Breten Vyghan, Little Britain; in French these Britons became Bretons and Breten became Bretagne (ibid.).

The United Kingdom of Great Britain and Northern Ireland, to give it its full name, has, under the Labour government elected in 1997, embarked on large-scale constitutional changes. Of these, Scottish devolution from 1999 is the most significant, but Welsh devolution from 1999, a new settlement in Northern Ireland (the Good Friday Agreement) in 1998, an elected mayor and assembly for London from 2000, and the establishment of English regional development agencies in 1999 all have their varying importance. There has also been a proposal, now in abeyance, for English regional assemblies. These reforms are taking place, moreover, within the larger context of moves towards the 'ever closer European union' anticipated in the Treaty of Rome to which the UK became a signatory in 1973, the enlargement of the European Union from 2004 to include eight post-communist and two other new members, and the proposed adoption of an EU constitution to give the potentially unwieldy union a better chance of working effectively. Before 1997 there had been protracted and extensive debate about national identities in Scotland, Wales, and Northern Ireland. It is hardly surprising that there has since also been a debate about national identity in England which extends far beyond the question of Britain's relation to the EU.

Anyone still wondering why the new Labour government elected in 1997 should have embarked on constitutional changes in Britain should look closely at Table 1.1 which sets out responses to the 'Moreno question' about alternative or dual national identities. The question is so-called after its use by Luis Moreno, a Catalan studying in Edinburgh who was familiar with the issue of Spanish and/or Catalan identity (cf. Moreno and Arriba 1996). When the peoples of England, Scotland, and Wales are asked to specify their national identity there are clear differences in the claims each makes with respect to Britishness or the lack thereof. The key finding in 1997 was this: almost two-thirds of those living in Scotland declared that they were Scottish not British, or more Scottish than British, whilst only a quarter of those resident in England made a similar claim about their Englishness. Welsh residents were midway between the two. Conversely more than two-thirds of respondents in England said they were equally British and English, more British than English, or British not English. By comparison, half the respondents in Scotland made the equivalent claim. Again respondents in Wales came between the two. Following devolution the number of Scottish residents saying they are Scottish not British has gone up from nearly a quarter

TABLE 1.1 National identity by country: 1992, 1997, 1999, 2001, and 2003

1992 and 1997: 'We are interested to know how people living in England/Wales/Scotland see themselves in terms of their national identity. Which of these statements best describes how you regard yourself?'

1999, 2001, and 2003: 'Some people think of themselves first as British. Others may think of themselves first as English, Welsh or Scottish. Which, if any, of the following best describes how you see yourself?'

X = British, English, Welsh, Scottish (%)

	England					Wales					Scotland				
	92	97	99	01	03	92	97	99	01	03	92	97	99	01	03
1. X not British	16	7	17	17	17	28	13	17	24	21	37	23	32	36	31
2. More X than British	12	17	15	13	19	20	29	19	23	27	27	38	35	30	34
3. Equally X and British	43	45	37	42	31	30	26	36	28	29	25	27	22	24	22
4. More British than X	10	14	11	9	13	7	10	7	11	8	4	4	3	3	4
5. British not X	15	9	14	11	10	14	15	14	11	9	5	4	4	3	4
6. None of these	3	7	7	8	10	1	7	7	3	6	2	4	4	4	5
Rows 1 + 2 ('A')	28	24	32	30	36	48	42	36	47	48	64	61	67	66	65
Rows 3 + 4 + 5	68	68	62	62	54	51	51	57	50	46	34	35	29	30	30
Rows 4 + 5 ('B')	25	23	21	20	23	21	25	21	22	17	9	8	7	6	8
A: B where B = 1	1.1	1.0	1.5	1.5	1.6	2.3	1.7	1.7	2.1	2.8	7.1	7.6	9.6	11.0	8.1

Sources: 1992 Rowntree Survey; 1997 British Election Survey; 1999 British Election Survey; 1999 British Social Attitudes Survey, Scottish Parliamentary Election Study, Welsh Assembly Election Study; 2001, 2003 British and Scottish Social Attitudes Surveys, Welsh Life and Times Surveys.

in 1997 to nearly a third in 2003, the number of Welsh residents saying they are Welsh not British, has risen from nearly an eighth to more than a fifth, and the number of English residents saying they are English not British, has doubled to nearly a sixth. The proportion declaring they were equally British, more British, or only British has fallen most sharply in England from over two-thirds to a bit more than half. Despite falls, the proportions remain substantial in Wales at a bit less than half and in Scotland at a bit less than a third. Comparing 1997 with 2003, the ratio of those saying they were English only or more English than British, to those saying they were more British or only British, went up from 1.0 to 1.6 : 1 while the equivalent Welsh figure went up from 1.7 to 2.8 : 1, and the much more striking Scottish figure went up from 7.6 to 8.1 : 1. In sum, England, Wales, and Scotland have different national profiles. Devolution has been accompanied by a weakening of Britishness and a strengthening of Scottishness, Welshness, and Englishness, but the changes have neither been large nor entirely consistent from survey year to survey year and even in Scotland there remains majority acknowledgement of Britishness to some degree. Answers to the Moreno question certainly do not (yet) point to the future break-up of Britain although they do indicate that young Scots and Welsh are more likely to disclaim Britishness than their elderly compatriots.

The government's General Household Survey introduced a question on national identity in 2001.[2] Respondents were asked to choose one or more identities from the following list: British, English, Scottish, Welsh, Irish, Other. The responses are given in Table 1.2. They are consistent with responses to the Moreno question in Table 1.1. Nearly half the people in Britain and in England gave British as an identity compared with little more than a third in Wales and a quarter in Scotland. Conversely 80 per cent of the people in Scotland gave Scottish as an identity compared with 62 per cent of those in Wales giving Welsh and 57 per cent of those in England giving English. Three other details are worth early comment. First, the English born in Scotland are, according to the 2001 census, 8 per cent of the total. Scots habitually refer to all Britons from England as English; Table 1.2 suggests only half of them choose to identify themselves as English, others opting for British. Second, about a fifth of the population of Wales identifies itself as English, a very significant proportion given the importance in Wales of issues of language and culture but also an under-researched one. Third, the 6 per cent of the population choosing an Other identity includes 19 per cent in

TABLE 1.2	National identity by country (%): GHS 2001			
	Britain	England	Wales	Scotland
British	46	48	35	27
English	51	57	19	4
Scottish	9	2	1	80
Welsh	4	1	62	0
Irish	2	2	0	1
Other	5	6	3	2

Source: National Statistics Living in Britain 2001, table 3.18 (part).

London in contrast to 5 per cent in the South-East and the West Midlands and lower percentages elsewhere.

Interestingly John Curtice (2003: 9) has reported findings from the 2001 British and Scottish Social Attitudes Surveys on 'feelings towards flags in England and Scotland' which are again consistent with responses to the Moreno question on national identity. Fifty-nine per cent of people in England felt very proud or a bit proud on seeing the Union Jack compared with 31 per cent in Scotland. Conversely 71 per cent in Scotland felt similarly proud on seeing the Saltire of St Andrew compared with 40 per cent in England on seeing the Cross of St George.

Differences in self-declared national identity may turn out to be less amenable to change than some Scottish and Welsh nationalists would like but the difference between Scotland on the one hand and England and Wales on the other is big enough and enduring enough to pose problems for any British government. Whether the devolution enacted by the current British government is the best way of addressing them is open to debate, but it would have been hard to defend doing nothing.

Perceived differences with respect to national identity, ethnic composition, economic interests, political values, and cultural forms between England, Scotland, and Wales have persuaded many recent commentators that Britain's days are numbered. It is no surprise that Tom Nairn, a supporter of Scottish independence who wrote The Break-Up of Britain as long ago as 1977, should entitle his latest book After Britain (2000). More telling is the shift in emphasis of Andrew Marr, a Scot who favours the union and now the BBC's political editor. Writing about *Ruling Britannia* in 1995, he allowed that, for all its democratic shortcomings, Britain could have a future and subtitled his book *The Failure and Future of British Democracy* accordingly. By contrast both his BBC television series in the autumn of 1999 and the subsequent book (2000) bore the title *The Day Britain Died*—even if the finality of that death was compromised by the queue of contenders for the day in question. Another journalist, Peter Hitchens, has assailed the liberal project that he holds responsible for *The Abolition of Britain* (1999) and all it stands for since the 1960s. Unsure of the difference between England and Britain, his particular conception of the British nation-state renders him unable even to engage with the case for devolution and unable to see the European Union as anything other than an emergent German-led federal state. Hitchens, a conservative utopian, offers shrewd comment on how Britain came to its current condition but is unable to indicate how it could be returned to its past virtue; all he can do is deplore. By contrast yet another journalist, Simon Heffer, in his *Nor Shall My Sword* (1999), respects the right of the Scots to go their own way if they so choose and calls, as his subtitle puts it, for *The Reinvention of England*. Also from the right, the former Conservative cabinet minister John Redwood has contributed *The Death of Britain?* (1999). His main fear is that the European Union will become a United States of Europe with Scotland, Wales, Northern Ireland, and England, or perhaps the English regions, merely regions of Europe. A devotee of the market, he believes small government is best, so the prospect of more government with ministers in Edinburgh, Cardiff, and Belfast as well as London appals him. His book is meant as a wake-up call to the mass of Britons who, he is confident, still cherish their nation-state but risk losing it. Lacking Hitchens's grasp of twentieth-century British political, economic, and social history, Redwood comes over as an exceptionally quirky national liberal who cannot understand how the current condition of Britain came about, other than to blame Tony Blair, but who also cannot accept that all is lost. His wake-up call seemed to have fallen on deaf ears, but the strong showing of the United Kingdom Independence Party in the 2004 Election to the European Parliament, with 16 per cent of the vote, will have strengthened the resolve of all who share his cause. The best-known contribution to an emergent debate specifically about England has come from the television journalist Jeremy Paxman. His book *The English* (1998) sold more than 300 000 in the first two years alone.

The recent debate about the demise of Britain among social scientists and political commentators addresses nation, state, and nation-state. Most participants at least agree that there has been a British nation, and not just a British state, even if, in their view, there is not one any longer or will not be one for much longer. There are historians, however, for whom Britain was never a nation and only ever a state. Hugh Kearney (1989) provides a particularly interesting example. In the introduction to *The British Isles*, he draws attention to well-known historians who have switched back and forth between England and Britain without any awareness of what they were doing, let alone justification. He also comments how national histories so often project current national boundaries back into the past regardless of whether they then had any relevance. So far, so fair. But it is one thing to reinstate the national histories of Scotland, Wales, and Ireland, and to emphasize their 'Britannic' context, and quite another to adopt the subtitle *A History of Four Nations*—England, Scotland, Wales, and Ireland—without ever allowing the existence of a fifth, Britain. Historians do seem to have had inordinate difficulty in addressing the five-nations possibility. No wonder David Cannadine (1995) has written about 'British history as a "new subject" ' (in a book edited by Alexander Grant and Keith Stringer (1995) with the thoughtful title *Uniting the Kingdom?*). It sometimes seems as if the Whig interpretation of English/British history which 'celebrated parliamentary government, the Common Law, the Church of England, ordered progress towards democracy, and the avoidance of revolution' (Cannadine 1995: 16) has gone into reverse. Where once Whig historians concentrated on what made England/Britain both unique and superior, there are now historians who emphasize the transience of Britain in the longer-term relationships between the peoples of these islands and those of continental Europe. Norman Davies (1999), for example, has quite deliberately called his monumental new history simply *The Isles* (1999).

Social scientists have also been insensitive to national variations within British society. The 1988 first edition of Nicholas Abercrombie and Alan Warde's much used sociology textbook, *Contemporary British Society*, gives no indication that Scotland and Wales might differ from Britain/England in any significant respect. The 'completely revised', 600-page, third edition of 2000 concedes that Scotland is 'very much a separate society' but omits to specify how separation can also mean difference except very briefly in the chapter on the state and politics (p. 17). The treatment of Wales is even more cursory with the Welsh language, the first language of one in five of the people of Wales, not rating a mention. Perhaps the best-known text-book on British politics, Bill Jones et al.'s *Politics UK*, does only a little better. The first edition of 1991 contains occasional references to the Scottish and Welsh nationalists but omits to address how or why Scottish and Welsh politics might be different. There is no mention whatsoever of the Scottish and Welsh Offices and the peculiarity of administrative devolution unaccompanied by political devolution. The 700-page fourth edition of 2001 boasts 'Full coverage of New Labour's first three years' and does at least have a chapter on devolution. This acknowledges that Scotland and Wales have identities of their own but omits to say what institutional, cultural, and economic differences underpin them. In both cases the authors might reply that their textbooks concentrate on structures and processes, but in their insensitivity to national differences they are not untypical of British sociology and political science. In England national variations within Britain have gone largely unnoticed. It could be argued that, although its different measures for Scotland, Wales, Northern Ireland, London, and the English regions do not add up to any consistent design, the new Labour government elected in 1997 at least knew better than most social scientists that it had to do something. When it came to addressing a constitutional future for Britain as a whole, British social scientists had extraordinarily little to offer.

No one can be sure how the constitutional reforms introduced by the new Labour government will work out. In particular, no one can be sure that they will issue in the dissolution of Britain, so why do so many commentators think it likely? This question will be explored at length in Ch. 2, but for the moment a simple answer will suffice. In many eyes Great Britain was basically an imperial project, and a post-imperial Britain that has still not come to terms with its reduced economic, political, and military standing is not worth having. Many of the things that have at different times made Britain distinctive and attractive to its population—such as the Protestant ascendancy, Empire, economic pre-eminence, military might, and the majesty of the monarchy—have either passed into history or no longer work very well. There are Scots, in particular, who argue that Scotland (or rather a Scottish elite) agreed to union in 1707 in expectation of economic advantage, and, after a slow start in the early eighteenth century, union (and Empire) did prove economically advantageous. In the second half of the twentieth century, however, the union ceased to offer economic advantage, leading many to conclude that it was time for Scotland to withdraw and make a different future. In these circumstances, it is understandable that there should have been in Scotland a cultural revival and a reassertion of a national identity. In Wales, too, there have been those who believe that a British government is insensitive to Welsh interests. A renewed pride in Wales has also accompanied a revival in the Welsh language and culture.

Dissociation from Britain is, however, much more problematic for the very many white English who have habitually conflated English and British. It also presents problems for, among others, those black British and Asian British who have come to identify with Britain at a time when many Scots and Welsh no longer do. There is a real sense in which the British Empire made them and they cannot 'revert' from British to English in the way that Scots or Welsh can re-embrace, or better reimagine, their Scottish or Welsh identities. There are also more mixed families of English, Scottish, Welsh, and/or Irish descent in England than elsewhere in the United Kingdom; they too have reason to think of themselves as British. It might well prove easier to take Scotland out of Britain than to take Britain out of England. Dissociation from Britain is also exceedingly problematic for Ulster unionists, even if many identify with a Britain that no longer exists.

Those who still share a national identification with Britain have not had the support of the BBC. In advice given by the BBC to its journalists and programme makers following the establishment of a parliament in Scotland and assemblies in Wales and Northern Ireland, broadcasters have been told, 'Don't talk about "the nation" when you mean "the UK".... The BBC provides programmes and services to people across the United Kingdom. We broadcast to an audience in the **nations** of England, Scotland and Wales' (BBC, 1999: 4–5). Northern Ireland is designated a province (p. 14). In the name of clarity, however, the BBC is disallowing the verbal association of Britain with nation, a practice that would, if there were no other factors at work, help to ensure that Britain ceased to be one. The BBC's world services would thus seem unable to live up to the corporation's own motto, 'Nation shall speak peace unto nation', in so far as the BBC no longer recognizes that there is a British nation to speak for. There is a curious reverse slight in this. For centuries Scots and Welsh have suffered the humiliating references made by people in England and overseas to England and the English where Britain and the British would have been correct. Now those in England and elsewhere in Britain who identify with a British nation and claim British nationality are regarded in some quarters as deluded. The poor fools have not grasped that British is only their state identity.

Tony Blair's call, after the 1997 General Election, for the rebranding of Britain as a 'young country' may have been crass but it is hard to deny that a reconstruction of some sort is necessary if Britain is to endure. Whether there can any longer be enough unity for a British union only time will tell. In the meantime, we can review the arguments and examine the evidence. Accordingly, the chapters that follow look at the historical, and, especially, the contemporary, similarities and differences between Britain as a whole and its constituent parts, and they will connect these to historical, and, especially, contemporary, constructions and representations of Britain, Scotland, Wales, and England as nations. Additional chapters will consider the English regions, and review the relations of Britain and its constituents to Ireland, the Commonwealth, and the European Union. The concluding chapter will return to the politics of representation and the current constitutional reforms. It will acknowledge that the break-up of Britain is certainly a possibility, but it will also assess the prospects for the 'asymmetrical federalism' to which the sum of these reforms might deliver us if nothing else intervenes, and consider comparisons with Canada and Spain. An asymmetrical federalism is one in which different component states or parts have different powers and different relations to the centre. As things currently stand, any such outcome would be the product of typically British muddling through—not design. No one has ever advocated it, nor has it ever figured in public debate.

Nations, nation-states, and nationalisms

Social scientists use concepts in conformity with the conventions of their disciplines and specialities, but they can never succeed in articulating a conceptual vocabulary of their own in complete detachment from political debate about how the social world is and how it could or should be because there is a two-way tie between their concepts and those in ordinary discourse, or what Anthony Giddens (1976) calls the double-hermeneutic.

When formulating their concepts, social scientists have to acknowledge that they draw upon the natural language concepts of ordinary citizens, even as they clarify, refine, amend, or supersede them; and when using their concepts, social scientists have to acknowledge that their usages may feed back into ordinary discourses and practices whether they want them to or not. That feedback potential, if actualized, may or may not amount to much. Actualization may be direct, or, more likely, mediated by pundits, professionals, politicians, or whoever, but the potential for actualization can never be discounted. Social-scientific discourse can therefore never divest itself of moral and political content and consequence. Social scientists thus have a practical interest, actual or potential, in the object of their studies as well as a cognitive one. On occasions it may suit them to adopt what Henry Kariel (1973) calls the 'indicative mode' and play this interest down, but even then they may find themselves drawn into his alternative 'transactional mode' regardless of their intentions. Debates about nations, national identities, and nationalisms are matters that clearly do not exercise just sociologists and political scientists, but are also very much the concern of politicians and citizens and all those who would influence them. Social scientists who address these matters have little chance of confining themselves to the indicative mode. Inevitably the terms of a debate of real political consequence—nation, nation-state, nationalism, ethnicity, sovereignty, federalism, devolution, and many more—are highly contested. This is, after all, a debate that challenges the taken-for-granted and gets down to fundamentals. David Easton's model of political decision-making indicates just what is at stake.

Easton (1965) argued that any functioning political system combines three levels of decision-making. At the top level decisions are made about who gets what, when, and how. Politics at this level is about the distribution of political power and economic resources, and it is driven by interests. Beneath this there is necessarily a middle level of decision-making about rules, procedures, and rights. These latter make up both the constitution and the institutional framework of the regime, and they are informed by reason. Then underpinning them there is the bottom level of decision-making; it addresses the composition of the 'we' whose polity has the constitution and the institutions within which normal distributive politics takes place. It is at this fundamental level that decisions are reached about identity, citizenship, and territory, and about the very social and cultural boundaries of the nation-state. In play here are passions. Most politics has to do with the top level—who gets what, when, and how. Sometimes the parameters within which normal politics is conducted are called into question and constitutional and institutional arrangements are amended, reformed, or superseded. Only rarely, Easton continued, does politics address questions at the most fundamental level of all—who are we?—because answers at that level are usually taken for granted. In similar vein, Chantal Mouffe (1995: 17) has reminded us 'that politics concerns collective and public action and that it always concerns collective identities'. Theorists of democracy might like to begin with the formula 'we the people', but the 'we' is never universal (all humankind), but always particular (a we marked off from the Other, us from them). Decisions as to who 'we' are, and who 'we' include and exclude from our number, may often be implicit rather than explicit, but they are never irrelevant. They also typically involve variations on the themes of unity in diversity and the accommodation of difference.

The politics of early 1960s America was more stable than most, and middle-, and even bottom-level political decision-making have been commoner than Easton anticipated. Indeed, shortly after he wrote, the civil rights movement challenged, and in due course transformed, the bottom and middle levels of politics in America itself. Be that as it may, Britain at the beginning of the new millennium offers a still relatively rare instance in which the politicians and citizens of a mature democracy ask themselves who they are, and whether or not they are one people. These are, as Easton says, matters of passion but it is possible to bring clarity to them by using social-science concepts with proper care.

It is not possible to review in a few pages how all the concepts central to a discussion of nations and national identities have been variously formulated by different social scientists at different times, but it is possible to make an instructive selection. A good place to start is with Max Weber who was interested in nation and state formation both in theory and in connection with the position of Germany as a major power in central Europe following unification in 1870. According to Weber, a nation is 'a community of sentiment which would adequately manifest itself in a state of its own; hence a nation is a community which normally tends to produce a state of its own' (Weber 1912 in Gerth and Mills 1948: 176).[3] A nation exists where a people claim to be one and succeed in that claim by securing recognition from others. National solidarity draws upon selected 'objective' factors, such as language, religion, customs, political memory and experience, and 'race', which make a nation different from others. These are the markers of community. But no single one of these, nor any particular combination of them, invariably defines a nation. There is thus always a subjective dimension to national solidarity. There has to be a valuation—enter intellectuals as well as (would-be) leaders—which makes one or more of these markers significant enough to make those who share it feel solidarity among themselves and difference from others. This is the source of sentiment. National identity is thus also a matter of pathos and of consciousness and lived experience. By taking this approach, Weber treats nations as constructions that some peoples make successfully and others not. Each is constructed in a unique way and each has an identity of its own. A nation is a *Gemeinschaft*, a community, and intellectuals are important in forming the language of solidarity, whereas the state is a *Gesellschaft*, an association, and an instrument of politicians. Nations usually, but not invariably, need a state to protect their integrity and interests; states usually need (to forge) a nation if they are to command allegiance.

Weber is a very good place to start because: (1) he allows the possibility of stateless nations (such as Scotland after 1707) and nationless states (such as Britain in 1707); (2) he recognizes that the status of 'nation' is about the making and conceding of claims (compare, for example, the very different standings of claims made for Croatia, Quebec, Wales, and Cornwall today); (3) he separates objective factors which recur in different constructions of nation at different times and places from the subjective factors of how each nation is valued, understood, and experienced on a continuing basis by people who claim to be one; (4) he treats each construction of nation as unique; (5) he regards 'race', or as we would now say 'ethnicity', as neither a necessary nor a sufficient constituent of nation; and (6) he acknowledges the part played by intellectuals in articulating conceptions of the nation. This last point can be broadened by turning to the concept of collective representations that originated with his contemporary Emile Durkheim.[4] Collective representations are the ways collectivities represent themselves to themselves and to others. Representation is both process and product. Intellectuals play a prominent part in the process—representation as generation, regeneration, transformation, transmission, and reception—but so do other influentials and indeed the people, whether as citizenry or *Volk*.

Symbolic representations of the nation—flags, anthems, monuments, and historic sites, for example—often have a particular potency. In today's idiom some are iconic. Representation can also be connected to the distinction between the cultural nation and the political nation. All nations are cultural nations; most nations also have a political expression and are thus political nations; some nations have a state of their own and are thus nation-states. Political representation refers to both how a people represents itself to itself and Others (such as sovereign, neutral, allied, victim), and to the representation of the people in parliaments and councils.

The second and fifth of Weber's points also feature in Ernest Gellner's approach to nations. Gellner, an anthropologist, famously wrote that 'Nationalism is not the awakening of nations to self-consciousness; it *invents* nations where they do not exist' (1983: 169). By this he means two things. First, there are vastly more separately identifiable peoples (what the French call *ethnies*) in the world than there are nations, so being a nation is something different from, and rarer than, being a people. Second, nationalists selectively draw upon the past and distinctively gloss the present to generate and regenerate (a sense of) nationhood. They thus do not invent nations out of nothing, as critics of Gellner sometime suppose, but rather 'need some pre-existing differentiating marks to work on' (ibid.). Anderson (1983: 135) has given a good example of this. 'In 1891, amidst novel jubilees marking the 600th anniversary of the Confederacy of Schwyz, Obwalden and Nidwalden, the Swiss state "decided on" 1291 as the date of the "founding" of Switzerland.' Similarly Poland's origin in 966 is an invention of nineteenth-century romantic intellectuals.

Gellner's reference to inventing nations (repeated in the Peter Scott quotation at the very beginning of this chapter) is, however, open to misunderstanding. Invention implies fabrication with its connotations of falsity and forgery. But some nations could only be false if others are true, which is exactly what Gellner wants to deny; there are, he insists, no primordial or authentic nations, only latter-day constructions. All claims to nationhood invoke some combination of objective and subjective factors, some more convincingly than others. Or as Anderson (p. 6) puts it, 'Communities are to be distinguished not by their falsity/genuineness, but by the style in which they are imagined.'

This takes us to the most influential book on nations and nation formation in recent times, Benedict Anderson's *Imagined Communities*

(1983). According to Anderson, a nation is 'an imagined political community—and it is imagined as both inherently limited and sovereign' (p. 6). It is imagined because most members of a nation never meet most others, 'yet in the minds of each lives the image of their communion' (p. 7). It is a community in that it is an imagined horizontal comradeship, or fraternity, for which members are on occasions willing to behave altruistically, even, in times of war, giving their lives. It is limited because it is finite and bounded, even if its boundaries are not fixed; in other words a nation is always one among others. It is sovereign in that it is free of impediments to self-determination; thus the 'gage and emblem of this freedom is the sovereign state' (ibid.). It is Anderson's basic argument that:

> the convergence of capitalism and print technology on the fatal diversity of human language created the possibility of a new form of imagined community, which in its basic morphology set the stage for the modern nation. The potential stretch of these communities was inherently limited, and, at the same time, bore none but the most fortuitous relationships to existing political boundaries (which were, on the whole, the high water marks of dynastic expansionisms). (p. 46)

In other words it was the circulation of texts that constituted the print communities out of which nationhood could develop. One does not have to accept that all nations originated this way to acknowledge a connection between printing and shared imaginings. The intellectuals who, according to Weber, are important to the generation of national solidarity were, after all, literate when others so often were not.

The association of print communities with the seeds of nationhood allows a compromise between the dominant modernists and the still-vocal medievalists on the entry of nations in the history of the West. Medievalists and modernists have debated whether there have been any pre-modern nations. For Adrian Hastings (1997) the prototype for all nations is England and pre-modern England at that. He is certainly right that there have been imaginings of an English nation from Bede in the eighth century onwards, but in medieval times, at least, they were the inconstant preoccupation of kings and bishops and were unknown to the poor and the illiterate—in other words almost everyone. For a people to be a nation there has to be an imagining of a national community in which all can join (cf. Anderson 1983). By contrast the evidence of an English nation that Hastings produces is largely evidence of what might be called a nation-in-itself rather than a nation-for-itself and it is with reference to the latter that the modernists make their claims. It is true that the development of printing, and especially the publication of works in English rather than Latin, enabled more of the population to imagine itself as part of a national community. But a nation is a whole people conscious of its difference from others and concerned to safeguard it. There is in the very idea of the people as a nation an expectation that the people's voice will be heard; this democratic turn may often have been thwarted but it has also proved remarkably insistent. In short, there is always a political dimension to nationhood, though no necessity that it takes the form of statehood. The combination of extensive popular conscious-ness, horizontal solidarity (in contrast to personal allegiance to a superior) and political expectation is, as John Breuilly (1982), Ernest Gellner (1983), Anthony Giddens (1985), and Eric Hobsbawm (1990) have all emphasized, a characteristic of modernity. From when, then, should modernity be dated? The modernists tend to look to developments following the American and French revolutions, but it could be argued that in the case of England the key date is much earlier. In 1534 Henry VIII broke with Rome thereby founding a national church, the Church of England, which was to go on to adopt a ver-nacular Bible and liturgy—this in an England that was post-feudal even if it was pre-modern.

The basic idea of an imagined political community has proved a powerful one, prompting researchers in many countries to ask who imagined what, why, and how, and how such imaginings are shared and transmitted from generation to generation. For example, is imagining gendered? The link with sovereignty, however, is a step backwards in so far as it ties nation to state. It encourages the notion that all states are nation-states. This con-nection has often been made unthinkingly. It is more disquieting when it is made deliberately, as in the work of Giddens. He refers to a nation as 'a collectivity existing within a clearly demarcated territory, which is subject to a unitary administration, reflexively monitored both by the internal state apparatus and those of other states' (1985: 116). A nation 'only exists', he adds, 'when a state has a unified administrative reach over the territory over which its sovereignty is claimed' (p. 119). He then declares that 'The nation-state, which exists in a complex of other nation-states, is a set of institutional forms of governance maintaining an administrative monopoly over a territ-ory with demarcated boundaries (borders), its rule being sanctioned by law and direct control of the means of internal and external violence' (p. 121).

By this reckoning Prussia, the Soviet Union, and the former Yugoslavia were not just nations but nation-states, there being no other kind, and so, incontestably, is Britain today. On the other hand, Russia before 1991 was not a nation, and nor is England, Scotland, or Wales, or Palestine, there being no possibility of a stateless nation. Giddens might well contend that his usage is justified by the existence of a global nation-state system as confirmed by international bodies such as the League of Nations and its successor, the United Nations, but it would be better to acknowledge that the global political order is really a global state system.

There is a different version of the nation/state pairing in the work of the historian Charles Tilly. In the introduction to the book he edited on *The Formation of National States in Western Europe* (1975), he remarks that 'nation' is a puzzling and tendentious term and then shifts his attention to states whilst also using 'national' to mean state-wide. This elision of nation and state also occurs in the branch of political science known as international relations and in most popular uses of the adjective 'international'. Tilly's use of national to mean state-wide is, however, problematic in Britain today. When a Scot refers to the national interest, for example, only the context will reveal whether the reference is to Scotland or Britain.

Weber recognized that each nation is unique but that does not preclude recurrent 'objective' features in their construction. In particular it is possible to distinguish two main types, the ethnic nation and the civic nation. Anthony Smith (1991: 21) lists six main attributes of an ethnic community (or *ethnie*):

1. a collective proper name
2. a myth of common ancestry
3. shared historical memories
4. one or more differentiating elements of common culture
5. an association with a specific 'homeland'
6. a sense of solidarity for significant sectors of the population.

Like Gellner, he acknowledges that not all ethnies are nations and not all nations have ethnic origins. Nations have five main attributes (p. 14):

1. an historical territory, or homeland
2. common myths and historical memories

3. a common, mass culture

4. common legal rights and duties for all members

5. a common economy with territorial mobility for members.

It is instructive to compare the two lists. First, the omission of 'a collective proper name' from the second list is surely an oversight. Second, 'one or more differentiating elements of common culture' in list one has become a 'common, mass culture' in list two. This suggests that nations are modern phenomena and that most of their populations, not just elites or intellectuals, identify with them. Anderson's print communities, the subsequent development of both mass media and easy travel (often following the building of railways), universal schooling, and for nation-states 'national service' in the armed forces, are only some of the most obvious generators of popular identification with the nation.

The references to common legal rights and duties and to a common economy in list two, however, are more problematic because they are defined in law which is more a matter of state than nation and they blur the distinction between citizenship and nationality. This does not make much difference in practice in nation-states but it does make a difference where nations are stateless (such as Scotland or, indeed, England) and states are nationless (such as the former Yugoslavia), multinational (such as the Soviet Union), or faced with a denial of their parallel nationhood by a significant fraction of their citizens (such as Britain or Spain today). Legal rights and duties pertain to citizenship which is primarily about attachment not to a nation but to a state. Ordinary English usage, and also British law, are misleading in so far as they confuse nationality and citizenship. Hotel registers typically ask for the nationality of their guests, when what they need to know is their citizenship, and thus, for foreigners, the state that issued their passports. We also often refer incorrectly to dual nationality instead of dual citizenship, though we always correctly describe people who do not have citizenship anywhere as stateless. But although our primary citizenship is defined by the state we are also citizens of other political communities to which legal rights and duties attach, for example Scotland or the city of Manchester. These other communities certainly now include the European Union. The idea of individuals having world citizenship, however, remains largely rhetorical in so far as it is about moral rights and duties (such as environmental stewardship of the Earth) which are not legally enforceable, and are not associated with any polity.

The reference to a common economy is also not straightforward. An economy is common in so far as internal barriers to trade and the movement of labour have been removed which is again a matter of law, and thus of the state. But we can and do also refer to economies whose boundaries do not coincide with those of the state such as the economy of Scotland, or the economy of the North-West region of England.

Perhaps the best example of the need not to confuse nationality and citizenship is that of Poland from the Third Partition of 1795 to the end of the First World War. During that period *all* of Poland was occupied and divided up by its neighbours, Prussia (after 1870 Germany), Russia, and Austria (after 1867 Austria-Hungary). The Polish state ceased to exist and Poland was part of three different jurisdictions and three different economies with tariffs and other barriers to exchanges between them. From the mid-nineteenth century onwards, however, it was increasingly recognized inside and outside Poland that there was a Polish nation, but there was no de facto restoration of a Polish state until 1918 and no agreement on its restoration until the Treaty of Versailles a year later.

The most important difference between Smith's two lists is the omission of a myth of common ancestry from the second. The significance of this omission is most apparent when the issue of descent is coupled with that of a homeland, and together these are considered in connection with the difference between ethnic and civic constructions of nation. First, it should be noted that exceptions to the attribution to all ethnies and nations of a homeland are exceedingly rare. The only obvious exception is gypsies. Interestingly Roma began in 2000 to make claims to be a nation—because nations get taken more seriously than ethnic minorities and everywhere Roma are a minority. Second, Smith's best-known book deals with *The Ethnic Origins of Nations* (1986) but he also recognizes that not all nations are derived from a single ethnie. The most obvious example of a nation whose people do not have any claim to a common ancestry is the USA. Third, ideas about nation inform laws determining citizenship. Where the principle of descent from common ancestors—*ius sanguinis*, or the law of the blood—takes precedence over other factors, constructions of nation tend towards the ethnic ideal-type. Where the principle of birth within a territory takes precedence—*ius soli*, or the law of the soil—constructions of nation tend towards the civic type. In practice today combinations of the two are usual, but in differing proportions; the dominant principle still greatly affects national self-understanding (Bryant 1997).

One of the clearest examples of a nation that does have a myth of common ancestry is that of Germany. German nationhood is vested in the *Volk*, an ethnic community, and citizenship is based on descent, the principle of *ius sanguinis*, as Rogers Brubaker (1992) has made clear in his celebrated comparison of citizenship and nationhood in France and Germany. Ethnic nations, then, are communities of descent. By contrast, civic nations are territorial communities, binding together all the people or peoples who live within a territory. Civic nations vary in their capacity to accommodate difference. One sub-type is the assimilationist of which France is the classic example. France is a civic nation willing since the Revolution of 1789 to bestow the honour and benefit of being French on all who were born there (the principle of *ius soli*), and to many who migrate there, in the expectation that they will acknowledge the honour and the benefit. Both Germany and France are currently experiencing great difficulties in maintaining their historically distinct constructions and are becoming more like each other. The other main sub-type, the pluralist, is by definition better placed to accommodate difference—but pluralism is itself a difficult concept in that it is used to refer to both plural societies and pluralist politics.

Plural societies display (degrees) of segmentation; (vertical) differentiation on the basis of race, ethnicity, language, or religion has high salience for all members—and for some at least, higher salience than the horizontal differentiation of class or stratum. In extreme cases a society can comprise a number of coexisting sub-societies. The Netherlands offers the closest approximation to this among European democracies from the inception of the 'pillarized' system there in 1917 to the partial depillarization from the mid-1960s onwards (Bryant 1981). Dutch society has made separate institutional provision (schools, social services, political parties, unions, television channels, etc.) for people of different religious and political persuasions. This system of institutional separation without geographical separation has interested commentators on both Northern Ireland and multi-ethnic parts of Britain.

Pluralist politics properly refers to more than the articulation of political differences and the legitimacy of opposition (the prevailing conception in

Eastern Europe since 1989). William Connolly sums up what was in origin a largely American approach to politics as follows.

> It portrays the system as a balance of power among overlapping economic, religious, ethnic, and geographical groupings. Each "group" has some voice in shaping socially binding decisions; each constrains and is constrained through the processes of mutual group adjustments; and all major groups share a broad system of beliefs and values which encourages conflict to proceed within established channels and allows initial disagreements to dissolve into compromise solutions. (Connolly 1969: 3)

This system of multiple group pressures is said to promote a plurality of legitimate and public ends. Crucially, all groups are assumed to have enough resources—votes, money, leaders, presentational and organizational skills, etc.—to affect outcomes.

Few contemporary democracies present segmentation or vertical differentiation on the scale associated with plural societies. On the other hand the benign assumptions of harmony and balance among competing interests favoured by supporters of the (American) notion of pluralist politics do not sit easily with contemporary struggles to secure an acceptable accommodation of differences of value, interest, culture, and consciousness—differences articulated in varying organizational forms and with varying degrees of success, and associated not only with the ethnicity, language, and religion of most concern to analysts of plural societies, but also with class, gender, region, and national identity. When speaking of pluralism it is thus necessary to come to terms with complex actualities that contain elements of both plural societies and pluralist politics. Pluralism is thus best regarded as a socio-political form.

It is possible to identify the principles of ethnic integrity, cultural assimilation, and institutional pluralism that have informed nationhood and citizenship in Germany, France, and the Netherlands. By contrast, confusion, muddling through, is a very visible practice in Britain, but hardly a principle. It can be, and often is, dignified as 'pragmatism'. Britain is in origin a territorial community with a civic conception of nation. The British state dates from 1707 and the Treaty of Union between England and Scotland. In the next chapter I will discuss the development of a British nation and national identity subsequent to 1707. For the moment, just let it be noted that, by guaranteeing the maintenance of the separate institutions of the Scots (the Church of Scotland, Scottish law and courts, the educational and local government systems, and the right of the banks to issue their own banknotes) the treaty effectively ensured that there would always be more than one way of being British. 'British' has always been a composite identity and it has long proved possible to extend it to cover citizens of other origins, from refugees in Victorian times to 'coloured' immigrants from the former Empire in the 1950s and 1960s. What one has in Britain is a civic nation that has proved capable of accommodating a large amount of difference. The notion of ethnic and other communities, of community relations and leaders, of different ways of being British—a notion, albeit for different reasons, without parallel in Germany and France—is to most Britons most of the time as 'natural', as unremarkable, as the equivalent is to the Dutch. Where the British differ is in the haphazard character of the civic nation. There is a *de facto*, and often contested, pluralism rather than, the Treaty of Union apart, a *de iure*, and universally endorsed, one.

Ernest Renan, in his famous essay 'What is a Nation?' (1882), referred to the existence of nations as an everyday plebiscite. Their continued existence depends on habits and sentiments of solidarity and community that are reaffirmed daily. Integral to this is what Michael Billig (1996) calls banal nationalism, the countless reminders of nation we rarely think about in everything from news reporting to flags and symbols in advertising and public places. But this daily reproduction of nation is not orchestrated by anyone and is never unchanging. Brubaker (1996: 13) is surely wrong to deny the reality of nations as 'substantial, enduring collectivities'—France, for example, has had a pretty long run—but he is right to draw attention to nations as contingent events in so far as they can develop in ways no one foresees, let alone intends. Historians often describe the development of nations, but if 'development' suggests direction and intention, Brubaker is right to stress the frequency of the alternative—things that just happen.

Finally, references to continuity, development, and change also invoke perhaps the biggest appeal of nations today. Nationhood is embedded in narratives of nation that connect past, present, and future. Ours is often characterized as a post-modern age in which the grand narratives of reason, science, and progress have lost their credibility. When all else has seemingly fragmented, grand narratives about the nation retain their appeal for many citizens in that they are understood to offer some cognitive and emotional order in which individuals can locate themselves and find some meaning to their lives. At the same time, loyalties to nation are more diverse in number and salience than heretofore. For some citizens they are fundamental to their very being; for others they are more like lifestyle choices which can be adopted and set aside to suit the circumstances of the moment. There are, for example, some citizens who are self-consciously British through and through. Others move easily from, say, an English to a British, even a European, identity according to circumstances. Sport is interesting in this context. FIFA rules allow a footballer to play for the country in which a grandparent was born. Jackie Charlton built the first Republic of Ireland side to reach the finals of the European Championship and World Cup with many players born outside Ireland who had sometimes not considered themselves Irish until the one-grandparent rule offered them an unexpected opportunity to play international football. There are also lots of weekend golfers not otherwise enamoured of Europe who identify with it when the biennial Ryder Cup match between America and Europe is played.

References have already been made in passing to nationalism, but one key feature may not yet have come through. If nations are, as Weber claimed, communities of sentiment, and if, as Anderson would have it, they are imagined communities, then the propagation and dissemination of these sentiments and imaginings constitutes nationalism. Very often, moreover, these sentiments and imaginings involve perceptions of national interest. Nationalisms make national sentiments and imaginings the springs of cultural and political mobilization. This mobilization can take many forms from top-down state nationalization to bottom-up cultural and political movements old and new. In short, nationalism has to be understood not only as ideology and shared understandings, but also as concerted action. This way of characterizing nationalism is consistent with A. D. Smith's definition of nationalism as 'an ideological movement for attaining and maintaining autonomy, unity and identity on behalf of a population deemed by some of its members to constitute an actual or potential "nation"' (1991: 73). Imagining, celebrating, and promoting one nation may or may not pose problems for an Other, and where they do pose problems these may or may not be regarded by both parties as legitimate. It is best to discard the notion, sometimes favoured on the left, that patriotism, love of country, is acceptable, but nationalism is not.

This section began by pointing up Weber's approach to nation which recognizes the variety of 'objective' and 'subjective' factors that have been invoked in the making and conceding of different claims to nationhood. Something similar happens among citizens, especially the citizens of multinational states, when individuals attribute nationality to each other. In their work on Scottish national identity, Kiely et al. (2001) refer to the markers and rules of national identity. The identity markers are the characteristics that are invoked in the making and conceding of claims to national identity by individuals—such as place of birth, ancestry, upbringing, place and length of residence, accent, commitments, etc. The rules are the rules of thumb individuals use when deciding which combinations of markers are sufficient to establish a claim. Birth, ancestry, upbringing, and residence together typically constitute an incontrovertible claim, but a claim based on other combinations, such as, in the Scottish case, ancestry and current residence without birth in Scotland and a Scottish accent, will often be contested. Markers and rules figure, of course, not only in how individuals decide national identity claims, but also in the making and conceding of regional and local identity claims (cf. Cohen 1985).

So far I have indicated my approach to questions of nation and national identity by selectively engaging with the theoretical and conceptual literature. I now want to go beyond that by adding a simple ordering device before engaging with the enormous literatures relevant to questions about the nations of Britain to be found in the social sciences, history, cultural studies, law, and journalism. Indeed, without some such device, it is hard to know how one could proceed at all systematically. To reduce to fundamentals, questions of nation are about time and place. Narratives of nation relate past, present, and future, and nations have homelands. Although I want to concentrate on contemporary constructions of the nations of Britain, there are differences in content and emphasis according to whether one looks back to the past or concentrates on the present and prospects for the future. There are also differences in content and emphasis according to how one views place. Attention can close in on home alone or it can open up to worlds beyond home.[5] In the cases of Scotland and Wales, Britain occupies a place beyond home. This simple rationale generates the orientation matrix in Table 1.3.

The matrix provides a maximum of six cells, and in the Scottish case all are used. Wales requires the modification indicated in Ch. 4. In the English

TABLE 1.3	Contemporary constructions of nation		

		Orientations to Place		
		Home	Britain	Abroad
Orientations to Time	Past			
	Present			

case Britain is omitted from the columns and there are only four cells. In all three cases each cell contains one or occasionally two ways of constructing or representing the nation. Britain itself is a special case and use of the matrix is deferred till the concluding Ch. 8. Each version refers to the nation as an 'imagined community', so long as 'imagined' is not opposed to 'real', and (*contra* Davey 1999) 'imaginary' is not substituted for 'imagined'. Construction and representation are matters of unending process without any final product. Nations as imagined communities never have a fixed form. Instead they are continuously reproduced and transformed by what people say and do, not just political and cultural elites but all citizens, in response to conditions at home and abroad. Sometimes the names used with cells will be familiar to all citizens, such as Celtic Scotland and Little England. On other occasions they will be familiar only to social scientists, such as Civil Scotland and Anglo-Britain, or to citizens of one of the nations of Britain only, such as Y Fro Gymraeg. On still other occasions, they are my invention, such as Cymru/Wales and Cosmopolitan England, but that invention is confined to putting a name to a version of the nation that is meant to be readily recognizable. In all cases, I would claim that the constructions and representations of nation distinguished in the chapters that follow have a contemporary currency.

Some of these constructions undoubtedly have greater currency than others but no attempt is made to quantify the currency of each. The main reason for this is the absence of data which would make accurate quantification possible—though evidence can sometimes be offered in support of trends. There is, however, a secondary reason which is very important: alternative versions of nation are not necessarily exclusive and citizens can and do switch their identifications between, and buy into and rework, (aspects of) different versions according to circumstance—which can make life hard for politicians intent on popularity. In the course of reflections on 'ethnicity, etc', Richard Jenkins (1997), a native of Swansea, produced the hierarchy of Welsh identity in Fig. 1.1 in which each level involves identification with one half of a binary. The figure illustrates Jenkins's claim that individuals can identify with the communal, the local, the national, and the global according to context and circumstance.

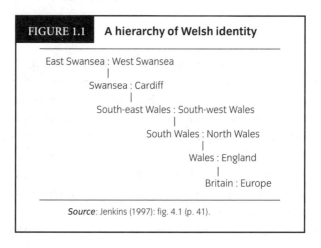

FIGURE 1.1   **A hierarchy of Welsh identity**

East Swansea : West Swansea
|
Swansea : Cardiff
|
South-east Wales : South-west Wales
|
South Wales : North Wales
|
Wales : England
|
Britain : Europe

Source: Jenkins (1997): fig. 4.1 (p. 41).

I also suggest that individual citizens use hierarchies of British identities but, as Fig. 1.2 illustrates, hierarchies afford more possibilities than Jenkins specifies. At each level there are (potentially) alternative constructions or representations of place/people. Some involve binaries, but others not. The salience of any one level varies both for individual citizens from time to time and between citizens at any one time. Some individuals disregard some levels—for example region and Europe—altogether. There are also citizens with dual or multiple identifications at particular levels—for example, place of upbringing and place of residence, or father's national identity and mother's national identity. Ethnicity, it should be noted applies to everyone and can be contestable. Many Muslims, for example, regard Muslim as an ethnic category although the Race Relations Act (1965) does not. In

---

FIGURE 1.2 **Hierarchies of British identity**

Local Community 1, 2, 3, ...
|
Town or City 1, 2, 3, ...
|
County 1, 2, 3, ...
|
Region 1, 2, 3, ...
|
Ethnicity 1, 2, 3, ... (e.g. census ethnicities)
|
England, Scotland, Wales, and/or Northern Ireland 1, 2, 3, ...
|
Britain 1, 2, 3, ...
|
Europe, 1, 2, 3, ...

---

sum, individuals have their own hierarchies even if they seldom articulate them as such, but they also share identities by engaging with and reworking the constructions and representations they encounter.[6] In giving voice to their identities they both take account of others and represent themselves to others. Nations are communities of sentiment, not collections of solipsists.

Finally, all constructions and representation of nation have their light side and their dark side. The tension can be between the good and the bad, the authentic and the distorted or perverted, or the shining ideal and the grubby reality. All too have normative dimensions and there is always room for argument as to whether the norms they supply or imply deserve respect, and, if they do, whether they get it. Of necessity nations appeal to the passions as well as reason and elicit emotional responses from love to hate. The very idea of an imagined *community* reflects a desire for community in modern life where it is otherwise mostly absent. But the longed-for is idealized, reality always falls short of it, and both reason and the passions are needed to cope with the difference. In sum, nations, including all versions of the nations of Britain, invite both celebration and criticism.

NOTES

1 Roy Strong (1996: 1) begins his *The Story of Britain* with the seemingly innocuous 'Britain is an island . . . ' Norman Davies in his acclaimed *The Isles* (1999: p. xxviii) objects that Strong uses Britain as shorthand for the United Kingdom, which includes Ireland from 1801 to partition in 1922 and Northern Ireland after partition, and the UK is not an island (in the singular). Sometimes Strong does indeed do this: 'In 1949 the Irish Free State became the Republic of Ireland. Northern Ireland remained part of Britain' (ibid. 541). And sometimes he does not: 'Although Ireland was never part of Britain it had been one part of what is designated the United Kingdom' (ibid. 469). That the British state tried and failed to incorporate Ireland, however, never stopped Britain from being an island. Davies also says that Britannia is the Latin for England (ibid. 1093), which is a nonsense. The Romans called both the island and the Roman province on the southern two-thirds of the island Britannia. They did not call England Britannia because there was no England in Roman times; Angles did not invade and settle on the island till after the Romans had left in 410. By contrast, in church and medieval Latin there was a need for a Latin name for England, and that name was Anglia.

2 All figures from the General Household Surveys for 2001 and 2002 have been taken from *Living in Britain* reports accessed via the website of National Statistics (www.

statistics.gov.uk/lib2001, accessed 28 May 2005).

3 Also see Weber (1922: 395–8 and 921–6), and Beetham (1974: ch. 5).

4 Durkheim's concept of collective representations had quite a complex career from its first appearance in 1897 till his death in 1917. See Lukes (1973: 6–8).

5 Timothy Garton Ash (2004) has used a similar device. He attributes to Britain a double Janus-like character, facing not two ways but four. The first pair are back and front, 'Island' and 'World'. Island, the more comforting, looks backward and inward; 'World', the more promising, looks forward and outward. The second pair are left and right, looking on the one side to America and on the other to Europe. Garton Ash does not distinguish between Britain and its constituent parts. His four possibilities are also really three, with looking forward and outward divided into looking out and left to America or right to Europe.

6 Brian Roberts (2004) has put forward a model for the systematic analysis of the fit between personal histories (what individuals say about their own experience) and communal narratives (what is said in public documents, at public sites, and on public occasions about the communities in which they have lived and worked).

REFERENCES

ABERCROMBIE, NICHOLAS, and WARDE, ALAN, with others (1988), *Contemporary British Society* (Cambridge: Polity), 3rd edn. 2000.

ANDERSON, BENEDICT (1983), *Imagined Communities: Reflections on the Origin and Spread of Nationalism* (London: Verso).

BBC (1999), 'The Changing UK', an unpublished BBC editorial guide for its staff (London: BBC).

BEETHAM, DAVID (1974), *Max Weber and the Theory of Modern Politics* (London: Allen & Unwin).

BILLIG, MICHAEL (1995), *Banal Nationalism* (London: Sage).

BREUILLY, JOHN (1982), *Nationalism and the State* (Manchester: Manchester University Press).

BRUBAKER, ROGERS (1992), *Citizenship and Nationhood in France and Germany* (Cambridge Mass.: Harvard University Press).

—— (1996), *Nationalism Reframed: Nationhood and the National Question in the New Europe* (Cambridge: Cambridge University Press).

BRYANT, CHRISTOPHER, G. A. (1981), 'Depillarisation in the Netherlands', *British Journal of Sociology*, 32: 105–28.

—— (1997), 'Citizenship, national identity and the accommodation of difference: reflections on the German, French, Dutch and British cases', *New Community*, 23: 1–16.

CANNADINE, DAVID (1995), 'British history as a "new subject": politics, perspectives and prospects', in Grant and Stringer (eds.), ch. 2.

COHEN, ANTHONY P. (1985), *The Symbolic Construction of Community* (Chichester: Ellis Horwood and London: Tavistock).

CONNOLLY, WILLIAM (1969) (ed.), *The Bias of Pluralism* (New York: Atherton).

CURTICE, JOHN (2003), 'Brought together or driven apart?', paper presented to the Joint RSE/British Academy Symposium on Anglo-Scottish Relations since 1914, Royal Society of Edinburgh, November 2003.

DAVEY, KEVIN (1999), *English Imaginaries: Six Studies in Anglo-British Modernity* (London: Lawrence & Wishart).

DAVIES, NORMAN (1999), *The Isles: A History* (London: Macmillan).

EASTON, DAVID (1965), *A Systems Analysis of Political Life* (New York: Wiley).

GARTON ASH, TIMOTHY (2004), 'The Janus dilemma', in *The Guardian Review*, 5 June 2004: 4–6.

GELLNER, ERNEST (1983), *Nations and Nationalism* (Oxford: Blackwell).

GIDDENS, ANTHONY (1976), *New Rules of Sociological Method* (London: Hutchinson).

—— (1985), *The Nation-State and Violence* (Cambridge: Polity).

GRANT, ALEXANDER, and STRINGER, KEITH J. (1995) (eds.), *Uniting the Kingdom? The Making of British History* (London: Routledge).

HASTINGS, ADRIAN (1997), *The Construction of Nationhood: Ethnicity, Religion and Nationalism* (Cambridge: Cambridge University Press).

HEFFER, SIMON (1999), *Nor Shall My Sword: The Reinvention of England* (London: Weidenfeld & Nicolson).

HITCHENS, PETER (1999), *The Abolition of Britain* (London: Quartet). Rev. edn. 2000.

HOBSBAWM, ERIC (1990), *Nations and Nationalism Since 1780: Programme, Myth, Reality*, Cambridge: Cambridge University Press.

JENKINS, RICHARD (1997), *Rethinking Ethnicity: Arguments and Explorations* (London: Sage).

JONES, BILL et al. (1991), *Politics UK* (Hemel Hempstead: Philip Allan), 4th edn. 2001.

KARIEL, HENRY (1973), 'Neither Sticks Nor Stones', *Politics and Society*, 3: 179–99.

KEARNEY, HUGH (1989), *The British Isles: A History of Four Nations* (Cambridge: Cambridge University Press).

KIELY, RICHARD; BECHOFFER, FRANK; STEWART, ROBERT; and McCRONE, DAVID (2001), 'The markers

and rules of Scottish national identity',
Sociological Review, 49: 33–55.

LUKES, STEVEN (1973), *Emile Durkheim: His Life and Work–A Historical and Critical Study* (London: Allen Lane/Penguin).

MARR, ANDREW (1995), *Ruling Britannia: The Failure and Future of British Democracy* (London: Penguin).

_____ (2000), *The Day Britain Died* (London: Profile).

MORENO, LUIS, and ARRIBA, ANA (1996), 'Dual identity in autonomous Catalonia', *Scottish Affairs*, 17: 78–97.

MOUFFE, CHANTAL (1995), 'Understanding nationalism and the nature of the political', in J. JENSEN and F. MISZLIVETZ (eds.), *East-Central Europe: Paradoxes and Perspectives* (Szombathely (Hungary): Savaria University Press), 13–22.

NAIRN, TOM (1977), *The Break-Up of Britain* (London: New Left Books).

_____ (2000), *After Britain: New Labour and the Return of Scotland* (London: Granta).

PAXMAN, JEREMY (1998), *The English: A Portrait of a People* (London: Michael Joseph).

PAYTON, PHILIP (2004), *Cornwall: A History* (Fowey: Cornwall Editions), 1st. edn. 1996.

REDWOOD, JOHN (1999), *The Death of Britain? The UK's Constitutional Crisis* (Basingstoke: Macmillan).

RENAN, ERNEST (French 1882), 'What is a nation?', in J. HUTCHINSON and A. D. SMITH (eds.), *Nationalism* (Oxford: Oxford University Press, 1994).

ROBERTS, BRIAN (2004), 'Biography, time and local history-making', *Rethinking History*, 8: 89–102.

SCOTT, PETER (1990), *Knowledge and Nation* (Edinburgh: Edinburgh University Press).

SMITH, ANTHONY D. (1986), *The Ethnic Origins of Nations* (Oxford: Blackwell).

_____ (1991) *National Identity* (London: Penguin).

STRONG, ROY (1996), *The Story of Britain: A People's History* (London: Hutchinson).

TILLY, CHARLES (1975), *The Formation of National States in Western Europe* (Princeton: Princeton University Press).

WEBER, MAX (German 1912), 'The nation', comments made at the 1912 meeting of the German Sociological Association, in H. H. GERTH and C. WRIGHT MILLS (eds.), *From Max Weber: Essays in Sociology* (London: Routledge & Kegan Paul, 1948), 176–9.

_____ (German 1922) *Economy and Society* (Berkeley, Calif: University of California Press, 1978), 395, 921–6.

WILLIAMS, GWYN A. (1991), *When Was Wales? A History of the Welsh* (London: Penguin). (First published London: Black Raven Press, 1985.)

2

Great Britain: The Post-Imperial Dilemma

Imperial Britain

Linda Colley's *Britons: The Forging of the Nation 1707–1837* (1992) is widely regarded as the best book on the original formation of a British national identity ever written. She argues that there was almost no prior understanding of a British nation when the union of England and Scotland came into being in 1707, despite the union of the crowns a century earlier, but there was a strong sense of British national identity by the time Victoria succeeded to the throne in 1837. The very idea that Britain is so recent a construction runs counter to the history many Britons learnt in school and offends those who have long elided their English and British history whilst holding Britain dear. Peter Hitchens (1999: 322) is one such and he can only respond by labelling Colley an ideologist of the left, a left, moreover, he sees as wittingly or unwittingly complicit in the abolition of Britain and all it stands for. But though Colley's book is about how and when a British nation was actually achieved, her metaphor of 'forging' does need to be treated with care. Colley means that British nationhood was hammered out in the heat of religious conflict, war, and imperial rivalry, not, as supporters of the dissolution of the union might suppose, that it was somehow counterfeited. Forging also covers a multitude of possibilities. Part of the British case consists of a state project to fashion a nation that supports it—an example of what Rogers Brubaker (1996), echoing Max Weber, calls 'state nationalisation'. But the state was not the only nation builder, and, additionally, there was also in Britain, as elsewhere, what Brubaker calls 'eventfulness', a reference to contingencies, to nation formation being less a project than something that just happens. These qualifications do not diminish Colley's basic argument that a British nation was forged out of four elements: Protestantism, trade and Empire, war and military service, and intermarriage among the landed classes of England, Wales, Scotland, and Ireland. Much of the time British identity crystallized in opposition to the Other, whether that other was Catholic Spain, Catholic or revolutionary France, or the colonized peoples of the Empire. She also emphasizes the importance of the monarch as a symbol of the nation, beginning with the latter part of the reign of George III. Each of these deserves separate comment.

England, Scotland, and Wales were all predominantly Protestant and the union of 1707 was explicitly a Protestant foundation, albeit with a Presbyterian established church in Scotland and an Anglican one in England and Wales. The (English) Act of Settlement of 1701 (which is still in force) laid down that the sovereign must be Protestant, and when Queen Anne died without an heir in 1714 the British government turned to the Lutheran Elector of Hanover to become King George I. Popular support for the Hanoverians grew with the defeat of the Jacobites, supporters of the Catholic James II and his descendants. James II had been forced from the throne in the 'Glorious Revolution' of 1688 and had fled to France. In 1716 and 1745 Jacobite armies invaded England from Scotland to reclaim the throne for the Stuarts. In 1745 Bonnie Prince Charlie's army of Catholic Highlanders got as far south as Derby before being chased back to Scotland and decimated at Culloden in 1746 (the last battle fought on British soil). And it was in 1745 that the entry of the king (to the Haymarket Theatre in London) was marked for the first time by the singing of 'God save the King'. The king, George II, might have been brought up in Hanover and spoken English imperfectly, but he was Protestant and that was what mattered when a Catholic was laying claim to the throne.

With the final defeat of the Jacobites, suspicion of Catholics slowly abated. In 1778, however, the passage of the Catholic Relief Act, when Britain was at war with Catholic France, met with huge opposition. In London, in 1780, it took the form of serious violence, the Gordon Riots, so-called after their leader, Lord George Gordon, a Scot; and in Scotland all attempts to implement the legislation were abandoned. Catholic emancipation was finally enacted in England and Wales in 1829. By then it was apparent to Parliament that Catholics had long ceased to be a threat to the established order—indeed many had (illegally) fought for Britain in the Napoleonic wars—and that the cession of civil rights to Catholics in Ireland necessary if civil war were to be avoided there could hardly be made without allowing

Catholic emancipation in Britain too. Even so, large-scale popular opposition to the measure found expression in petitions to Parliament from all parts of Britain. Following emancipation, all Catholic males in Britain and Ireland were now citizens in so far as they could vote, stand for Parliament and occupy most public offices on the same bases as Protestants. Colley adds one delightful detail. In 1834 Parliament burnt down. The architect for the new, neo-Gothic, Palace of Westminster, the Houses of Parliament as we know them today, was Charles Barry, and the designer of the equally celebrated interior and fittings was Augustus Pugin—a Catholic.

So Great Britain was a Protestant foundation, but why was it founded at all? When Elizabeth I died in 1603 without an heir, her ministers had arranged that James VI of Scotland, a Protestant, would succeed her as James I of England. James (who preferred the title James I of Great Britain and who introduced the Union Jack to ships of the English and Scottish navies) had hoped that the union of the crowns would be followed by a union of the states, but opposition to this proved too great in both kingdoms. In 1707, by contrast, the Treaty of Union was agreed. The Scottish treasury was near bankrupt, Scotland was poor and Scottish economic interests wanted access to the English market and the English empire (in North America and the Caribbean). In turn, the English Parliament wanted military security and an end to the threat from the north and the auld alliance between Scotland and France without which imperial adventures abroad could have been jeopardized by instability at home. A deal was done by the two political elites. Given that England was more powerful, rich, and populous, and that government would be based in London (as the court had been since 1603), the Scots took the larger risk—but not that large a risk. The terms of the union provided for the retention by the Scots of their own established church, legal and educational systems, and local government and for their banks to continue to issue their own notes. The significance of this in terms of the subsequent development of a distinctive Scottish civil society will be discussed in the next chapter. The union also provided for the removal of all internal barriers to free trade throughout Britain and for uniform taxation. In this the Scots saw economic advantage and they were right. If the benefits to Scotland and Scots were small at first, they expanded greatly after 1746. There were indeed profits for Scottish businessmen in the larger home market and in the expanding British Empire. Talent came south, went overseas, and did well. Scots may still sometimes have met prejudice and discrimination in

England—though their success was great enough for John Wilkes to lead bitter English nationalist complaints by the 1760s—but this seems only to have spurred them to find fortune abroad. Scots were disproportionately well represented in imperial service in India and elsewhere, and in the officer corps of the British army.

The third constituent in the formation of a British nation was service in the British army and navy and in imperial administration and participation in imperial trade. This is a different point from the attractive opportunities for individual advancement that the armed forces and Empire offered. The army, navy, and Empire afforded a common experience of opposition to the (often Catholic) Other in war and trade. The differences among Britons seemed insignificant compared with the differences between Britons and Others, between us and them. In the 130 years from the foundation of the union to Victoria's accession in 1837 Britain was at war with France alone for 51. And whilst the loss of the American colonies by 1783 signalled the contraction of the 'first empire', Britain quickly acquired a second one in India, Quebec and Western Canada, South Eastern Australia, and Cape Colony. Acquisition of both the first and the second empires would not have been possible without the supremacy of the Royal Navy over all others. This, as well as freedom at home, was thought to rest on God's blessing for a Protestant people. These sentiments are expressed in the words of a song written by James Thompson, the son of a Protestant minister in the Scottish Lowlands, in 1740.

> When Britain first, at Heaven's command,
> Arose from out the azure main,
> This was the charter of the land,
> And guardian angels sang this strain—
> Rule, Britannia! Britannia, rule the waves,
> Britons never, never, never will be slaves.

Colley's fourth element in the forging of a British nation was the scale of intermarriage, and the joining of estates, between the noble and landed classes of England, Scotland, Wales, and Ireland. The reasons for this are too complex to elaborate here but the consequence is simple enough, the development of a truly British ruling class. Colley further argues that the Scots, Welsh, and Irish who figured in its formation should not be thought of as Anglicized or Anglicizing. For most of them, 'dual nationality became a highly profitable reality. They could partake of London's bounty to a considerable extent, while still retaining considerable autonomy in their own countries' (1992: 162). There were some non-English who described themselves as English—the Anglo-Irish Lord Palmerston was one—but they were the exception.

The final part of Colley's thesis concerns the use of the monarchy. Colley describes how in the second half of George III's reign—after his recovery from 'madness' in 1789—successful attempts were made to re-present the king, already acknowledged as a good family man, as a symbol of the nation visible to, quite literally seen by, Britons everywhere. The modern practice of royal visits and the idea of an exemplary royal family date from then. 'Ritual splendour, an appearance of domesticity, and ubiquity: this was the formula that George taught and bequeathed to his royal successors. That it made them captives after a fashion, at the same time as it captivated large numbers of Britons, was the price of its success' (p. 236). For social scientists, at least, this is not a new argument. Thirty years before Colley, Jürgen Habermas (1962) analysed changes in the conduct of kings in connection with the emergence of a public opinion formed in coffee houses and salons and articulated in newspapers, a public opinion they could not ignore with impunity. There is, incidentally, an interesting treatment of the public role of the monarch in a film about George III, *The Madness of King George* (1994), and also in *Mrs Brown* (1997), a film about Queen Victoria's re-entry into public life in the 1870s after her long withdrawal following the death of Albert, the Prince Consort, in 1861.

It is important to note the precise character of Colley's claim that a British national identity, absent in 1707, had been forged by 1837. She treats Britishness as a superimposition upon other identities, including Englishness and Scottishness. She specifically rejects the idea that Britishness was a blend of Englishness, Scottishness, and Welshness—or that Britain was a kind of melting-pot. She also dismisses the idea that an imperialistic English core displaced Celtic interests and identities, the internal colonialism argument of Michael Hechter (1975) discussed below. Nor would she agree with Stephen Haseler (1996) or Jeremy Paxman (1998) that the British Empire was really an English empire—indeed, so great was the involvement of the Scots in the Empire that she gives a part of one chapter the title 'A Scottish Empire?', thereby anticipating two books by Scots a decade later, Michael Fry's *The Scottish Empire* (2001) and T. M. Devine's *Scotland's Empire 1600–1815* (2003)—or that the union and the Empire represented 'the expansion of England' of which Bill Schwarz (1996) speaks. But that still leaves open the question whether this overlay of Britishness attached to other identities in the same way, to the same degree, and with the same effects and long-term consequences in all parts of Britain. One of the problems here has always had to do with English domination of the union in terms of greater population (a domination that has increased since 1707), proportionately greater wealth (a domination that has decreased), and the doubling of the English capital, London, as the capital of Britain. The treaty of 1707 did not secure a union of equals in all significant respects. 'Putting it perhaps too boldly', Keith Robbins (1998: 264) concedes, 'the English had little incentive to understand Scotland but the Scots had little alternative but to understand England if they were to play an effective part in a Britain moulded by England'. This may be so, but, crucially, the Scots did play an effective part, so much so that Britain could not in the longer run properly be characterized as simply a product of the English. The term Anglo-Britain acknowledges that in some respects the English contribution to the making of Britain overshadows that of the Scottish and Welsh but it does not suppose England and Britain are synonymous.

Arthur Aughey (2001) has argued that the criticisms of Colley are of three kinds. First, Colley is sometimes better on what Britain was against than what it was for. Colley, of course, stresses that Britain was a Protestant nation, but, for Aughey, Protestantisms divided the British even as Protestantism united them (while dividing the Irish). This is true, but the divisions mattered less than the common opposition to Catholicism. But was Britain only about Protestantism, Empire, and profit? Aughey's own main addition is constitutionalism. Another possibility is represented by the figure of John Bull with his union-jack waistcoat. Here the American, Gerald Newman (1987), is interesting despite his inattention to any difference between England and Britain. Newman argues that the aristocracy's obsession with French fashion and taste provoked a bourgeois and yeoman 'English' reaction from the mid-eighteenth century onwards. French luxurious excess, political venality, and moral dissolution were contrasted with English solidity, practicality, steadfastness, and moral concern; effete French nobles were no match for John Bull, who was 'largely an invention of the 1750s (though with roots earlier)' and who 'was already by the sixties acquiring definition in English periodical literature as "a very worthy, plain, honest old gentleman of Saxon descent" ' (p. 116).

Second, post-1707 Britishness was not the first. Simon Partridge (1999), for example, draws attention to Roman Britain; Celtic Britain before the invasions of Angles, Saxons, and Jutes; the Greater Britain popularized by Geoffrey of Monmouth in the twelfth century in his *A History of the Kings of Britain* including King Arthur; new references to Britain among Welsh writers after Henry VII, the first of the Tudors (a dynasty of Welsh origin), won the English throne in 1485, and after Henry VIII annexed Wales to England in 1536; and the thwarted British ambitions of James VI of Scotland and I of England following the union of the Scottish and English crowns in 1603. All this is true, but also marginal—distant history, occasional writers, and missed opportunities. It is particularly notable that the desire of James VI and I for a union of states went unsatisfied.

Third, describing the forging of Britain in terms of factors all of which have since gone, are going, or are a shadow of what they once were, implies Britain has no future. This is true only if it is assumed that no other factors since 1837 have contributed, or could contribute, to the (re)forging of Britain, and it raises questions beyond the scope of Colley's book. Colley took a lot of unfair criticism from Conservatives who largely failed to engage with its actual content. (Her own position on the reforgeability of Britain is discussed in the concluding Ch. 8.) All in all, Colley's book has survived extensive critical attention, some of it politically partisan, with its reputation largely intact.

There is no account of the development of the British nation and national identity after 1837 comparable to Colley's. Later writers such as David Powell (2002) who covers 1800–2000 and Richard Weight (2002) who covers 1940–2000 discuss the vicissitudes of Britishness and the unmaking of Britain as much as the making. But it is easy enough to itemize many of the factors that continued to incline Britain towards one community of sentiment—though these in no way preclude significant variations in the British overlay in different parts of the kingdom at different times. (1) Britain not England, was the first industrial nation. The central Forth-Clyde belt in Scotland, and later South Wales, were as industrialized as anywhere in England, and industrialization gave rise in due course to a British labour movement and a Labour Party which, for all the talk of internationalism, has proved staunchly unionist. (2) The British Empire continued to expand, particularly in the Indian subcontinent, Africa, and Australasia. The Scottish stake in the Empire was very evident. According to Keith Robbins

(1998: 214), 'In 1901 . . . Scots formed 15 per cent of the British born in Australia, 21 per cent in Canada and 23 per cent in New Zealand, whereas Scots constituted some 10 per cent of the United Kingdom population.' (3) The British armed forces continued to fight numerous wars, mostly on the winning side. Service in the armed forces was part of the common experience of every family in Britain. In particular Britain did stand alone in the war against Hitler's Germany in 1940, and it did eventually triumph in the defeat of hateful regimes in Germany and Japan. It was a victory in which Britons could and did take great pride. (4) The Great Reform Act of 1832 and the equivalent Scottish act signalled the development of a truly common parliamentary system with a common struggle for a universal franchise. (5) From Victoria's return to public life in the 1870s, the royal family, with its homes in England and Scotland, visibly presided over all Britain. (6) Following receipt of its royal charter in 1927, the BBC, under the direction of a Scot, Lord Reith, addressed all Britain at the same time and in the same terms. (7) The development of the welfare state by the Labour government after 1945 was a great British project which won majority support in all parts of the kingdom. Support for the National Health Service, founded in 1948 by a Welshman, Aneurin Bevan, has proved particularly strong and enduring. (9) Finally, and no small matter, internal migration and intermarriage continued on a large scale for all classes.

It is true Protestantism declined in significance after the emancipation of Catholics in England and Wales in 1829—the Vatican restored the Catholic episcopacy in England in 1850 and Scotland in 1878—but not necessarily by much. In England the continued establishment of the Church of England, with the monarch as its supreme governor, ensured Protestant domination in public life, while north of the border Presbyterian doubts whether Catholics in Scotland—mostly Irish immigrants—could or should be regarded as Scottish Catholics confirmed Protestant domination in public debate (Robbins 1998: 258). In short, common industrial, labour, imperial, military, royal, cultural, familial, and, still to an extent, religious experiences continued to do a great deal to make Britain one community of sentiment, to use Weber's expression, or nation. Britons could identify with the British Empire, with Britain as a great power and with Britain as a civilized country. Belief in British superiority over other nations and cultures was commonplace. For most Britons, Britain was self-evidently best. But for all that Britain was 'unified but not uniform', as Robbins puts it (1995: 253).

David Marquand (1993 and 1995) has described the British nation up until the 1950s as Whig imperialist. Let Marquand's own words convey the imperialist component.

The new British state ... acquired a new and special legitimacy: the legitimacy of imperial success. Its justification was that it was a better predator than other states; that the pickings of its Empire were richer; that the blaze of glory surrounding it was brighter. Later when success had bred more success, when the global preeminence of the British state seemed beyond challenge, a more relaxed tone came to predominate. Now its justification was the pax Britannica: its role as the guarantor and linchpin of the global market which the guns of the Royal Navy had brought into being.   (Marquand 1995: 287)

The Whig component has to do with assumptions about Britain as the embodiment of progress, the rule of law, constitutional achievement, and, though this was a bit battered by the end, economic success. In particular, England/Britain had for centuries been renowned for the liberty of its people. The text which represents the Whig high point is Winston Churchill's loyal parliamentary address to King George VI in 1945 at the conclusion of the Second World War. It includes the following self-congratulatory lines.

If it be true ... that every country gets the form of government it deserves, we may certainly flatter ourselves. The wisdom of our ancestors has led us to an envied and enviable situation. We have the oldest, the most famous, the most secure, the most serviceable monarchy in the world. King and parliament both rest safely and solidly upon the will of the people expressed by free and fair election on the basis of universal suffrage. Thus this system has long worked harmoniously, both in peace and war.   (Churchill 1945, in Giles and Middleton (eds.) 1995: 139)

There is a second text from the same period which celebrates the sum of Britain's achievement and which in its own way is just as famous as Churchill's—T. H. Marshall's lectures on 'Citizenship and Social Class' delivered at Cambridge University in 1949. It may seem odd to attribute to Marshall, a sociologist and supporter of the post-war Labour government, subscription to a version of the Whig view of history but the lectures were, though calm and measured, both self-congratulatory and complacent. Marshall argued that a full development of citizenship was in prospect that would greatly benefit the working class and render class conflict, in all its destructiveness, unnecessary. He took citizenship to have three dimensions, civil, political, and social. The civil element in citizenship he associated with 'individual freedom—liberty of the person, freedom of speech, thought and faith, the right to own property and to conclude valid contracts and the right to justice' (Marshall 1949: 74). These rights had largely been established in the eighteenth century, and the institutions that deal most directly with them are the courts. The political element has to do with the right to vote and the right to be elected. This was mostly put in place in the nineteenth century and the institutions connected with it are parliament and local councils. Lastly, the social element refers to 'the whole range from the right to share to the full in the social heritage and to live the life of a civilized being according to the standards prevailing in the society' (ibid.). The educational and social services are the institutions that sustain it and its development is largely a twentieth-century affair with Clement Attlee's 1945–51 Labour government effecting a huge step forward by establishing the welfare state. Marshall's analysis has framed a vast amount of subsequent research and comment. It is also obviously flawed. In its timings, in particular, it is a male story; it sometimes suggests rights were bestowed by the enlightened when actually they were fought for by the excluded; and, significantly, it assumes that the progressive development of citizenship is irreversible. Above all, it is a confident success story.

There are four problems with a Whig imperialist version of Britain today. The first is that the Empire has gone. The second is that Britain is no longer obviously in the van of progress. The third is the linkage with constitutional and political practices, such as the unitary state, the sovereignty of parliament (as distinct from people), and Britain's world role, which no longer fit British circumstances. The fourth is that developments that seemed like irreversible achievements, such as the construction of the welfare state, turned out, beginning with the Conservative governments of Margaret Thatcher, not to be.

Post-imperial Britain: first thoughts

Whig imperialism gave way to decolonization. The status of Britain changed over time but four dates best signify that change. In 1947 the jewel in the imperial crown, India, was partitioned and granted independence. In 1956, Britain and France invaded Egypt to reverse Egyptian nationalization of the Suez Canal. The invasion was disowned by the United States and the invaders were obliged to withdraw. In the shocked stocktaking that followed, Britain, supposedly still a world power, abandoned its global pretences and within a decade had decided British forces would no longer operate east of Suez. The year 1973 saw Britain at last join the European Economic Community, confirming that its future rested with Europe—not that hangover of Empire, the Commonwealth—even if many of its citizens then and since have begged to differ. Finally, between 1989 and 1991 the Soviet bloc collapsed and the Cold War came to an end, thereby rendering irrelevant that last vestige of world power status, the British nuclear deterrent.

Little of what once gave Britain its identity still works, or at least works as well as it once did. After reviewing popular culture and newspaper coverage for the period from 1940 to 2000, Weight (2002) confirms that most citizens of Britain know this well enough from their own experience. Protestantism is a spent force. The Church of England is increasingly marginal and fractious and probably heading for disestablishment. The assembly of the Church of Scotland has lost its role as a surrogate parliament for Scotland now that a real one has been restored. And, whilst attendance at mass is falling, Roman Catholics are now more visible in public life than at any time since the Reformation. Britain today is not a Protestant nation, but is rather a largely secular society (much to the discomfort of many Muslims). The Empire is also history. The last significant bit went with the return of Hong Kong to China in 1997. British economic decline is more complicated. Imperial trading patterns have largely gone, and the economic decline of Britain relative to other countries from the third quarter of the nineteenth century onwards is incontestable. Britain fell from first in the world to eighteenth in per capita GDP in just over a century. The *de facto* integration of the economies of England, Scotland, and Wales still provides ties that bind, but the home market is now the European Union as a whole. Some of the Thatcherite and new Labour reconstruction of the British economy, however, has paid off; unemployment is lower than in most other EU countries, the pound is strong, and inflation is low. Unfortunately investment in manufacturing is also low, and industrial productivity remains lower than in many other pre-2004 EU countries, notably Germany and France. In 1981 Andrew Gamble could famously, unambiguously, and justifiably write about *Britain in Decline*. A quarter of a century later, however, the performance of the British economy compares favourably with other big economies in the EU. Britain's relative economic fortunes may at last be changing for the better and there may be some Scots and Welsh who were formerly disposed towards separation but who are now inclined to leave well alone. The idea of identifying with British economic success, so long far-fetched, is less far-fetched than it used to be.

For most families, military service is a thing of the past, national service having been abolished by 1960. The British armed forces are in any case diminishing in size. They are no longer big enough to fight another campaign like that in the Falklands. Britain's fully professional forces are efficient by comparison with most others, and especially by comparison with conscript armies, but they can only act alongside others in NATO, in UN peacekeeping forces, or as the US's (over-)faithful ally. Nuclear weapons are unusable militarily but they continue to buy a seat on the UN Security Council. The former Conservative Foreign Secretary, Douglas Hurd, plausibly claimed that Britain punches above her weight in international affairs. There is also some sentimental attachment to British armed forces among those who served in them, and very real respect for the part they played in the defeat of Nazi Germany and Japan in the Second World War. The British are good at fighting and have taken pride in it, but by comparison with America Britain is now very obviously an also-ran. Turning to the royal family, there is not much majesty in a royal dysfunctional family reduced to a soap opera. And as for the BBC, it now has to compete to be heard as satellite communication and digitization ensure the broadcast media go on multiplying. Forty years of English as the world's first language has also proved a mixed blessing. The ever-reducing need to speak a foreign language has left Britons less sensitive to other cultures than might otherwise have been the case, and the loss of English to the world has rendered it unusable in fashioning a distinctively British identity. In short, in post-imperial Britain the things that forged British identity from 1707 to 1945 are diminishing assets at best and at worst irrelevancies.

In addition one other factor that helps to reinforce nations as a single community of sentiment is not always available to Britain. The success of the British teams at the Sydney and Athens Olympics in 2000 and 2004 may have heightened pride in Britain but in many team sports, including football, rugby union, and netball, England, Scotland, and Wales have their own national teams and matches against England have a special edge. Similarly, in many sports for individuals, such as golf and snooker, competitors are routinely identified as English, Scottish, or Welsh. And the summer 'national sport' of cricket is primarily an English one although first-class cricket is also played in Wales. The most significant of these sporting non-identifications with Britain is certainly that of football given the global significance of the World Cup, the Continent-wide interest in the European Championship, and the massive popular interest in, and media coverage of, the separate English and Scottish leagues and cups, and the separate English, Scottish, and Welsh representation in the two European club competitions. The opposition of both officials and fans to a combined British football team rules out participation in the Olympics. Part of that opposition has to do with a fear that if a British football team were to compete in the Olympics, FIFA and UEFA, football's world and European governing bodies, would each demand a single united British membership of their organizations, an all-British league, and British national and representative club teams in all their competitions. Almost all football followers view such a prospect with horror.

More than two decades ago Ralf Dahrendorf (1982) noted early in his Reith lectures *On Britain* that, unlike many Continental countries, Britain had long avoided any 'national question'. Instead the British question that taxed him and so many others at that time referred to the seemingly intractable problem of the country's relative economic decline—a decline that was a century old and still continuing. Britain with its poor economic growth, even poorer industrial relations, and a propensity for wage inflation was often portrayed as the sick man of Europe. Now it is the other way round. The British question is no longer economic, but political. The governments of Margaret Thatcher and Tony Blair, Conservative and new Labour, have gone a long way towards transforming the British economy at least in terms of securing a performance comparable to, sometimes conspicuously better than, those of other members of the European Union. But Britain now has a national question of real difficulty. In 1982 Dahrendorf could write, 'devolution may be an issue, but the nation is not. Felix Britannia!' (p. 15). Today no such easy happiness is possible.

National and regional differences

Many differences between the nations of Britain and the regions of England that have a bearing on national identities will be discussed in the chapters that follow, but four issues are worth brief comparative examination at the start. Before turning to them, however, it is necessary to indicate why use will not be made of Michael Hechter's *Internal Colonialism* (1975) thesis. Hechter, an American who had not then set foot in Britain, caused a stir with his thesis that the Celtic fringe of Scotland, Wales, and Ireland remained the colony of England it had been for centuries. Some nationalists in Scotland and Wales adopted it as a stick with which to beat the English, but it did have the undoubted virtue of drawing attention to economic and cultural relations between different parts of the kingdom. Hechter's thesis starts by treating capitalist development in terms of core and periphery. The core develops the periphery to meet its own needs, not the periphery's. It exploits the periphery and renders it dependent upon it, the core having a diversified economy and the periphery an economy over-reliant on one or two products. The core also portrays the culture of the periphery as backward and inferior. In other words it turns the relation between core and periphery into a cultural division of labour in which the self-proclaimed culturally superior core calls the shots and tells the periphery that it can only overcome its inferiority by embracing the modern ways of its master. Eventually, however, the periphery comes to reject its economic dependency and challenge its supposed cultural inferiority. A nationalist movement then reasserts its culture and nationalist parties demand political autonomy or independence.

For Hechter, England was the core and he often refers to the government of England, not Britain, in the centuries after 1707. Whenever governors of 'England' turn out not to have been English they are said to have been Anglicized; the same is said of the capitalists and leading lights of Scotland, Wales, and Ireland. Hechter acknowledges that Scots, Welsh, and Irish have derived economic benefits from the British Empire, but that only means that Britain's Celtic fringe was a (seemingly homogenous) colony within the core of the world economic system; his main concern was economic relations *within* Britain and Ireland, beginning with England's 'union' with Wales in 1536, but focusing mostly on capitalist industrial development from the late eighteenth century to the time of publication. Hechter's biggest fault is that he seems not to have grasped at the outset that the Scottish Lowlands were not Celtic and that they were as much part of the core in the industrial development of Britain as the North and Midlands of England. He also underestimates the distinctiveness and durability of Scottish civil society and the significance of an established church in Scotland that, unlike those in Ireland and Wales, was not Anglican. The Scottish Enlightenment, too, was hardly the product of a backward people. David McCrone, in his celebrated *Understanding Scotland: The Sociology of a Stateless Nation* (1992: ch. 3), examines economic data for the nineteenth and twentieth centuries and concludes that, contrary to Hechter's attribution of peripheral status, the Scottish economy, unlike the Welsh, has not been markedly less diversified than the English. Reconsidering his thesis some time after its original publication, Hechter (1982: 9) decided that Scotland perhaps presented a case not of underdevelopment but rather of 'an overdeveloped peripheral region'. McCrone is unimpressed: 'Describing Scotland as "overdeveloped" as an explanation for neo-nationalism when "underdevelopment" does not do the job does not ring true' (1992: 62). Hechter is on better ground when discussing the Scottish Highlands, though he misleads in so far as he presents the lairds who perpetrated the Highland clearances (the displacement of tenant farmers to make way for more profitable sheep grazing) as simply Anglicized. He is also on better ground when considering Wales where by the nineteenth century the gentry were indeed Anglicized (mostly both English-speaking only and Anglican) but the people were not, and measures were taken to suppress the Welsh language. Nevertheless Graham Day in his impressive *Making Sense of Wales: A Sociological Perspective* (2002: 62) observes that 'The omission from the internal colonial model of any reference to the transfer payments made by the British state [in the second half of the twentieth century] to support living standards and welfare in Wales was an especially glaring weakness'; far from being exploited, Wales was, by then at least, in receipt of subsidies. And with respect to Ireland, Hechter seems not to realize that Ulster Scots outnumber 'Ulster English' by two to one. (No doubt he thinks Ian Paisley is an English name.) A final comment: the forms of first English, then British, government, and the condition of first subjects, then citizens, since the unions of 1536 (Wales), 1707 (Scotland), and 1801 (Ireland) have not been colonial and to say they have is a rhetorical excess with a political charge. Hechter's fusion of a Marxist theory of capitalist exploitation with a theory of the cultural division of labour to generate a theory of internal colonialism and peripheral nationalism is certainly novel, but the application of the theory to the British case has not stood the test of time. There are too many misconceptions and historical errors (as well as too many doubts about the proxy measures Hechter uses to test his theory against historical evidence).

The first of the four issues for brief comparative examination is population, given that unions of partners grossly unequal in size are difficult to manage. In the British case England has always had by far the largest population and England's share of the total British and UK populations has grown significantly over the last two centuries (see Table 2.1). When England annexed Wales in 1536 it had an estimated population of 3.75 million compared with Wales's 0.28 million according to John Davies (1993: 233). John Guy (1984: 224), following Wrigley and Schofield (1981), gives a much lower figure for England in 1541 of 2.77 million. The England–Wales population ratio was thus about 10–13 : 1 in 1536 compared with the 16.9 : 1 indicated by the 2001 census. In 1688 Gregory King estimated the population of England and Wales to be 5.5 million and in 1755 Alexander Webster estimated the population of Scotland to be 1.26 million.[1] At the time of the union of England and Scotland in 1707 the population of England would have been considerably more than 5 million and the population of Scotland a little more than 1 million. The England–Scotland ratio would thus have been about 5 : 1 compared to the 9.7 : 1 indicated by the 2001 census. The year of the union of Britain and Ireland to form the United Kingdom, 1801, was also the year of the first census in Britain (though not Ireland). The population of Britain was recorded as 10.59 million, that of England as 8.31 million; that of Ireland was estimated at 5.22 million. The Britain–Ireland and England–Ireland ratios were thus about 2.0 : 1 and 1.6 : 1 compared with ratios of 14.4 : 1 and 8.3 : 1 indicated by the 1921 census in Britain and the 1926 censuses in Ireland shortly after partition. Ireland lost 19.9 per cent of its population between 1841 and 1851, and 46.3 per cent between 1841 and 1911, the last census before partition, to emigration and to starvation following the failure of the potato crop in the 1840s. By contrast in the nineteenth century Scotland's population grew by 278 per cent, Wales's by 342 per cent, and England's by 367 per cent. In the twentieth century growth was much smaller but England's was still greatest. The population of Scotland grew by 11.3 per cent, that of Wales by 14.4 per cent and England's by 16.0 per cent.

In terms of politics today the most sensitive statistic in Table 2.1 is the decline in the Scottish share of the British population from 15.31 per cent in 1801 to 8.87 per cent in 2001. It is made even more sensitive by projections for future population. The Statistical Office population projections for 2021

TABLE 2.1	The UK population: Censuses of 1801–2001 (millions, and England, Wales, and Scotland as % of GB)					
	1801	1851	1901	1921	1951	2001
United Kingdom	15.74m	27.37m	41.46m	44.03m	50.23m	58.87m
Great Britain	10.50m	20.82m	37.00m	42.77m	48.86m	57.15m
England	8.31m	16.77m	30.52m	35.23m	41.16m	48.18m
	79.13%	85.30%	82.47%	82.38%	84.25%	86.06%
Wales	0.59m	1.16m	2.01m	2.66m	2.60m	2.90m
	5.59%	5.92%	5.44%	6.21%	5.32%	5.08%
Scotland	1.61m	2.89m	4.47m	4.89m	5.10m	5.06m
	15.31%	14.70%	12.01%	11.41%	10.43%	8.87%
Ireland	5.22m[*]	6.56m[†]	4.46m[†]	2.97m[‡]		
Northern Ireland				1.26m[‡]	1.37m	1.69m

Source: Derived from Annual Abstract of Statistics, no. 139, London: TSO, 2003, table 5.1, p. 26.
[*]Derived from C. Harvie (1984), p. 425.
[†]Derived from Annual Abstract of Statistics, no. 84 (1935–46), London: CSO, 1947, table 6, p. 7.
[‡]1926 censuses. Obtained from the website of CAIN: http://cain.ulst.ac.uk/ni, accessed 28 May 2005.

(in the Annual Abstract of Statistics, 140 (2004), 26) are for increases to 63.24 million in the United Kingdom, 61.14 million in Great Britain, 53.43m in England, and 3.04 million in Wales. By contrast the population of Scotland is projected to continue to fall. The census population of Scotland peaked at 5.24 million in 1971. It had fallen to 5.06 million in 2001 and is projected to fall further to 4.91 million and 8.00 per cent of the British population in 2021. Scotland entered the union as the formal equal of England. In practice, Scots accepted the status of junior partner in the union and its project of Empire but have always been sensitive about the persistent English conflation of England and Britain. The near halving of the Scottish share of the British population in the last two centuries has made it both easier for the English, on occasions, to leave Scotland out of account and even more necessary that Scots should contest the slight.

The most profound of the other three issues in its implications for national identity is that of differences in the ethnic composition of the nations and regions. Cardiff and Glasgow aside, concentrated non-white ethnic minorities are largely an English phenomenon. Economic inequalities have also been a sensitive issue, especially in Scotland following the discovery of 'Scotland's oil', although it is Wales that more often compares badly with English regions. There is also the related question of different levels of public spending across the nations and regions, with Scotland in particular faring better than poorer English regions. Devolution has also raised awkward questions about the representation of the people at Westminster. Scottish 'overrepresentation' is now being ended. These comparisons also begin to reveal how different London is from everywhere else.

Constitutional reform has to take into account the very different ethnic composition of the populations of England, Scotland, and Wales. That many black and Asian British identify themselves as such diverts attention from the very different ethnic compositions of England, Scotland, and Wales. The 2001 Census recorded non-white population percentages as:

9.0 in England,
2.1 in Wales,
2.0 in Scotland.[2]

The English percentage covers very big regional and metropolitan county variations, for example:

28.8 in Greater London,
11.3 in the West Midlands metropolitan county,
2.3 in the South-West.

These percentages indicate the upper range for selected districts and counties:

60.6 in the London borough of Newham,
54.7 in the London borough of Tower Hamlets,
36.3 in Slough,
36.1 in Leicester,
29.1 in Birmingham,
21.7 in Bradford,
19.0 in Manchester.

By contrast there is the lower range:

1.5 in Norfolk,
1.3 in Dorset,
1.0 in Cornwall,
1.0 in Northumberland,
0.7 in Cumbria.

These are the largest percentages in Wales and Scotland:

8.4 in Cardiff,
5.5 in Glasgow.

The striking feature of the non-white population in terms of national identity, as recorded by the General Household Survey for 2001 (table 3.19), is that on the one hand 51 per cent defined themselves as British only, compared with 29 per cent of the white population, while on the other 32 per cent chose an identity which was neither British, nor English, Scottish, Welsh, or Irish, compared with just 2 per cent of the white population.[3] In other words, half the black and Asian population identifies with Britain rather than any of its constituents, while a third identifies neither with Britain nor any of its constituents. That third, around a million-and-a-half people, poses a worrying challenge to integrationists.

The uneven distribution of the ethnic minority population of Britain is also very significant, in so far as talk of multiculturalism is consistent with the daily experience of most people in Inner London, but not that of most people in, say, Devon and Cornwall or Norfolk (cf. Younge 2000). Politicians and media commentators based in London who routinely refer to multiculturalism do not always remember that. On the other hand people living outside London—now, it is claimed, the most ethnically diverse city in Europe—seldom appreciate just how different London is from other regions with major non-white populations, such as the West Midlands, let alone regions without them, such as the North-East or the South-West. Combined figures for both the 2001 and 2002 General Household Surveys indicate that London's 13 per cent of the total population of Britain is made up of these percentages of the totals for each ethnic group:

white British	9
other white	39
mixed	32
Indian	36
Pakistani and Bangladeshi	25
Other Asian	49
black Caribbean	56
black African	80
other black	80
other	46

As Table 2.2 shows, England has a higher per capita GVA and per capita disposable income than Scotland, Wales, or Northern Ireland.[4] If one breaks England down into the English regions, however, it becomes evident that this is due mainly to the prosperity of London, the South-East, and the East (which includes part of the London commuter belt). Scotland had a higher per capita GVA in both 1991 and 2001 than six of the nine English regions. Wales had a lower figure than any English region in 1991, and a figure higher than only one English region in 2001. Scotland also had a higher per capita disposable income than six English regions in 1991 and five in 2001. Wales had a higher figure than two English regions in 1991 but a figure lower than any English region in 2001. Turning to unemployment, England had a lower unemployment rate in 1999 and 2003 than any of the other three parts of the United Kingdom, but again Scotland had a lower rate than two English regions in 1999 and three in 2003. Wales had a higher rate than any English region in 1995 but a lower rate than five regions in 2003 and a lower rate than England as a whole. England had a lower rate of unemployment benefit claimants than any other part of the UK in both 1998 and 2002. The Scottish rate was higher than only one English region in both years and the same as a second. The Welsh rate was exceeded by only one English region in 1992, but in 2002 two English regions had a higher rate and two more the same rate as Wales.

One other politically sensitive measure of the economic fortunes of the nations and regions of Britain is public expenditure per head. Table 2.3 compares 1998–9 with 2002–3. Public expenditure in Scotland remains higher than in any English region and is 21 per cent higher than in England as a whole. Public expenditure in Wales is nearly as high as in Scotland and

| TABLE 2.2 | Economic trends by nation and English region |

	GVA per head (UK = 100)		Gross Disposable Income per head (UK = 100)		Unemployment rate (%)		Unemployment claimant count rate (%)	
	1991	2001	1991	2001	1999	2003	1998	2002
United Kingdom	100.0	100.0	100.0	100.0	6.2	5.1	4.6	3.1
North-East	84.5	76.4	88.3	88.9	10.1	6.6	7.1	5.2
North-West	90.8	89.8	94.2	93.7	6.5	5.1	5.1	3.6
Yorks & Humber	90.4	86.4	93.7	91.9	6.7	5.5	5.4	3.7
East Midlands	94.9	91.9	95.0	92.8	5.3	4.3	4.0	2.9
West Midlands	92.0	90.4	88.7	94.1	6.9	5.9	4.5	3.5
East	109.4	110.1	109.7	104.9	4.4	4.2	3.3	2.1
London	130.5	133.2	117.8	120.4	7.8	7.1	5.2	3.6
South-East	110.2	120.1	109.9	109.0	3.8	3.9	2.6	1.7
South-West	92.9	89.3	101.4	99.3	5.0	3.9	3.4	2.0
England	101.8	102.5	101.3	101.4	6.0	5.1	4.3	3.0
Wales	83.3	78.9	89.8	87.5	7.4	4.6	5.5	3.6
Scotland	99.5	94.7	96.3	97.3	7.5	5.7	5.4	3.7
Northern Ireland	76.4	78.4	85.1	88.7	7.6	5.4	7.3	4.5

Source: Derived from Regional Trends, 38, tables 12.1, 2.7, 5.18, and 5.19 (London: National Statistics, 2004).

is similar to that in the English region with the highest spending, namely London where government spends a lot on itself.

Taking all these measures together Scotland fares better than some English regions and decidedly better than Wales where per capita disposable income remains lower than in any English region, though the fall in unemployment there has been proportionately higher than in England. That public spending in Scotland is higher than in England is only to be expected in so far as the Barnett formula introduced in 1978 entrenched a premium in the base of the Treasury block grant for Scotland both in recognition of

TABLE 2.3	Total identifiable expenditure on services by nation and English region (index)	
	1998–9	2002–3
United Kingdom	100	100
North-East	110	114
North-West	107	107
Yorkshire & the Humber	98	98
East Midlands	89	89
West Midlands	95	95
East	84	83
London	114	115
South-East	85	83
South-West	91	98
England	96	96
Wales	114	115
Scotland	116	116
Northern Ireland	133	129

Source: Derived from HM Treasury Public Expenditure Statistical Analyses 2004, table 8.2 (London: National Statistics, 2004), Cm 6201.

greater need and in order to spike nationalist guns. Oil in Scottish waters has long prompted Scots to ask whether their economy would not do better in an independent Scotland, but most commentators are agreed that it is not economic grievance that drives Scottish and Welsh separatists.

The Barnett formula and how it has worked, has not worked, and could be made to work is a difficult and contentious issue, but Robert Twigger (1998), Iain McLean (2000, 2003), Timothy Edmonds (2001), and Peter Jones (2002) offer some enlightenment. The main features of the story are these: in 1978 Joel Barnett, the Labour Chief Secretary to the Treasury, introduced a formula to allocate annual increases in block grant to Scotland and Wales in order to avoid continued wrangles with the nationalists.

The Treasury had in 1976–7 made an assessment of relative need in England, Scotland, Wales, and Northern Ireland in anticipation of the devolution to Scotland and Wales then proposed (but subsequently rejected in the referendums of 1979). This assessment (not published at the time) indexed needs in England at 100 with figures of 116 for Scotland and 109 for Wales, compared with actual spending per head indexed at 100 for England with figures of 122 for Scotland and 106 for Wales (McLean 2000: 83). Barnett took the actual spending as the base thereby advantaging Scotland and disadvantaging Wales.[5] Barnett then used the ratio 85 : 10 : 5 to divide the annual British addition to the base between England, Scotland, and Wales respectively. The ratio was supposed to reflect the distribution of population, but Barnett applied it in a way that did not. He 'decided Scotland should get 10/85 (11.79%) and Wales 5/85 (5.88%) of the English increase'; 11.79 per cent was greater than Scotland's 11.1 per cent of the British population (Jones 2002: 192). The formula did not apply to English regions, for which there had been no assessment of relative need. Over time the proportion of the total represented by the base (which reflected need) would diminish as annual formulaic increases (which did not) were added and there would thus be convergence—except that there was not. The reasons for this are complicated but basically the working of the formula (base plus accumulated annual increases made according to the ratio) was not adjusted for Scotland's decline in population after 1978 relative to England until 1992. There have also been separate payments for items specific to Scotland (and Wales) such as public water authorities (water authorities in England have been privatized) and occasional special in-year increases outside the formula. Four other points are important. First, the formula only applied to block grant expenditure, around 60 per cent of the total; among expenditure omitted is that on social security and defence. Second, the base assessment of need has never been revised notwithstanding 'Scotland's huge relative improvement in GDP per head' (McLean 2000: 87). Third, the incorporation since 1997 of an annual review of population figures has resulted in what in Scotland is portrayed as 'the Barnett Squeeze'. 'In rough terms, a 4 per cent increase in England translates into a 3 per cent increase in Scotland' (Jones 2002: 193). The squeeze is portrayed in some Scottish quarters as an English inflicted injustice, not the English catch-up it is. But the 1 per cent difference can bite hard where increases are not much more than inflation (not currently the case in health and education); not much more in England translates into next-to-nothing, and adverse comment, in Scotland. Fourth, academic commentators are agreed that the Barnett formula is broken. Opinion differs on whether repair or replacement is the better course. Most argue that either way reform will require a new needs assessment that takes account of English regional variations for the first time (Jones 2002; McLean 2003).

The differences in parliamentary representation between England on the one hand, and Scotland and Wales on the other, are more significant. The overrepresentation of Scotland, Wales, and Northern Ireland at Westminster by comparison with England is shown in Table 2.4. Before devolution few English politicians or voters seemed to mind, but the 1998 act which provided for devolution also required the Boundary Commission for Scotland to apply the same electoral quota (average electorate) to Scotland as is applied to England. This will reduce Scottish seats by a fifth to fifty-nine at the next general election. The anomaly of Scottish and Welsh MPs voting on English domestic affairs when their English counterparts cannot vote on Scottish and Welsh domestic affairs because responsibility for these has been devolved to Edinburgh and Cardiff will remain. This has not proved an issue yet, but it will if and when a contentious measure pertaining to England only, and supported by a majority of English MPs, is lost because enough Scottish and Welsh MPs oppose it. At the moment this

TABLE 2.4 Distribution of UK parliamentary seats by country and average electorate in 2003

	No. of seats	Average electorate
England	529	69,981
Scotland	72	53,583
Wales	40	55,499
Northern Ireland	18	59,309
United Kingdom	659	67,311

Source: Richard Cracknell, 'Electorates—2003', Standard Note sn/sg/02165, London: House of Commons Library, 8 March 2004.

is unlikely because Labour governments since 1997 have enjoyed big majorities in Scotland, Wales, and England—indeed this is one of the reasons why the heat has been taken out of the nationalist cause in Scotland and Wales—but it does have a bearing on the plight of the Conservative Party and its stance on English nationalism.

General election results in Britain are distorted by the simple majority voting system, and complicated by the presence of nationalist parties in Scotland and Wales. Even so there is clearly a difference in political culture between England on the one hand and Scotland and Wales on the other. Thatcherite neo-liberalism found much more favour in England. In Scotland and Wales what grated between 1979 and 1997 was government by a Conservative Party that had been unambiguously rejected at the polls. The Conservatives lost all their MPs in Scotland at the 1997 general election (the culmination of four decades of decline from 1955 when they were the largest party with thirty-six seats) and in 2001 they regained just one constituency. In 1997 they also lost all their seats in Wales and they failed to win any back in 2001. By contrast, they only lost half their MPs in England in 1997, and although they made no net gains in 2001 they remain more likely to recover lost ground there than in Scotland or Wales. Were the Conservatives sometime in the future to win in England but lose in Britain overall because of opposition in Scotland and Wales, political representation in Britain following devolution might quickly become a major issue. Historically the Conservatives have also been the Unionist Party, but their leader between 1997 and 2001, William Hague, flirted with the idea of an English parliament. Were some future demand for an English parliament to succeed there would be devolution all round. Where that would lead—federation, dissolution of the union, or something novel—it is impossible to foresee.

Can Britain be reforged?

Establishment of the British state preceded formation of a British nation, but British national identity has helped to secure that state. The Treaty of Union, however, has ensured that British national identity could only be an overarching, not an exclusive, one. It inserted the precedent of group rights—the separate institutions and identity of the Scots—from the start. Accommodation of non-territorial groups was always possible, though not necessarily easy, once it was clear all Britons were not going to be the same. The British Empire, all of whose subjects had a right of entry to Britain, only confirmed that. For the union of Britain to continue, however, there does have to be a content to an overarching British identity—and Protestantism, Empire, and military and economic might no longer provide it. Negative British responses to both Commonwealth immigration and the development of the European Community/Union reflect, at least in part, the unease of those who are no longer confident about their nation's identity and who seek to strengthen it by recalling, or reimagining, the past. How, or even whether, British national identity can be reconstructed in a secular and post-imperial society of diminished economic standing relative to others is an open question.

The chapters that follow begin by discussing separately Scotland, Wales, and England in that order. The discussion starts with Scotland because that is where the future of the union will be decided. Scotland could choose independence—it is both politically possible and practically feasible—and if it were to do so it is hard to see how it could be denied it for long. Whether it will do so is quite another matter. The discussion then turns to Wales. It is very unlikely that Wales would opt for independence if Scotland had not already done so, but Welsh national consciousness is in the ascendant. Where does a conspicuous strengthening of Scotland and Wales as communities of national sentiment which has already issued in devolution leave the English? At a minimum, it leaves (some of) them rediscovering Englishness and reconsidering Britishness at a time of constitutional change in London and talk of change in the English regions (though the latter cause suffered a very major setback with the 'no' vote on establishment of an assembly in the North-East in November 2004). It is only after working through aspects of the past, present, and future in Scotland, Wales, and England as they are seen today that one can properly return to the question of the future of Britain. It is not hard to think of elements that could in principle figure in the reforging of Britain, but whether they will do so in practice only time will tell. In principle reconstruction might be possible in terms of some distinctive configuration of common culture, the riches of multiculturalism, differences from Europe, the product of internal migration and intermarriage, and positively valued aspects of Britain's historical legacy. There are plenty of commentators—and not all of them Scots—who expect the dissolution of Britain within a generation or two, but it is by no means a foregone conclusion.

NOTES

1 On King, see George (1953: 14–19 and appendix). On Webster, see Smout (1972: 241–5).

2 2001 census figures have been obtained via the websites of National Statistics <www.statistics. gov.uk/census2001> and the General Register Office for Scotland <www.gro-scotland.gov.uk/census 2001>, both accessed 1 June 2005.

3 All figures from the General Household Surveys for 2001 and 2002 have been taken from *Living in Britain* reports accessed via the website of National Statistics <www.statistics.gov.uk/lib2001>, accessed 1 June 2005.

4 Instead of GDP, some British official statistics now refer to GVA. Gross Value Added is Gross Domestic Product at value added instead of at market prices. When grossing the value of all products, taxes (such as VAT) and subsidies are excluded. GVA thus measures what firms add in value to products, or what final users pay minus taxes and subsidies.

5 The Conservative government elected in 1979 did the same, because to do otherwise would have required a greater reduction in public expenditure in Scotland than Margaret Thatcher intended for Britain as a whole and this was deemed too provocative.

REFERENCES

AUGHEY, ARTHUR (2001), *Nationalism, Devolution and the Challenge to the United Kingdom State* (London: Pluto).

BRUBAKER, ROGERS (1996), *Nationalism Reframed: Nationhood and the National Question in the New Europe* (Cambridge: Cambridge UP).

COLLEY, LINDA (1992), *Britons: Forging the Nation 1707–1837* (New Haven Conn.: Yale University Press).

DAHRENDORF, RALF (1982), *On Britain* (London: BBC).

DAVIES, JOHN (1993), *A History of Wales* (London: Penguin), 1st Welsh edn. 1990.

DAY, GRAHAM (2002), *Making Sense of Wales: A Sociological Perspective.* (Cardiff: University of Cardiff Press).

DEVINE, THOMAS M. (2003), *Scotland's Empire 1600–1815* (London: Penguin—Allen Lane).

EDMONDS, TIMOTHY (2001), 'The Barnett Formula', *House of Commons Library Research Papers*, no. 01/108.

FRY, MICHAEL (2001), *The Scottish Empire* (Phantassie (East Lothian): Tuckwell, and Edinburgh: Birlinn).

GAMBLE, ANDREW (1981), *Britain in Decline* (London: Macmillan).

GEORGE, M. DOROTHY (1953), *England in Transition*, rev. edn. (Harmondsworth: Penguin), 1st edn. 1931.

GILES, JUDY, and MIDDLETON, TIM (1995) (eds.), *Writing Englishness 1900–1950: An Introductory Sourcebook on National Identity* (London: Routledge).

GRANT, ALEXANDER, and STRINGER, KEITH J. (1995) (eds.), *Uniting the Kingdom? The Making of British History* (London: Routledge).

GUY, JOHN (1984), 'The Tudor age', in Morgan (ed.), ch. 5.

HABERMAS, JÜRGEN (German 1962), *The Structural Transformation of the Public Sphere* (Cambridge: Polity, 1989).

HARVIE, CHRISTOPHER (1984), 'Revolution and the rule of law (1789–1851)', in Morgan (ed.), ch. 8.

HASELER, STEPHEN (1996), *The English Tribe: Identity, Nation and Europe* (Basingstoke: Macmillan).

HECHTER, MICHAEL (1975), *Internal Colonialism: The Celtic Fringe in British National Development, 1536–1966* (London: Routledge & Kegan Paul).

——— (1982), 'Internal colonialism revisited', *Cencrastus*, 10: 8–11.

HITCHENS, PETER (1999), *The Abolition of Britain* (London: Quartet), rev. edn. 2000.

JONES, PETER (2002), 'Barnett plus needs: the regional spending challenge in Britain', in J. TOMANEY and J. MAWSON (eds.), *England: The State of the Regions* (Bristol: Policy Press), ch. 14.

McCRONE, DAVID (1992), *Understanding Scotland: The Sociology of a Stateless Nation* (London: Routledge).

McLEAN, IAIN (2000), 'A fiscal constitution for the UK', in S. CHEN and T. WRIGHT (eds.), *The English Question* (London: Fabian Society), ch. 6.

——— (2003), 'Public finance in a union state: Goschen, Barnett and beyond', paper presented at the British Academy/Royal Society of Edinburgh Symposium, Anglo-Scottish Relations since 1914, Edinburgh, November 2003.

MARQUAND, DAVID (1993), 'The twilight of the British state? Henry Dubb versus sceptred awe', *Political Quarterly*, 64: 210–12.

——— (1995), 'How united is the United Kingdom?', in Grant and Stringer (eds.), ch. 16.

MARSHALL, THOMAS H. (1949), 'Citizenship and social class', in his *Sociology at the Crossroads and Other Essays* (London: Heinemann, 1963), ch. 4.

MORGAN, KENNETH O. (1984) (ed.), *The Oxford Illustrated History of Britain* (Oxford: Oxford University Press).

NEWMAN, GERALD (1987), *The Rise of English Nationalism: A Cultural History 1740–1830*, 2nd edn. (Basingstoke: Macmillan).

PARTRIDGE, SIMON (1999), 'The British Union State: Imperial Hangover or Flexible Citizens' Home?', *Catalyst Papers*, 4 (London: Catalyst Trust).

PAXMAN, JEREMY (1998), *The English: A Portrait of a People* (London: Michael Joseph).

POWELL, DAVID (2002), *Nationhood and Identity: The British State since 1800* (London: I. B. Tauris).

ROBBINS, KEITH (1995), 'An imperial and multinational polity: the "scene from the centre"', in Grant and Stringer (eds.), ch. 14.

——— (1998), *Great Britain: Identities, Institutions and the Idea of Britishness* (London: Longman).

SCHWARTZ, BILL (1996) (ed.), *The Expansion of England: Race, Ethnicity and Cultural History* (London: Routledge).

SMOUT, T. C. (1972), *A History of the Scottish People 1560–1830* (London: Fontana).

TWIGGER, ROBERT (1998), 'The Barnett Formula', *House of Commons Library Research Papers*, 98/8.

WEIGHT, RICHARD (2002), *Patriots: National Identity in Britain 1940–2000* (London: Macmillan).

WRIGLEY, E. A., and SCHOFIELD, R. S. (1981), *The Population History of England 1541–1871: A Reconstruction* (London: Edward Arnold).

YOUNGE, GARY (2000), 'On race and Englishness', in S. CHEN and T. WRIGHT (eds.), *The English Question* (London: Fabian Society), ch. 8.

3

....

Claiming Scotland

Introduction

The union of England and Scotland from 1707 conserved, or more accurately allowed further development of, a distinctively Scottish civil society that in turn generated and regenerated a Scottish identity. Scots could and did become British but few forgot that they were also still Scots. But with the British Empire gone and Britain's relative economic decline seemingly without end, it is hardly surprising that from the 1950s onwards many Scots should have revisited their Scottishness. In 1992 David McCrone published a seminal account of the part played by a distinctive Scottish civil society in sustaining Scotland as a stateless nation, and Lindsay Paterson (1994) and Tom Devine (1999) have shown why for so long most Scots thought devolution or independence unnecessary. Basically, Scotland had its own institutions run by Scots, the UK governing party up to 1979 had nearly always been the same as the leading party in Scotland, and Scotland got (more than) fair treatment in terms of measures to support its economy and share of public expenditure. Many recent publications have explained how and why this has now changed dramatically. The majority of the people in Scotland now support devolution, a minority favour independence, and only a few seek a return to the status quo ante. Only time will tell whether devolution will facilitate maintenance of the union of England and Scotland or turn out to be a step towards the independence of a 'sovereign' Scotland.

When the people of England, Scotland, and Wales are asked to specify their national identity there are clear differences in the claims they make. Surveys in 2003 found that 65 per cent of Scottish residents declare themselves Scottish only or more Scottish than British, compared with 36 per cent of English residents, and 48 per cent of Welsh, who made a similar claim about their Englishness or Welshness (see above, Ch. 1, Table 1.1). Scots may strongly affirm the primacy of their Scottish identity, but who do they think they are? The debate in Scotland over the last three decades has been intense and extensive but it has not yielded a single simple answer for a number of reasons. First, there has been ambivalence in Scotland about Britain and the British. On the one hand Britain has historically afforded Scots economic and other opportunities, though less now than when the Empire was at its height, but on the other the English have dominated Britain often to the point of not knowing or even caring whether they themselves were English or British and thus also to the point of gross insensitivity to Scottish identity and distinctiveness. So what Scots think about Scotland is related to what they think about Britain and that itself is complex. Britain for most people in Scotland is neither truly home nor really abroad. Until 1994 there was an annual football competition between England, Scotland, Wales, and Northern Ireland called the Home Internationals. 'Home international' is a very odd concept but it does capture something of Scotland's relation to Britain.

Second, Tom Nairn (1977) long ago pointed out that nationalism is not just about the burnishing of a distinctive national identity, it is also about the mobilizing myth of 'the people'. But the English constitutional settlement of the Glorious Revolution in 1688 established the sovereignty of (the crown in) parliament, not the sovereignty of the people, and thereby diverted the English from thinking then and since in republican terms about 'we the people' as the foundation of democracy and thus about who we the people are. Following the union of the crowns in 1603 and the union of parliaments in 1707, the settlement discouraged Scots, too, from thinking in terms of 'we the people' much of the time. The English/British formula of the crown in parliament has been convenient in so far as there has been ambivalence in Scotland about Scotland and the Scots. If Scotland since the Reformation has been a Presbyterian nation how can the millions descended from nineteenth-century Irish Catholic immigrants be part of it? What too of the English in Scotland (as Britons from south of the border are labelled irrespective of how they identify themselves) or other minorities? Scots can easily agree that they are not English but talk of 'we the Scottish people' can quickly expose divisions of class, ethnic origin (Scottish, Irish, English, Other), religion, and occasional residues of the once significant division between the Highlands and the Lowlands.

Third, running counter to the demobilizing invocation of the crown in parliament, but also complicating argument, there has in Scotland additionally been, as Jonathan Hearn (2000) has reminded us, a tradition of covenants and claims of right. The National Covenant of 1638 bound the signatories to defend Presbyterianism and oppose Catholicism. The Solemn League and Covenant of 1643 'pledged mutual support between the Covenanters and the English parliament in the same cause' (p. 105). The Claim of Right of 1689 'prohibited royal prerogative from overriding parliamentary law in Scotland, thus setting Scotland's terms for the accession of William and Mary' (p. 60). The Claim of Right of 1842 'was drawn up by the General Assembly of the Church of Scotland to voice objection to Westminster interference in Church matters' (ibid.). The Scottish Covenant of 1949 committed signatories to doing all in their power to secure a Scottish parliament, and the Claim of Right for Scotland of 1988 (which included rejection of the crown in parliament) was drafted by a group of eminent men and women demanding a Scottish assembly.[1] In short, at key junctures in Scottish history (would-be) influential men and women have combined to make covenants and claims of right in order to assert and safeguard (true) Scottish identities and interests. This Presbyterian informed counter-tradition to that of the crown in parliament still has a resonance—though its historical associations are unlikely to have as much appeal to Catholics as to Presbyterians.

Fourth, there is the problem of what Neal Ascherson (2002) calls St Andrew's fault. The debate about Scotland, Scottishness, and a Scottish parliament has, at least until recently, had much greater salience for the professional classes than the rest of the people. McCrone (1992) drew attention to Scotland's distinctive civil society and public administration and the distinctive professional classes associated with them. The latter ran the numerous Scottish institutions, which are different from those in England including the separate legal, church, education, and local government systems guaranteed by the Treaty of Union of 1707 and the devolved state administration of Scotland before and after the establishment of the Scottish Office in 1887. It is among the professionals and public administrators that interest in Scottishness has been greatest—institutional Scotland, after all, had been their preserve. In other words the debate about Scottishness has sometimes divided Scots on class lines with middle-class Scots deliberating whether devolution would enable them to run Scotland better and hard-pressed working-class Scots just taking their Scottishness for granted. The fifth, and related, reason is that the separate system of Scottish public administration without, until 1999, any accompanying devolved parliament, was in many ways so peculiar as to frustrate clear discussion and defy the classifications of polities made by social scientists. It is part of the 'when is autonomy not autonomy?' issue discussed below

The sixth reason why the question is difficult is that when Scots think about Scotland there is more than one possibility with which to engage. I cannot overemphasize that the seven alternatives are not necessarily exclusive—quite the contrary, most Scots, in their identifications, switch between (aspects of) them according to circumstances—and, with perhaps one exception, each enjoys considerable currency in practice if not in name.

The seven constructions are: two versions of Independent Scotland (Celtic Scotland and Scotland the Brave), Civil Scotland, Scotland in the Empire, Little Scotland, Self-Governing Scotland and Scotland in Europe. They can be differentiated on two dimensions as Table 3.1 illustrates, orientation to time and orientation to place, with Britain in an ambiguous position between home and abroad. The first version of (1) Independent Scotland, (1a) Celtic Scotland, is one of the three main constructions of Scotland's past. It emphasizes developments within Scotland itself. Celtic Scotland is more Highland, Gaelic, and, sometimes, Catholic. It shades into (1b) Scotland the Brave following the wars of independence with England.

TABLE 3.1	Contemporary constructions of Scotland by time and place		
		Orientations to place	
		Home	*Britain*	*Abroad*
Past	1. Independent Scotland	2. Civil Scotland	3. Scotland in the Empire
Orientations to Time	*Present*	4. Little Scotland	5. Scotland: Civic and Self-Governing	6. Scotland in Europe

Scotland the Brave is a source of Scottish heroes. (2) Civil Scotland, by contrast, is more Lowland, Scots, and Presbyterian. It is an auld Scotland ('auld' is Scots for 'old') that originated before the union with England but only fully developed after it and in some respects as a consequence of it. It has had a highly distinctive civil society, so that what Ulrich Beck (1986) would call its 'sub-politics', politics in all settings other than British parliamentary democracy, are its own, and it can be said to have been self-managing—but it was still a stateless nation only. (3) Scotland in the Empire was more than a junior partner in the union, it was a vigorous and disproportionately large partner in the British Empire. Civil Scotland and Scotland in the Empire both look backwards. Civil Scotland also looks outward to Britain, and Scotland in the Empire looked outward beyond it. Both acknowledge that the union was a marriage of convenience from which the partners have historically benefited. Whether the union is still convenient, with the Empire long gone, is now questioned but the answers are varied. (4) Little Scotland—not a term with much currency but one chosen by loose analogy with Little England—refers to a contemporary Scotland preoccupied with itself and suspicious of Britain, Europe, and foreign entanglements generally and also of those in its midst who are not true Scots. By contrast (5) Civic and Self-Governing Scotland is confident and at ease in a redefined union, whilst (6) Scotland in Europe is outward-looking, confident, and expansive. For supporters of the union as well as advocates of Scottish independence it provides an alternative to looking to Britain and it opens Scottish life and culture to diversification (in the relative absence of the diversity presented by ethnic minority communities in England).

Two of these characterizations need a further comment. For Lindsay Paterson (1994), as for Jaroslav Krejčí and Vítězslav Velímsky (1981) before him, what I have called Civil Scotland amounted to an 'autonomous' Scotland, but whether autonomous is the right word is arguable. Scotland may have had its own jurisdiction and law (the literal meaning of 'autonomous'—*nomos* is Greek for law) but it was not self-legislating because, having no parliament from 1707 to 1999, it was not self-governing (the usual meaning of autonomous). What I have called call Self-Governing Scotland I had intended to call Autonomous Scotland because I think it has similarities with what in Spain is called the autonomous community of Catalonia (Catalunya) (see Ch. 8), but have desisted because Paterson's work is well known. By 'self-governing' I mean not 'independent' or 'sovereign' but an autonomous Scotland with a parliament.

The location of Britain between Home and Abroad in this table is highly appropriate. In some ways Britain has been an extension of Home, as in a home language area, a home market, and a home polity; but in other respects Britain is not-quite abroad, a place where non-Scots predominate and where England is the primary Other. (For the English, Scotland is almost never the Other; vastly commoner candidates are France, Germany, or 'Europe'.)

1 Independent Scotland

There are constructions of Scotland that find in the past the inspiration for Scotland to be a nation again. One is Celtic Scotland as an alternative to Anglo-Saxon England and Anglo-Britain. The other is Scotland the Brave, which fought England to safeguard its independence and won.

1.1 Celtic Scotland

Scotland emerged from the settlements and kingdoms of indigenous Picts north of the Forth-Clyde, Scots (whose forebears had migrated from the north of Ireland and extended the kingdom of Dalriada to Argyll and beyond), indigenous Britons (i.e. the Celts, or Galls, who were the inhabitants of Britain south of the Forth-Clyde when the Romans invaded and whose name lives on in Galloway), Northumbrian Angles in south-east Scotland between the Forth and the Tweed, and Norsemen (who originated in Scandinavia) in the Northern Isles and the far north of the mainland. At the time of the Norman invasion of England in 1066 it was unclear which lands south of the Forth-Clyde and north of the Ribble-Tees would finally be incorporated in Scotland and which in England. Following the union of the Picts and Scots traditionally attributed to Kenneth Mac Alpin between 843 and 847, 'Scotland' referred to lands north of the Forth; 'it is not until the late twelfth or even the thirteenth century that the term Scotia, Scotland, begins to acquire . . . the connotations and range we associate with it' today (R. Davies 1999: 56). English and Continental writers sometimes refer to Scotland, Wales, and Ireland as Britain's Celtic fringe. This is misleading in different ways in each case. It is misleading in the Scottish case in so far as Celtic Scotland represents only one part of Scotland's past, albeit a part that figures prominently in the contemporary branding of Scotland for commercial, tourist, and other purposes (McCrone, Morris, and Kiely 1995). Three aspects of Celtic Scotland are particularly important for this discussion: the Gaelic language, the changing valuation of the Highlands, and the iconography of tartanry.

At their maximum extent in the first millennium BC Celtic speakers are thought by some scholars to have inhabited lands across Europe including Britain and Ireland, much of Iberia (where they have given their name to Galicia in north-west Spain), most of France (Gaul), lands along the Danube as far as the Black Sea, lands north of the Carpathians (where they have given their name to Galicia in southern Poland), and much of Anatolia (Galatia) in Turkey (Robb 2002: 235). Other scholars think that these far-flung Celts were simply barbarians, Keltoi, to the Greeks and not a single people or group of people at all (Harvey et al.: 2). What is not in dispute is that related 'Celtic' languages were once spoken throughout Britain and Ireland, even if they were only labelled as such for the first time in the early eighteenth century. It is not clear 'whether Celtic [the language] was brought over [to Britain and Ireland from the Continent] as late as the second-half of the first millennium BC, as some distinguished Irish scholars have supposed, or whether it had gradually evolved *in situ* from late western Indo-European over many millennia from 4500 BC, as argued by Colin Renfrew' (Sims-Williams 1998: 21). The Celtic languages fall into two groups in terms of phonetic development: the Goidelic (or Gaelic or Q-Celtic), which survives as Irish, Scottish Gaelic, and Manx; and the Brittonic (or British or P-Celtic), which survives as Welsh, Breton, and Cornish.

It is also not entirely clear whether the Picts in the Highlands of Scotland were a pre-Celtic or a Celtic people, but such linguistic evidence as suggests they were Celtic also suggests their language was Brittonic. The language of the Norsemen was Norse, that of the Celts of the south-west Cumbric, a Brittonic language, and that of the Angles Northumbrian English. Scottish Gaelic was thus the language of only one of the five peoples who constituted early Scotland, but it was the language of the one whose kings were to become kings of all Scotland and who gave their name to the country, and by the eleventh century it was the most widely spoken. MacKinnon (2000: 44) repeats a standard claim associating Scotland with Gaelic.

The Gaelic language came to Scotland around 500 AD with the expansion of the northern Irish kingdom of Dàl Riata into the western Highlands and Islands ... The expansion of this settlement and the subsequent absorption of the Pictish kingdom in Northern Scotland, the British kingdom of Strathclyde in south-western Scotland and part of Anglian Northumbria in the south-east, established a largely Gaelic-speaking Scottish kingdom [Alba], largely co-terminous with present-day Scotland, by the eleventh century.

Scotland may have been largely Gaelic-speaking in the eleventh century but the absorption of English-speaking northern Northumbria was highly significant. At its greatest Northumbria stretched from the Humber to the Forth. Northumbrians captured what we now know as the castle rock in Edinburgh from the Picts in 638. Edinburgh in the historical record was an English-speaking settlement from the start. The Northumbrians did not stop at the Forth. They sought to trade and dominate across the Forth in Fife and across the Tay in Angus, but were defeated in battle by the Picts in 685 and withdrew from north of the Forth. English traders continued to penetrate the east side of Scotland, however, even after the Northumbrians were driven back to the Tweed by Scottish kings late in the tenth century. The Northern Isles of Orkney and Shetland were also never Gaelic-speaking; they only became part of Scotland in 1468.

It was the Norman invasion of England in 1066 that was to make English, or an English dialect, the language of Lowland Scots.[2] King Malcolm III Ceannmor (Canmore) who ruled from 1057 to 1093 was a Celt and spoke Gaelic. In 1068 he married for a second time. His new wife, Margaret, was English, indeed a descendent of Alfred the Great of Wessex, and she was accompanied to Scotland by her brother Edgar, the heir to King Harold who was killed at the Battle of Hastings. Other English fled to Scotland at the same time. Margaret was a pious and gentle woman and Malcolm seems to have been in awe of her. He changed to speaking English, he accepted the English and Anglo-Normans who filled her court, and he turned from the Celtic church and followed her in embracing Roman ways. They had six sons, none of whom was given a Celtic name. Malcolm's brother Donald Bane, the last Gaelic-speaking king of Scotland, contested the succession and twice ruled briefly in the 1090s. Three sons of Malcolm and Margaret reigned between 1097 and 1153, the first of the whom, Edgar (who ruled from 1097 to 1107), moved the family home from Dunfermline to Edinburgh. They took further developments their father had begun which made the Lowlands predominantly English-speaking, thereby accentuating the difference between the Lowlands and the Highlands. Together they continued the Normanization of Scotland, basically the establishment of a feudal order in the countryside, incorporated and English-speaking burghs, and a Roman church. They and their courtiers intermarried with the English, held lands south of the border, and invited Norman and English families to settle in Scotland as the bearers of new skills and a more refined culture. Indeed Rees Davies (1999: 144) has argued that, 'regardless of the role played by [Norman] personnel in the leadership, momentum and documentation' of the movement of people, 'it was the English who were the numerically dominant and critical group'.

The English were most prominent in the south-east but were also found in southern Galloway (where settlement dated from the tenth century) and along the east coast. By the 1180s their absorption into a unitary Scottish kingdom was well underway. Gaelic, Davies argues, 'probably reached its maximum area of currency in the early twelfth century; thereafter the story is that of the advance of English and the retreat of Gaelic and Cumbric' (ibid. 157). Davies (ibid.) further claims that 'native society' in the south and east was 'party to a process of acculturation and cultural surrender, abandoning many of the crucial features of Gaelic culture (including classes of hereditary *judices* and poets, and offices such as that of *mair*), contracting mixed marriages, giving Anglo-Norman names to its children, and adopting English terminology for its urban and trading activities'. In addition, 'the law of Scotland, or at least of royal and lowland Scotland, was substantially reshaped on the English model from the mid-twelfth century onwards' (p. 106). By the beginning of the fourteenth century, Scotland also had twenty-six shires on the English model. For Davies all this is part of an Anglicization of the whole British Isles, but it was in the most populous and prosperous parts of Scotland 'that the influence of England—in law, institutions, tenurial custom, burghal development, coinage, trade patterns, language, and so forth—was arguably most profound' (pp. 170–1). This was, moreover, much more than just a reflection of English royal might and commercial acumen. 'It was also the triumph of the fashionable, the innovative, the exciting, the technologically more advanced, the wealth-creating, the transformative' (p. 170).

From the beginning of the twelfth century Scotland had English-speaking kings and an English-speaking court. Statutes of the Scottish parliament were written in English from 1382. Rule in Gaelic was limited to the Lordship of the Isles (the Hebrides and west coast of the Highlands) and even that was forfeited when the lordship lost its semi-autonomous status in 1493. The likeliest source of rebellion and disorder feared by these English-speaking kings was in the Gaelic-speaking Highlands. Measures to promote education in the medium of English were first enacted in the Scottish parliament in the late fifteenth century. 'By the 17th century Gaelic had retreated to the Highlands and Hebrides, which still retained much of their political independence, Celtic culture and social structure' (McKinnon 2000: 45). Further measures to promote English and suppress the Gaelic language and the culture of the clans culminated in the punitive acts of the British parliament after the failure of the 1745 rebellion led by Bonnie Prince Charlie. In the nineteenth century, at the time of the depopulation of the Highland clearances (the expulsion of the crofters by the lairds (lords) in order to make way for more profitable sheep-farming), successful voluntary Gaelic schools were started. But they were superseded after 1872 by universal free primary schooling in the medium of English. From then on Gaelic was largely a language of home and Calvinist church.

Gaelic remains the first language of a majority of the people of the Western Isles and parts of Skye—the Gaidhealtachd—and is widely spoken throughout most of the rest of the western Highlands, but the number of Gaelic speakers has declined sharply over the last century. According to the 2001 Census there were only 58,650 Gaelic speakers in Scotland—1.16 per cent of the total population—compared with 65,978 in 1991, a decline of 11.1 per cent in just a decade, and with 254,415 in 1891. Three-fifths of the speakers live in the Gaidhealtachd, but (the families of) most of the rest have left it for the Lowlands. Sentimental regard for Gaelic as the language of the Scots may be widespread, but few suppose its decline can be reversed. The Highland Gaelic-speaking population is ageing and Lowland Gaelic speakers are scattered, but there are some Gaelic radio programmes, publications, and columns in newspapers, and some new learners in primary schools (Robertson 1999; Macdonald 1999; MacKinnon 2000). Together these should save the language from unwanted extinction—but only as a marginal feature of Scottish life. Other aspects of the (supposed) culture of the Highlands—kilt, tartan, and bagpipes—have fared much better, and indeed have come to represent Scotland as a whole at home and abroad. This is the unlikely story of 1745 and 1822.

Tom Devine (1999: 231) has noted that the very notion of the Highlands does not appear in the written record before the fifteenth century (see also Withers 1992). Its growing use thereafter referred to an area of Scotland that was as much socially and culturally as geographically distinct and Gaelic was only ever part of the difference. For Lowland Scots and the English there have been three successive representations of the Highlands, the barbarous Highlands, the Jacobite Highlands, and the romantic Highlands. *The barbarous Highlands* were the Highlands of the clans, traditional authority, clan warfare (the last clan battle was fought as late as 1688), lawlessness, the absence of learning, and economic backwardness. Highlanders were regarded as uncivilized and the mountains were seen as dark, threatening, and forbiddingly hard to penetrate. Devine (1999: 232) notes that

In the early modern period, Highland instability was seen as a major obstacle to the effective unification of the country. After the Reformation, the Highlands were not properly evangelized for the new faith and were regarded as irreligious, popish and pagan for generations thereafter. For the Scottish political elites and the Presbyterian Church before 1700, the Highlands were alien and hostile, in need of greater state control and both moral and religious "improvement". The consensus was that the society had to be assimilated to the social and cultural norms that prevailed in the rest of Scotland because it was both inferior and dangerous.

Scotland may originally have been a Highland kingdom but learning, wealth, and the civility of civil society were features of the Lowland burghs. By the time of union the Highlands had become the Other Scotland, and not much valued.

The Jacobite Highlands were the site of rebellion against the crown and of consequent repressive measures that changed them forever. In 1603 James VI of Scotland had ascended the English throne as James I of England, or, as he preferred, Great Britain. The English Act of Succession of 1701 required that the monarch be a Protestant. When Queen Anne died childless in 1714, the Protestant succession was only secured by passing over the close claims of Catholic pretenders of the Scottish House of Stuart in favour of the distant claim of the Protestant Elector of Hanover who reigned as George I. In 1715 supporters of Prince James Edward Stuart, 'the Old Pretender'—mostly Highlanders and Catholic but including some Protestant Episcopalians and anti-unionists—mounted a rebellion. It was poorly led and easily defeated. The subsequent punitive measures were light by the standards of the time.

The last of four Jacobite rebellions in 1745 was a different story. The Young Pretender, Prince Charles Edward Stuart ('Bonnie Prince Charlie'), led an army raised in the Highlands on a march on London to claim the throne for his father. He got as far south as Derby before being chased back to Scotland and overwhelming defeat at Culloden, near Inverness, in 1746.

At the height of the 1745 emergency, George II went to a performance at the Haymarket Theatre in London. The audience responded with huge enthusiasm to the singing of 'God Save the King', a song that had existed in various versions for half a century (including a Jacobite one responsible for the line 'Send him victorious'—send him, that is, to claim his throne from the usurper). After 1745 what was to become known in the early nineteenth century as the national anthem acquired a verse that, unsurprisingly, is no longer sung.

> God grant that Marshall Wade,
> May by thy mighty aid,
>   Victory bring,
> May he sedition hush,
> And like a torrent rush,
> Rebellious Scots to crush,
>   God save the king.

Not all Scots were branded rebellious Scots, as some untutored Scottish nationalists now like to suppose, only the Jacobites—mostly Catholics and Episcopalians and mostly Highlanders. Their defeat at Culloden was at the hands of a Hanoverian army commanded by an Englishman, the Duke of Cumberland, but three of its four regular regiments were of Lowland Scots. The duke was congratulated on his success by the General Assembly of the Church of Scotland. McCrone, Morris, and Kiely (1995: 192) note how historians regard the '45' and its defeat as 'more of a civil war within Scotland than a national fight for independence between Scotland and England, yet the prevailing myth is that it represented a military defeat for Scotland and its final incorporation into the "English" state'. This time the punitive measures following rebellion were certainly severe. Cumberland decided on a scorched earth policy—burning, clearance, and pillage. The estates of those who backed the '45' were confiscated. In addition, all clan chiefs were deprived of their hereditable jurisdictions, their legal authority over their clansmen, and all clansmen were forbidden to carry arms or to wear the Highland dress of tartan, kilt, and plaid. The blow to Highland pride was immense. Steps were also taken to facilitate the spread of Presbyterianism, including penal restrictions on the Episcopal Church.

Given that Lowland Scots rejoiced at the defeat of the primitive High-landers as much as did the English, the revaluation, indeed celebration, of the Highlands by the early nineteenth century requires explanation. First, the Highlands by then no longer represented a threat to the Protestant as-cendancy. Helpfully, emigration had also ensured that there were now fewer Highlanders than before. Second, the romantic movement changed the per-ception of the mountains and glens from bleak and threatening to beautiful and inspiring. Third, the backward Highlander, once despised and feared, was now something of a noble savage—or at least brave, proud, and loyal to tradition. The Waverley novels of Sir Walter Scott played a significant part in this revaluation. Fourth, the raising of Highland regiments had provided an outlet for hitherto warring clansmen that proved of great value in the British Empire and during the Napoleonic wars. All agreed Highlanders were fine soldiers—and they looked splendid in their tartan dress. That dress, however, was not ages old but part of what Eric Hobsbawm and Ter-ence Ranger (1983) were the first to call an 'invented tradition'.

Highland dress before 1746 was plain and dull and its main item was a belted tunic, the plaid, the lower half of which was like a skirt. According to Hugh Trevor-Roper (1983), one of the main contributors to Hobsbawm and Ranger's seminal work, the kilt had only recently been invented and was not widely worn, and there were no bright tartans, let alone a distinctive pattern, or sett, for each clan. Some Highland regiments after 1745 adopted the kilt for convenience—others wore tartan trousers or trews. Either way, each regiment had a bright pattern of its own. The act forbidding civilians from wearing Highland dress was repealed in 1782, and the romanticization of the Highlands made the wearing of Highland dress among the fashion-able classes popular. Differentiation of tartans by regiment extended to dif-ferentiation by clan. There was no historical basis for these differences but Celtic romantics, and canny manufacturers in Lancashire as well as Scot-land, each had an interest in inventing them. In 1842 the fantasists John and Charles Allen, who had taken the name Sobięski Stuart, claiming to be grandsons of the Young Pretender whose mother was Polish, published the *Vestiarum Scoticum*, a book of setts supposedly derived from a manu-script of 1721 in turn supposedly derived from a compilation made in 1571. It was quickly shown to be a forgery. This invention of brightly coloured clan tartans was part of a larger invention of a Highland tradition the most notorious element of which concerned the supposed poems of Ossian published in the 1760s. This episode involved two unrelated Scots by the name of Macpherson who 'discovered' and 'contextualized' purportedly ancient Scottish Gaelic poems of great literary merit (Trevor-Roper 1983; Chapman 1978: ch. 2; W. Ferguson 1998: ch. 11). In 1805 Sir Walter Scott showed the poems to be fabrications derived from ancient Irish poems. They were a part of a larger claim that Scottish Gaelic culture was older and richer than Irish culture, a reversal of the usual claim and not one that any Celtic scholar today accepts.

The revaluation of the Highlands was enhanced by a visit to Scotland by George IV in 1822 orchestrated by Sir Walter Scott. 'Scott had wished the visit to be a "gathering of the Gael", but what his Celtic fantasy had in fact produced was a distortion of the Highland past and present and the projection of a national image in which the Lowlands had no part' (Devine 1999: 235). The king heightened the pageantry by himself appearing in Highland dress—and pink tights. And in 1848 Queen Victoria sealed the revaluation of the Highland by the purchase of her estate at Balmoral (and the commissioning of a tartan). The once barbarous Highlands were now fit for a queen. It is worth noting that the 1822 extravaganza had followed one of the most notorious of all Highland clearances, in Sutherland, between 1807 and 1821. The emptying of the glens and the ruining of cottages throughout the nineteenth century seems only to have added to the romantic appeal of the Highlands. John Morrison (2003: 158) notes how mid-Victorian Scottish artists 'painting the nation' as anything other than the romantic Highlands were felt to have fallen 'little short of treachery'. Royal approval of the Highlands opened the way to a representation of all Scotland featuring tartanry, bagpipes, ceilidhs, whisky, and oat cuisine which persists, though not without challenge, to this day. The kitschification of Scottish culture—Nairn's 'tartan monster'—offends many Scots (Nairn 1977: 162). Others acknowledge tartanry—sometimes ironically—recognizing that in marketing terms it has helped to establish Scotland the brand the world over. Tartan also now has the value of being classless and timeless. Predictably it figures in the official Scottish equivalent to St Patrick's Day in the United States—Tartan Day (Hague 2002).

There is a parallel here with England. The Highlands often stand for Scotland although most of the people do not live there, just as the countryside often stands for England—'the green and pleasant land', 'our England is a garden'—although most of the English do not live there either. Indeed Scotland and England already had urban majorities by the time of the 1851 census. The identification of the Highlands with all Scotland also shifted the great dividing line from Highland/Lowland to Scotland/England. Lowlanders once believed themselves to have much more in common with the English than with Highlanders, but not so now. Despite this the symbolic appropriation of the Highlands for most Scots takes forms way short of the Celtophile, including the knowing and the ironic. But for some Celtophiles, as Malcolm Chapman (1992) has noted, there is an opposition between the Celt, 'a magical figure, bard, warrior and enchanter', and the Anglo-Saxon, 'disfigured by every wart and sore that industry, cities, pollution, capitalism and greed can cast upon his countenance' (p. 253). In the Scottish context one might add that the opposition might more plausibly be between the Celt and all the heirs and beneficiaries of the Scottish Enlightenment (of which more below). For other, less confrontational Celtophiles there is at least a celebration of 'Celtic' music, poetry, and design and an identification with the 'Celts' who have long created them (Harvey et al. 2002). Quite where the dour, narrow, and evangelical Presbyterianism that had won over most Highlanders by the end of the eighteenth century fits in all this goes unsaid.

1.2 Scotland the Brave

The Normanization of Scotland led to the claims of English kings that Scottish kings owed them fealty, to the claims of Scottish kings that lands in Northumbria and Cumbria where they were lords were part of Scotland, to border wars, and to eventual confirmation of Scottish independence. The border between England and Scotland has followed the current line with little variation since the Treaty of York in 1237, the main exception being the border town of Berwick, which changed hands many times before finally becoming part of England in 1482. The Wars of Independence and the subsequent history of an independent Scottish state offer Scots much to celebrate but have also sown the seeds of national self-doubt.

The celebrations have often to do with Scottish victories over the English. One of these was won by William Wallace, the Braveheart of the 1995 film, at Stirling Bridge in 1297. Wallace styled himself Guardian of Scotland following his victory. He was executed by the English at the Tower of London in 1305. Anglo-Norman, later English, claims to overlordship in Scotland, or to the Scottish crown, were pursued with greatest vigour by Edward I, the Hammer of the Scots. His son, Edward II, suffered their most famous reverse at the hands of Robert Bruce at the Battle of Bannockburn in 1314. Scottish lords and bishops petitioned the Vatican in the Declaration of Arbroath in 1320 to recognize Scottish independence. The declaration acknowledges Robert Bruce as King of Scotland but also places this famous limitation on his power.

Yet if he should give up what he has begun, and agree to make us or our kingdom subject to the King of England or the English, we should exert ourselves at once to drive him out as our enemy and a subverter of his own rights and ours, and make some other man who was well able to defend us our King; *for as long as but a hundred of us remain alive, never will we on any conditions be brought under English rule.* It is in truth not for glory, nor riches, nor honours that we are fighting, but for freedom—for that alone, which no honest man gives up but with life itself.[3]

These sentiments had no relevance to unfree Scots—the serfs who were most of the population—but they do have a ring that has crossed the centuries. The italicized words are inscribed in the entrance to the first room of the superb new Museum of Scotland opened in 1998. The Vatican endorsed Scottish independence in 1323 (having already recognized a Scottish church not subject to the archbishops of York in 1192), France recognized it in 1323, and England conceded it in 1326 and wrote it into the Treaty of Northampton of 1328. In practice it did not stop English kings from making claims to overlordship of Scotland, but none succeeded for long. Thus from 1326 to 1707 Scotland enjoyed an independent statehood recognized not only by England but also throughout Europe.

The celebrated figures of Wallace and Bruce appear at the beginning of the story of Scottish independence (W. Ferguson 1998). Interestingly Wallace was of British and Bruce (de Brus) of Norman descent. Wallace is commemorated in many places, but most notably by the large Wallace Monument just north-east of Stirling which was completed in 1869 at a time when many proud Scots thought Union and Empire had enabled Scotland to fulfil its destiny (Morton 2001); and Bruce is commemorated by the great equestrian statue at the (now disputed) site of the Battle of Bannockburn. Both are remembered in Robert Burns's famous poem 'Scots wha hae'. Scots supporting their national football team today recall the former independence of Scotland and the age of such heroes as Wallace and Bruce when they wave the flag of the Scottish kings, a red lion rampant on a gold field. In the early 1990s, chafing under Conservative governments that they had not voted for, and enjoying a resurgence of Scottish culture and identity, Scottish bodies, beginning with the Scottish Rugby Union, adopted as a Scottish national anthem the folksong 'Flower of Scotland' written by Roy Williamson of The Corries in the 1960s (it had been sung by the Murrayfield crowd at the 1990 rugby grand slam decider against England which Scotland won). The flower of Scotland refers to those who fought and died at Bannockburn. The second verse refers to 'land that is lost now | Which those so dearly held'—but no land has been lost to Scotland except for Berwick. The third verse says this:

> Those days are passed now
> And in the past
> They must remain
> But we can still rise now
> And be the nation again.

What we have here is a lament for the lost independence of Scotland, a claim that it amounted to a national (and cultural?) subjugation (and humiliation?), and a call for Scotland to assert itself and be a nation again. The popularity of Flower of Scotland is a reminder of how much the careless conflation of England and Britain made by the English slights the Scots. It leaves many today not just at odds with the English but indignant that their forebears put up with it for so long. 'Rise now and be the nation again' is at a minimum a demand for Scottish self-respect, for care for Scottish institutions, culture and traditions, and for the self-government that goes with them.[4]

Once the Scottish court moved to English-speaking Edinburgh early in the twelfth century, the process which made a version of English, Scots, the dominant language of Scotland by the time of the union of the Scottish and English crowns in 1603 was underway. Crucially English was the language of commerce. Whether Scots should be regarded as an English dialect or a separate language is disputed (Smith 2000). Calling it Scottish originated in the late fifteenth century; hitherto Scottish had referred to Gaelic as distinct from English (Templeton 1973: 6). After 1603, and even more the union of the states in 1707, Scots gave way among the educated to what has become known as Scottish Standard English—English with a Scottish accent and the continued use of some Scots words. Thereafter Scots mainly survived as a spoken language among the working class, in verse (that of Robert Burns being the best known), as a prose tradition in fiction and the popular press in the nineteenth century, and as Lallans (Lowlands) a synthetic twentieth-century attempt to produce a prestigious written Scots which, according to Smith, is now in decline. Scots, especially exiled Scots, gather for Burns Night suppers on Burns's birthday, 25 January, for a traditional meal of haggis and bashed neeps and potatoes, served with a whisky and to the accompaniment of bagpipes.

The continued celebration of the greatest writer in Scots is a reminder that there is more to Scottish iconography than tartanry, but it is the selective re-construction and re-presentation of elements of Celtic Scotland, Scotland the Brave, and Jacobite Scotland that figure most prominently in the brand-ing of Scotland and depictions of Scottish heritage. For Historic Scotland, the public agency responsible for many historic sites and buildings, 'Scot-land is a land of castles' (quoted in McCrone, Morris, and Kiely 1995: 93). And just as those castles recall an independent Scotland, so the battlefield at Culloden has come to represent its loss. McCrone, Morris, and Kiely (ibid. 195) have described how Culloden

has taken on an elegiac quality, through both the defeat of the 'real' Scotland, and the place's association with Jacobitism which . . . is still a powerful myth north of the border. What was a military defeat has been turned into a moral victory, over-coming contrary historical evidence that whatever else it was about, it was not a Scottish–English battle. Now it has come to stand for Scotland, especially as it has acquired the patina of heritage. Its power as an icon derives from its contemporary cultural-political significance rather than its eighteenth-century significance.

It would seem long to have appealed to all those who see Scotland as vic-tim, tricked out of its statehood, denied its royal line, and economically ex-ploited for the benefit of the English and those Scots who threw in their lot with them. Murray Pittock (1991: 107–8) put it like this:

since the Union, pro-Jacobite ideology had argued that if Scotland yielded to com-mercial priorities, she could expect only commercial exploitation, having aban-doned the older values of nobility and liberty . . . The Clearances sadly fulfilled the Jacobite prophecy. The oldest and noblest kind of Scot (the Highlander/Jacobite patriot) was being exiled from the land of his birth in the interest of a money-based (i.e. British) society in which Scotland was participating, having sold out to corrupt values in 1707.

Pittock notes how 'the Jacobite idea of a radical community struggling for liberty against a moneyed oppressor' acknowledged by Robbie Burns, a Lowlander, at the end of the eighteenth century was taken up again by Hugh MacDiarmid, poet, nationalist, and radical, in the twentieth century (p. 135). One of MacDiarmid's contemporaries, Edwin Muir, another poet, revealed, however, just how divisive Jacobitism could be. According to Pittock (p. 140):

In his largely fatalistic poetry, Muir accuses the reformation of having for ever destroyed Scotland's ability to be "a tribe, a family, a people"; he declares that the divisions it brought to Scotland helped to "fell the ancient oak of loyalty" (the Stuart cause and badge), and replace it with the "Golden Calf" of Presbyterian mercantilism which put money before independence.

Today Jacobite sentiments can sometimes be discerned among Scottish nationalists, and Scottish anti-capitalists, but they have had little appeal to a Scottish National Party which campaigned so successfully with the slogan 'It's Scotland's oil'.

2 Civil Scotland

In 1707 Scotland entered into union with England. It did so out of weakness. The country was poor and undeveloped by English standards. A disastrously unsuccessful attempt to establish a Scottish colony at Darien in the isthmus of Panama had all but bankrupted it. The union was deemed an 'incorporating union', not a federal one. It established a single parliament and government in London because that was the only way the English thought they could ensure a government for Scotland strong enough to meet their interests there. These interests were largely in the maintenance of order, and the end of the auld alliance between Scotland and France and the consequent threat from the north. But in other respects 'incorporation' is a misnomer. In contrast to England's annexation of Wales enacted in 1536 and 1542, the key feature of the union of England and Scotland is precisely that it did not presage the extension beyond England of English law, the English church, and English local government. Instead the terms of the union guaranteed Scotland retention of its own church, its own law, and its own systems of local government and education. It also guaranteed the right of Scottish banks to issue their own banknotes (which they still do, albeit under the supervision of the Bank of England—the central bank for the whole of the UK). The forfeit of Scottish statehood was controversial in Scotland because the richer English outnumbered the Scots by five to one and thus might have been expected to dominate them. The circumstances in which the Scottish parliament voted to dissolve itself are disputed but certainly some who voted in favour had succumbed to English financial blandishments. But in the end the parliament voted itself out of existence by a big majority because many members thought the union offered economic advancement for Scots and Scotland via tariff-free access to the English market and colonies without loss of the distinctively Scottish institutions that mattered most to them. And if initial economic expectations went largely unfulfilled, from the middle of the eighteenth century onwards the calculation increasingly looked to have been right.

It is sometimes argued that the maintenance of separate and distinctive Scottish institutions guaranteed by the Treaty of Union ensured the perpetuation of the Scottish nation. This assumes that there was one in 1707. Nationalist historians have made claims for the formation of a Scottish nation in medieval times. Indeed one, David Murray, has gone so far as to make Scotland *The First Nation in Europe* (1960). Neil Davidson (2000) has pointed out that any such claim depends on a feudal conception of what makes a people distinguishable (loyalty to a king whose subjects then constitute the community of the realm) which would also apply to other cases than Scotland. If we take a nation to be a people—and not just educated, propertied, and ruling elites—who understand themselves to be a single people different from other peoples then it is open to question whether this describes all the inhabitants of Scotland in 1707. Loyalties were too often local and the differences between the Gaelic-speaking and largely Catholic Highlands and the Scots-speaking and Calvinist Lowlands too great for the notion of a single people to mean much to most of them. Although the Calvinist reformation had marked most people in the burghs of the Lowlands and the East Coast, it was the privileged few who staffed the institutions of the church, the law, local government, and commerce who were most interested in the maintenance of distinctively Scottish institutions. As it happens many of these could also see advantage in the union and were among its staunchest supporters after 1707. But if claims for the antiquity of the Scottish nation are sometimes overdone, no one disputes that the development of a distinctively Scottish civil society after 1707 was also crucial to the development of Scottish nationhood. Distinctively Scottish professions had an influential presence in every city, town, and village. Each deserves some comment.

The Scottish church rejected the authority of the pope in 1560. The reformers were led by John Knox who had been inspired by Calvin's achievements in Geneva. There followed a struggle between Episcopalians and Presbyterians, which ended in the re-establishment of the Presbyterian Church of Scotland in 1690. (The Presbyterian churches of the Reformed, or Calvinist, tradition have a collegial type of church government by pastors and lay elders, or presbyters.) At the time of union the kirk had the greatest impact on the lives of Scots of all the distinctively Scottish institutions—so much so that Devine (1999) refers to the 'parish state'. 'The minister was usually supported by a kirk session or permanent committee of lay elders, who were elected into their office for life; and they were usually individuals of merit, piety or social standing in the local community' (p. 84). The kirk session organized the collection and distribution of funds for the relief of the poor, it managed the parish school (often the clerk to the session was himself the local schoolmaster) and maintained a curriculum derived in large part from the Bible and the catechism, and it supervised the moral behaviour of parishioners by hearing cases of breaches of church discipline and referring more serious cases to the civil authorities. It made great use of naming and shaming. It was not possible for a man or woman to move from one parish to another without a certificate of good behaviour signed by the minister. This maintenance of Godly discipline, and punishment of offenders, was important to a community because of its commitment to the rooting out of sin. Toleration of sinners was incompatible with membership of the true church to which the elect, who would enjoy salvation, belonged. All others, the reprobates, would suffer eternal damnation. Not surprisingly, Calvinist churches (in the Netherlands as much as in Scotland) have displayed a propensity to schism in which self-designated true believers accuse their co-religionists of departures from the straight and narrow and either expel them or leave to set up a new church.

Calvinist elders jealously guard the right to determine who their minister should be. It was this Presbyterian principle that underpinned the rejection of bishops and opposition to patrons, usually local landowners, whose right to nominate ministers had been restored by (the Westminster) Parliament in 1712. The latter issue led eventually to the Disruption of 1843 in which over a third of the clergy and laity, the Evangelicals, left the Church of Scotland to form the Free Church of Scotland. Those that remained, the Moderates, 'had a much more easy-going attitude towards dogma and personal behaviour' (Kellas 1968: 53). Many Moderate ministers 'were closely identified with their patrons, and they shared some of the aristocratic tastes in recreation, culture and wine'. Their close relations with landlords ensured that Highlanders joined the seceders en masse. The third main Calvinist church, the United Presbyterian Church, was formed in 1847 from the merger of a number of 'voluntary' churches. Patronage in the Church of Scotland was at last abolished in 1874. In 1900 the Free Church and the United Presbyterian Church merged to form the United Free Church. In 1921 the Church of Scotland secured complete independence from parliament on matters of doctrine (whilst remaining nominally established) and this opened the way to union with the United Free Church in 1929. The reconstituted Church of Scotland would, its supporters hoped, be better able to keep the Roman Catholic Church from invading the mainstream of Scottish life. Since 1929 the Church of Scotland has been referred to as the 'national church'. Dissenters to Free Church participation in the 1900 merger with the United Presbyterians kept a rump Free Church and found themselves labelled 'the wee frees'. The famously strict, Sabbatarian, and anti-papist wee frees remain prominent in the Western Highlands and Islands to this day.

There are five reasons why this church history is still relevant today. The first is that Scotland differs from England in terms of religion in so far as it has a Presbyterian establishment not an Anglican one and the difference has got bigger since the union. Pittock (1997: 10) estimates that between a third and a half of Scots at the time of union were Episcopalian. By contrast, Kellas (1998: 52) put Scottish Episcopal Church numbers in the 1960s at 1.6 per cent. It also differs in so far as hostility to Catholics (discussed below) has been more intense and more enduring. The second is that the annual General Assembly of the Church of Scotland served as a surrogate parliament in which the particular affairs of Scotland could be debated, but its authority was greatly diminished after the 1843 schism and further diminished by the later growth of the Catholic population. Even so it had right up until devolution a vastly greater significance in Scottish life than the Synod of the Church of England has in English life. The third is that the dourness, industry, sobriety, respectability, and civil responsibility associated with some manifestations of Scottish character owe a good deal to Calvinism. In addition 'The influence of Presbyterianism on Scottish institutions is important, for it provided the basis of a conception of "civic duty" which emphasised communal values and social responsibility' (McCrone 1992: 120). The fourth is that the rigours of Calvinism have historically been responsible for greater hostility to Roman Catholicism than is found among most other Protestant denominations including Anglicanism/Episcopalianism and Lutheranism. This remains a major issue in Northern Ireland, and was formerly a problem in the Netherlands. It is of diminishing significance in Scotland but it has by no means disappeared altogether. That the place of Catholics in Scotland today is still a matter of real sensitivity was confirmed by the furore following a speech by James MacMillan, the composer, at the Edinburgh Festival in 1999 in which he called continuing hostility to Catholics and their schools 'Scotland's shame'. The fifth has to do with the distinctive religious profile of the Highlands even today. On the one hand, parts of the Highlands remain Catholic. On the other, the rest is stricter in its Presbyterianism than elsewhere in Scotland. After 1745 the broader Episcopalian Church, many of whose bishops and priests had remained loyal to the Stuarts, was undermined by punitive restrictions. The Church of Scotland moved to fill the gap only to lose almost all it had gained in 1843. In 1929 it recovered its position, so to speak, but the stricter Presbyterianism of parts of the Highlands remains. In particular, there are isolated parts of Scotland—particularly Skye and the Western Isles—where the strength and conviction of the wee frees can still surprise the outsider. In 1990 the wee frees expelled their most distinguished member, Lord Mackay of Clashfern, the last Conservative Lord Chancellor (the head of the judiciary in England), for attending the funeral of a Catholic colleague. Sabbatarians have long prevented ferries to the mainland from operating on Sundays and they recently tried unsuccessfully to stop the introduction of a Sunday flight to Stornoway, the main town in the Outer Hebrides (Seenan 2002).

The separate education system guaranteed by the terms of the union (and reviewed at length by Tom Bryce and Walter Humes (1999)) has contributed greatly to the development of Scottish identity in five different ways. The first and simplest is that the Scottish school and university system, examinations, and teachers' qualifications and unions always have been different from the English (Anderson 1999; L. Paterson 1999). To give just one example, school leavers in Scotland enter university at 17, and obtain a masters degree after four years' successful study, whereas school leavers in England and Wales enter university at 18 and obtain a bachelors degree after three years' successful study. There is thus a fundamental sense in which pupils and students experience a distinctively Scottish education. The second is that teachers, like clergy, are part of a distinctively Scottish professional class (Livingstone 1999). The third is that Scots claim historically to have valued education more than the English. One manifestation of this is that Scotland, a poorer and much less populous country, had five ancient universities at the time of union (Edinburgh, Glasgow, two colleges in Aberdeen, and St Andrew's) compared with England's two, Oxford and Cambridge. Another is the meritocratic myth of the 'lad o' pairts' and the greater opportunities for advancement afforded in Scotland. The lad o' pairts was a boy from a small town or rural area with the talent but not the means to go to university who is nonetheless enabled to do so because the local schoolmaster persuades local worthies to pay for him. Most were the sons (there was no lass o' pairts) of ministers, teachers, farmers, shopkeepers, and artisans, and they were all Protestant (Anderson 1985: 100). In the late nineteenth century there were proportionately 5.8 times as many university places in Scotland as England (McCrone 2001a: 94). More than a century later it is open to question whether there is greater educational opportunity in Scotland than elsewhere in Britain, but the belief that there is persists and Scotland has already achieved the university participation rate (50% of the population by the age of 30) which is the controversial goal for England of the current Labour government. It is also notable that one of the first initiatives of the Scottish parliament was the abolition of university tuition fees for Scottish residents. The fourth has to do with belief in the high standard of Scottish education in general and its superiority to education in England in particular (whether that belief is still warranted or not). The fifth pertains to a national curriculum in Scotland which in some subjects, such as history, differs from that in England (and which is also not formally prescribed as in England). Humes and Bryce (1999: 106) draw attention to

the development of curricular materials with a strong Scottish flavour across a range of subjects in primary and secondary schools. Scottish history is now well-established as a field of study in schools and universities, and the use of

Scottish texts in drama and literature courses is widespread. Add to this the wider cultural renaissance in Scotland, which includes art, music and media, and the argument that Scottish society and Scottish education are dominated by English values and institutions seems hard to sustain.

There is no doubting the past glories (Broadie 2001). The eighteenth century saw a concentration of scholars—Adam Smith (economics), David Hume (philosophy), Adam Ferguson and John Millar (sociology), William Robertson (history), Francis Hutcheson (moral and political philosophy), and James Hutton (geology) are merely the most renowned—who have come to be known as the Scottish Enlightenment. In the late eighteenth, the nineteenth, and the twentieth centuries the story continues with a succession of distinguished figures from James Watt (designer of the steam engine), and Archibald Buchanan (originator of the integrated cotton mill), to William Thomson (ennobled as Lord Kelvin—discoverer of absolute zero), John Logie Baird (pioneer of television), and Alexander Fleming (discoverer of penicillin). So many were the achievements of the greats of the Scottish Enlightenment, and of their successors, that Duncan Bruce entitles his book *The Mark of the Scots: Their Astonishing Contributions to History, Science, Democracy, Literature and the Arts* (1997). Similarly, Stewart Lamont's title *When Scotland Ruled the World* (2001) refers to the two centuries after 1750 as a golden age of 'genius, creativity and exploration'. In addition Arthur Herman subtitles his book on the Scottish Enlightenment *The Scots' Invention of the Modern World* (2002) and James Buchan (2003) subtitles his book on the capital *How Edinburgh Changed the World*. These 'hagiographers', Devine (2003: 171) comments, 'fructify and feed the collective ego of a small nation which, while taking on challenging responsibilities in the post-devolution era, is still somewhat lacking in confidence'. Well may be, but it is incontestable that Scotland has a pantheon of philosophical, scientific, and technological giants very much its own.

The glories of the Scottish Enlightenment have done much for Scottish pride but did little for Scottish nationalism. Devine (1999: 81) notes how 'The dominant figures of the Enlightenment were integral parts of the political establishment, virtually all Whig Hanoverians who regarded Jacobitism as a deadly threat to Protestant liberties and freedoms.' Far from being inimical to Scottish achievement, the union of 1707 was thought protective of it. Colin Kidd (1993) argues that the Scottish Whigs in effect folded the seventeenth-century Scottish Whig-Presbyterian interpretation of history into the eighteenth-century English Whig-libertarian interpretation of history, thereby contributing significantly to the formation of an Anglo-British political culture attractive enough to divert Scots from flirtation with any romantic Scottish nationalism in the mid-nineteenth-century springtime of nations.

Scotland's own law and legal system is guaranteed by the Treaty of Union. The courts have different names and competences (Kellas 1980). Most criminal cases that would be heard by a crown court in England and Wales are heard by a sheriff court in Scotland. Instead of barristers, as in England and Wales, there are advocates, and the defendant in an English court is the accused in a Scottish criminal case and the defender in a civil one. In contrast to civil law where appeal to the House of Lords in London is possible, criminal law allows no appeal beyond the High Court of Justiciary in Edinburgh. Juries have fifteen members (not twelve as in England) and majority verdicts have always been accepted. In addition to 'guilty' and 'not guilty' a verdict of 'not proven' is possible in rare circumstances. In terms of content, Scottish law retains some features of Roman law that English law has long lost, but differences between the common law of Scotland and that of England and Wales are few. On the other hand the feudal elements of Scottish land and property law make it both markedly different from English law and more controversial. Kellas (1998: 49) commented that 'There is little evidence that the ordinary Scot feels much pride in the Scottish legal system', but court reports in the media remind Scots every day that theirs is a distinctive law and legal system.

Scotland has also long had its own dense network of professional, voluntary and sporting associations. It has also, very significantly, long had its own media. There are three Scottish daily papers—*The Herald, The Scotsman*, and the *Daily Record* and Scottish editions of some of the British papers—as well as Scottish commercial television companies and Scottish BBC broadcasting including Scottish edited news programmes. In sum, most of Scottish life has been lived within a framework of public administration, civil organization, and media presentation that has been distinctively Scottish. In this respect there are obvious major continuities with Civic and Self-Governing Scotland after 1999.

I have followed McCrone and Paterson in emphasizing that it was and is the strength of Civil Scotland that has sustained Scotland as a distinct nation within Britain, but there are also doubters. Might Civil Scotland have been an institutional success story but at the same time a cultural nonentity? Craig Beveridge and Ronald Turnbull (1989) argue scathingly that far too many Scots have thought so, albeit wrongly. They deplore Scotland's own *trahison des clercs*, the 'inferiorism' of its academics and its 'anglicised' intellectuals. Scottish inferiorism regards pre-union Scotland as superstitious, poor, uncultured, and unruly and post-union Scotland as improving and modern, the beneficiary of an opportunity to catch up with superior English ways in agriculture, industry, government, broad churchmanship, practical knowledge, and social manners (cf. Fry's (1992) account of the Whig interpretation of Scottish history). Beveridge and Turnbull argue that pre-union Scotland was not that bad, and much improvement after the union would have happened anyway. Worse, the nineteenth- and twentieth-century intellectuals who succumbed to metropolitanism (variously a Home Counties, English, British, or unsourced vice) disdained Scottish practices of value, ignored Scottish intellectuals of stature, and thereby fed Scots' doubts about their capacity for independence. One of their particular gripes concerns the decline and fall of the general philosophy courses that once graced all Scottish degree programmes but that are held (wrongly according to L. Paterson 1994: 66) to have been displaced by the late nineteenth-century switch to excessively specialized degrees copied from England. George Davie (1961) had associated this philosophy course with a kind of levelling—professor and student, tutored and untutored, could all have their say—and thus with reproduction of the democratic intellect, no less. How pernicious of the English to prompt its demise! As with many polemics, Beveridge and Turnbull's is hit-and-miss. They are right, however, that there always was more to Scottish literature than the 'kailyard' (cabbage-patch) stories of homely decency and well-earned local success which were so popular from the 1880s to the 1930s; and more to philosophy in Scottish universities in the mid- and later twentieth century than the logical positivism and linguistic philosophy that prevailed in Oxbridge (as there was, too, in many other English universities). But if they feared fondness for kitsch and kailyard had deformed Scottish culture and sapped Scottish political will beyond repair, the renewed vigour of Scottish arts over the last quarter-century and the achievement of devolution has proved them wrong.

3 Scotland in the Empire

Michael Fry's massive *The Scottish Empire* (2001), and Tom Devine's elegant *Scotland's Empire 1600–1815* (2003) document in great detail Scottish
imperial ventures in Ulster following the union of the crowns in 1603 and
just about everywhere following the union of the parliaments in 1707. The
first gave us the Ulster Scots (and later the Americans the Scotch-Irish), the
second gave us the significant Scottish presence in America (since overshadowed by Irish immigration), and the huge Scottish presence in the West
Indies, India, Canada, Hong Kong and the Far East, New Zealand, and
to a lesser extent Australia. Scots went to trade—and trade very successfully—and to settle. Marjory Harper (2003) documents the pull as well as
the push factors even for displaced Highlanders; there were adventurers as
well as exiles. In addition, Scottish missionaries went to convert the hea-
thens as in Livingstone's work in East Africa and the evangelization of the
South Pacific. For long periods there were cities such as Calcutta, Madras,
Dunedin, Hong Kong, and the Anglophone half of Montreal that were conspicuously Scottish. The same might be said of the East India Company and
of Nyasaland. Scottish participation in Empire was proportionately greater
than English in most respects—settlers, soldiers including officers, administrators including the highest ranks, governors, traders including owners
and senior managers of the greatest companies, shippers, bankers, civil en-
gineers, teachers, and missionaries. For Christopher Harvie and Peter Jones
(2000: 20), 'The Scots were, in general, the governing class of the "white
dominions". They were usually radical in fighting off aristocratic interference from London, though they could be near-racist in expropriating native
people.' The success of the Scots had much to do with Calvinist discipline,
an education system better developed than in England, a spirit of enterprise that could not be satisfied in Scotland or England, and, after 1745, the
fighting spirit of the Highland regiments. 'A British imperium', Linda Colley (1992: 130) argues, 'enabled Scots to feel themselves peers of the English
in a way still denied them in an island kingdom' before Victoria. Even today
English and foreigners alike are inclined to refer to England instead of Britain, but, tellingly, references to the Empire are always to the *British* Empire.

In these post-colonial times, there has been an understandable distaste
for the celebration of Empire, but there is also now the beginnings of a

renewed interest in Empire which recognizes the achievement as well as the exploitation. The recent Channel 4 television series *Empire: How Britain Made the World* (2002) and the accompanying book (2003) were, fittingly, both the work of a Scot, Niall Ferguson, and any Scottish reconsideration of Empire can hardly fail to notice the scale of Scottish achievement as well as the parts Scots played in slavery, exploitation, and atrocity. Fry notes how the orientalists, the respecters of local culture, among the Scottish imperialists gave way over time to the modernizers, who, heeding the Scottish Enlightenment, thought they could bring reason, justice, and progress to all.

Empire made its mark on Scotland not just by reinforcing the adage 'get on, or get out' (to Ireland, England, America, or the colonies) but also by ensuring that a small nation was outward looking and internationally connected. The economics of Empire also, of course, generated growth in Scottish cities and towns—especially Glasgow and the Clyde, which benefited from the slave trade, then tobacco importation, and later textiles and ship-building and other heavy industry—and the improvement of agriculture following the purchase of estates by sugar and tobacco lords and others who profited abroad. Fry rates Empire alongside the Reformation, Union, and the Enlightenment as one of the four greatest contributors to the formation of Scotland, and Devine (2003: 353) argues that the scale and success of Scottish participation in 'the imperial project in the long run massively increased the nation's sense of self-esteem'. It was certainly a matter of great national pride to nineteenth-century Scots and it was also no surprise that, on its foundation in 1934, the Scottish National Party declared its aim to be 'self-government for Scotland on a basis which will enable Scotland as a partner in the British Empire with the same status as England to develop its National Life to the fullest advantage' (quoted ibid. 388).

John MacKenzie (1998) surmises that the Empire, rather than help forge a British national identity as argued by Colley (1992), gave Scots the means ('a loop beyond the English') to sustain and strengthen their own distinctive national identity. Graeme Morton (1999) argues that it did both.

4 Little Scotland

I have coined the term Little Scotland by analogy with Little England to refer to a contemporary Scotland preoccupied with itself and suspicious of

Britain, Europe, and foreign entanglements generally (Bryant 2003). I am not sure that it has much support but surmise that it does have some on the unfavoured side of St Andrew's fault among the poor and the badly housed whose ambitions do not run much further than survival in changing times and a deindustrialized economy, and those who still doubt the Scottish credentials of Catholics of Irish descent. Certainly there are accusing references to it in the contributions to Tom Devine and Paddy Logue's *Being Scottish* (2002). The most vivid is in the personal reflection of Charles Kennedy (p. 114), MP for Ross, Skye and Inverness and Leader of the Liberal Democratic Party. He quotes the following 'beautiful' lines about Scotland and Scottishness written by Hugh MacDiarmid

> The rose of all the world is not for me,
> I want for my part only the little white rose of Scotland,
> That smells sharp and sweet,
> And breaks the heart.

and adds that they are 'wrong'. 'That is introspective, self-regarding, solipsistic Scotland turning its back on the world and stumbling into a Celtic twilight—a temptation for Scots, I know, but one that should be resisted.'

Scottish nationalists opposed to the Scottish National Party's commitment to the European Union might endorse Little Scotland. Alice Brown et al. (1999) report that 9 per cent of respondents in the 1997 Scottish Referendum Survey, asked about their preferred constitutional status for Scotland, opted for 'Scotland should become independent, separate from the UK and the European Union' (table 7.4, p. 147). Little Scotland might also be the default Scotland of those unconfident about any future. It would be interesting to know more about the 40 per cent who did not vote in the 1997 referendum on a Scottish parliament, the 41 per cent who did not vote in the 1999 Scottish parliamentary election, and the 51 per cent who did not vote in the 2003 Scottish parliamentary election. One might hypothesize that there are some among the poor and the badly housed on the 'wrong' side of St Andrew's fault. According to Ascherson (2002: 84–5):

The wholesale uprooting of Scottish society within a few years and its forcible replanting in physically transformed landscapes, in new industrial cities or in other hemispheres altogether, has left a persistent trauma. . . .

The Scottish trauma is to do with self-doubt (sometimes masked in unreal self-assertion), with sterile speculations about national identity and—as I guess—with suspicions of 'otherness' which so often poison relationships between Scottish neighbours. But above all, the trauma shows in a chronic mistrust of the public dimension.

The self-doubt to which Ascherson refers might be deemed the inferiorism of the locals in contrast to Beveridge and Turnbull's inferiorism of the cosmopolitan intellectuals. The chronically mistrustful would seem unlikely to vote, or to place confidence in Edinburgh, London, or Brussels.

In 2002 the Glasgow newspaper *The Herald* (7 August) reported the complaint of James MacMillan, the composer whose denunciation of anti-Catholicism in Scotland (discussed below) had generated fierce debate three years earlier, about a 'Little Scotland' mentality which was associated with a growing anti-Englishness as part of a wider xenophobia.

5 Scotland: civic and self-governing

Civic and Self-Governing Scotland is the successor to Civil Scotland.[5] The distinctive institutions of Civil Scotland—church, education, and law—are as significant as ever. So too is the vast number of distinctive organizations and voluntary associations. There are some all-British bodies prominent in Scotland—such as the BBC, British Airways, the British Olympic Committee, and the British Red Cross Society (interestingly the last two are all-British because the International Olympic Committee and the International Red Cross require them to be so)—but there are many more that are Scottish only. The National Trust, which owns and conserves stately homes and other heritage properties and parts of the countryside and coastline of great natural beauty, for example, only operates in England, Wales, and Northern Ireland, there being a separate National Trust for Scotland. Scotland mostly has its own sports governing bodies and leagues such as the Scottish Football Association and the Scottish Premier League and its own cultural institutions such as the National Gallery of Scotland and the Museum of Scotland. Scotland looks distinctive (the topography of the Highlands and Islands; the vernacular architecture of tenement houses, 'baronial' castles, and much else; tartanry; even the banknotes), and it sounds distinctive (accents and some vocabulary; pipes and drums). Scotland is another country.

It could be argued that Scotland has long been another country but that it was only in the late 1990s that it had the need, the confidence, *and* the opportunity to become self-governing. Even so the establishment of a Scottish parliament in 1999 is the culmination of developments that began in the 1970s. Economics were at their heart. On the one hand there were ultimately unsuccessful attempts to arrest the decline of traditional industries such as shipbuilding, steel, and coal, a failure made sharper by memories of red Clydeside and the key parts played by Scottish political activists and trade unionists in the development of the British labour movement (Harvie 1981; Foster 1992). There were also unsuccessful attempts to establish new manufacturing industries, such as car production. On the other, there were successful initiatives, such as the development with inward investment from America, of electronics in 'Silicon Glen'. Following mergers and takeovers of Scottish firms in other sectors, Scottish plants, as in Silicon Glen, were increasingly branch plants of companies headquartered in Britain or abroad. Crucially, there was, too, the discovery of North Sea oil, but the tax revenues it generated passed to the British treasury (even if some returned in funds for the Scottish Development Agency established in 1985). Together they suggested that Scotland had lost control over its economy and they prompted a widespread demand for economic sovereignty. The Scottish National Party exploited this brilliantly with it slogan 'It's Scotland's oil'. The union with England seemed to many Scots to have outlived its economic usefulness.

Associated with the economic issues was a political divergence from England. The first Scottish National Party MPs were elected at a by-election in 1973 and the general election in 1974.[6] The British Labour government was rattled and responded by proposing devolution. In a referendum on devolution in 1979, 51.6 per cent voted in favour with a turnout of 63.6 per cent, but the proposal was lost as the terms of the referendum required a minimum of 40 per cent of the electorate to vote in favour for the proposal to succeed and only 32.8 per cent had done so. Subsequently, the majority of Scottish voters rejected the Conservative Party of Margaret Thatcher in the British general elections of 1979, 1983, and 1987, and of John Major in 1992, only to find themselves with a Conservative government each time because support for the Conservatives in more populous England outweighed Scottish opposition. This is highly significant. It had last happened in 1959 but there was not then an electorally significant Scottish National Party to cry foul. Ironically it was the fiercely anti-devolution unionist, Mrs Thatcher, who confirmed the need for Scotland to be self-governing. Dismayed by the 1987 rebuff to Scottish voters, eminent Scots drafted a Claim of Right for Scotland in 1988 which proposed the establishment of a constitutional convention to draft proposals for a Scottish assembly. The Labour, Liberal Democrat, Green, and Communist parties, fifty-nine of Scotland's sixty-five local, regional, and island councils, the Scottish Trades Union Congress, the Scottish churches, and the Scottish Convention of Women agreed to participate in the convention. The Conservative and Scottish National Parties did not. In 1990 the convention published its proposals, but it took till 1997, and the landslide victory of new Labour, before a government was elected that was committed to Scottish devolution. Dissatisfaction with the political representation of Scottish interests at Westminster coupled with stronger expressions of Scottish cultural identity and greater confidence in Scottish capacity for self-government ensured a significantly different result in the second devolution referendum held the same year. In the 1997 referendum, 74.3 per cent voted in favour of a Scottish parliament with a turnout of 60.4 per cent (44.8% of the electorate), and 63.5 per cent voted in favour of it having tax-varying powers (38.4% of the electorate). This time it was agreed that it was the settled will of the Scottish people that there should be a Scottish parliament and the first was duly elected in 1999.

The collapse of the Conservative Party in Scotland has been spectacular. In 1955 it was the only party in Scottish electoral history to poll more than half the vote—50.1 per cent winning thirty-six of the seventy-one seats. Thereafter its vote fell steadily to 31.4 per cent in 1979 when Margaret Thatcher came to power and 17.5 per cent in 1997 when the Conservatives lost power and failed to win a single seat in Scotland. Given class structure (larger working class) and housing tenure (more council tenants), what is surprising is that the Conservatives once had greater success in post-war Scotland than in England. McCrone (2001a) reviews survey evidence that provides an explanation. The Conservative Party was the party most associated with union, Empire, Protestantism, and the army. Unionist-nationalism—the belief of proud Scots that Britain and its empire offered Scotland its best prospects for development—dates back, as Morton (1999) shows, to the mid-nineteenth century. It is unsurprising that the owners and managers of great firms supported the Conservatives, but the Conservatives also mobilized the Protestant working class. The end of Empire, the ending of conscription, secularization, and the move to a branch-plant economy, however, combined to undermine the party. In 1964 the Unionist label was dropped. Additionally Scottish conservatism stressed civic duty and social responsibility, and was ill-prepared for Margaret Thatcher's neo-liberal transformation of Conservatism south of the border and her wilful refusal to countenance what A. D. R. Dickson (1988) calls 'the peculiarities of the Scottish' despite the electoral evidence that she should. Here at least Scottish complaints about English arrogance were well founded.

As the Conservative Party declined Labour and the Scottish Nationalists offered alternative versions of Scottishness that emphasized discontinuities with Britishness. The Scottish National Party made its big breakthrough in February 1974 winning 21.9 per cent and seven seats. Since then it has had a high of 30.4 per cent and eleven seats in October 1992 and a low of 11.7 per cent and two seats in 1983. Originally more a middle-class Protestant Party, it has since moved to the left and succeeded in appealing to Catholic workers. The Labour Party, once heavily dependent on the support of Catholic workers, has succeeded in appealing to Protestant workers and professionals, and it has delivered devolution.

In general, Scotland's politics are different from those of England as a whole in more ways than just the vigorous presence of a nationalist party, the dynamics of four-party politics, and the all-pervasive sensitivity to Scottish interests and identity. There has been more support for the left, the public sector and public authority, for comprehensive schools, and for progressive taxation and levels of taxation sufficient to pay for better services, and less support for neo-liberal individualism, though differences with the north of England are much smaller than with the south-east. Support for the left, however, has not deflected Scots from taking advantage of Margaret Thatcher's decision to sell off council housing to tenants at large discounts, thereby shifting housing tenure from under one-third owner occupation to nearly two-thirds (Harvie and Jones 2000: 125). The findings of the 2000 and 2002 British and Scottish Social Attitudes Surveys also suggest that while support for redistribution of income is stronger in Scotland, differences on most left–right and liberal–authoritarian measures are now small.

Ross Bond (2000: 20) notes that it would be reasonable to suppose that 'those who strongly assert their Scottish identity in response to survey questions will also be very likely to be supporters of the SNP and independence;

in other words, these three indicators of Scottish nationalism/national identity should be strongly aligned'. Inspection of evidence from three election
surveys in the 1990s, however, tells a different story—what Bond calls 'the
political non-alignment of Scottish identity'. Basically, a third of Labour
voters support independence and half of SNP voters do not. In practice,
most voters for all parties, including the Conservatives, strongly assert their
Scottish identity; Labour and the SNP compete for the left-of-centre vote
consistent with Scottish political values; there is strong support for devolution in all parties; and there is also some recognition that independence
and sovereignty are not absolutes. Drawing on later surveys, Ross Bond and
Michael Rosie (2002: 46–7) confirm the earlier findings but are also able
to add that in 1999, asked which will have the most influence over the way
Scotland is run, the Scottish Parliament, Westminster, local councils, or the
European Union, 42 per cent said the Scottish parliament and 39 per cent
Westminster. Asked in 2001 which has the most influence, 15 per cent said
the Scottish parliament and 66 per cent Westminster. The perceived, but
unexpected, dominance of Westminster is significant politically because in
both 1999 and 2001 74 per cent said the Scottish parliament should have
the most influence. No wonder the percentage saying the Scottish Parliament should have more powers grew from 56 per cent in 1999 to 68 per cent
in 2001 (ibid. 48). The failure of the alignment thesis can be construed as
evidence of the sophistication, not the confusion, of the Scottish electorate
and of the likely durability of self-government within the union. Agreement
to more powers for the Scottish parliament is evidence of the strength of
support for the parliament irrespective of the reasons why it has so far not
proved able to do all that was expected of it.

It is likely that the reduced turnout of 49 per cent in the 2003 Scottish parliamentary election reflects more disillusionment in practice than in principle. The Scottish parliament has taken some important initiatives. More
generous financial provisions for the elderly in care and for Scottish residents who go to university have attracted a lot of publicity, but there are many
others from a reform of Scottish land law to a different way of organizing
the National Health Service. But there have also been adverse reactions to
the big increase in salaries members (MSPs) voted themselves in 2002, to
the decision in 2003 not to implement the formula that had been expected
from the outset to reduce the number of MSPs, and above all to the fiasco of
the mismanaged construction of the new parliament building at Holyrood

which opened three years late in 2004 at a cost, not of £40 million as the Scottish public had originally been told, but of £431 million.

Civic and Self-Governing Scotland, as successor to Civil Scotland, upholds a basically civic, rather than ethnic, conception of the Scottish nation. It emphasizes attachment to the homeland, participation in its associational life, generation and regeneration of its culture, and subscription to its values. Surveys reported by McCrone (2001b: 20) indicate that Scots think the key markers defining who is a Scot are birth, ancestry, and residence. Eighty-two per cent think birth in Scotland is very or fairly important, 73 per cent regard ancestry (i.e. having Scottish parents or grandparents) as very or fairly important, and 65 per cent say residence in Scotland is very or fairly important. Taking into account all three markers, McCrone has devised the typology of Scots in Table 3.2. Three of McCrone's types are problematic. Are all people born in Scotland of parents themselves born in Scotland, but of Irish Catholic descent, regarded as pure Scots by other Scots and do they always so regard themselves? Are all people born in Scotland of parents born abroad, in Pakistan for example, regarded by other Scots as real Scots and do they so regard themselves? Are all first-generation immigrants regarded as (new) Scots by other Scots, including not just, say, Pakistanis, but the English, and do they so regard themselves? Questions such as these prompt others. How does a Scotland as a civil nation accommodate difference? Does it demand the assimilation of all individuals who are not pure Scots, or does it provide for the integration of communities determined to safeguard (some) aspects of their collective identity which mark them out as

TABLE 3.2	**Types of Scot**			
	Born in Scotland		Not born in Scotland	
	Scottish lineage	*Not Scottish lineage*	*Scottish lineage*	*Not Scottish lineage*
Living in Scotland	'Pure' Scots	'Real' Scots	'Returning' Scots	'New' Scots
Not living in Scotland	'Expatriate' Scots	'Accidental' Scots	'Heritage' Scots	N/A

Source: McCrone (2001b): 21

different? Can there be a Cosmopolitan Scotland? To begin to answer such questions, I will consider the circumstances of Catholics of Irish descent, the English, and Asians and blacks who live in Scotland.

There was massive Irish emigration to Scotland in the nineteenth century. It was concentrated in Glasgow and west-central Scotland, but included significant movements to Edinburgh and Dundee. Most immigrants came from Ulster—in the middle decades between a fifth and a quarter were Scotch Irish Protestants, the descendants of Scots who had settled in Ulster in the seventeenth century—and they brought with them their sectarian animosities, the Green and the Orange. Devine (1999: 163) estimates that in mid-nineteenth-century Glasgow about a third of the population was Irish born or of Irish descent. By the end of the twentieth century, three-quarters of Scottish Catholics lived in the west-central region where they constituted a quarter of the population (Rosie and McCrone 2000: 204). Irene Maver (1996: 271) notes that the Catholic population of Scotland in 1900 was about 10 per cent of the total, and most would have been of Irish descent. Devine (1999: 386) gives the number of Catholic church members in 1939 as 614,469, and Iain Paterson (2000: 220) gives the number for 1997 as 705,650. According to the 2001 Census the Scottish population of 5,062,011 included 803,732 Catholics, 15.9 per cent of the total.

Integration of Irish Catholics has not been easy for a number of reasons. First, most Irish labourers in the nineteenth century were deemed too poor, ill-educated, and feckless to be acceptable. Second, most Irish Catholics could not identify with a Scotland 'which, as a stateless nation, derived its collective identity from Presbyterianism, a creed whose adherents regarded Catholicism as at best superstitious error and at worst as a satanic force' led by the Antichrist, the pope of Rome (Devine 1999: 488). Third, Pope Pius IX's *Syllabus of Errors* (1864) enjoined Catholics everywhere to reject the modern world in so far as its liberalism and progressivism threatened traditional values. One immediate consequence was Catholic insistence on separate Catholic schools and encouragement of Catholic welfare and leisure associations in order that Catholics could learn and socialize with their co-religionists and not have their salvation jeopardized by unnecessary contact with Protestants and secularists. In Scotland the result was a large measure of Catholic self-separation (Rosie 2004). Third, most Scottish Presbyterians, proud of appointing their own ministers, could not identify with a people seemingly in thrall to their priests. Fourth, the unresolved question of Irish home rule in the half-century before the First World War undermined integration in so far as most Irish Catholics supported the Irish cause and followed Irish, not British or Scottish, politics. Fifth, a third of Irish immigrants to Scotland were Presbyterian and they played their part in reproducing in Scotland the division between the communities they had known in Ulster. Sixth, 'The terrible carnage of the Great War, followed by economic depression, mass unemployment, and a huge increase in Scottish emigration, created a grave crisis of national insecurity' (Devine 1999: 498: cf. Walker 1996). Indicative of the times, the Church and Nation Committee of the Church of Scotland in 1923 approved the infamous report *The Menace of the Irish Race to Our Scottish Nationality* 'which accused the Irish Roman Catholic population of taking employment from native Scots, of being part of a papist conspiracy to subvert Presbyterian values, and the main source of intemperance, improvidence, criminality and much else besides' (Devine 1999: 499). To deal with this, the report proposed deportations of Irish prisoners and Irish in receipt of poor relief and job reservation for true Scots. Although such racist sentiments found little support in the main political parties or the press, they did reflect the views of enough Scots to reinforce the fortress mentality of Irish-born Catholics and Catholics of Irish descent.

By contrast shared service in the British army in the Second World War, and shared privations on the home front, did contribute to integration—as did full employment in the post-war reconstruction and the efforts of the Labour Party in Scotland, to which most Catholics gave their votes, in building up the welfare state in the late 1940s. Two decades ago Steve Bruce (1985) argued that theologically grounded anti-Catholicism was a feature of the strict Calvinism of the Highlands—but there were very few Catholics there of Irish descent and there thus had, historically, been negligible scope for communal conflict. In the Lowlands, by contrast, the Presbyterian churches had been, for the most part, middle-class and disinclined theologically, and socially, to engage in anti-Catholicism. Instead Baptists had provided much of the hard anti-Catholic leadership, whilst the working class was largely alienated from religion. But it was working class 'Protestants' (i.e. non-Catholics) who had had to compete with Catholics of Irish descent for jobs and housing and the basis of conflict between them was thus better regarded as ethnic than religious. However, the Moderator of the Church of Scotland's polite reception of John Paul II at the Mound in Edinburgh, next to the statue of John Knox, during the papal visit to Britain in 1982, confirmed that times had changed markedly. Secularization has also lowered the religious temperature in Scottish life.

The Labour Party had also contributed to integration by introducing comprehensive schools in the 1960s. Lindsay Paterson (2000) notes how Catholic comprehensives offered *all* Catholic pupils for the first time the opportunity to obtain the qualifications that would secure them both better jobs and the chance to enter universities and other tertiary colleges. For many Scots, Catholics and Protestants alike, better education to higher levels, upward social mobility, and evident prosperity have combined to generate a social and cultural expansiveness in which old conflicts rooted in defensive enclaves and the insecurities of the vulnerable have no place. So the short answer to Raymond Boyle and Peter Lynch (1998), who asked whether Catholics are now 'out of the ghetto', has to be 'yes'. But if one were to ask whether Catholics of Irish descent are fully accepted as Scots and whether they fully identify with Scotland, the answers would be more complex—'yes but', and 'yes but'.

In the 2001 census only 1 per cent of those resident in Scotland ticked Irish as their ethnic group, but 7 per cent of Catholics claimed Irish as a national identity in the Scottish Social Attitudes Survey of the same year (Rosie 2004: 66). But does 'full' identification with Scotland exclude any identification with Ireland? If identities, including ethnic and national identities, can be both multiple and layered, then, just as many Scots identify on some occasions and in some contexts with Britain, some may be expected to identify in some contexts with Ireland (cf. Bradley 1995, 1998). In this way we can in principle reconcile data confirming the convergence of Scottish Catholics with all Scots on many issues germane to national identity as reported by McCrone and Rosie (1998) and Rosie (2004), with the evidence of our eyes when, for example, we see on television among flags waved by the tens of thousands of Celtic supporters at the UEFA Cup Final in Seville in May 2003 countless Irish tricolours but barely a Scottish saltire or lion rampant.[7] But can we in practice?

In August 1999 the distinguished composer, James MacMillan, gave a lecture on 'Scotland's shame' at the Edinburgh Festival in which he described Scotland as a land of 'sleep-walking' anti-Catholic bigotry. He also deplored 'a very Scottish trait—a desire to narrow and restrict the definition of what it means to be Scottish' (MacMillan 2000: 1). In similar vein, Andrew O'Hagan (2000: 25) has written that 'Scotland is a divisive, bigoted society'.

In the passionate debate that followed in the Scottish media there were many who disagreed with MacMillan. Among them there was at least one Catholic, Owen Edwards (2000: 20), who deplored 'the sickness of modern Scottish Catholic culture'. The harsh stridency of many of the opinions voiced served only to confirm that old animosities were far from dead. One episode held to encapsulate the problem had occurred earlier in May 1999. Donald Findlay QC, Vice-Chairman of Rangers FC and outgoing Rector (the elected chief representative of the students) of St Andrews University, was videoed at a private party celebrating Rangers' championship of the Scottish Premier League singing 'The Sash', an anti-Catholic song with the most offensive of lyrics. He was forced to resign and forfeited the honorary degree at St Andrews he would otherwise have received. At about the same time two Catholic boys wearing Celtic colours had been killed in separate attacks by Protestant thugs. Donald Findlay had been the defence counsel for the perpetrator of a similar killing in 1996. Are these killings ugly anachronisms or are they symptomatic of something persistent and pervasive—anti-Irish racism and anti-Catholic sectarianism, both individual and institutional—which it is more comfortable to deny?

Some critics of MacMillan charge that he made the right accusation two or three decades too late. Others suggest that what might sometimes still be true of west-central Scotland is not necessarily true of the rest. Prejudice and discrimination against Catholics used to be major phenomena in Scottish life, the rejoinder goes, but they are now negligible. Catholic school leavers now do as well in terms of examination passes and entry to tertiary education as non-Catholics and younger Catholics have an occupational profile comparable to that of all Scots (I. Paterson 2000); Catholics are just as likely to declare themselves Scots, not British, or more Scottish than British, as other Scots (Brown, McCrone, and Paterson 1999: 63; I. Paterson 2000: 227); and they are as positive as other Scots in their attitudes towards the Scottish National Party—which used to be perceived as a vehicle for a Presbyterian Scottish national identity—though they are still less likely to vote for it (Rosie and McCrone 2000; Rosie 2004). All commentators agree that the 1918 Education Act which provided public money for Catholic schools was crucial in lifting the crippling burden of paying for separate schools from the Catholic community, and that Catholic schools have a good educational record. But many Scots believe the separate education of Catholics to be divisive. Maintenance of Catholic schools with their distinctive ethos remains a cause dear to the Catholic clergy and a majority of the laity but in a 1997 survey 45 per cent of Catholics opted for phasing them out compared with 78 per cent of all Scots (Rosie and McCrone 2000: 207). Rosie and McCrone entitle their chapter in Devine's (2000) book on the MacMillan debate 'The Past is History'; Rory Williams and Patricia Walls (2000), who challenge aspects of their data sources and the use they make of them, concede that Catholic disadvantage in Scotland is going but insist that it has not yet gone. A System Three poll reported in *The Guardian* of 26 May 2003 found that 13 per cent of Scots claim to have experienced some form of religious bigotry.

In terms of national identity perhaps the most significant finding is that Catholics respond to the Moreno question about Scottish and British identities much as other Scots do. Those who keep asking the question always have the devolution/independence issue in mind. It is notable that they never ask self-declared Catholics a similar question about Scottish and Irish identities. Might that introduce considerations of different ways of being Scottish at a time when evidence of convergence between Catholic and non-Catholic Scots on political and social issues has seemed of greater political significance? Joseph Bradley (2000: 42) argues that it is Celtic FC, rather than the RC church, that provides an 'anchor of identity' for many Catholics in west-central Scotland, though the club discourages those who regard it as 'a recreational substitute for Irish nationalism'. He adds that 'Not a few Celtic fans will urge on whatever team defeats Scotland, especially if it is from a Catholic country, as was the case with Costa Rica in the 1990 World Cup.' More seriously, Irish Republicans and Ulster Loyalists in Northern Ireland both have their supporters in the west of Scotland where Irish republican networks and the Orange Order are both active. The republican networks include the rebel music scene studied, with increasing distaste, by Mark Boyle (2002)—himself a Scot of Irish Catholic descent. Rebel bands glorify the IRA and vilify the British.

Clearly the religious issue in Scotland continues to raise difficult questions of interpretation. Commentators differ on the significance of (1) discrimination against Catholics even if the incidence is nothing like as great as it once was, (2) separate schools for Catholics, (3) contemporary clashes between Rangers and Celtic (football rivalry, community conflict, a cultural overhang from an otherwise discarded past, and/or an opportunity for ironic partisanship and a raucousness absent from polite society?), and

(4) identification by Scots with Britain and Ireland. My own outsider's risky assessment is that today's religious differences are more evidence of pluralism than division, but that the accommodative big picture should not blind us to stubborn residues of sectarianism (cf. Finn 1999). Reference to sectarianism, however, is not uncontroversial. For Rosie (2004) sectarianism is a myth, though bigotry, whilst now much less common than often supposed, is not. Rosie follows John Brewer (1992) in arguing that sectarianism is like racism in that it is manifest in pejorative beliefs, inequality, discrimination, and harassment and he assembles evidence with respect to housing, education, jobs, income, and life chances that suggests that differences between Catholics and non-Catholics are now negligible or non-existent. There is still some bigotry, and the bitter memory of much more, and there is still some separation of Catholics and non-Catholics, particularly in schools, but that is not sectarianism and the hostilities at old-firm football matches is better regarded these days as just football rivalry. The latter is thus redefined as an unusual case of smoke without fire. The problem with this analysis is that ordinary usage, at least as defined by the *Concise Oxford Dictionary*, connects sectarianism not with inequality and discrimination but with bigotry and this, Rosie concedes, does persist.

In percentage terms the next largest group to consider is the English in Scotland. According to the 2001 census 408,948 residents of Scotland were born in England, 8.1 per cent of the total population.[8] An NOP poll for *The Sunday Times* of 28 June 1998 indicated that 43 per cent of Scots thought that anti-English sentiment was increasing among Scots. Paterson et al. (2001) have noted that election surveys have shown an increase in the percentage of Scots saying conflict between the Scots and the English is 'very' or 'fairly' serious from 15 per cent in 1979 to 43 per cent in 1999 (table 79, p. 116)—but that could just reflect Scottish hostility to the Conservative governments of Margaret Thatcher and John Major which they never supported. Accusations of anti-English prejudice and discrimination, albeit on a small scale, are persistently made, and there are Scots, such as James MacMillan, who think they are justified. Anthony Cohen (1996: 806), writing for an American readership, acknowledged in Scotland 'an almost palpable dislike for, or resentment of, the English, even in the most civil of settings'. He also suggested that the inclusive Scottishness, and the anti-anti-Englishness, of liberal Scottish nationalism had more support in the seminar room than on the street (Cohen 2000: 147). According to Michael Keating (2001: 220), 'A diffuse anti-English sentiment does exist within Scottish society but it tends to be aimed at the structures of the British state rather than English people as individuals or a race.' It probably does, but the Commission for Racial Equality [in] Scotland has upheld complaints from English residents about discrimination and it has made a point of reminding Scots that discrimination against the English is unlawful. The commission's annual report for 2002 notes that 8 per cent of enquiries complained about anti-English discrimination though most were outside the scope of the Race Relations Act (p. 13). It is certainly the case that very many Scottish football and rugby fans cheer England's defeats and support their opponents whoever they are, which could be considered unneighbourly. There is little systematic evidence of anti-Englishness beyond the sporting arena but research on nations and regions currently being conducted by a team at the Institute of Governance at Edinburgh University led by David McCrone should clarify the issue. An NOP poll in 1998 indicated that 16 per cent of Scots chose 'arrogant' as an adjective to sum up the English (*Sunday Times*, 28 June 1998). Scottish preoccupation with the English is simply not reciprocated.

McCrone (2001a: 170), citing M. B. Dickson (1994), notes how 'English-born immigrants to Scotland tended to "go native", and to adopt political and social attitudes much more similar to native Scots than to the English population they had left behind.' For Dickson himself the Scottishing of the English in Scotland was more obvious than the feared Englishing of Scotland. Subsequently the support for devolution among the English in Scotland has been nearly as strong as that of the electorate as a whole. What the English in Scotland have not done is form any associations or communities of their own—hence their description by Murray Watson (2003) as Scotland's invisible minority. Watson conducted lengthy, unstructured interviews with fifty-eight English-born men and women who had moved to, and remained in, Scotland. Quite how they were selected is not made clear beyond a claim that they were representative of the English-born in Scotland in terms of location, gender, and occupation according to the 2001 census. The interviewees had migrated for (often complex combinations of) job, personal, and lifestyle reasons but with no expectations of joining other English there. They were dispersed, there being no English *community* as such to speak of. From inspection of censuses Watson estimates that one-third of English-born migrants to Scotland return to England. But the stayers merge into Scottish society and become largely invisible. Certainly most are *not* 'white settlers' in the Highlands (cf. Jedrej and Nuttall 1996); and many of the 'counterurbanists' in the Highlands are Lowland Scots. That the English-born were and are able to blend in indicates both their readiness to integrate and the willingness of Scots to let them. Watson's research confirms the Scottishing Dickson had noted. Some of the English-born did comment on anti-Englishness—mostly verbal taunting—but it was more an occasional irritant than a confidence-sapping threat. They had made their lives in Scotland and felt committed to it. Ian McIntosh, Duncan Sim, and Douglas Robertson (2004) reach broadly similar conclusions in their study of the English in thirty households in central Scotland and Greater Glasgow, although their interviewees did find the common low-level anti-Englishness tiresome.

Devine (1999) discusses new Scots in his history of the Scottish nation in terms of Catholic Irish and Protestant Irish, but also Lithuanians, Italians, and Jews in Glasgow. The small, non-white population of Scotland has not received much attention. About a third of this population is Pakistani in origin with a concentration in Glasgow. In a small study of Glasgow secondary school pupils with Pakistani backgrounds, Amir Saeed, Neil Blain, and Douglas Forbes (1999) found that, unprompted, most identified themselves as 'Muslim', but asked directly about ethnic identification and offered alternatives, including hybrids (though not 'Asian British'), many opted for 'Scottish Pakistani'. In their very much bigger study of adult Pakistanis and English in Scotland, Asifa Hussain and William Miller (2003) also found that by far the most favoured self-identification among Pakistanis is Muslim, but that offered four hyphenated alternatives (see table 9), 40 per cent chose Scottish Muslim, 24 per cent British Muslim, 15 per cent British Pakistani, and 14 per cent Scottish Pakistani. Of those born in Scotland 50 per cent opted for Scottish Muslim and only 9 per cent British Pakistani. Given that a majority of Scottish residents declare themselves Scottish only or more Scottish than British, the responses of Pakistanis in Scotland could be said to be the conformist ones. Almost half said that they or someone in their household had been harassed or discriminated against because they were Pakistanis and/or Muslims, and that the perpetrators were almost always ordinary people, not employers, police, or government officials. Most considered such treatment annoying more than frightening and most, too, thought relations between Muslims and non-Muslims were worse in England. Rowena Arshad and Fernando Diniz (1999: 882) report consultations with 'key organisations across Scotland' that indicate that 'Black pupils are still viewed as "incomers", "foreigners" or alternatively are endowed with an assimilated "Scots" or "New Scots" identity; how they define themselves has not been given much attention by curriculum developers and researchers. It is still not part of the hegemony that one can be brown or black skinned Scottish.' Only a quarter of Hussain and Miller's Pakistani respondents thought incomers should 'adapt and blend' with other Scots (what James Kellas (1998: 65) calls inclusive civic nationalism in which anyone can 'adopt the culture and join the nation'), whilst half preferred to 'add variety' (what Bhikhu Parekh (2000) regards as the multicultural alternative to both ethnic nationalism and liberal civic nationalism). It is the Kellas option, not the Parekh option, however, that Lindsay Paterson (2002: 125) argues Scots endorse. England, he says, is more comfortable with multiculturalism than Scotland. Scots support the rights of individual members of ethnic minorities to join the majority, to become full members of the national community; what they are uncomfortable with are ethnic minority group rights, the right to sustain alternative communities.

By English standards, or more precisely the standards of London and English regions such as the West Midlands, the East Midlands, and Yorkshire and the Humber, Scotland cannot be said to be a cosmopolitan country. The 2001 census has shown that non-white groups made up 9 per cent of the population of England but only 2 per cent of the population of Scotland. Within England the figure for London was 28.8 per cent, for the West Midlands 11.3 per cent, and for both the East Midlands and Yorkshire and the Humber 6.5 per cent. No one can know, however, how Scotland would have managed black and Asian immigration on the English scale as it has not experienced it. But some sense of the capacity of Scotland today to accommodate difference can be obtained by considering the experience of Catholics of Irish descent, the English in Scotland, and the relatively small numbers of Asian and black Britons. The record is mixed.

It is sometimes suggested that racial intolerance is a peculiarity of the English as they fail to come to terms with the end of Empire and not something that disfigures Scotland. That does seem a conceit (quite apart from the difficulty in distinguishing anti-Catholic sectarianism from anti-Irish racism (Kelly 2003)), and there is bitter testimony to the contrary (for example Qureshi 2002). Racial incidents recorded by chief constables rose from 299 in 1988 to 1,271 in 1998 (Kelly 2000: 159), and a System Three poll in September 2002 for the Scottish Executive found that 24 per cent of Scots describe themselves as 'slightly racist' and 1 per cent 'strongly racist' (*The Scotsman*, 25 September 2002). The Scottish Executive has responded by launching a 'One Nation, Many Cultures' campaign. Noting that Scotland's population fell between 1991 and 2001, that it is projected to fall further, and that it is ageing, the first minister, Jack McConnell, has also proposed that Scotland should seek immigrants. That entrepreneurship among non-white immigrants is reportedly twice as high as among indigenous Scots adds weight to his cause (*The Guardian*, 26 February 2003).

6 Scotland in Europe

In 1988 Jim Sillars won a by-election for the Scottish National Party using the slogan 'independence in Europe'. Thereafter the party adopted it as policy partly out of wishful thinking that an independent Scotland could somehow do as well out of the European Community economically as the Republic of Ireland had done, and partly out of an expectation that an independent Scotland would have a louder voice in the European Community than it had in Margaret Thatcher's Britain, but also as an affirmation that independence would not mean (self-imposed) isolation. Scotland in Europe recalls old Scottish traditions. There are Scottish quarters and streets in many European cities—Gdansk and Vienna spring immediately to mind—which date back to the enterprise of Scottish traders before the union. The Scottish contribution to the Enlightenment is also widely acknowledged in Europe to have been immense.

Atsuko Ichijo (2001) has given more definition to Scottish integration in Europe. Reflecting on thirty-six in-depth interviews with (unnamed) members of the 'Scottish intelligentsia', she distinguishes three 'visions' of Scotland in Europe. In all three cases Europe provides Scotland with an alternative reference point to Britain and English 'Euroscepticism' serves only to increase the attraction of Europe to Scots. Brussels is not London. The first vision presents the EU as a means by which Scotland can achieve greater autonomy (Europe of the regions) or independence (maximum political change with minimum economic disruption). The second regards the EU as a progressive project in which European commitments to social democracy, justice, and welfare are truer to Scottish traditions of civic responsibility than the Thatcherite neo-liberalism that persists in England. The third recalls Scottish alliances with, and trading communities in, European countries before the 1707 union, acknowledges that these were superseded by massive and successful Scottish participation in Empire, and argues that, with Empire gone, it is now Europe that again presents a theatre of opportunity for ambitious and enterprising Scots. In sum, Scotland should return to its European destiny. I will refer to representations of Scotland linked to Europe as Scotland in Europe irrespective of whether Scotland remains part of the United Kingdom or not and without suggesting that it is in any way the preserve of the Scottish National Party.

SNP leaders and Ichijo's interviewees among the Scottish intelligentsia might be agreed that where it once looked outward to Union and Empire, Scotland now, with or without Union, looks outward to Europe. But how widely this sentiment is shared is hard to say. In response to a 1994 Scottish poll that asked about national identity and allowed European to be chosen in combination with Scottish, or with British, or with Scottish and British, or not chosen at all, only 26 per cent of those polled opted for a European combination—10 per cent with Scottish, 5 per cent with British, and 11 per cent with Scottish and British (Brown et al. 1996: table 9.8, p. 211). The figure may not have shifted much since. Lynn Jamieson and Sue Grundy (2003) have reported EU-funded survey research on 'Orientations of Young Men and Women to Citizenship and European Identity' conducted in ten cities and districts in four pre-2004 members of the EU (Austria, Germany, Spain, and Britain), and two of the 2004 entrants (Czech Republic and Slovakia). In seven of the ten cities and districts between two-thirds and a half of 18–24-year-olds felt strongly or very strongly about being European. The figures for the remaining three were 38 per cent in Bilbao in the Basque Country, 30 per cent in (Greater) Manchester—and 23 per cent in Edinburgh. Scotland in Europe would still seem a minority vision. The number of school pupils achieving a Higher grade examination pass in a foreign language has also fallen sharply since 1970, and there is scant evidence of any increase in the number of Scottish graduates seeking employment in other countries of the EU. Pittock (2001: 8) comments that 'Europe is, like Gaelic bilingual signposting, a chic designer accessory to contemporary Scottish cultural nationalism not altogether sustained in society at large.'

The pluralism and diversity integral to a Scotland open to Europe is inconsistent with sectarianism and racism. Racism in Scotland is a relatively small problem compared with many other countries in the European Union but, by the same token, sectarianism, even if it is very much less evident now than formerly, is a larger one. Having said that, the idea of a nation confident of its place among other European nations and open to exchanges of all kinds with them as an alternative, or at least as a complement, to an unequal relation with England, has an appeal that will endure. Europe can also be a successor to Empire as a site of Scottish endeavour. Scotland in Europe may largely be an aspiration, but it also has its modern inspirations as well as its ancient ones. The renown of the Edinburgh Festival, now the largest arts festival in Europe, and the success of Glasgow as European City of Culture in 1990, are two such.

Conclusions

Unlike the majority of Scots in the 1997 Scottish Referendum Survey I do not think it very likely or quite likely that Scotland will become completely independent from the United Kingdom within twenty years (Brown et al. 1999: table 7.3, p. 147). What I do think is that in the last half-century more and more Scots have increasingly come to view economic, political, social, and cultural affairs through a Scottish lens first and a British one second (if at all), and that this is now so much the norm that it is only the exceptions that are remarked upon. It is thus irrelevant that on some economic measures Scotland is no longer the poor relation but rather comparable to a number of English regions, or that on some measures the superiority of Scottish education compared with English is more contestable that many Scots suppose. What matters is that the disjuncture between Scottish sensibilities and Thatcherite neo-liberalism moved very many Scots to think in Scottish terms first much more than they had hitherto and this is likely to prove irreversible. I expect Scotland to remain part of Britain—but only because Scots judge it in their interests for it to do so. Pittock (2001: 143–4) argues that under the Pax Britannica of the Empire there was room for 'local nationalities' such as Scotland's, but the end of Empire saw British Conservative governments opt not for a new internationalism in Europe but a narrow English nationalism. This would have left little room for a local Scottish nationality if, slighted, the Scots had not fought back by vigorously reasserting it. What needs to be said in response to Pittock is less that Britain now has a Labour government that delivered devolution, than that England is increasingly multicultural. Scots being different will not bother the English. They will just add it to the differences evident within England. The Pax Britannica is now an internal one.

Gerry Hassan and Chris Warhurst (2002b: 5) comment that 'Scotland is slowly becoming a different country place from the rest of the UK: a society and body politic with a different set of priorities, debates and policies.' But there is no homogenous 'rest of the UK' with which Scotland can be compared and contrasted—quite the opposite. Scotland is homogenizing at a time when England, in particular, is becoming more diverse. The old divisions between Gaelic and Scots/English speakers, Highlands and Lowlands, Calvinists and Catholics, Scots and Irish, and East and West have never had less significance (cf. Keating 2001: 235). But, prompted by family history and life experience, there are still different constructions of Scotland with which Scots can engage, and different ways of representing England/Britain within them (most of which do not exclude some identification with it). Multiple and layered ethnic and national identities are thus a feature of today's Scotland as they are of most other societies (cf. McCrone et al. 1998).[9] James Mitchell (2004: 39) comments that 'The jury is still out as to whether devolution will undermine or underline the union' (Curtice 2003). As it will take more than one generation to explore the possibilities and limitations of an autonomous Scotland with its own parliament it will be out for many years yet. The break-up of Britain having so far eluded him, Nairn (2002: 240) now speaks of 'late Britain' but today's Britain may prove not terminal but changing. Europe offers Scots an alternative point of reference to England/Britain and another opportunity to locate Scotland in a pluralist discourse, but whether Scots are ready to accept the immigration that will be necessary to counter the fall in population remains to be seen.

NOTES

1 The claim is reprinted in full in Devine (1999: 610–11).

2 On medieval and independent Scotland, I have used Kearney (1989), Lynch (1992),

R. Davies (1992), W. Ferguson (1998), N. Davies (1999), and Schama (2000).

3 The declaration was written in Latin. This English wording is taken from *The Declaration of Arbroath 1320 — Facsimile and Translation*, HMSO.

4 The haunting reference to 'the nation again' invites recovery of something that was lost. It is not a new one. In 1842 the Irish poet James Clancey Mangan stirred the cultural nationalists of the Young Ireland movement by publishing the ballad 'A Nation Once Again'.

5 Marr (1992) on *The Battle for Scotland*, and Harvie and Jones (2000) on the *The Road to Home Rule*, have given engaging book-length accounts of the struggle for autonomy/independence. Harvie and Jones comment that Scottish nationalism is 'deeply unstraightforward' (p. 2). There is a briefer account in Brand and Mitchell (1997).

6 Strictly speaking these were not the first. Robert McIntyre won a by-election for the SNP in Motherwell in 1945 but lost the seat at the general election two months later.

7 It should be added that Rangers supporters are the only ones in Scotland to wave the Union Flag as well as the Scottish saltire. Rangers has historical associations with working-class unionism and pride in Glasgow as the second city of the British Empire. For McCrone (2001a: 25) the offensive songs and taunts of the rival fans at 'Old Firm' matches are largely 'nostalgic echoes of another time and another place'. For Bradley (1995) they are more disturbing.

8 For all Scottish census figures in this chapter, see *Scotland's Census 2001: The Registrar General's 2001 Census Report to the Scottish Parliament*.

9 To give just one example, Charles Kennedy (2002: 115), MP for Ross, Skye and Inverness and Leader of the Liberal Democratic Party, says he is 'with no sense of contradiction, a Highlander, a Scot, a Briton and a European'.

REFERENCES

ANDERSON, ROBERT D. (1985), 'In search of the "lad of parts": the mythical history of Scottish education', *History Workshop Journal*, 19: 82–104.

—— (1999), 'The history of Scottish education, pre-1980', in Bryce and Humes (eds.), ch. 20.

ARSHAD, ROWENA, and DINIZ, FERNANDO A. (1999), 'Race equality in Scottish education', in Bryce and Humes (eds.), ch. 98.

ASCHERSON, NEIL (2002), *Stone Voices: The Search for Scotland* (London: Granta).

BECK, ULRICH (1986), *Risikogesellschaft: Auf dem Weg in eine andere Moderne* (Frankfurt: Suhrkamp).

BEVERIDGE, CRAIG, and TURNBULL, RONALD (1989), *The Eclipse of Scottish Culture* (Edinburgh: Polygon).

BOND, ROSS (2000), 'Squaring the circles: demonstrating and explaining the political "non-alignment" of Scottish national identity', *Scottish Affairs*, 32: 15–35.

—— and ROSIE, MICHAEL (2002), 'National identities in post-devolution Scotland', *Scottish Affairs*, 40: 34–53.

Boyle, Mark (2002), 'Edifying the rebellious Gael: uses of memories of Ireland's troubled past among the west of Scotland's Irish Catholic diaspora', in Harvey et al. (eds.), ch. 11.

Boyle, Raymond, and Lynch, Peter (1998) (eds.), *Out of the Ghetto? The Catholic Community in Modern Scotland* (Edinburgh: John Donald).

Bradley, Joseph M. (1995), *Ethnic and Religious Identity in Modern Scotland: Culture, Politics and Football* (Aldershot: Avebury).

—— (1998), 'Images, perceptions and the ghetto: conformity and invisible identity', in R. Boyle and P. Lynch (1998: ch. 5).

—— (2000), 'Catholic distinctiveness: a need to be different?', in Devine (ed.), ch. 13.

Brand, Jack, and Mitchell, James (1997), 'Home rule in Scotland: the politics and bases of a movement', in J. Bradbury and J. Mawson (eds.) *British Regionalism and Devolution: The Challenges of State Reform and European Integration* (London: Jessica Kingsley and Regional Studies Association), ch. 2.

Brewer, John D. (1992), 'Sectarianism and racism, and their parallels and differences', *Ethnic and Racial Studies*, 15: 352–64

Broadie, Alexander (2001), *The Scottish Enlightenment: The Historical Age of the Historical Nation* (Edinburgh: Birlinn).

Brown, Alice; McCrone, David; and Paterson, Lindsay (1996), *Politics and Society in Scotland* (Basingstoke: Macmillan).

—— —— —— and Surridge, Paula (1999), *The Scottish Electorate: The 1997 General Election and Beyond* (Basingstoke: Macmillan).

Bruce, Duncan (1997), *The Mark of the Scots: Their Astonishing Contributions to History, Science, Democracy, Literature and the Arts* (New York: Citadel).

Bruce, Steve (1985), *No Pope of Rome: Anti-Catholicism in Modern Scotland* (Edinburgh: Mainstream).

Bryant, Christopher G. A. (2003), 'These Englands, or where does devolution leave the English?', *Nations and Nationalism*, 9: 393–412.

Bryce, Tom G. K., and Humes, Walter M. (1999) (eds.), *Scottish Education* (Edinburgh: Edinburgh University Press).

Buchan, James (2003), *Capital of the Mind: How Edinburgh Changed the World* (Edinburgh: John Murray).

Chapman, Malcolm (1978), *The Gaelic Vision in Scottish Culture* (London: Croom Helm).

—— (1992), *The Celts: The Construction of a Myth* (London: Macmillan).

Cohen, Anthony P. (1996), 'Personal nationalism: a Scottish view of some rites, rights, and wrongs', *American Ethnologist*, 23: 802–15.

—— (2000), 'Peripheral vision: nationalism, national identity and the objective correlation in Scotland', in id. (ed.), *Signifying Identities: Anthropological Perspectives on Boundaries and Contested Values* (London: Routledge), ch. 6.

Colley, Linda (1992), *Britons: Forging the Nation 1707–1837* (New Haven, Conn.: Yale University Press).

Curtice, John (2003), 'Brought together or driven apart', paper presented to the joint Royal Society of Edinburgh/British Academy symposium on Anglo-Scottish Relations since 1914, Edinburgh, 6–7 November 2003.

Davidson, Neil (2000), *The Origins of Scottish Nationhood* (London: Pluto).

DAVIE, GEORGE (1961), *The Democratic Intellect* (Edinburgh: Edinburgh University Press).

DAVIES, NORMAN (1999), *The Isles: A History* (London: Macmillan).

DAVIES, REES R. (1999), *The First English Empire: Power and Identities in the British Isles 1093–1343* (Oxford: Oxford University Press).

DEVINE, TOM M. (1999), *The Scottish Nation 1700–2000* (London: Penguin).

_____ (2000) (ed.), *Scotland's Shame? Bigotry and Sectarianism in Modern Scotland* (Edinburgh: Mainstream).

_____ (2003), *Scotland's Empire 1600–1815* (London: Penguin—Allen Lane).

_____ and FINDLAY, RICHARD J. (1996) (eds.), *Scotland in the 20th Century* (Edinburgh: Edinburgh University Press).

_____ and LOGUE, PADDY (2002) (eds.), *Being Scottish: Personal Reflections on Scottish Identity Today* (Edinburgh: Polygon).

DI DOMENICO, CATHERINE; LAW, ALEX; SKINNER, JONATHAN; and SMITH, MICK (2001) (eds.), *Boundaries and Identities: Nation, Politics and Culture in Scotland* (Dundee: University of Abertay Press).

DICKSON, A. D. R. (1988), 'The peculiarities of the Scottish: national culture and political action', *Political Quarterly*, 59: 358–68.

DICKSON, MALCOLM B. (1994), 'Should auld acquaintance be forgot? A comparison of the Scots and English in Scotland', *Scottish Affairs*, 7: 112–34.

DONNACHIE, IAN, and WHATLEY, CHRISTOPHER (1992) (eds.), *The Manufacture of Scottish History* (Edinburgh: Polygon).

EDWARDS, OWEN D. (2000), 'Is the cardinal Anti-Catholic?', *Scottish Affairs*, 32: 1–22.

FERGUSON, NIALL (2003), *Empire: How Britain Made the World* (London: Allen Lane).

FERGUSON, WILLIAM (1998), *The Identity of the Scottish Nation: An Historical Quest* (Edinburgh: Edinburgh University Press).

FINN, GERRY P. T (1999), ' "Sectarianism" and Scottish education', in Bryce and Humes (eds.) ch. 97.

FOSTER, JOHN (1992), 'Red Clydeside, Red Scotland', in Donnachie and Whatley (eds.), ch. 7.

FRY, MICHAEL (1992), 'The Whig interpretation of Scottish history', in Donnachie and Whatley (eds.), ch. 5.

_____ (2001), *The Scottish Empire* (Phantassie (East Lothian): Tuckwell, and Edinburgh: Birlinn).

HAGUE, EUAN (2002), 'The Scottish diaspora: Tartan Day and the appropriation of Scottish identities in the United States', in Harvey et al. (eds.), ch. 9.

HARPER, MARJORY (2003), *Adventurers and Exiles: The Great Scottish Exodus* (London: Profile).

HARVEY, DAVID C.; JONES, RHYS; McINROY, NEIL; and MILLIGAN, CHRISTINE (2002) (eds.), *Celtic Geographies: Old Culture, New Times*, London: Routledge.

HARVIE, CHRISTOPHER (1981), *No Gods and Precious Few Heroes* (London: Edward Arnold).

_____ and JONES, PETER (2000), *The Road to Home Rule: Images of Scotland's Cause* (Edinburgh: Polygon).

HASSAN, GERRY, and WARHURST, CHRIS (2002a) (eds.), *Tomorrow's Scotland* (London: Lawrence & Wishart).

_____ (2002b), 'Future Scotland: the making of the new social democracy', in Hassan and Warhurst (eds.), 5–25.

HEARN, JONATHAN (2000), *Claiming Scotland: National Identity and Liberal Culture* (Edinburgh: Polygon).

HERMAN, ARTHUR (2002), *The Scottish Enlightenment: The Scots' Invention of the Modern World* (London: HarperCollins).

HOBSBAWM, ERIC, and RANGER, TERENCE (1983) (eds.), *The Invention of Tradition* (Cambridge: Cambridge University Press).

HUMES, WALTER M., and BRYCE, TOM G. K. (1999), 'The distinctiveness of Scottish education' in Bryce and Humes (eds.), ch. 10.

HUSSAIN, ASIFA, and MILLER, WILLIAM (2003), 'Implementing the oxymoron: the progress of multicultural nationalism in Scotland', paper presented to conference on Anglo-Scottish Relations Since 1914, Royal Society of Edinburgh, 6–7 November 2003.

ICHIJO, ATSUKO (2001), 'Scottish identity in the age of European integration', in Di Domenico et al. (eds.), 83–99.

JAMIESON, LYNN, and GRUNDY, SUE (2003), 'Orientations of young men and women to citizenship and European identity', paper presented to 6th Biennial Conference of the European Sociological Association, Murcia, September.

JEDREJ, M. CHARLES, and NUTTALL, MARK (1996), *White Settlers: The Impact of Rural Repopulation in Scotland* (Luxembourg: Harwood Academic).

KEARNEY, HUGH (1989), *The British Isles: A History of Four Nations* (Cambridge: Cambridge University Press).

KEATING, MICHAEL (2001), *Nations Against the State: The New Politics of Nationalism in Quebec, Catalonia and Scotland*, 2nd edn. (Basingstoke: Palgrave).

KELLAS, JAMES (1968), *Modern Scotland: The Nation Since 1870* (London: Pall Mall).

—— (1998), *The Politics of Nationalism and Ethnicity*, 2nd edn. (Basingstoke: Macmillan).

KELLY, ELLINOR (2000), 'Racism, police and courts in Scotland', *Scottish Affairs*, 30: 41–59.

—— (2003), 'Challenging sectarianism in Scotland: the prism of racism', *Scottish Affairs*, 42: 32–56.

KENNEDY, CHARLES (2002), 'Charles Kennedy' in Devine and Logue (eds.), 117–20.

KIDD, COLIN (1993), *Subverting Scotland's Past: Scottish Whig Historians and the Creation of an Anglo-British Identity, 1689–c1830* (Cambridge: Cambridge University Press).

KREJČÍ, JAROSLAV and VELÍMSKY, VÍTĚZSLAV (1981), *Ethnic and Political Nations in Europe* (London: Croom Helm).

LAMONT, STEWART (2001), *When Scotland Ruled the World: The Story of the Golden Age of Genius* (London: HarperCollins).

LIVINGSTONE, GEORGE (1999), 'Teachers' professional organizations', in Bryce and Humes (eds.), ch. 109.

LYNCH, MICHAEL (1992), *Scotland: A New History*, rev. edn. (London: Pimlico), 1st edn. 1991.

McCRONE, DAVID (1992), *Understanding Scotland: The Sociology of a Stateless Nation* (London: Routledge).

—— (2001a), *Understanding Scotland: The Sociology of a Nation*, 2nd edn. of (1992) (London, Routledge).

—— (2001b), 'Who are we? Understanding Scottish identity', in Di Domenico et al. (eds.), 11–35.

—— and ROSIE, MICHAEL (1998), 'Left and liberal: Catholics in modern Scotland", in Boyle and Lynch (eds.), ch. 4.

____ MORRIS, ANGELA, and
KIELY, RICHARD (1995), *Scotland—the
Brand: The Making of Scottish Heritage*
(Edinburgh: Edinburgh University
Press).

____ STEWART, ROBERT; KIELY,
RICHARD, and BECHHOFER, FRANK
(1998), 'Who are we? Problematising
national identity', *Sociological Review*, 46:
629–52.

MACDONALD, SHARON (1999), 'The
Gaelic Renaissance and Scotland's
Identities', *Scottish Affairs*, 26: 100–18.

MCINTOSH, IAN; SIM, DUNCAN; and
ROBERTSON, DOUGLAS (2004), ' "We hate
the English, except for you, cos you're
our pal": identification of the "English"
in Scotland', *Sociology*, 38: 43–59.

MACKENZIE, JOHN M. (1998), 'Empire
and national identities: the case of
Scotland', *Transactions of the Royal
Historical Society*, 6th series, 8: 215–31.

MACKINNON, KENNETH (2000), 'Scottish
Gaelic', in GLANVILLE PRICE (ed.)
Languages in Britain and Ireland (Oxford,
Blackwell), ch. 4.

MACMILLAN, JAMES (2000), 'Scotland's
shame', in Devine (ed.), ch. 1. (Public
lecture given in 1999.)

MARR, ANDREW (1992), *The Battle for
Scotland* (London: Penguin).

MAVER, IRENE (1996), 'The Catholic
community', in Devine and Findlay
(eds.), ch. 14.

MITCHELL, JAMES (2004), 'Scotland:
expectations, policy-types and
devolution', in A. TRENCH (ed.), *Has
Devolution made a Difference? The State of
the Nations 2004* (London: Imprint
Academic and The Constitution Unit,
2004), ch. 1.

MORRISON, JOHN (2003), *Painting the
Nation: Identity and Nationalism in
Scottish Painting, 1800–1920* (Edinburgh:
Edinburgh University Press).

MORTON, GRAEME (1999),
*Unionist-Nationalism: Governing Urban
Scotland 1830–1860* (Phantassie (East
Lothian): Tuckwell).

____ (2001), *William Wallace: Man and
Myth* (Stroud: Sutton Publishing).

MURRAY, DAVID (1960), *The First Nation
in Europe: A Portrait of Scotland and the
Scots* (London: Pall Mall).

NAIRN, TOM (1977), *The Break-Up of
Britain* (London: New Left Books).

____ (2002), 'Disorientations from Down
Under: The Old Country in retrospect',
in Hassan and Warhurst (eds.), 234–52.

O'HAGAN, ANDREW (2000), 'Into the
Ferment', in Devine (ed.), ch. 2.

PAREKH, BHIKU (2000), *Rethinking
Multiculturalism: Cultural Diversity and
Political Theory* (Basingstoke:
Macmillan).

PATERSON, IAIN R. (2000), 'The pulpit
and the ballot box: Catholic assimilation
and the decline of church influence' in
Devine (ed.), ch. 17.

PATERSON, LINDSAY (1994), *The
Autonomy of Modern Scotland*
(Edinburgh: Edinburgh University
Press).

____ (1999), 'Educational provision' in
Bryce and Humes (eds.), ch. 2.

____ (2000), 'Salvation through
education? The changing social status of
Scottish Catholics', in Devine (ed.),
ch. 12.

____ (2002), 'Scottish social democracy
and Blairism: difference, diversity and
community', in Hassan and Warhurst
(eds.), 116–29.

____ et al. (2001), *New Scotland, New
Politics* (Edinburgh: Polygon).

PITTOCK, MURRAY G. H. (1991), *The
Invention of Scotland: The Stuart Myth
and the Scottish Identity, 1638 to the
Present* (London: Routledge).

_____ (1997), *Inventing and Resisting Britain: Cultural Identities in Britain and Ireland, 1685–1789* (Basingstoke: Macmillan).

_____ (2001), *Scottish Nationality* (Basingstoke: Palgrave).

QURESHI, ROBINA (2002), 'Robina Qureshi', in Devine and Logue (eds.), 217–19.

ROBB, JOHN G. (2002), 'A geography of Celtic appropriations', in DAVID C. HARVEY, RHYS JONES, NEIL MCINROY, and CHRISTINE MILLIGAN (eds.), *Celtic Geographies: Old Culture, New Times* (London: Routledge, 2002), ch. 14.

ROBERTSON, BOYD (1999), 'Gaelic education', in Bryce and Humes (eds.), ch. 23.

ROSIE, MICHAEL (2004), *The Sectarian Myth in Scotland: Of Bitter Memory and Bigotry* (Basingstoke: Palgrave).

_____ and MC CRONE, DAVID (2000), 'The past is history: Catholics in modern Scotland', in Devine (ed.), ch. 16.

SAEED, AMIR; BLAIN, NEIL; and FORBES, DOUGLAS (1999), 'New ethnic and national questions in Scotland: post-British identities among Glasgow Pakistani teenagers', *Ethnic and Racial Studies*, 22: 821–44.

SCHAMA, SIMON (2000), *A History of Britain, i. At the Edge of the World: 3000BC–AD1603* (London: BBC).

Scotland's Census 2001: The Registrar General's 2001 Census Report to the Scottish Parliament (2003) (Edinburgh: General Register Office for Scotland).

SEENAN, GERARD (2002), 'Thou shalt not land', *The Guardian (G2)*, 25 October 2002, pp. 4–5.

SIMS-WILLIAMS, PATRICK (1998), 'Celtomania and Celtoscepticism', *Cambrian Medieval Celtic Studies*, 36: 1–35.

SMITH, JEREMY J. (2000), 'Scots' in GLANVILLE PRICE (ed.), *Languages in Britain and Ireland* (Oxford, Blackwell), ch. 13.

TEMPLETON, JANET M. (1973), 'Scots: An Outline History', in A. J. AITKEN (ed.), *Lowland Scots*, Occasional Papers, 2 (Edinburgh: Association for Scottish Literary Studies), 4–19.

TREVOR-ROPER, HUGH (1983), 'The invention of tradition: the Highland tradition in Scotland', in Hobsbawm and Ranger (eds.), ch. 6.

WALKER, GRAHAM (1996), 'Varieties of Scottish Protestant identity', in Devine and Findlay (eds.), ch. 13.

WATSON, MURRAY (2003), *Being English in Scotland* (Edinburgh: Edinburgh University Press).

WILLIAMS, RORY, and WALLS, PATRICIA (2000), 'Going but not gone: Catholic disadvantage in Scotland', in Devine (ed.), ch. 18.

WITHERS, CHARLES (1992), 'The historical creation of the Scottish Highlands', in Donnachie and Whatley (eds.), ch. 9.

4

Voicing Wales

Introduction

England annexed Wales by means of acts of the Westminster parliament in 1536 and 1542. Annexation incorporated Wales within the English systems of law, government, and public administration but did not lead to the loss of a separate Welsh identity. The single most important reason for this was language. Almost all the people of Wales continued to speak Welsh. Although Henry VIII made English the sole language of state and justice (in principle if not always in practice), Elizabeth I enacted in 1567 that church services be provided in Welsh where parishioners were Welsh-speaking. Religious texts were translated into Welsh and Bishop Morgan's complete Welsh Bible of 1588 was one of the first translations into a non-state language anywhere in Europe.

Adding Welsh in church to Welsh at home effectively guaranteed the continuation of the language. Janet Davies (2000: 83) estimates that about 80 per cent of the population spoke Welsh in 1800, including 10 per cent who were bilingual. But according to censuses, by 1901 just half the population spoke Welsh (49.9%) and by 2001 only a fifth (20.8%).[1] Even so, without anything comparable to the distinctive civil society that the Scots developed further after the union of 1707, Welsh identity has continued to centre on matters of language and culture and these in turn have long been contained by the British state without undue difficulty. In the late twentieth century, however, deindustrialization, or at least the rapid ending of coal mining and the big contraction of tinplate and steel production, called in question the future of Anglo-Wales (areas where most people speak English only) whose progressive 'modern' economy had hitherto been contrasted with the traditional rural economy of Welsh Wales (areas where most people's first language is Welsh). Economic dislocation was now added to cultural difference. And then from 1979 to 1997 Wales was subject to the Conservative governments of Margaret Thatcher and John Major after rejecting the Conservatives at the polls. Government from London by a party other than the one which had won the most votes in Wales was not new, but the clash between the communal and solidary values of the Welsh and Thatcherite neo-liberalism was very sharp. Matters of culture, economics, and politics combined to set Wales apart from Anglo-Britain, a Britain in which England predominated.

In these circumstances it might be thought unsurprising that there should have been the developments that culminated in the establishment of the National Assembly for Wales in 1999. Support for political devolution was, however, decidedly limited. The Welsh language issue divided the Welsh as much as it united them and there was no resource akin to 'Scottish' oil that nationalists could claim would facilitate the regeneration of the Welsh economy. In the 1997 referendum on Welsh devolution just 50.3 per cent voted in support of establishment of a Welsh assembly on a 51.3 per cent turnout. This compared favourably with the 20.9 per cent who had voted in support on a 58.8 per cent turnout in the 1979 referendum on devolution, but unfavourably with the 74.3 per cent who voted in support of establishment of a Scottish parliament on a 60.1 per cent turnout in 1997. In the capital, Cardiff, those opposed to an assembly outvoted those in favour by 55.4 per cent to 44.6 per cent. The lack of enthusiasm in Wales compared with Scotland prompted John Curtice (1999: 125) to ask 'Is Scotland a nation and Wales not?' He did not answer his own question, but instead noted that the 1997 Scottish and Welsh referendum surveys found that, whilst 66 per cent of Scottish electors considered themselves Scottish only or more Scottish than British, only 43 per cent of Welsh electors considered themselves Welsh only or more Welsh than British.

Although the people of Wales affirm their particular identity less strongly than the people of Scotland affirm theirs, only 12 per cent of the electorate in the same 1997 survey described themselves as British only. So who do the Welsh think they are? The debate over the last three decades has not yielded a single simple answer for six main reasons. First, there has been ambivalence about Britain and the British, though it has a different cast from that in Scotland. For the Welsh to dissociate themselves from Britain jars in so far as they lay claim to being the descendants of the Britons who occupied

all of what is now England, Wales, and the western lowlands of Scotland before they were either displaced, or absorbed, by invading Saxons and Scots.
The Welsh language is derived from British, the language of the Britons, and
belongs to the Brittonic branch of Celtic languages. Wales was also annexed
by a Tudor, Henry VIII, and the Tudors made political capital out of their
descent from Cadwaladr, the last British king to succumb to the Saxons, and
made visible their Welsh origins by adopting as a supporter for the royal
arms the red dragon of Cadwaladr to accompany the English lion.[2] It was
also Welsh subjects of the Tudors, John Dee and Humphrey Lhuyd, who
originated the notion of a British Empire. After annexation there was nothing to stop English-speaking Welshmen making their way in England and
for centuries many have; and the impediments to English-speaking Welsh
women were the same as for women generally. Over the centuries England,
Britain, and the British Empire have afforded the Welsh opportunities on a
large scale, but at the same time the Anglicization of Wales has undermined
the Welsh language and eroded traditional culture; more often than not,
too, the Welsh economy has been peripheral to that of England (the great
days of coal and steel being the main exception). To summarize, the Welsh
lay claim to have been British for longer than the English and recognize that
England, Britain after 1707, and the Empire have provided opportunities,
but, at the same time, they resent English descriptions of Britain as England
which leaves them out of account and know only too well that Anglicization
has made Welsh the language of a minority and diminished traditional rural
culture. So what the Welsh think about Wales is related to what they think
about Britain and that itself is complex.

Second, Welsh confidence in Wales as a single political entity different
from England is, in some respects, relatively recent. There never was a single
kingdom of Wales or an all-Wales state (and as a consequence there is not
a Welsh component in the union flag or the royal standard). In 1216 Llywelyn ap Iorweth (Llywelyn I, the Great) was acknowledged by other Welsh
princes as the overlord of all Welsh lands not held by the English crown or by
Anglo-Norman lords and by 1234 these lands constituted about two-thirds
of all Wales but none of the south.[3] Llywelyn's heartland was in the north
in Gwynedd. Thereafter some lands were lost to the English but Llywelyn's
grandson, Llywelyn ap Gruffudd (Llywelyn II), reversed the losses, and the
lands confirmed by the Treaty of Montgomery in 1267 as, in effect, Welsh,
were the most extensive of any Welsh regime—but still excluded the south.

The treaty required Llywelyn II to acknowledge King Henry III of England as his lord, but granted that he was Prince of Wales. Again lands were lost thereafter, and in 1283–4 Edward I completed the conquest of Wales. Beginning in 1400 Owain Glyn Dŵr led an uprising against English rule that briefly succeeded in uniting all Wales except the south-west, but he was defeated in battle in 1405 and by 1415 the last of the revolt was over. Owain Glyn Dŵr summoned the first Welsh parliament at Machynlleth in 1404 whose six-hundredth anniversary has just been celebrated. It is also significant that from 1120 all the Welsh bishops were obliged to swear allegiance to the archbishop of Canterbury. Attempts to get the Vatican to accept a church in Wales separate from that in England failed.

In making Wales an extension of England in 1536–42, Henry VIII ended the distinction between the royal principality in the north and west—the shires of Caernarvon, Merioneth, Flint, Cardigan, and Carmarthen created in 1284—and the marches of the east and lordships of the south where the local lords had exercised their powers and privileges. The latter were divided in 1536 into the shires of Denbigh, Montgomery, Radnor, Brecknock, Glamorgan, and Monmouth (with a handful of lordships added to the English shires of Shropshire, Worcester, and Gloucester). All the shires except Monmouthshire were included in one of the four new Welsh court circuits in 1543. These Courts of Great Session applied English law but were different from the courts in England and thus gave Wales as a territory some legal identity of its own. The Courts of Great Session were abolished in 1830 despite Welsh protests. After the 'acts of union' the Welsh shires and boroughs sent representatives to parliaments at Westminster. The Council of the Marches was also re-formed as the Council of Wales and the Marches with responsibility for good order in both Wales and the border counties of England. It had its seat in Ludlow in Shropshire, and was answerable to the Privy Council. Having long since been marginalized, it was finally abolished in 1688.

Monmouthshire was attached to the court system of neighbouring English counties and taxes in the shire were paid directly to the English treasury, not to one of the new treasuries in Wales. In effect Monmouthshire was made part of England even though most of the people in the west of the shire spoke Welsh. Monmouthshire was thus an anomaly. When, for example, a university college was established in Cardiff in 1883, it was called the University College of South Wales and Monmouthshire; or to give another example

Newport Rugby Football Club was once a member of both the Welsh and English rugby unions. It was only in 1974, as part of the local government reform in England and Wales, that Monmouthshire was unambiguously returned to Wales—with the ancient name of Gwent.

If the homeland of the Welsh is Wales, many would say the heartland of Wales is Y Fro Gymraeg, Welsh-speaking Wales, and some would add that the heartland of the heartland is Gwynedd in the north-west. The mountainous terrain of Wales has made internal communication difficult; the main rail and road routes link the north and south coasts of Wales to England. There is no rail route from south to north except via Shrewsbury in England and there is no fast road from south to north. All nations have their regional differences but that between North and South Wales is more marked than most and has historical connections to economics, politics, language, and culture. In some respects the differences between west and east Wales are also marked and have prompted references to inner and outer Wales. Much of the middle of the country is very sparsely populated. Difficult internal communications have contributed to strong local loyalties, and these have led to one construction of Wales as a (somewhat elusive) community of communities, with a principal city, Cardiff, not easily accessed from the northern heartland. There is thus good reason why Thompson, Day, and Adamson (1999) should point to the continuing *local* production of Welsh identities.

Cardiff, unlike London, Edinburgh, or Dublin, is not a city that has been at the heart of a nation's history for centuries. In the seventeenth and eighteenth centuries there were very many more Welsh in London than any Welsh town, and the London Welsh pioneered more developments in Wales than the Welsh of any Welsh town. Cardiff grew from a small to a large town only when the exploitation of the South Wales coalfield in the Victorian era required a coal-exporting port. Its population grew almost ninefold in the six decades to 1911 (Day 2002: 30). Many incomers migrated from England and Ireland, and much less Welsh was spoken in Cardiff than in most of the rest of the country. Cardiff acquired city status only in 1905, and the status of capital—Wales's first—in 1955.

Beginning in the late nineteenth century there were occasional political developments that acknowledged Wales as a territory different from England. Foulkes, Jones, and Wilford (1986: 276) note that the Welsh Intermediate Education Act of 1889 'virtually created the modern system of

Welsh secondary education', that the Central Welsh Board, an inspecting and examining body, was set up in 1896 to administer the act, and that in 1907 a Welsh Department was established at the Board of Education. Other ministries acquired Welsh sections beginning with Health and Agriculture in 1919, and by 1945 there were fifteen such. After the Second World War both the Treasury and the National Health Service made Wales a region, and from 1951 the UK government included a junior minister for Welsh affairs. In addition the Church (of England) in Wales had been disestablished in 1920. But all these, and a few other lesser developments, were minor compared with the separate provisions made for and in Scotland. Wales became really visible in terms of administrative devolution only with the establishment of the Welsh Office and a Secretary of State for Wales in 1964.

It could be said that the English conquest of Wales robbed Wales of its future as a nation-state. Without a history of statehood, with ambiguity about its border the product of annexation by England, with difficult internal communications and strong local loyalties to match, and with a modern capital without a long history of national significance and one in which English has long been the predominant language, Wales as a nation has been enough of an enigma for Gwyn Williams (1991) to write a book entitled *When Was Wales?* in 1985, and for Dai Smith (1984) to choose a book title with not just a question but also an exclamation, *Wales? Wales!*.

The third point has a parallel with Scotland. Tom Nairn (1977), to repeat, long ago pointed out that nationalism is not just about the promotion of a distinctive national identity, it is also about the mobilizing myth of 'the people'. But the English constitutional settlement of the 'Glorious Revolution' in 1688 established the sovereignty of (the crown in) parliament, not the sovereignty of the people, and thereby diverted both the English and the Welsh from thinking then and since in republican terms about 'we the people' as the foundation of democracy, and thus about who we the people are. But, fourth, and running counter to the English tradition of the crown-in-parliament there has been the Welsh concept of the *gwerin*. The *gwerin* refers to the folk, the Welsh as an inclusive community that transcended differences of class (whilst excluding the Tory and Anglican gentry who were few in number) and which drew strength from Welsh culture, respected learning, lauded self-improvement, resented snobbishness, and prompted a genial solidarity.[4] This is a cherished concept but also one whose extension beyond traditional Welsh Wales has always been problematic and whose time had passed by the First World War (Day 1984). But the myth and memory of the *gwerin* still has a resonance; it can prompt the populist thought that the Welsh are a people who should determine their own future.

Fifth, the language fault line among the Welsh divides Welsh speakers, the bilingual Welsh Welsh, from unilingual English speakers, the Anglophone Welsh.[5] On the one side it generates suspicions, especially in Gwynedd and Dyfed, that government from cosmopolitan Cardiff cannot be relied upon to protect the Welsh language and traditional culture; on the other it generates anxiety that the bilingual Welsh will be unfairly advantaged in politics and the labour market. The language issue is central to Welsh national identity and will be discussed more fully later. The paradox is that it both unites the Welsh — most Anglophone Welsh endorse efforts to secure the future of the language, and divides them — with some of the Welsh Welsh dismissive of the culture of the Anglophone Welsh and vice versa. It leaves the Anglophone Welsh in an ambivalent position between the Welsh Welsh and the third main group in Wales, the English.

The sixth reason why the question is difficult follows from much of the above; when the Welsh think about Wales there is more than one possibility with which to engage — hence Dai Smith's (1984: 1) comment that Wales is 'a singular noun but a plural experience'. My aim in this chapter is to clarify the debate about Wales by specifying five alternative ways of representing or constructing Wales and Welshness. Far from the five versions of Wales being necessarily exclusive, most Welsh, in their identifications, switch between (aspects of) more than one of them according to circumstances and each enjoys considerable currency in practice if not in name. I must emphasize that, unlike the Waleses in Denis Balsom's three-Waleses model, they are representations of Wales as a whole rather than constructions of particular regions.

Balsom (1985), on the basis of ability to speak Welsh as identified by the 1971 census and self-declared national identity as ascertained by the 1979 Welsh Election Survey (WES), distinguished three different Waleses: Y Fro Gymraeg (Welsh-speaking Wales), i.e. north-west and west Wales; what he called Welsh Wales, i.e. Llanelli, Gower, Swansea, and the Valleys; and British Wales, i.e. east Wales from Clwyd to Monmouth and the far south of Wales from Newport, through Cardiff to the Vale of Glamorgan and on to an outlier in Pembrokeshire. In Y Fro Gymraeg two-thirds of the population spoke Welsh, and, asked to choose a single national identity from Welsh,

British, English, or something else, two-thirds opted for Welsh. In Welsh Wales, only a minority spoke Welsh but two-thirds still gave Welsh as their identity. In British Wales, only a minority spoke Welsh and only half gave Welsh as their identity, most of the rest opting for British. I shall argue that Balsom's three Waleses can be reworked as three constructions of Wales (among others) with application to the whole of the country. The partisans of Y Fro Gymraeg in Cymdeithas yr Iaith Gymraeg (The Welsh Language Society), for example, want to reverse its historical contraction and make Welsh speaking the norm wherever they can—a process that has been called recymrufication. Balsom's Welsh Wales is also misleadingly named in so far as most of the Welsh, and most commentators Welsh and non-Welsh, refer to Y Fro Gymraeg as Welsh Wales; it is better designated Labour Wales. Labour Wales has had its heartland in industrial South Wales but has also appealed beyond it. Finally the idea of British Wales may have found favour among, for example, most people in Radnor, but British Wales is really a kind of plural Wales which has a currency beyond just the east and the parts of the south where Balsom locates it.

What I propose has more affinity with another analysis derived from the 1979 WES that Balsom did jointly with Madgwick and Van Mechelen (1984). This distinguished Cymrics (23% of the WES sample) who identified themselves as Welsh and could speak Welsh, Anglo-Welsh (5%) who identified themselves as British or English but could speak Welsh (not the usual definition of Anglo-Welsh), Welsh (34%) who identified themselves as Welsh but could not speak Welsh, and British (38%) who identified themselves as British or English and could not speak Welsh. Even if, by these definitions, the Cymrics at 55 per cent constituted the biggest fraction of the population in north-west and west Wales, the Welsh at 48 per cent the biggest fraction in upper South Wales (Swansea and the Valleys), and the British the biggest fraction at 49 per cent in north-east and mid-Wales and 46 per cent in lower South Wales, the percentages for the smaller fractions add up to more than half the population in three regions and nearly half in the other. The 1979 WES was conducted at a time when national confidence was low following the decisive rejection of devolution at the 1974 referendum, and the percentages in the four categories today would be different with more Cymrics and Welsh, but all four categories would still figure in all four regions. But in proposing five contemporary constructions of Wales I want to do more than just escape from thinking in terms of regions and lines on maps, I want also to acknowledge that people in Wales can and do engage with different aspects of different constructions at different times.

The five contemporary constructions are: Y Fro Gymraeg, Labour Wales, Anglo-British Wales, Cymru-Wales which is civic and bilingual, and Modern Wales which is diversified and cosmopolitan. They can be differentiated on two dimensions as Table 4.1 illustrates, orientation to time and orientation to place. Looking back, an orientation beyond Britain is, however, less significant to Welsh identities than it is to Scottish and I have not separated Britain and Abroad. I also have not separated them when looking to the present and future because to do so requires specification of two varieties of economic and cultural openness when there is evidence only of one. Looking back (1) Y Fro Gymraeg is one of three main constructions of Wales. It centres on Welsh language and culture and rural life. (2) Labour Wales also looks back. It centres on working class solidarity and is both fiercely Welsh in its historical memory and British in its belief that its welfare is inextricably connected to the fortunes of the labour movement throughout Britain. It thus straddles the Home and Britain and Abroad cells. (3) Anglo-British Wales also has a take on the past. It accepts that England, Britain and the Empire have long re-formed Wales in terms of language, culture, economy, and demography. The other two constructions are oriented to the present. (4) Cymru-Wales revolves around bilingualism and bilingual

TABLE 4.1	Contemporary constructions of Wales by time and place		
		Orientations to Place	
		Home	*Britain and Abroad*
Orientations to Time	*Past*	1. Y Fro Gymraeg	2. Labour Wales	3. Anglo-British Wales
	Present	4. Cymru-Wales (civic and bilingual)		5. Modern Wales (diversified)

education and public administration, and emphasizes development of a distinctively Welsh civil society and devolved government. (5) Modern Wales is cosmopolitan, derives benefit from a plural society that is about more than language, and is committed to a diversified economy. It has a positive outlook on Britain, Europe, and beyond. Cymru-Wales and Modern Wales are compatible in most respects but not all.

1 Y Fro Gymraeg

Y Fro Gymraeg, Welsh-speaking Wales, has been in retreat for centuries but is still at the heart of debates about Welsh national identity. And of the three Waleses that look back, it is the one that looks back furthest. The Britons of Wales were cut off from those in Cornwall and the south-west by the Saxon victory at Dyrham near Bath in 577 and from those in Cumbria and the north-west by the Saxon victory at Chester in 616, and were shut off in the late eighth century from the territory the Saxons had acquired by Offa's Dyke, the boundary constructed by the Saxon king of Mercia to keep the displaced Welsh to the west at bay (Bowen 1986: 68). The Saxons called the people beyond the dyke Wallas, or 'strangers'; these strangers, or 'Welsh', referred to each other as 'fellow-countrymen', or Cymry (ibid.). Their language was Welsh, or British as the act of 1536 was to call it. Mostly upland, Wales proved hard to unite but came nearest to unification under Prince Llywelyn ap Gruffudd in the late thirteenth century before succumbing to one or other of the two forms of rule the Normans had sought to impose from 1067, the year after their conquest of England. The east and south of Wales constituted Marchia Wallie, the Welsh Marches, and was made up of lordships whose lords were granted their Welsh estates, mostly in the half-century following 1067, in return for fealty to the king and the maintenance of order. Some of these lords found it hard at times to hang on to their lands in the face of Welsh opposition. The marches were not part of England and each lord held his own courts. Together the marcher lords secured a buffer between the kingdom of England and Pura Wallie, the territories beyond the marches. These were mainly the territories of the Welsh princes but included fortified crown holdings at points on the coasts. Norman and Plantagenet kings set out to acquire the lands of the Welsh princes and, not without reverses, bit by bit they succeeded, but it was not until 1292–3 that Edward I completed the Anglo-Norman conquest of Pura Wallie and built or rebuilt the castles to enforce his rule, including those at Beaumaris, Caernarfon, Conwy, and Harlech which still impress more than seven hundred years later. These lands were again not part of England, but rather part of the royal domain, and the law applied in them was a mixture of English statute and the laws of Wales but not the common law of England. They were consolidated as a principality in 1284 and in 1301 Edward I made his eldest son prince of Wales, as monarchs still do.[6] In both parts of Wales the language of rule and administration was English, as was the language of the new towns (from which the Welsh could be excluded), but the language of the people remained Welsh. The language of the law was variously English and Welsh depending on which body of law it was and to whom it was being applied. In particular the English in Wales could be tried only in English and according to English law.

The act of 1536 by which Wales was annexed to England—annexed is the word used in the preamble to the act—came to be known as the act of union only in the nineteenth century, and it effected a union of the principality and the marches as much as it made England and Wales one. When Henry VIII broke with Rome in 1534 and made himself supreme governor of the Church of England he could not leave intact the Roman Catholic Church in Wales. It thus suited him to incorporate Wales as an extension of England and to make the boundaries of the kingdom and the national church the same. Unlike the kings of the twelfth century he had the means to hold the marches without the aid of the marcher lords; there were also practical advantages in applying the same systems of government and law in both countries.

Economically and politically Wales benefited from the union with England, but culturally it did not. The gentry had to acquire English to discharge their public offices in Wales, and to take advantage of the new opportunities open to them in England. Over the centuries they were Anglicized. Their patronage of the Welsh poets had fallen away by the end of the seventeenth century and increasingly bilingualism gave way to the speaking of English only. Many did well enough in business in Wales and in England to become wealthy and a gulf opened up between this thin Anglicized ruling class and the Welsh-speaking people, the *gwerin*. The idea of Y Fro Gymraeg, the Wales not just of Welsh speakers but of the *gwerin*, was at its most potent in the hundred years or so that ended with the First World War. Prys Morgan (1986*a*: 35–6) says this of the *gwerin*:

Gwerin in Welsh means a mass, so the word means the masses of common people, as opposed to aristocrats or clergy. Nonconformist and Radical publicists came to use this word more and more frequently as the nineteenth century advanced, excluding the aristocracy from the Welsh nation entirely, and most Anglicans for good measure, and the nation became a nation of the *Gwerin*, poor labourers, craftsmen, merchants, even capitalists, together with their printers, preachers, publicists, performers, all united in their Welsh self-consciousness as expressed in the life of the chapel. The Welsh saw themselves as the most virtuous and hard-working people in Europe, in farm, mine and factory, the most God-fearing, the best at observing the Sabbath, the most temperate and abstinent with regard to drink, the most deeply devoted to educational improvement and to things of the mind, the most constant in their support in country and town for the Liberal or Radical political cause, the most classless and egalitarian in spirit. The *Gwerin* thus embraced a very broad spectrum of the Welsh people, at their most anglicized the *Gwerin* were merely a Welsh aping of Victorian middle class *mores*, but at their least anglicized, the leaders of the *Gwerin* could be very anti-English and anti-capitalist.

In the twentieth century the myth of the *gwerin* retained an appeal even as the substance receded. Three features of the Wales of the *gwerin* require particular attention: language and culture, religion and education, and the economy and politics.

Language and culture

I have already noted that, in the absence of distinctive institutions comparable to those of Scottish civil society after 1707, language and culture have been central to Welsh national identity. Gwyn Williams (1991: 121) comments that Bishop Morgan's Bible of 1588 'proved the sheet-anchor of a threatened language'. Welsh was the spoken language of home, but it was the church, and later the chapel, that were to make it a language widely read and written. At the beginning of the nineteenth century four-fifths of the people of Wales spoke Welsh but at the beginning of the twenty-first century only one-fifth do. Non-Welsh speakers have always posed a threat to the integrity of Y Fro Gymraeg, and their increasing numbers in the nineteenth and twentieth centuries, even in Gwynedd and Dyfed, have given real cause for alarm. The most extreme counter to this threat has been the burning of second homes owned by families in England *pour décourager les autres*.

Prys Morgan (1983) has given a fascinating account of 'the hunt for the Welsh past in the romantic period' in the eighteenth and nineteenth centuries, a tale of ancient practice and invented tradition. The collection of folk-tales, drawn from fourteenth-century manuscripts and now known as the *Mabinogion*, is only the most famous item in a rich tradition of Welsh literature. Traditional Welsh poetry and music have been celebrated for centuries at competitions, *eisteddfodau* (literally sessions), throughout Wales. The competitions were conducted according to rules set by the bards, but assemblies of bards had died out by the end of the sixteenth century. *Eisteddfodau* were revived in the eighteenth century with the encouragement of Welsh societies. The most famous of these was the Honourable Society of Cymmrodorion, founded in 1751, a charitable and dining society dedicated to the promotion of all things Welsh and involving leading figures in London as well as Wales. The society's name refers to the Welsh as the aboriginal people of Britain. Beginning in 1815, and at the instigation of a stonemason, Edward Williams, who had taken the name Iolo Morgannwg, *eisteddfodau* have included a *gorsedd* (literally a throne), or assembly, of bards. Morgannwg was a fine poet and folklorist, but also a forger extraordinary who claimed to be reviving the rites of the Celtic priesthood of the druids but was actually making them up. Gwyn Williams (1985: 165) says this of him.

He had an intuitive grasp of the historical function of Welsh traditions and of their functional utility to the half-starved and often self-despising Welsh of his own day. Welsh poets, he perceived, had not been 'poets' as the English used the word. They had been the rib-cage of the body politic, remembrancers, a collective memory honed for historic action. So he invented a *gorsedd*, a guild of those 'bards' who would be so much more than poets, antiquarians or historians, a directive and democratic elite of a new and democratic Welsh nation, conceived in liberty, deploying a usable past in order to build an attainable future (a kind of collective Owain Glyn Dŵr who'd served a proper apprenticeship, in short).

The annual National Eisteddfod, held alternately in North and South Wales, dates in its present form from 1861. 'At the Chester Eisteddfod [in 1866], Hen Wlad fy Nhadau (Land of my Fathers), composed in 1856 by Evan and James James of Pontypridd, was sung with such passion that it was adopted forthwith as the national anthem' (ibid. 417). Since 1951 the language of the National Eisteddfod has been Welsh only. Attendances remain high but for many Welsh the sight of the bards in their faux druidic robes is a matter for mockery. There has also been since 1947 an International Eisteddfod each year in Llangollen.

The *gorsedd* of bards in their colourful robes are not the only Welsh figures in concocted garb. There is also Dame Wales in the national costume invented around 1840 by Lady Llanover in romantic vein and for the benefit of tourists. She and her friends 'evolved a homogenized national costume from various Welsh peasant dresses, the most distinctive features of which were an enormous red cloak worn over an elegant petticoat and bedgown *(pais a betgwn)* and a very tall beaver hat, in the style of Mother Goose' (Prys Morgan 1983: 82).

The National Eisteddfod was not the only achievement of the cultural nationalists. In 1872 they founded Aberystwyth College which became the University College of Wales, Aberystwyth, in 1885. University colleges were also founded at Bangor (1883), Cardiff (1883), and Swansea (1920). Together the colleges constituted the federal University of Wales which dates from 1893. The National Library of Wales at Aberystwyth dates from 1916 and the National Museum of Wales in Cardiff from 1927. In addition there is the Welsh Folk Museum at St Fagans near Cardiff which opened in 1948, and is now the Museum of Welsh Life. The renaming was controversial in so far as Welsh life aside from Y Fro Gymraeg and the *gwerin* once had little place at St Fagans but that is no longer the case (see Brewer 1999).

The original exclusion is symptomatic of a more general one. In 1937 Saunders Lewis, the leading nationalist of his day, famously asked: 'Is there an Anglo-Welsh literature?', and answered that there was not. Tony Bianchi (1986: 73) summarizes his argument—'as literature is the product of an organic community and industrialism the destroyer of such communities, no national literature in English, the language of industrial Wales, could possibly emerge'—and notes how it was used by 'a Welsh-speaking intelligentsia jealously pressing the claim that it and it alone could speak for the whole of Wales'. Similar claims have often been made since. Anglo-Welsh literature, it is said, is just an unworthy substitute and poor solace for the loss of Welsh. The one exception, for those of this persuasion, proves the rule. R. S. Thomas was a great poet because he was a superb translator; he had a unique ability to render experience of Welsh rural life in an English idiom. It also helped that he learned Welsh at the age of 30 even if he never felt able to write poetry in it. Not that he was an easy adoptee. His biographer, Byron Rogers (2000), said this of him in an obituary: 'To adapt what someone said of de Gaulle, Thomas had one illusion, Wales, and one hate, the Welsh, who had been born into a tradition they neglected, and which he, like a tramp at Christmas, was doomed to stand outside.'

The Cymdeithas yr Iaith Gymraeg (Welsh Language Society) was first founded in 1885 to campaign for teaching in the medium of Welsh. It had its successes but did not last. The Cymdeithas was re-formed in 1962 to campaign for the use of Welsh in public life and has had major successes. The Welsh Language Act of 1967 provided that Welsh should have the same legal force as English. The fourth television channel in Wales, Sianel Pedwar Cymru (S4C), which consolidated and extended Welsh-language television, began broadcasting in 1982. Above all the Welsh Language Act of 1993 (discussed below) is changing the face of Wales, but that Wales is not Y Fro Gymraeg revived but a new bilingual Wales—in effect Cymru/Wales.

Religion and education

Religion in Y Fro Gymraeg (and in Labour Wales) has been a complicated story. From the end of the eighteenth century, the industrialization of Wales widened the economic and social distance between the Anglicized and Anglican landowning class who reaped the big rewards from their new investments and the workers, farm labourers, and small tenant farmers who did not, with artisans and professionals in between but more often of small means than not. It was in this context that Baptists, Congregationalists, and later Methodists won their converts on a huge scale. With their lack of ostentation and inattention to class, their regard for work, self-improvement, and sobriety, and their focus on the Welsh Bible, they had an appeal the established Church of England could not match and it is this commonality rather than the differences between, and varying fortunes of, the many different denominations and groupings that matters most in understanding Welsh identity. Protestantism helped bind Wales to Britain but from the eighteenth century onwards its predominant form was Nonconformist and it was chapel that was at the heart of Welsh life, not church. This is despite the historic role of the church in sustaining the Welsh language via translations of religious texts, the significant participation of Anglicans in the revival of *eisteddfodau*, and the strong support of Anglicans for establishment of the University of Wales and other Welsh cultural institutions.

Three things told against the church. First, the Anglican church was more than just the church of the Tory gentry, but the patronage of the gentry rendered it increasingly unacceptable to the *gwerin* (and in due course to the workers of industrial Wales). Second, none of the church's bishops from the early eighteenth century to the late nineteenth spoke Welsh. Third, the church's commitment to English-medium church schools in Wales, reassuring to the establishment in Wales and England, though well meant, was not always well received. In 1843 Hugh Owen had published a letter to the Welsh in which he urged that they apply for newly available Privy Council grants to organize schools. Though many schools were started this way, they were greatly outnumbered by schools run by the church. The church believed English was the language of the modern economy and Welsh children needed to learn it if they were to get the best jobs they could. The case was not made with much tact. The (blue-bound) Report of the Commissioners on Education in Wales, produced for the Privy Council in 1847, massively documented the wholly inadequate provision of schools in much of Wales, but also in one brief but misguided section the English and Anglican commissioners seemed to imply that ignorance and sexual impropriety were associated with Nonconformity and the limited world of the unilingual Welsh. This antagonized opinion formers across Wales as nothing had done before. In angry response Welsh-speaking Nonconformists condemned 'the treachery of the Blue Books' and portrayed the church as an English church hostile to the Welsh language and the traditional ways of the people.

Almost all schools in Wales, before and after the 1870 Education Act that provided for universal elementary schooling in Wales (and England), taught in the medium of English. Welsh could be left to Sunday schools. Many families accepted that English-medium education was the key to advancement for their children. The frequency and severity with which children were punished for speaking Welsh at school may also subsequently have been exaggerated. But many Nonconformist parents resented having to send their children to a church school for want of any other in the locality. The Education Act of 1902 compounded the offence by extending public funding from board schools to all schools; Nonconformists objected to Anglican schooling on the rates. From the 1880s onwards there was some teaching in Welsh in some schools. Advocates of Welsh-medium teaching argued that it could be employed as a step towards mastery of English and public funding was made available to that end. Comment on the Victorian imposition of English-medium teaching for Welsh-speaking children in the cause of a modern economy consistent with the ambitions of British imperialism could still be bitter over a century later. Phylip Rosser (1985: 185) describes Wales as a victim of Empire: 'Through the educational system, the Empire set out to murder the Welsh language, callously imposing the badge of inferiority and spreading a social stigma across countless Welsh families who persisted in using their own language.'

The controversy over church schools had long fuelled the demand for the disestablishment of the Anglican Church in Wales and in 1920 the church was disestablished and reconstituted as the Church in Wales with its own archbishop. Ironically this turned it into a Welsh national institution, as Chris Harris and Richard Startup (1994) have pointed out, but it did not save it from a continuing decline in the number of churchgoers. Of much greater national significance, the twentieth century also saw an unrelenting decline in chapel membership and with it further evidence of the passing of the *gwerin*.

Regard for education has been high in Wales (even if secondary school examination pass rates throughout the second half of the twentieth century were consistently lower than those in England). The 1889 Welsh Intermediate Education Act set up a system of county schools across Wales far superior to the provision made for secondary education in England. The 1944 Education Act abolished the county schools but Welsh local education authorities (LEAs) then made available proportionately more grammar school places than their English counterparts. For much of the twentieth century Wales also produced more trained teachers than it could employ. The 1944 act allowed LEAs to develop teaching of and in Welsh in response to parental demand. The upshot was a wide diversity of practices including Welsh-medium teaching, Welsh for native speakers, Welsh for learners, and, very often, no Welsh at all. The big change came with the 1988 Education Reform Act. It placed Welsh in schools on a new footing, but in so doing it did not so much give strength to Y Fro Gymraeg as provide for the new bilingual Wales I call Cymru-Wales and discuss below.

Economy and politics

Historically Y Fro Gymraeg has had a rural and small town economy. Following Howell (1977: 21), Graham Day (2002: 142) notes 'that in the middle of the nineteenth century 60 per cent of Welsh land was under the control of just 1 per cent of landowners, each of whom possessed estates of 1,000 acres or more'. Tenant farmers and agricultural labourers combined, however, were able to supplant the landowners and by the 1920s the great estates had been broken up and sold off and were now in the possession of hundreds of small family farmers. Prolonged agricultural recession, the effects of the First World War, and death duties, effected nothing less than 'the ejection of the landlord class from the social structure of rural Wales' (ibid.), and thus, one might suppose, the triumph of the *gwerin*. In practice, it was not quite like that. English continued to make inroads. The religious revival of 1904 was the last; thereafter chapelgoing declined. People left the depressed countryside of the 1930s to find work elsewhere. Agriculture has supported ever fewer people and come to depend on public subsidy. And although agriculture remains by far the most subsidized industry in the European Union, the level of subsidy has started to fall and can be expected to go on doing so. The prospects for Welsh agriculture are difficult. Hill farming, in particular, is barely viable even with public subsidy. In rural Wales unilingual English retirees, rural retreatists, and second-homers may sometimes price young locals out of the housing market; but they seldom take jobs from them. The problem for those dismayed by the contraction of Y Fro Gymraeg is how to secure a successful modern economy throughout Wales in which most producers, exchangers, and consumers speak Welsh most of the time at work and in public places as well as at home. They find it near impossible to present scenarios whereby this might credibly be brought about.

Distanced from the gentry, Y Fro Gymraeg has also been radical in its politics, voting mostly Liberal until the First World War, then increasingly Labour and latterly Plaid Cymru and Labour—especially now that Plaid Cymru has clearly positioned itself as a left-of-centre party. This time the problem for those who cherish Y Fro Gymraeg is that Plaid Cymru, renamed Plaid Cymru, the Party of Wales for the 1999 Welsh Assembly Election, has also, as electoral logic always demanded it eventually would, and as Phillip Rawkins (1979) anticipated, committed itself to enhancing the prospects of all the people in a bilingual Wales. The survival, indeed strengthening, of Welsh in a bilingual Wales would be, I suspect will be, a great achievement, and one in which all those who have resisted the seemingly irresistible decline of the language can take special pride. But a bilingual Wales is very different from Y Fro Gymraeg.

Day (2002: 142) comments that 'the existence of a classless gwerin provided the foundations for one of the dominant versions of Welshness and Welsh nationhood, and it makes frequent appearances more or less at the margins of social science writing on Wales'—a wary formulation if ever there was one. The legacy of the *gwerin* has its attractive and its ugly components. In one form it celebrates classlessness, the fortitude of *pobl bach*, the little people, and devotion to the integrity of a distinctive but threatened culture. It values hard work, thrift, education, and individual and communal responsibility—and it has sustained a rich literature on rural Wales. In another it lays claim to true Welshness in a way that excludes most of the Welsh, and in particular the working class in industrial Wales, as unWelsh, or renders them inferior, lesser Welsh—and it denies that Anglo-Welsh literature (literature written by Welsh authors in English) has any place in the national culture. It also presents the English as the enemy. David Adamson (1991: 106) put it like this: 'The imagery of resistance is of a Welsh tenantry oppressed and exploited by an English landed class. That class imposes a foreign religion in an alien language on a culturally and religiously homogenous people, the Welsh.' That this is a distortion is irrelevant. With the landed class gone, the English enemy has taken a succession of new forms, such as profit-obsessed industrialists, white settlers, and carriers of an insidiously meretricious culture. The latter version has occasionally come uncomfortably close to notions of cultural, if not, racial purity. Either way Y Fro Gymraeg is oriented to the past; it celebrates what was.

2 Labour Wales

From the beginning of iron production in Merthyr Tydfil in the eighteenth century through the spectacular rise, decline, and eventual closure of the South Wales coalfield in the nineteenth and twentieth centuries to the development and huge contraction of steel production in the second half of the twentieth century, industrial Wales is basically a story of metals and coal, not manufacturing. It is, too, primarily a story of South Wales (although coal and steel were also the main industries in north-east Wales), but one with cultural, social, and political consequences for all Wales. There was nothing new in a significant difference between North and South Wales, but the industrialization of the south-east intensified it dramatically. 'The ratio of population in Glamorgan and Monmouthshire to all other Welsh counties changed between 1801 and 1911 from one to four to three to one' (Smith 1984: 21). Population growth led to dense urban concentrations in the Valleys and Wales's first big towns, Cardiff, Newport, and Swansea, with Cardiff, the largest, overtaking Merthyr Tydfil, by the 1881 census. Immigrant labour came from the rest of Wales, England (especially the adjoining counties), Ireland, and beyond. Some non-Welsh immigrants learned Welsh, but more did not and over time the predominant language of industrial South Wales shifted from Welsh to English, albeit a bit less so in the west. With the exception of Cardiff, the new urban and industrial South Wales was a near one-class region—working class.

Urban and industrial Wales gave rise to a 'vision' of Wales with, according to Day (2002: 15), 'a set of attributes which, for a given period of time, appear to have defined some of the basic features of Welsh society: predominantly working-class, well-organized, self-assertive, intensely solidary and politically Labourist'. The reference to class is crucial. Both the Wales of the *gwerin* and Labour Wales have taken pride in community and solidarity and shown strong commitment to education and self-improvement, but while the former paid little attention to class differences in Wales while supporting a Welsh cultural nationalism, the latter knew it was engaged in a class struggle, relished the hugely important part it played in the British labour movement, and endorsed a labour internationalism (cf. Adamson 1991 and 1999). There is a real edge to this difference. At one extreme there were cultural nationalists who ignored the working class, its history, and its politics, even though the workers and their families were most of the population; at the other there were revolutionary socialists who were internationalist in outlook and had scant regard for their own Welsh identity. From the second half of the nineteenth century onwards Labour Wales was also as much secularized as chapelgoing, and its most celebrated recreational pursuits, rugby and male voice choirs, were not those of Y Fro Gymraeg. 'Modern' Labour Wales, with the Valleys at its heart, has offered a proud alternative to traditional Welsh-speaking Wales, and in Dai Smith (1980, 1984, 1986, and 1999) it has had someone committed to giving eloquent testimony to its vibrancy and the value of the literature it has inspired.[7] If the Museum of Welsh Life at St Fagans is the iconic heritage centre for Y Fro Gymraeg, the Big Pit is the equivalent for Labour Wales at Blaenavon.

The universal franchise gave industrial Wales its political voice and it was Labour. The Liberal ascendancy in Wales peaked at the 1906 general election when the party won every constituency except Merthyr Tydfil, the seat of Keir Hardie. After 1918 Labour grew in dominance in industrial areas and made inroads elsewhere. As Smith (1984: 155) says, 'Two generations of trade union leaders and socialist politicians, from A. J. Cook in 1926 to Aneurin Bevan in 1945, became synonymous with Welsh politics, as David Lloyd George had been before.' More than that, Bevan founded the National Health Service in 1948, the pillar of the welfare state established by the 1945 Labour Government that enjoys by far the most popular support over half a century later. Charlotte Aull Davies (1989: 101) argues that Labour's great welfare state project unwittingly gave a structural stimulus to Welsh nationalism by prompting Welsh welfare bureaucracies within the welfare state and matching Welsh welfare associations outside it, and by enabling a degree of Welsh economic planning in the guise of regional development.

In 1966 Labour took thirty-two of the thirty-six Welsh constituencies at the general election, but later that year Plaid Cymru won for the first time at a by-election in Carmarthen and embarked on an electoral strategy that was to win them support in industrial South Wales as well as Welsh Wales. The times they were achanging. It was a Welshman, Neil Kinnock, who as leader of the party from 1983 to 1992, began the transformation of Labour that led to the new Labour victory under Tony Blair in 1997. But the politics of new Labour are not those of Labour Wales.

There is a strong sense of changing times and the rethinking of national identity in Brian Roberts's account of 'Welsh identity in a former mining valley' (1994) based on fieldwork in 1990–1 including eighty in-depth interviews and a postal survey in Blaina and Nantyglo, a part of Gwent in which little Welsh had been spoken for more than a century. Respondents acknowledged that the community and solidarity of old was based on mining and, with the mines closed, was irrecoverable. They all affirmed their Welshness, often with a new heightened reflectiveness, and knowingly marked themselves off from the English and the more Anglicized Welsh of Balsom's British Wales. But they knew, too, that for many in west and north Wales the Valleys are doubtfully Welsh. So what did *they* think made them Welsh? Basically they were Welsh because they were not English, they were local—and each particular locality was in the Valleys and the Valleys were unlike anywhere else. Their families had for generations been part of a hard but proud industrial past, and the hillsides still bore the scars of that industry even as the greening of the valleys confirmed its passing. They approved of Welsh language classes and school *eisteddfodau*. Their responses suggested an openness to a future different from the past, definitely Welsh in character if hard to specify, together with a judgement that political independence for Wales was an economic non-starter.

3 Anglo-British Wales

Those who construct a Wales in which the Welsh language is the foremost, or even just a highly significant, constituent, render the Anglophone Welsh a secondary population in their own country at best and a threat to the very integrity of the nation at worst. Indignant at such slights, and mindful of their massive contribution to the development of modern Wales, modern Britain, and, via Welsh coal, the British Empire, non-Welsh speakers have identified with a vigorous alternative, Labour Wales. Turning to Anglo-British Wales, however, it is not easy to find articulations of Wales made by academic commentators or the Anglophone Welsh that omit references to both the Welsh language *and* labourism, but one such, that of David Howell and Colin Baber (1990), distinguishes Wales by reference to its 'separate history, instinctive radicalism in religion and politics, contempt for social pretentiousness, personal warmth and exuberance, sociability, love of music and near obsession with rugby' (quoted in Day 2002: 244). The first five items figure in both Y Fro Gymraeg and Labour Wales but here extend beyond them. It is worth adding that secularization has made radicalism in religion increasingly but a memory, and the radicalism in politics that culminated in the failure of the Conservatives to win a single seat at the 1997 General Election also brought electoral success for new Labour, whose radical credentials are more neo-liberal than socialist or even social-liberal, as well as the prominence of a now left-of-centre Plaid Cymru. The last two are not so straightforward. The traditional music of *eisteddfodau*, especially the singing of folk stanzas to a harp accompaniment, *penillion telyn*, is very different from the male voice choir tradition of the industrial south. And football, not rugby, is the preferred winter sport in North and mid-Wales.

Howell and Baber's characterization is also a somewhat male one, and I will take up the issue of women and Welsh identity below.

Notwithstanding these qualifications, Howell and Baber's characterization of Wales and the Welsh is both distinctive and inclusive. It is also augmentable. In addition to identification with Welsh history or historical memory, they could, arguably should, have added identification with the land. Most of Wales is mountainous and looks different from the England that adjoins it and the Romantic Movement from the late eighteenth to the mid-nineteenth century generated a love of mountains in Wales as elsewhere. When asked to name three things that made them proud of Wales, Balsom, Madgwick, and Van Mechelen (1984: 174–5) found that their respondents said the environment more often than anything else (with a quarter of all mentions). That the soils of upland Wales are poor, and that life there has often been a struggle, only adds to the resonance. Even the horrendously scarred Valleys—the only part of Wales the Wales Tourist Board omits from its 2004 promotion—are unlike any others in Britain and undeniably memorable, and the English painter L. S. Lowry made them into works of art. There are also parts of Wales that the Welsh regard as English and the English as Welsh which suggests they have a character of their own. Aitchison et al. (1989) found respondents who regarded much of Radnor as one such.

There does not seem to have been much research on constructions of Wales that had a currency among the Anglophone Welsh who did not identify with an Y Fro Gymraeg which excluded or marginalized them or with a Labour Wales whose principles were not their own. Perhaps they just kept their distance from questions of national identity, or perhaps they identified with Britain (as did 18% of Welsh speakers according to Balsom (1984)). The Welsh bourgeoisie may historically have been small, but it would still be interesting to know more about the representations of Wales it favoured. Then, too, there have always been Welsh Conservative voters in Wales as well as English. What of their Wales? James Davies (1986: 55) argues that 'A sense of Welshness as a bourgeois bastion in the west was fundamental to [Dylan] Thomas's career' but Thomas's writings have no clear political import.

There has been almost no interest in the views of Wales held by the English in Wales. The English who move to Wales cannot go native in the way, accent apart, so many of the English who move to Scotland do (see Watson 2003). In Scotland the English are dispersed—there are no English communities as such—and they participate in, and come to identify with, the separately organized institutions and associations of Scottish civil society which have since 1707 been the key to the maintenance of Scottish national identity. In Wales incomers may not form English communities as such but there are concentrations of retirees along the coasts of North and South Wales. They also cannot go native in the sense of participating in most of the key cultural features of Welsh life that have sustained a Welsh identity since 1536 without learning Welsh, which exceedingly few do. They thus have a choice between understanding themselves as permanent outsiders, even interlopers, in another country, Wales, or as residents in a distinctive region of their own country, Britain. The latter requires the representation of Wales as a British Wales in which people of different identities live and to whose fortunes all contribute; it allows the English in Wales, as the Welsh invariably call them, to consider themselves British if they so wish.

The elaboration of British Wales as Anglo-British Wales calls to mind not Britain after the Romans left but before the Normans invaded, but the Britain that developed from the unions of 1536 and 1707 in which England is always the senior partner. The annexation of 1536 intensified the Anglicization of Wales and the treaty of 1707 led to a Britain and a British Empire in whose formation the English played the greatest part even if Scotland's contribution to Empire was proportionately larger than its population would have suggested. The notion of British Wales has a common currency; Anglo-Britain, and hence Anglo-British Wales, is an academic construction only.

4 Cymru-Wales

Cymru-Wales is the first of two constructions of Wales oriented to the present and possibilities for the future. This does not means that it has no foundations in the past. On the contrary the four events of founding significance for Cymru-Wales were the establishment of the Welsh Office in 1964, the Education Reform Act of 1988, the Welsh Language Act of 1993, and the opening of the National Assembly for Wales in 1999. Together they have given basic shape to the civic and bilingual Cymru-Wales of today.

The Education Reform Act of 1988 applied to England and Wales but allowed developments peculiar to Wales (Farrell and Law 1997). In particular it introduced the national curriculum in a manner that made possible the specification of a dedicated national curriculum for Wales. There are two components to the latter. First, it made teaching in and/or of Welsh a requirement in all schools for the first time (though its implementation in Gwent and some other areas has proceeded only as fast as the supply of teachers of Welsh could be increased). Second, in the subject areas of history, English, art, and music, it took the form of a Curriculum Cymreig which required attention to Welsh history, Anglo-Welsh authors, and Welsh cultural forms. Gareth Rees and Sara Delamont (1999) note that since the 1988 Education Reform Act much attention has focused on pupils in Welsh-medium schools whose parents do not speak Welsh. It has yet to be seen whether these pupils (have sufficient opportunity to) keep up their Welsh on leaving school. Opportunities to do so at university are very limited. There is some teaching in the humanities and social sciences in the medium of Welsh, and there are Welsh language halls of residence at the university colleges in Aberystwyth and Bangor; but half the students in Welsh universities are English (and half of all Welsh students go to university in England), and Welsh higher education is basically Anglophone. Outside traditional Welsh-speaking areas, the use of Welsh in the workplace and in public life is still more the exception than the norm.

The Welsh Language Act of 1993 stipulates that every public body in Wales shall show how it gives effect to 'the principle that in the conduct of public business and the administration of justice in Wales the English and Welsh languages should be treated on the basis of equality' (quoted in Aitchison and Carter 1999: 96) and it established the Bwrdd yr Iaith Gymraeg (Welsh Language Board) to that end and to promote Welsh language use generally. The act requires that anyone dealing with any public body, including the courts, in any capacity shall be able to do so in Welsh if he or she so chooses and it ensures that all public documents and forms are available in both languages as are all public signs including road signs. Coupled with education measures discussed below these developments have, according to Aitchison and Carter (1999), led some Welsh speakers to claim the fight for the language has been won. They will have been heartened by the 2001 census finding that 20.8 per cent of those aged 3 and over said they were able to speak Welsh compared to 18.7 per cent in 1991, with the biggest increases in terms of age among 10–14-year-olds and in terms of place in Gwent where Welsh-speakers are fewest. Others are more sceptical. Although 23.6 per cent said they could understand spoken Welsh, only 16.3 per cent said they could speak, read, and write it and some of those will have been less than fully proficient. Hywel Williams (2004) in *The Guardian* recently dismissed Welsh speakers who just 'do pidgin Welsh'. More temperately, Aitchison and Carter refer to 'semi-speakers' but acknowledge the possibility that some of these may go on to acquire fluency. What is not always clear is how the 1993 language act is being implemented in both reality and perception. What level of proficiency in Welsh is required for which jobs in the public sector and where, given labour market realities? How many of the Anglophone Welsh parents who choose Welsh-medium schools for their children do so in the belief that this will improve their employment prospects?

Despite these uncertainties the representation of Wales as a bilingual nation will endure. All those whose first language is Welsh are bilingual, and all children whose first language is English learn (some) Welsh in schools. In addition most Anglophone Welsh believe the Welsh language should be enabled to survive and prosper and be heard in public life and seen in public places.

Turning now to public administration and government, in 1964 the Labour Government established the Welsh Office in Cardiff and appointed the first Secretary of State for Wales with a seat in the cabinet (see Deacon 2002 for this and much else in this paragraph). There had been calls for such an initiative since the previous century but Labour only adopted the cause in the late 1950s and then somewhat diffidently. Labour had established an Advisory Council for Wales of little consequence in 1949. In the 1950s the Conservatives had made the first ministerial appointments for Wales, but in 1957 they refused a call from the council for the appointment of a Welsh secretary of state with a seat in the cabinet, whereupon the entire council resigned. Some Labour figures were more sympathetic to the call, believing government decisions sometimes favoured Scotland because there was a Scottish secretary in the cabinet to argue for them, and on returning to power in 1964 Labour created the post. The initial responsibilities of the Welsh Office were limited—mainly housing and local government, some environmental matters, regional economic planning, and the Welsh language, National Museum, and National Library—but after a low-key beginning much more followed. The Welsh Secretary and Welsh Office began to make visible the notion that Wales was not only a territorial unit but also potentially a political nation. As it accumulated more functions, the ministry created quangos beginning with the Welsh Arts Council in 1967. Developments of particular significance included the transfer of responsibility for primary and secondary education in 1970, the establishment of the Welsh Development Agency and the Development Board for Rural Wales in 1976, the transfer of responsibility for agriculture in 1978, the transfer to the Welsh Office of almost total responsibility for deciding how the Treasury's allocation of funding for Wales, the Welsh 'block grant', be spent in 1980, the establishment of separate funding councils for further and higher education in Wales in 1993, and the transfer of responsibility for determining the structure of local government in Wales in 1994. So many quangos were created in the 1980s under Margaret Thatcher that Osmond (1995: 43–52) refers to 'living in quangoland', J. Barry Jones (2000: 20–1) refers to 'the Welsh quango state' and Deacon (2002: 38) refers to 'the decade of the quango'.

The Welsh Office in Cardiff itself gave a *raison d'être* for the further development of civil society in Wales. Welsh associations and organizations old and new geared up to engage with the expanding Welsh Office and its proliferating quangos. Many British associations and organizations had also to put in place dedicated Welsh branches or sections. There thus began both the gradual shift from civil society in Wales to a Welsh civil society, and the development of dedicated Welsh policy communities with government, academic, voluntary association, and business participation. Administrative devolution on its own also led to the complaint, already familiar in Scotland, that what became known as a democratic deficit could be remedied only by an accompanying political devolution. The Conservatives' appointment of party sympathizers to quangos in the 1980s in order to give the party an influence it could not secure at the ballot box only added to the deficit.

Reflecting in 1988 on the Welsh Office, the Select Committee on Welsh Affairs at Westminster, the Wales TUC, the Welsh Arts Council, and other Welsh bodies, J. Barry Jones reached an uninspiring conclusion.

... Wales is an incomplete political community. It lacks the full range of institutions and those it does possess ... are frustrated from exercising their role in sustaining and enhancing the national identity—as they have, manifestly, in Scotland. It is difficult to argue, therefore, that Welsh public institutions either moderate political excesses or consolidate social norms. In these circumstances, it may be precipitate to talk of Welsh institutions reinforcing the Welsh identity and replacing such declining social factors as nonconformity and the Welsh language as a but-tress for the Welsh 'way of life'. Given the weak autonomy of many Welsh insti-tutions, they may simply serve to integrate Wales more fully into the British State. (J. B. Jones 1988: 59)

J. Barry Jones was right that the new institutions of Welsh public adminis-tration and civil society could not buttress the old Welsh way of life of Y Fro Gymraeg or Labour Wales. Since 1988, however, these institutions have grown stronger and in 1997 the attempt was made for the first time to mo-bilize Welsh civil society in support of devolution. The closeness of the ref-erendum result confirmed that Welsh civil society was still weak in compar-ison with Scotland but Lindsay Paterson and Richard Wyn Jones (1999: 175) were in no doubt that 'The establishment of the assembly will surely serve as a catalyst for the development of Welsh civil society.' The establishment of the National Assembly for Wales has made Wales a more complete polit-ical community, arguably something that, contrary to J. Barry Jones, serves Welsh *and* British interests.

Denis Balsom (2000) mapped districts voting 'yes' and 'no' in the 1997 referendum and compared the result with the three Waleses model he had published in 1985. The fit was very close. Basically his Y Fro Gymraeg and his Welsh Wales (Llanelli, Swansea, and the Valleys) voted 'yes' and his Brit-ish Wales voted 'no'. The main exceptions were Conwy and Torfaen in the 'no' camp and Bridgend in the 'yes' camp. Jones, Tristan, and Taylor (2000: 170–1) also report interesting findings from the 1997 Welsh Referendum Survey. Of those who claimed they turned out,[8] voters born in Wales were almost twice as likely to say they voted 'yes' as those born in England; flu-ent Welsh-speakers (16% of the total) voted 'yes' by 77 per cent to 23 per cent; non-fluent Welsh-speakers (12%) voted 'no' by 52 per cent to 48 per cent; and unilingual English speakers (73%) voted 'no' by 58 per cent to 42 per cent. The assembly thus came into being with the active support of only a quarter of the electorate, and with that support itself disproportionately given by a minority of the population—Welsh speakers. The assembly was going to have to prove itself. In one respect the first elections to the assembly added to the pressure to succeed. By comparison with the 1997 British Gen-eral Elections results, the big winners in the 1999 Welsh Assembly Elections were Plaid Cymru whose vote went up from 9.9 to 28.4 per cent and the big losers were Labour whose vote went down from 54.7 per cent to 37.6 per cent (Johnston et al. 2000: 183). The implication of this is that many voters thought a Welsh party would put Wales first more reliably than the Welsh branch of a British party. New Labour in London had made this seem all the more plausible by foisting Tony Blair's nominee for the leadership, Alun Michael, on a reluctant party in Wales (who were later to get the leader they wanted, Rhodri Morgan, after Michael lost a vote of confidence in the assembly's first year).[9]

The assembly inherited all the responsibilities of the Welsh Office, thenceforth known as the Wales Office, but it has no powers to make primary legislation or levy taxes. Its initial form was also unclear. The Government of Wales Act 1998 envisaged something akin to a county council with decisions finally made in full council headed by a first secretary. Once elected, however, members agreed to delegate to the first secretary powers to appoint the members of a Welsh Assembly Government and from 2002 the first secretary has been styled first minister. This odd formulation acknowledges that the movement to something like the Scottish first minister and Scottish Executive depends on a delegation of the powers of the whole assembly. In March 2004 a commission chaired by Lord Richard recommended that the assembly be given law-making powers in education and health and that the executive and legislature be separated. The response from Welsh MPs at Westminster has been mixed. Some reform is expected, but, as of March 2005, quite what remains unclear.

Cymru-Wales is a version of Wales in which women seek visible participation as never before. Where were the sisters in the land of their fathers? Princes, bards, preachers, politicians, miners, rugby players—the key figures in constructions and representations of Wales have long been men. There has been mam at home in the Valleys and the colourful woman in Lady Llanover's 'national costume' of kitsch Welsh doll fame but not much else. Deirdre Beddoe (1986: 227) could not have put it more bluntly: 'Welsh women are culturally invisible.' In recent decades, however, women in Wales have striven not just for equal opportunities but also for visibility and recognition. In *Our Sisters' Land: The Changing Identities of Women in Wales* (1994) Aaron et al. signalled a different Wales, and in *Our Daughters' Land* (1996) Sandra Betts's contributors looked to changes that the next generation of women might expect. Teresa Rees (1995) documented change over the last half-century and in a more recent essay (1999: 265) pointed to the lead the National Assembly can give in securing full equality for women by embedding equality in its own practice as well as in policy delivery and in organizing itself in a family friendly way. The election of women to half the seats in the assembly in the 2003 elections was an auspicious moment.

That Cymru-Wales is bilingual *and* civic is best confirmed by the dual role of the National Assembly for Wales. The assembly is both the guarantor of the future of the Welsh language via the requirement that it be taught in all schools and the enforcement of the equal status provisions of the 1993 Welsh Language Act, and it is the advocate and promoter of the development of a Welsh civil society to supersede the language as a basis for Welsh national identification. The latter is hard for some Welsh speakers to accept. 'The jettisoning of language as the qualifier of a unique claim to national space is', as Colin Williams (1999: 131) says, 'a very radical proposition in the Welsh context'. Day (2002: 253–4) recognizes that some Welsh speakers will resist it, but Plaid Cymru nationally, if not always locally, has accepted it and there is no going back. The difference between the resisters and the proponents of a bilingual and civic Wales is nicely illustrated by two papers on north-west Wales. In one, Fiona Bowie (1993) describes the aggrieved defensiveness of particular Welsh-speaking localities in Gwynedd. The locals disliked the 'English' (English speakers of any provenance) and had little to do with them, but then they did not like any outsiders much and were opposed to economic developments which would bring in more of them. In the other, John Borland, Ralph Fevre, and David Denney (1992) include discussion of the idea of an 'open community' advanced by the Plaid Cymru MP for Meirionydd Nant Conwy, Dafydd Elis-Thomas, in 1987. An open community welcomes all incomers who, while sensitive to Wales as a country with cultural traditions of its own, have something to contribute. It is a difference between the excluders and the includers and economic development and electoral politics are on the side of the includers.

5 Modern Wales

The focus of Cymru-Wales is on cultural and political representation. The focus of Modern Wales is on economic and social composition. Modern Wales is cosmopolitan, derives benefit from a plural society that is about more than language, and is committed to a diversified economy. It has a positive outlook on Britain, Europe, and beyond.

Wales has a lower per capita GDP than any English region and higher unemployment than any English region except the North-East, but it has had some significant economic success since the 1980s (Hill 2000*b*). Economic problems have for two centuries prompted demands that Wales must modernize if it is to prosper. The argument used to be that a 'traditional' agrarian and small town economy was progressively overshadowed in the nineteenth century by a 'modern' industrial and urban economy based on metals and coal. Then when this narrowly based economy imploded in the last third of the twentieth century, the promoters of a new modern economy turned to manufacturing and the attraction of foreign direct investment (FDI). They met with some trend-bucking, if controversial, success. Wales managed to expand manufacturing when it was contracting in the English regions after the 1979–83 recession. Ralph Fevre (1999: 59) cites studies indicating that 'between 1986 and 1996 Welsh manufacturing employment grew by 6 per cent whereas in the UK it fell by 16 per cent', so that 'by 1995, Wales had 5.0 per cent of the UK population but 5.7 per cent of UK manufacturing employment'. FDI was crucial to this success; investors were offered more financial incentives than were available in any English region. 'The Welsh proportion of all UK FDI projects peaked in 1991/2 at over 20 per cent, but the Welsh proportion of all jobs created by FDI continued to increase' (p. 61). By the mid-1990s over a third of those working in manufacturing plants that had opened between 1966 and 1992 were working for foreign-owned companies. The new plants were mostly located near motorways and, according to Max Munday (2000: 40), 'foreign firms in Wales tend to be significantly larger, more productive and higher paying than domestic firms'.

The success has always been controversial because it is connected to footloose capital and branch plant operations by transnational companies; there is always a fear that firms attracted to Wales by development grants and tax breaks have no commitment to the country and will swiftly pull out if the accountants in some faraway headquarters judge that production could more profitably be located elsewhere—a fear that will intensify following the admission to the European Union in 2004 of former Soviet-bloc countries with cheaper but well-educated labour forces. It is also argued that the job mix is weighted towards the lower-skill end with the strategic management and research and development always abroad. More than that, Wales increased its stake in manufacturing at a time when more advanced economies were seeking their growth in the service sector. Is not that what a modern economy should now concentrate on? Supporters of diversification can here point to some success in financial services in Cardiff, and in the marketing of Wales to tourists, while arguing that the service sector is still comparatively small. What is important in all this is not the fortunes of any particular industry or sector as such but the inescapable general conclusion: Wales has had to reinvent itself in very major ways in the economic past and it is going to have to go on doing so if it is to obtain a prosperity comparable to the leading English regions or the stronger Continental economies.

Of necessity Modern Wales is oriented to Britain, the European Union, and beyond (Day and Rees 1991). It has to be open to cultural exchange and the mobility of labour. Is this version of Wales compatible with Cymru-Wales? In many respects it is but there are points of tension. There is no obvious reason why the gradual shift to a Welsh civil society should impair the development of a Modern Wales, nor why a National Assembly for Wales and a structure of local government adopted with only Wales in mind should not issue in better government. The points of tension have to do with language and labour. I will express them as questions because there is not yet much research that would provide answers. Basically where employers are obliged to employ Welsh-speakers they have to recruit from a smaller pool of labour than would otherwise have been the case. Do they sometimes end up hiring labour less talented or skilled than they might otherwise have done and pay a price in subsequent performance? If they do, the problem is greater in the public sector where the requirement to hire Welsh-speakers is more often found and it may be greatest outside Cardiff. The growth of Welsh-speakers in public service in Cardiff could be draining the rest of Wales of talent. And do the imperatives of bilingualism deter Anglophone outsiders from investing in Welsh-speaking areas?

There is also an argument that ethnic diversity and cultural difference can be economic assets—sources of entrepreneurship, innovation, scarce skills, and willing labour; importers of ideas and other ways of seeing; catalysers of cross-overs and hybrids of remarkable value. Clearly the particular forms ethnic divisions have taken in some northern English towns such as Oldham and Burnley—divisions that have led to riots and the presence of the far-right British National Party—are anything but assets, but at the other end of the spectrum London is by far the most ethnically diverse city in Britain and has a notably vibrant culture and Britain's most buoyant economy.

Cardiff, the city in Wales with the strongest economy is, significantly, also the one with the biggest ethnic minority population. Some commentators have described Wales as a plural society to the (limited) extent that the Welsh Welsh, the Anglophone Welsh, and sometimes too the English, have different cultures, institutions, associations, and social networks (cf. Giggs and Pattie 1992). But Modern Wales goes beyond this in its accommodation of differences other than those pertaining to the Welsh and English languages. It uses all the talents it can muster and welcomes more.

'The Welsh have traditionally regarded themselves as a welcoming and tolerant people viewing with contempt the narrow xenophobia and overt racism of much of English nationalism' (Charlotte Williams 1999: 269). But by far the biggest ethnic minority in Wales is the English and there is evidence that hostility towards the English does not count in most Welsh eyes as racial prejudice although English complaints to the Commission for Racial Equality in Wales (CREW) are increasing (Charlotte Williams 2003). Indeed some in Wales have argued that as the victims of English racial oppression, the Welsh cannot themselves ever be racists—not a position consistent with academic scrutiny (Evans 2003) or CREW experience. Non-white minorities constitute only 2.1 per cent of the total population according to the 2001 census, though 8.4 per cent in Cardiff. Accommodating them is thus a much smaller issue than accommodating the English, and it is sometimes overlooked altogether. Nevertheless, nostalgists for Y Fro Gymraeg and the *gwerin* see blacks and Asians in Wales as just as non-Welsh-speaking as the English and even less often Christian Nonconformist in their religion. As Charlotte Williams (1999: 277) says, 'the gwerin is based on the idea of cultural homogeneity'; it is inimical to multiculturalism. Identifiers with Modern Wales, however, take pride in black and Asian achievers, such as the Cardiff-born black world record holder for the 110 metres hurdles, Colin Jackson (on sport see Evans and O'Leary 2003).

6 Conclusions

It is common enough for Welsh men and women to take pride in and feel nostalgia and respect for Y Fro Gymraeg and Labour Wales, but in so doing they look back. When identifying with Wales today and tomorrow, they have available to them instead Cymru-Wales and Modern Wales, the one constructed around cultural and political representation and the other economic and social composition. There are also many English in Wales, and some Welsh, who identify more with Britain than Wales, and many Welsh and some English for whom local identities are stronger or who have little interest in national identity and political devolution. These are a reminder that the national question in Wales does not have high saliency for everyone.

The 1987 Education Act and the 1993 Welsh Language Act have taken much of the heat out of the language question by providing a linguistic settlement for Wales today and tomorrow. They have already arrested the decline of the Welsh language and give reason to expect that the numbers speaking it will go up in future. They have also enhanced the status of the language by making it a language of public administration. Cymru-Wales has a bilingual foundation even if it is unevenly bilingual in practice and likely to remain so. The Welsh language is part of the enduring reality of Wales with which all who live there have rightfully to come to terms in one way or another. Conversely, to embrace Anglo-Welsh literature is to welcome a rich addition to literature in Welsh.

Day, Dunkerley, and Thompson (2000) have reminded us that civil society in nineteenth-century rural Wales, and to a lessening degree thereafter, was more obviously Welsh, and that civil society in the Labour heartland of industrial South Wales in the first six decades of the twentieth century was more obviously both strong and in its alternative way Welsh, than civil society in late twentieth-century fragmented Wales with its privatized citizenry is either Welsh or strong. In some respects the oft-desired shift towards a distinctively Welsh civil society is only recovering lost ground and still has a long way to go. Be that as it may, the direction of change in recent decades towards a Welsh civil society is incontestable, and the assembly will inevitably quicken the pace. Certainly, the more powers the assembly acquires the more bearing Cardiff rather than London will have on civil society. It is also worth noting that the assembly is formally committed to 'partnership' with civil society. Partnership is more easily pronounced than achieved, but the assembly recognizes in its first strategic plan that it needs partners if it is to make progress with respect to 'sustainable development, tackling social disadvantage and addressing equal opportunities. Moreover, partnership has moved on from mere rhetoric, as seen in the initiative to develop a variety of compacts and agreements with the voluntary sector' (Day, Dunkerley, and Thompson 2000: 31; Dicks, Hall, and Pithouse 2001; Osmond 2004). Effective partnership with business is proving harder (K. Morgan and Rees 2001).

Osmond (1998: 15) goes so far as to claim that the assembly 'will be the essential instrument to ensure that in the coming decades a Welsh democracy and a Welsh civil society will come into being'. In the mean time Keith Patchett (2000) is not alone in arguing that the assembly needs to make an early impact even though its powers are limited. Politicians and journalists routinely proclaim the establishment of the assembly to be central to a new-found national confidence in Wales, but the voters would seem less enamoured. The low turnout of 45.9 per cent in the first assembly elections in 1999 was followed by an even lower turnout of 38.2 per cent in the second elections in 2003. Significantly the biggest fall, from 60.3 per cent in 1999 to 45.0 per cent in 2003, was in Caernarfon as it was in Gwynedd that approval for the new assembly was greatest in the 1997 referendum.[10] Osmond (2004: 75) reports survey evidence that suggests that support for independence remained constant between 1997 and 2003 with about a seventh of respondents supporting it, 14.1 per cent in 1977 and 13.9 per cent in 2003, as did support for the assembly at about a quarter, 26.8 per cent in 1997 and 27.1 per cent in 2003. The change has been in those not wanting any elected body, who have halved from two-fifths to one-fifth, 39.5 to 21.2 per cent, and those preferring a parliament with its additional power, who have doubled from one-fifth to two-fifths 19.6 to 37.8 per cent. The 2003 turnout suggests the assembly has yet to prove itself. The survey evidence suggests a parliament with law-making and taxing powers might find it easier to do so, though the Scottish precedent cautions that it still would not be easy.

Politicians are not currently in much favour anywhere in Britain and it is possible that Modern Wales is of more interest to voters. There are plenty of voices saying that Wales's recent economic success has been exaggerated (cf. Lovering 1999) and that scenarios in which Wales catches up economically with more prosperous parts of Britain and the Continent are improbable (cf. Hill 2000a), but Modern Wales does represent maximized investment of financial and human capital in the Welsh economy and it does accommodate diversified cultural consumption. Both have their appeal.

NOTES

1 All details pertaining to language and the 2001 Census have been taken from Bwrdd yr Iaith Gymraeg (The Welsh Language Board) (2003).

2 The dragon was replaced by a Scottish unicorn when James VI of Scotland acceded to the English throne as James I of England in 1603. A year later James VI and I adopted the style James I of Great Britain.

3 On the history of Wales, I have made particular use of Kenneth Morgan (1981), Gwyn A. Williams (1991), and John Davies (1993).

4 This is not to say that there is no social inequality within rural communities in post-war Wales. David Jenkins (1960) and others since have distinguished between two lifestyle groups, buchedd A and buchedd B. Those attached to buchedd A conform to Nonconformist expectations and enjoy higher social standing. They are chapelgoing, diligent, respectable, self-improving, supportive of education beyond the school leaving age, more often sabbatarian and teetotal, and more likely to take leading roles in community organizations. Those attached to buchedd B are more secular, easy-going and likely to socialize in the pub, are likely to prefer an early job and earnings to an extended education, and are content to let others provide local drive and leadership. In some accounts they are the heirs of pre-Puritan merry Wales and they have more fun. Graham Day and Martin Fitton (1975) argue that these two status groups have a connection to the wider British class structure. Buchedd A is predominantly middle class and skilled working class, whilst buchedd B consists mainly of unskilled workers. Reporting on her fieldwork Emma James (2003) indicates that cultural judgements of a buchedd kind were still being made about locals and incomers in three villages in south-west Wales at the turn of the millennium.

5 The more usual term 'Anglo-Welsh' has been used by some Welsh Welsh to question the Welsh credentials of non-Welsh speakers. To avoid the 'only half-Welsh' connotation which many non-Welsh speakers find offensive, I refer to 'Anglophone Welsh'.

6 Queen Elizabeth II made Charles, her eldest son, Prince of Wales in 1956 and his investiture took place at Caernarfon in 1969. The proceedings followed a tradition largely invented by Lloyd George for the investiture of 1911.

7 I first encountered Dai Smith's *Wales! Wales?* (1984) in the Salisbury Collection of books on Wales at Cardiff University. Four previous readers had embellished the title page. One had written 'Sais' (English). Another had added 'so what?'. A third explained: 'Beware of this little guy's anti-Welsh hang-ups! Wales for him is all about egg-chasing at the Arms Park'. The fourth knew the type: 'Member of the Labour Party then.' What, I asked myself, was I getting into?

8 Sixty-one per cent claimed to have voted. The actual turnout was 51.3 per cent.

9 The general point that nationalist parties in Wales and Scotland fare better in elections for the devolved assembly and parliament than they do in British general elections has now been confirmed in two rounds of elections to Westminster and to Cardiff and Edinburgh. Conversely some voters would seem to reason that their interests are better served by a British party at Westminster than by a nationalist party of marginal consequence.

10 For a summary of the 2003 results and a comparison with 1999, see Young (2003).

REFERENCES

AARON, J., REES; T., BETTS, S.; and VINCENTELLI, I. (1994), *Our Sisters' Land: Changing Identities of Women in Wales* (Cardiff: University of Wales Press).

ADAMSON, DAVID L. (1991), *Class, Ideology and Nation: A Theory of Welsh Nationalism* (Cardiff: University of Wales Press).

—— (1999), 'The intellectual and the national movement in Wales', in Fevre and Thompson (eds.), ch. 3.

AITCHISON, JOHN, and CARTER, HAROLD (1999), 'The Welsh language today', in Dunkerley and Thompson (eds.), ch. 6.

—— DAY, GRAHAM; EDWARDS, B.; MOYES T.; and MURDOCH, J. (1989), *The Upper Ithon Valley: A Social and Economic Survey* (Aberystwyth: Rural Surveys Research Unit).

BALSOM, DENIS (1985), 'The three-Wales model', in Osmond (ed.), ch. 1.

—— (2000), 'The referendum result', in J. B. Jones and Balsom (eds.), ch. 9.

BALSOM, DENIS; MADGWICK, PETER; and VAN MECHELEN, DENIS (1984), 'The political consequences of Welsh identity', *Ethnic and Racial Studies*, 7: 160–81.

BEDDOE, DEIDRE (1986), 'Images of Welsh women', in Curtis (ed.), 225–38.

BETTS, SANDRA (1996) (ed.), *Our Daughters' Land: Past and Present* (Cardiff: University of Wales Press).

BIANCHI, TONY (1986), 'R. S. Thomas and his readers', in Curtis (ed.), 69–95.

BORLAND, JOHN; FEVRE, RALPH; and DENNEY, DAVID (1992), 'Nationalism and community in North West Wales', *Sociological Review*, 40: 49–72.

BOWEN, E. G. (1986), 'The geography of Wales as a background to its history', in Hume and Pryce (eds.), ch. 3, first published in Welsh in 1964 and in English in 1976.

BOWIE, FIONA (1993), 'Wales from within: conflicting interpretations of Welsh identity', in S. MACDONALD (ed.), *Inside European Identities* (Oxford: Berg), ch. 8.

BREWER, TERI (1999), 'Heritage tourism: a mirror for Wales?', in Dunkerley and Thompson (eds.), ch. 9.

BRYAN, JANE, and JONES, CALVIN (2000) (eds.), *Wales in the 21st Century: An Economic Future* (Basingstoke: Macmillan).

CHANEY, PAUL; HALL, TOM; and PITHOUSE, ANDREW (2001) (eds.), *New Governance—New Democracy? Post-Devolution Wales* (Cardiff: University of Wales Press).

CURTICE, JOHN (1999), 'Is Scotland a nation and Wales not?', in Taylor and Thomson (eds.), ch. 6.

CURTIS, TONY (1986) (ed.), *Wales: The Imagined Nation—Studies in Cultural and National Identity* (Bridgend: Poetry Wales Press).

DAVIES, CHARLOTTE AULL (1989), *Welsh Nationalism in the Twentieth Century: The Ethnic Option and the Modern State* (New York: Praeger).

DAVIES, JAMES A. (1986), 'A picnic in the orchard: Dylan Thomas's Wales', in Curtis (ed.), 43–65.

DAVIES, JANET (2000), 'Welsh' in G. PRICE (ed.), *Languages in Britain and Ireland* (Oxford: Blackwell), ch. 7.

DAVIES, JOHN (1993), *A History of Wales* (London: Allen Lane), translated by the author from the Welsh edn., 1990.

DAY, GRAHAM (1984), 'Development and national consciousness: the Welsh case', in H. VERMEULEN and J. BOISSEVAIN (eds.), *Ethnic Challenge: The Politics of Ethnicity in Europe* (Göttingen: Herodot), 35–49.

—— (2002), *Making Sense of Wales: A Sociological Perspective* (Cardiff: University of Wales Press).

—— and FITTON, MARTIN (1975), 'Religion and social status in rural Wales: "buchedd" and its lessons for concepts of stratification in community studies', *Sociological Review*, 23: 867–91

—— and REES, GARETH (1991) (eds.), *Regions, Nations and European Integration: Remaking the Celtic Periphery* (Cardiff: University of Wales Press).

—— DUNKERLEY, DAVID; and THOMPSON, ANDREW (2000), 'Evaluating the "new politics": civil society and the National Assembly for Wales', *Public Policy and Administration*, 15: 25–38.

DEACON, RUSSELL M. (2002), *The Governance of Wales: The Welsh Office and the Policy Process 1964–99* (Cardiff: Welsh Academic Press).

DICKS, BELLA; HALL, TOM; and PITHOUSE, ANDREW (2001), 'The National Assembly and the voluntary sector: an equal partnership?', in Chaney, Hall, and Pithouse (eds.), ch. 5.

DUNKERLEY, DAVID, and THOMPSON, ANDREW (1999) (eds.), *Wales Today* (Cardiff: University of Wales Press).

EVANS, NEIL (2003), ' Immigrants and minorities in Wales, 1840–1990: a comparative perspective', in Charlotte Williams, Evans, and O'Leary (eds.), ch. 1.

—— and O'LEARY, PAUL (2003), 'Playing the game', in Charlotte Williams, Evans, and O'Leary (eds.), ch. 7.

FARRELL, CATHERINE M., and LAW, JENNIFER (1997), 'A more separate education system for Wales', *Contemporary Wales*, 10: 170–81.

FEVRE, RALPH (1999), 'The Welsh economy', in Dunkerley and Thompson (eds.), ch. 4.

—— and THOMPSON, ANDREW (1999) (eds.), *Nation, Identity and Social Theory: Perspectives form Wales* (Cardiff: University of Wales Press).

FOULKES, DAVID; JONES, J. BARRY; and WILFORD, R. A. (1986), 'Wales: a separate administrative unit', in Hume and Pryce (eds.), ch. 13.

GIGGS, JOHN, and PATTIE, CHARLES (1992), 'Wales as a plural society', *Contemporary Wales*, 5: 25–63.

HARRIS, CHRIS, and STARTUP, RICHARD (1994), 'The Church in Wales: a neglected Welsh institution', *Contemporary Wales*, 7: 97–116.

HERBERT, TREVOR, and JONES, GARETH ELWYN (1995) (eds.), *Post-War Wales* (Cardiff: University of Wales Press).

HILL, STEPHEN (2000a), 'Shaping the future', in Bryan and Jones (eds.), ch. 11.

—— (2000b), 'Wales in transition', in Bryan and Jones (eds.), ch. 1.

HOWELL, DAVID W. (1977), *Land and People in 19th Century Wales* (London: Routledge & Kegan Paul).

—— and BABER, C. (1990), 'Wales' in F. M. L. THOMPSON (ed.), *The Cambridge Social History of Britain 1750–1950*, i. *Regions and Communities* (Cambridge: Cambridge UP).

HUME, IAN, and PRYCE, W. T. R. (1986) (eds.), *The Welsh and their Country: Selected Readings in the Social Sciences* (Llandysul (Dyfed): Gomer).

JAMES, EMMA (2003), 'Research on your own doorstep: Welsh rural communities and the perceived effects of in-migration', in C. A. DAVIES and S. JONES (eds.), *Welsh Communities: New Ethnographic Perspectives* (Cardiff: University of Wales Press), ch. 3.

JENKINS, DAVID (1960), 'Aberporth: a study of a fishing village in south Cardiganshire', in E. DAVIES and A. D. REES (eds.), *Welsh Rural Communities* (Cardiff: University of Wales Press).

JENKINS, RICHARD (1997), *Rethinking Ethnicity: Arguments and Explorations* (London: Sage).

JOHNSTON, RON; TRYSTAN, DAFYDD; PATTIE, CHARLES; and JONES, RICHARD WYN (2000), 'From parliament to assembly: changing voter behaviour in Wales between the 1997 General Election and the 1999 National Assembly Election', *Contemporary Wales*, 13: 182–202.

JONES, [J.] BARRY (1988), 'The development of Welsh territorial institutions: Modernization theory revisited', *Contemporary Wales*, 2: 47–61.

_____ (2000), 'Changes to the government of Wales 1979–1997', in Jones and Balsom (eds.), ch. 2.

_____ and BALSOM, DENIS (2000) (eds.), *The Road to the National Assembly of Wales* (Cardiff: University of Wales Press).

JONES, RICHARD WYN; TRISTAN, DADYDD; and TAYLOR, BRIDGET (2000), 'Voting patterns in the referendum', in Jones and Balsom (eds.), ch. 10.

LOVERING, JOHN (1999), 'Celebrating globalism and misreading the Welsh economy: the "new regionalism" ', *Contemporary Wales*, 11: 12–60.

MORGAN. KENNETH O. (1981), *Rebirth of a Nation: Wales 1880–1980* (Oxford: Clarendon, and Cardiff: University of Wales Press).

MORGAN, KEVIN, and REES, GARETH (2001), 'Learning by doing: devolution and the governance of economic development in Wales', in Chaney, Hall, and Pithouse (eds.), ch. 6.

MORGAN, PRYS (1983), 'From a death to a view: the hunt for the Welsh past in the romantic period', in E. HOBSBAWM and T. RANGER (eds.), *The Invention of Tradition* (Cambridge: Cambridge UP), ch. 3.

_____ (1986a), 'The *gwerin* of Wales: myth and reality', in Hume and Pryce (eds.), ch. 5.

_____ (1986b), 'Keeping the legends alive', in Curtis (ed.), 17–41.

MUNDAY, MAX (2000), 'Foreign direct investment in Wales: lifeline or leash?, in Bryan and Jones (eds.), ch. 4.

NAIRN, TOM (1977), *The Break-Up of Britain* (London: New Left Books).

OSMOND, JOHN (1985) (ed.), *The National Question Again: Welsh Political Identity in the 1980s* (Llandysul (Dyfed): Gomer).

_____ (1995), *Welsh Europeans* (Bridgend: Seren).

_____ (1998), 'Introduction', to J. Osmond (ed.), *The National Assembly Agenda* (Cardiff: Institute of Welsh Affairs), 1–15.

_____ (2004), 'Nation building and the assembly: the emergence of a Welsh civic consciousness', in A. TRENCH (ed.), *Has Devolution Made a Difference? The State of the Nations 2004* (London: Imprint Academic and The Constitution Unit), ch. 3.

PATCHETT, KEITH (2000), 'The new Welsh constitution: the Government of Wales Act 1998', in Jones and Balsom (eds.), ch. 14.

PATERSON, LINDSAY, and JONES, RICHARD WYN (1999), 'Does civil society drive constitutional change? The cases of Wales and Scotland', in Taylor and Thompson (eds.), ch. 8.

RAWKINS, PHILLIP M. (1979), 'An approach to the political sociology of the Welsh nationalist movement', *Political Studies*, 27: 440–57.

REES, GARETH, and DELAMONT, SARA (1999), 'Education in Wales', in Dunkerley and Thompson (eds.), ch. 14.

REES, TERESA (1995), 'Women in Wales', in Herbert and Jones (eds.), sect. C.

—— (1999), 'Women in Wales', in Dunkerley and Thompson (eds.), ch. 15.

REES, WILLIAM (1951), *An Historical Atlas of Wales* (London: Faber & Faber).

ROBERTS, BRIAN (1994), 'Welsh identity in a former mining valley: social images and imagined communities', *Contemporary Wales*, 7: 77–95.

ROGERS, BYRON (2000), 'R. S. Thomas', an obituary, *The Guardian*, 27 September.

ROSSER, PHYLIP (1985), 'Growing through political change', in Osmond (ed.), ch. 10.

SMITH, DAI (1980) (ed.), *A People and a Proletariat: Essays in the History of Wales 1780–1980* (London: Pluto).

—— (1984), *Wales? Wales!* (London: Allen & Unwin).

—— (1986), 'A novel history', in Curtis (ed.), 129–58.

—— (1999), *Wales: A Question of History* (Bridgend: Seren).

TAYLOR, BRIDGET, and THOMSON, KATARINA (1999) (eds.), *Scotland and Wales: Nations Again?* (Cardiff: University of Wales Press).

THOMPSON, ANDREW; DAY, GRAHAM; and ADAMSON, DAVID (1999), 'Bringing the "local" back in: the production of Welsh identities', in A. BRAH, M. J. HICKMAN, and M. MAC AN GHAILL (eds.), *Thinking Ethnicities: Ethnicity,*

Racism and Culture (Basingstoke: Macmillan), ch 3.

WATSON, MURRAY (2003), *Being English in Scotland* (Edinburgh; Edinburgh University Press).

Welsh Language Board (2003), 'Census 2001: Main statistics about Welsh', issued 23 September 2003, <www.bwrrd-yr-iath.org.uk>, accessed 1 June 2005.

WILLIAMS, CHARLOTTE (1999), ' "Race and racism": what's special about Wales?', in Dunkerley and Thompson (eds.), ch. 16.

—— (2003), 'Claiming the national: nation, national identity and ethnic minorities', in Williams, Evans, and O'Leary (eds.), ch. 13.

WILLIAMS, CHARLOTTE; EVANS, NEIL; and O'LEARY, PAUL (2003) (eds.), *A Tolerant Nation? Exploring Ethnic Diversity in Wales* (Cardiff: University of Wales Press).

WILLIAMS, COLIN H. (1999), 'Governance and the language', *Contemporary Wales*, 12: 130–54.

WILLIAMS, GLYN (1978) (ed.), *Social and Cultural Change in Contemporary Wales* (London: Routledge & Kegan Paul).

WILLIAMS, GWYN A. (1991), *When Was Wales? A History of the Welsh* (London: Penguin) (first published London: Black Raven Press, 1985).

WILLIAMS, HYWEL (2004), 'Heirs of Gwrtheyrn', *The Guardian*, 10 February 2004.

YOUNG, ROSS (2003), 'Welsh Assembly Elections: 1 May 2003', *House of Commons Library Research Papers*, 03/45.

5

Speaking for England

Introduction

The new Labour government of the United Kingdom elected in 1997 began a process of extensive constitutional reform including devolution to Scotland and Wales. In May 2003 the people of Scotland had the second elections to their parliament, and the people of Wales similar elections to their assembly, but those who lived in England had no equivalent opportunity to give political expression to an English national identity. Tristram Hunt, the historian, writing in *The Guardian* on St George's Day, 23 April 2003, regretted this. Simon Partridge, the advocate of assemblies for the English regions, in a letter to *The Guardian* three days later, did not: 'The bad news for aspiring English nationalists like Hunt is that not feeling very English seems to be the predominant aspect of living in England.' Partridge cited in support a BBC poll in 2002 on regional devolution which found that 'Only 27 per cent saw themselves as English', as distinct from identifying with a region, Britain, or the world (Strickland and Wood 2002: 40). This was disingenuous. The poll required respondents to choose a *primary*, not a *single*, identity from four: provincial, English, British, or cosmopolitan. Identities are not necessarily exclusive, and pollsters, and those who make use of their work, mislead if they do not make this plain. Those without multiple, layered, and variable identities may be more the exception than the rule. As yet there is negligible popular demand for any new constitutional settlement for England, such as an English parliament or assemblies for the English regions (cf. Harding 2000; Stoker 2000), but there is now a debate about national identity in England.[1] Jeremy Paxman's *The English* (1998) has attracted the most attention, selling more than 300,000 copies in the first two years. *England: An Elegy* (2000) by the political philosopher, Roger Scruton, has also sold well. Robert Colls'

Identity of England (2002) and Krishan Kumar's *The Making of English National Identity* (2003) are especially good. But these contributions are only four of many.[2] It is, however, one thing to rescue the notion of English national identity from those, like Partridge, who would discard it, and quite another to articulate it clearly, let alone progressively—which is what Hunt calls for.

Who do the English think they are? This is a difficult question for the English in at least four ways. First, the English, even more than the Scots and the Welsh, are not used to questioning their identity. As Tom Nairn (1977) has long since argued, nationalism is not just about the celebrating national identity, it is also about the mobilizing myth of 'the people'. But the constitutional settlement of the 'Glorious Revolution' in 1688 established the sovereignty of (the crown in) parliament, not the sovereignty of the people, and thereby diverted the English then and since from thinking in republican terms about 'we the people' as the foundation of democracy and thus about who we the people are. Second, what Krishan Kumar (2000: 589–90) calls the 'ruling authorities' of the union of England and Scotland recognized from the outset the need to restrain the claims of the English 'as the wealthiest, most numerous, and most powerful group within the United Kingdom' and to build up instead 'loyalty not to a people but to its institutions. Britain and the British came to be identified with the Crown, with Parliament, with the Protestant religion, and with the worldwide British Empire.' For the English, Britishness came to subsume Englishness so that the two were often indistinguishable; for the Scots, the Welsh, and later the Irish, Britishness was much more of an overlay. The consequences of this are still with us today. Those who live in England are twice as likely to think of themselves as British only, or more British than English, as those in Scotland are likely to think in equivalent terms (Curtice and Heath, 2000: 158). Many in England are unwilling to surrender a British national identification, however much this would suit Scottish nationalists. In other words, what it means to be English has less salience for them than what it means to be Scottish has for most Scots. Third, Scots, Welsh, and Irish within the United Kingdom have been partly prompted to think of themselves in contradistinction to the dominant English. Without an equivalent Other, many of the English have thought of who they are in regional terms. Natives of the North-East, Yorkshire, and Cornwall, and residents of London are perhaps the most obvious examples. In political terms English regionalism largely remains, despite the measures taken by the new Labour government, what Harvie (1991) called it more than a decade ago—'the dog that never barked' (see Ch. 6). Nevertheless regional loyalties can still be strong enough to dilute interest in the identification of any common Englishness.

The fourth reason why the question is difficult is that when the English do think about England there is more than one possibility with which to engage. My aim in this chapter is to clarify the debate about England by specifying four alternative ways of constructing or representing England and Englishness: English England, Anglo-British England, Little England, and Cosmopolitan England. They can be differentiated on two dimensions as Table 5.1 illustrates, orientation to time and orientation to place. (1) English England is the England with all the attributes the English suppose to be peculiarly, quintessentially, emblematically or just evocatively English. It evokes an England older than Great Britain and lauds a land, liberties, and customs hallowed by age. One variant of English England is Old England. Another is England: the Green and Pleasant Land. (2) Anglo-British England is the England that was at the heart of the making of Great Britain and the Empire, the one in which the differences between England and Britain disappear or are marginalized. It is proud of its past but is also outward-looking. The legacies of what some, such as Bill Schwarz (1996), echoing John Seeley (1883), have called 'the expansion of England' are still often obvious. (Schwarz, like Tomlinson (1982), also now refers to the contraction of England.) (3) Little England is the England of those who would turn their backs on overseas adventures. There have been versions of Little England

TABLE 5.1	Contemporary constructions of England by time and place		
		Orientations to Place	
		Home	*Abroad*
Orientations to Time	*Past*	1. English England	2. Anglo-British England
	Present	3. Little England	4. Cosmopolitan England

for as long as there have been imperialists, but it is not past foreign entanglements that exercise little Englanders but present ones—especially today the European Union. (4) Finally there is another England, a Cosmopolitan England, more oriented to Europe, the Commonwealth, and the world, and more open to a diversity of peoples and cultures. Accommodation of diversity is, however, not the same as indiscriminate acceptance of difference. Defining the terms and limits of accommodation is one of the most urgent and complex challenges England's citizens must address.

Before turning to the four different constructions of England, it is worth noting survey findings about the political attitudes of the English. Even if more people in England proclaim their Britishness than do people in Wales and, especially, Scotland, there are some in England who think of themselves as English only. In the 1997 British Election and 1999 British Social Attitudes surveys, John Curtice and Anthony Heath (2000) combined responses to the Moreno question[3] about British and/or English, Scottish, and Welsh identities with responses to the following alternative:

Please say which, if any, of the words on this card describes the way *you* think of *yourself*. Please choose as many or as few as apply. PROBE: Any other?
British,
English,
European,
Irish,
Northern Irish,
Scottish,
Welsh,
Other answer

Responses in England to the alternative measure are set out in Table 5.2. The percentage thinking of themselves as English rose between 1997, the year of the Scottish and Welsh devolution referendums, and 1999, the year of the first elections to the Scottish Parliament and the National Assembly for Wales, by 10 per cent and the percentage thinking of themselves as British only fell by 13 per cent.

Curtice and Heath combined the two sets of responses to generate a category of 'Unambiguously English' who said they were 'English only' in answer to the Moreno question and English alone in answer to the alternative question, and a category of 'Ambiguously English' who answered English alone to the first and English plus something else to the second. They have also constructed analogous categories of Unambiguously British and Ambiguously British to make seven in all: Unambiguously English,

TABLE 5.2	National identity in England: an alternative measure, 1997 and 1999		
	1997	1999	Change
% who think of themselves as			
British	73	70	−3
English	47	57	+10
% answering			
English only	18	21	+3
English and British	36	44	+8
British only	40	27	−13
N	3,150	2,718	

Source: 1997 British Election Survey, 1999 British Social Attitudes Survey.

Ambiguously English, More English than British, Equally English and British, More British than English, Ambiguously British, Unambiguously British. The Unambiguously English, so identified, were, when compared to all other categories, more English nationalist, more in favour of English devolution, more opposed to immigrants, and more Eurosceptic. Table 5.3 compares the scores for the Unambiguously English with those of all respondents in England.

What Curtice and Heath do not highlight is that the Unambiguously English constituted only 253 of their 2,718 respondents in England, i.e. 9.3 per cent. And although their scores were usually the highest or lowest of all the seven categories, some of them were still quite low or high respectively. For example 74 per cent of the Unambiguously English *disagreed* that it was bad that ethnic minorities had got ahead, and 76 per cent *disagreed* that being white mattered a great deal to being English. It would thus be quite wrong to suppose that all the Unambiguously English are hostile to non-whites in their midst although they may be cultural assimilationists.

1 English England

There is a construction of England that looks back both to Early England and Old England and to England: The Green and Pleasant Land of more

TABLE 5.3 English political attitudes, 1999		
	Unambiguously English	All
% who		
are very proud of being English	69	44
are very proud of being British	39	43
support Scottish team/athlete against foreign competition (when no English participation)	36	42
prefer Scottish independence	37	24
prefer Scottish devolution	42	54
prefer English parliament	25	18
prefer English regional government	18	15
prefer to keep the pound sterling	73	60
prefer to leave the EU	22	15
think immigrants take jobs	70	40
think it bad that ethnic minorities have got ahead	26	16
think equal opportunities have gone too far	46	34
think themselves very or little racially prejudiced	37	28
say it matters a great deal to being English to:		
be born in England	51	29
have English parents	41	25
have lived most of one's life in England	32	23
be white	24	12
Base	253	2,718

Source: Derived from Curtice and Heath (2000), tables 8.4, 8.5, 8.7, 8.9, 8.10, 8.11, and 8.12.

recent times. It values lands, liberties, and customs hallowed by age and it respects tradition. It is the England in which English men and women, the notable and the praised, the common and the unsung, locate things they mostly cherish, occasionally deplore, as peculiarly, quintessentially, emblematically, or just evocatively English—a process often intensified by encounters with Others in Britain, Ireland, the Empire, and Europe, in peace and in war. Theirs is an English England.

1.1 Early England and Old England

Celebrants of English England have to contend with the difficulty that much of the early history of England is in some ways not very English. Bede finished writing his magnum opus *The Ecclesiastical History of the English People*—the earliest surviving reference to an *English* people—in Latin in 731. Shakespeare wrote the historical plays that helped to generate a popular sense of English identity, and thereby please Elizabeth I, in the 1590s. Telling an *English* story that spans the centuries from the Anglo-Saxons to the Tudors, however, is not unproblematic. Much of the intervening period is a tale of Danes and Normans, of kings of England who lived for most (Cnut, Richard I) or much (William I and II, Henry I and II) of their reigns outside the realm, and of royal, legal, and official life conducted in French. When was England? Where were the English? Where was English?

It is not possible here to do more than give a brief and partial summary of matters germane to the Englishness or otherwise of the early and medieval history of England, but the following gives an idea of some of the events and developments at issue.[4] In 410 the Romans left Britain and the Romano-British had thenceforth to defend themselves. In the fifth century there began a process of invasion and settlement by, as Bede (731: 15) says, 'three very powerful Germanic tribes', the Jutes, the Angles, and the Saxons. By 600 this had extended to most of what we now know as England—the exceptions were Devon and Cornwall (the British kingdom of Dumnonia), lands bordering Wales, and lands in the north to the west of the Pennines—and to a small part of today's Scotland in the eastern Borders and Lothian. By 700 it took in the whole of England except Cornwall and a sizeable part of Scotland, the lands south of the Forth and north of the Solway Firth. Bede states that the Jutes (from Jutland—the north of what is today mainland Denmark) prevailed in Kent as well as settling on the Isle of Wight and lands north of the Solent, the Angles (from what today is the south of mainland Denmark and the west end of Germany's Baltic coast) settled Mercia (or Middle Anglia, today's Midlands), East Anglia, and Northumbria (all today's North and much of the south of Scotland), and Saxons (from what today is Lower Saxony) settled Sussex, Wessex, and Essex (p. 27). By the eighth century there had emerged seven (often warring) kingdoms without fixed boundaries—the famous heptarchy of Kent, Sussex, Wessex, Essex, East Anglia, Mercia (which had absorbed Lindsey), and Northumbria (which had absorbed the British kingdom of Elmet and united Deira in the south and Bernicia in the north). Of these Mercia was the most powerful. As such its king was for a while a sort of overking *(Bretwaldas)* whose supremacy the others (fitfully) conceded. It was Offa, King of

Mercia from 757 to 796, who built the great dyke on the west of his kingdom to keep the Welsh at bay, thereby establishing a border with Wales still familiar over twelve centuries later. Offa was the first king to use the title King of the English in his charters.

The Romano-British and the Celts viewed the settlement of the pagan and illiterate Anglo-Saxon raiders who had destroyed villas and monasteries and looted their contents as an invasion of barbarians with an inferior culture. The Anglo-Saxons in the south were converted by missionaries of the Roman church first sent by Pope Gregory in 597. The most important, St Augustine, is buried in Canterbury Cathedral, in the see he founded in 601. The Anglo-Saxons in the north, and later the west, were first converted to Christianity by missionaries of the Celtic church. The most important, St Aidan, came at the behest of King Oswald who had won control of Northumbria in 633. The differences in the role of bishops, calendar, liturgy, etc. of the Celtic and Roman churches were ended in favour of Roman practice at the Synod of Whitby in 664. Thereafter there was one church in England though the primacy of the archbishop of Canterbury over the archbishop of York was not agreed until 1072. The Anglo-Saxon invaders used the runic alphabet for inscriptions and were thus not the illiterates their detractors suggested. Following conversion by missionaries from the Roman church, however, they developed writing in the Latin alphabet. There were big differences in regional dialects, but Bede in 731 writes, quite simply, that the language of the Anglo-Saxons was English. Even so, the first great literary work in Old English, the poem Beowulf, composed some time in the last third of the first millennium, draws on the oral tradition of the Angles and recounts a fabulous history of warriors and a monster in what is now southern Sweden and Denmark. The first great story in English is thus not set in England. As for the inferior culture, the Anglo-Saxons had laid waste to the towns of Roman Britain but they also produced remarkable artefacts of their own, as evidenced, for example, by the treasure found at the Sutton Hoo ship burial site of Raedwald, King of East Anglia, who died c.624.

In the first part of the ninth century Mercian supremacy gave way to that of Wessex. Wessex in turn found its high position threatened, but this time not from a rival Anglo-Saxon kingdom, but from the Vikings from Denmark and what is now Norway and Sweden. The Viking raids on England, Scotland, and Ireland began in 789 and ended in full-scale invasion in

865. The plundering included the sacking of the great abbeys of Lindisfarne (793), Jarrow (794), and Iona (795). In 865 the Danish 'Great Army' invaded East Anglia, fought its way north and in 869 captured York. East Anglia and Northumbria were now under Danish rule. In 871 a second Danish army invaded and by 874 the Danes had added Mercia to their lands. They had then only to defeat Wessex to complete their domination of England. In this they failed. After suffering two reverses, King Alfred of Wessex finally routed the Danes against the odds in 878 and then concluded in 880 the treaty that confined them to the east and north. A century later the magnitude of his achievement was more obvious than it had been at the time and there began references to Alfred the Great.

The Danes ruled east and north of a line from the Thames just downstream of London to the south of Shropshire. In this territory, the Danelaw, they applied their own law. The Anglo-Saxons viewed the Vikings (literally plunderers) as a pagan and illiterate people with an inferior culture, much as the Roman-British had once regarded them. The Vikings struck fear, destroyed Anglo-Saxon centres of piety and learning, and extorted protection money—the Danegeld. In due course, they too were converted, and produced remarkable artefacts of their own, and they too acquired the Latin alphabet—though they showed little interest in writing. There is no corpus of texts in Old Norse comparable to that in Old English.

In 886 Alfred captured London from the Danes and handed it over to Mercia thereby sealing Mercian recognition of his overkingship. He had contained Danish settlement and secured the supremacy of Wessex in most of the rest of England. Alfred secured his half of England by developing fortified towns, training a militia, and building the first navy to defend the long English coastline. He also generated a cultural renaissance after the destruction and pillage wrought by the Danes. He developed law and codified it in English, translated Latin works, including Bede's *History*, into English, and oversaw within his court the compiling of the Anglo-Saxon Chronicles. In support of the Roman church, he wanted his priests to be proficient in Latin but for other purposes he promoted English. He was the first writer to refer to Angelcynn, the land of the English. The reigns of his successors saw the reconquest of the Danelaw, a process completed by victory over the last Viking King of York in 954. One of those successors, Athelstan, already king of Wessex and Mercia, established direct rule over Northumbria in 927, thereby effectively creating for the first time the Kingdom of England, though a Norse army from Ireland returned to York soon after Athelstan's death in 939. In the tenth century the Wessex administrative structure of shires, hundreds, and parishes was extended to all England. By the standards of the time England had a remarkably centralized state and was unusual in its use of a vernacular language, not Latin, in royal and state administration. The liberties of the English, however, were few beyond one inestimable blessing—life subject to the rule of law.

By the beginning of the eleventh century the names 'England' for the country (Engla land in Old English) and 'English' for its people were standard. But why England when the country had been unified not by Angles but by the Saxon house of Wessex? The answer may lie with the influence of Pope Gregory in Rome and Bede in Anglian Northumbria. Bede recounts the story that Gregory had seen fair-haired slaves in a market in Rome and had asked where they had come from. He was told they were Angli (English), and replied that they looked more like Angeli (angels). When later Gregory sent Augustine to Britain he did so as a missionary to the English even though Augustine would begin in Jutish Kent before proceeding to Saxon London. 'England' and 'English' thus had the approval of the church and this may have been the crucial factor. Additionally the Anglian Mercian kingdom had had supremacy before Wessex and had set the precedent of referring to all the non-British people of Britain as English, just as Bede had referred to their language as English. In any case, by the eleventh century there had long been intermarriage between Angles, Saxons, and Danes.

In 991 the Danes returned, defeating the English at Maldon. More raids followed and in 1002 King Aethelred ordered a massacre of all Danes living in England. It was not fully implemented, but it still prompted a series of Danish invasions. These were rebuffed until 1014 when Cnut became King of England, beginning a dynasty that lasted till 1042. In that year, the Wessex dynasty, in the person of Edward the Confessor (founder of Westminster Abbey) recovered the throne. In 1066 Edward's successor Harold hurried from victory at Stamford Bridge in Yorkshire over yet more Viking invaders to Hastings on the south coast to repel what Kumar (2003: 42) strikingly calls 'the last of the Viking raids'—the invasion by his distant cousin William of Normandy and his army. Harold and William both claimed to have been chosen by Edward the Confessor, who had died the previous year, as his successor. On acquiring the throne half a century earlier, Cnut had kept the Anglo-Saxon administrative structure, issued laws, founded monasteries, and mostly behaved like a civilized king. William of Normandy did the same, with one crucial, often brutal, difference. He replaced almost the entire Anglo-Saxon 'ruling class' with one of his own, and English as a language of rule, law, and literature gave way to French.

There was once a view—Michael Wood (1999) describes how it originated with the Levellers in the seventeenth century—that all that was oppressive in English rule flowed from conquest by Norman despots and their imposition of the Norman yoke. This absurdly exaggerated the virtues of Anglo-Saxon England where the lords and clergy had their privileges but the people were certainly not free. What changed under the Normans is that the English lords and clergy lost their ascendancy. William of Normandy and his successors dispossessed almost all the great Anglo-Saxon landowners and replaced them with Norman knights. Almost all English judges, administrators, bishops, and abbots were also replaced by appointees from the Continent, and the language of the royal court, the law courts, and official records changed to Norman French. The last of the remarkable chronicles written in English, the Peterborough chronicle, ceased in 1154 when a French bishop replaced that rarity, an English bishop. The origins of parliament in the early fourteenth century are still debated, but the language of parliament was certainly French until 1362. Norman Davies (1999) points up the Frenchness of the kings of England from William the Conqueror to Henry IV by referring to them throughout by their French names, in these cases Guillaume le Conquérant and Henri IV.[5] The royal court spoke French until the early fifteenth century. In sum, the language of authority was French, even while the language of the people remained English. Kings of England for five hundred years after the Conquest also had lands in France, and between 1337 and 1453 they fought the Hundred Years War to defend or extend them. In 1340 Henry II claimed the throne of France and quartered his coat of arms with the fleur de lys, as did all subsequent monarchs till 1801. The French motto 'Dieu et Mon Droit' has been retained on the royal arms of the United Kingdom to this day. The relative importance of England and French lands to English kings varied according to the wealth of each at the time and the scale of the French ambitions of the king in question, but England had a French cast for centuries.

The re-Englishing of England took place over three-quarters of a century from the second half of the fourteenth century to the first quarter of the fifteenth. Parliament was opened in English for the first time in 1362, the same year as there appeared the earliest-known version of William Langland's *Vision of Piers Plowman*. The 1362 parliament required that thenceforth the law courts should conduct their proceedings in English. Geoffrey Chaucer wrote the Canterbury Tales in English between 1386 and 1400. A translation of the Bible into English instigated by John Wyclif was completed in 1396. Henry IV, the first king of England since the Conquest to speak English as his first language, addressed parliament in English in 1399 following the abdication, also in English, of Richard II. And after Henry V came to the throne in 1413, the royal court switched from French to English as did the production of official documents by the scribes in Chancery.

From a twentieth-century English point of view, England is only unambiguously English following the re-Englishing of England which began in the late fourteenth century. From a twentieth-century Welsh, Irish, and Scottish point of view, the Englishing of Britain and Ireland had begun much earlier. The Normans set out to conquer Wales in 1068, a process that took the 'English' two-and-a-half centuries to complete but was well underway before what I have called the re-Englishing of the English. In Ireland, Henry II (Davies's Henri II) invaded in 1171 thereby beginning the 'English conquest'. And Scottish success in the Wars of Independence (1296–1371) is the success of Scottish kings of Norman descent over their English counterparts. R. R. Davies (2000) refers to an Anglicization of Scotland that begins in the eleventh century. What he also calls the First English Empire—the English domination of Britain and Ireland—was indubitably the work of kings of England but at the outset and for long afterwards was dubiously English. One indicator of this is the difficulty today in naming great English figures in the first two centuries after the Conquest. The two greatest authentically English figures in pre-Conquest England are Bede and Alfred the Great. After that the most celebrated figures are arguably John Wyclif (died 1384, posthumous Bible), Geoffrey Chaucer (*Canterbury Tales* from 1386) and Henry V (reigned 1413–22), and Henry V's wars and marriage would probably have won him the throne of France if he had not died of dysentery before he could inherit. By contrast for many Scots their two greatest heroes William Wallace (1272–1305) and Robert Bruce (reigned 1306–29) belong to the earlier age of the Wars of Independence.

The Wars of the Roses (1399–1485) are hardly a cause for celebration. It is only with the Tudors (1485–1603) that one finds an unambiguously

English age with English figures still widely celebrated by the English today. It is significant that this is the age that gave England one of its most familiar emblems, the Tudor rose. Henry VIII and Elizabeth I are regarded as great nation-building monarchs, William Shakespeare is acclaimed as a great writer, perhaps the greatest ever writer, in the English language, and the seafarers Sir Francis Drake and Sir Walter Raleigh are revered for their exploration of the world and their defence of the realm. Henry VIII's break with Rome in 1534 gave rise to the Church of England, a key component in the formation of the English nation. The foundation of what became a Protestant church for a Protestant nation was however, political, not theological, and it is notable that the Church of England is not associated with any theological figure of the stature of John Knox in Scotland, although the prayerbook of Thomas Cranmer (1549) is still remembered. There is also still a liking for the half-timbered architecture of the Tudor era, and for the finest of English pre-Renaissance architecture represented by Hampton Court Palace (given to Henry VIII in 1528 and twice extended by him), Hardwick Hall (1587), and the Jacobean Hatfield House (1607–11).

In the seventeenth century, the last century of England before Britain, there are English giants of science, especially Sir Isaac Newton, of philosophy, especially Thomas Hobbes and John Locke, and of literature, especially John Milton. The King James Bible of 1611 is also perhaps the single most significant text in the history of English. There are also great architects of the Renaissance, notably Sir Christopher Wren, whose St Paul's Cathedral in London (built 1675–1701) has iconic status. In terms of politics, the most significant figure, Oliver Cromwell, is lauded by some and reviled by others. The reframing of the English Civil War as the War of the Three Kingdoms (of England, Scotland, and Ireland) is a reminder that Cromwell had a stage larger than England and that there is less praise and more revulsion at his name beyond England's borders. The sovereignty of parliament finally secured in the Glorious Revolution of 1688 has certainly been one of the most celebrated achievements of the English—at least by English commentators. Elsewhere the sovereignty of the people has often seemed a better principle.

All in all, there is an England before Britain—an old England, a medieval England, and an early modern England—to be celebrated. It is just that there is rather less of it than is often supposed.

1.2 England: the green and pleasant land

There have always been some English capable of thinking about an England carefully distinguished from Britain. One such was Ernest Barker whose edited volume on *The Character of England* (1947) looks at the historical development and contemporary character of a wide range of institutions and forms of life with quiet pride. Even here, however, there are problems. G. M. Young (1947) on government, for example, elides the government of England and the British Government. But if it is one thing to try to define the character of England and quite another to specify the institutions or practices that are truly the peculiarities of the English—only the Church of England, public schools, pubs, cricket, and foxhunting spring to mind—there continues to be what Kumar calls an English cultural nationalism in which regard for language, literature, and landscape figures prominently.[6] But first let us note the five peculiarities.

Linda Colley (1992) is right to have stressed the centrality of Protestantism in the forging of a British identity after 1707, but the profile of Protestantism was and is different in England, Scotland, and Wales. In particular, the Church of England is established in England only. It has today few worshippers but its clergy are still visible on many public occasions such as commemorations of the war dead and they do perform rites of passage, especially weddings and funerals, for the many non-churchgoing English who declare a belief in God and tick 'C of E' when asked their religion on forms (such as on admission to hospital). Its theology is unimportant to most, including, it sometimes seems, its bishops and parish priests. There is nothing new in this. Kenneth Medhurst and George Moyser (1988) argue that its source is not only Elizabeth I's determination to find a middle way between reforming Protestants and (Catholic) traditionalists but also her demand for public conformity and support for the church of which she was head and her indifference to strictly private belief. Thereafter, 'it seems that the Anglican Church's continuing unity [has been] more the product of adhesion to a given ecclesiastical polity than of theological consensus' (ibid. 7). G. W. E. Russell would have agreed. In his wonderful poem 'Lines from a Parish Magazine' (1901) (in Ingrams 1989: 217), the 'loyal Anglican' rector declares that:

> To pick the best from every school
> The object of my art is,

> And steer a middle course between
> The two contending parties.

> My own opinions would no doubt
> Be labelled 'high' by many;
> But all know well I could not wish
> To give offence to any.

Indeed his success depends on 'this golden rule of action':

> See us from all men's point of view,
> Use all men's eyes to see with,
> And never preach what anyone
> Could ever disagree with.

The Church of England has for many long been a familiar and comfortable church. This is why the controversies over the ordination of women in recent decades and now the appointment of gay bishops have seemed so unseemly (see Bates 2004). In his portrait of an uncomfortable church, Michael De-la-Noy (1993: 324, 325) excoriates dogmatic 'evangelical fundamentalism' and its 'fascist mentality' and calls instead for 'a revival of undogmatic Anglo-Catholicism', thereby, impervious to irony, displaying a fundamental antidogmatism. The Church of England remains a significant part of village life, and its churches and cathedrals are often much loved buildings and the focal points of villages, towns, and cities, but there are now intemperate figures and forces within the church who are insensitive to what has historically made it a peculiarity of the English.

A century and a half ago, Howard Staunton (1865: p. ix) was already able to celebrate another peculiarity of the English: 'Nothing out of England corresponds to or resembles the English endowed school.' The oldest public school, Winchester, admitted its first scholars in 1393. Eton was founded in 1440. But it was the nineteenth century that saw the big expansion of public schools to cater for the growing middle class (cf. Chandos 1984). Public schools once educated almost all the establishment and still educate much of it (cf. Johnson 1977). They also provided governors for the Empire. As boarding schools with emphases on learning, chapel, and games, they were, and still are, regarded as character-forming, but their greatest achievement was, and still is, to impart confidence. They have also done much to reproduce those English obsessions, snobbery and class distinction.

Pubs—public houses—have a character different from the bars and coffee houses of other countries as any foreign visitor will confirm. The pubs especially associated with England are picturesque country pubs that are important to village life, and town pubs with a regular clientele from the local community. Either way, pubs are hubs—centres of social life—with historic or colourful names. They originated as farmhouses selling beer to rural labourers, inns where travellers could find lodgings, taverns that sold wine, and alehouses that supplied beer to the urban proletariat in the nineteenth century (M. Smith 1983). Their history is the history of the common man, less often the common woman. Much of it is about alcoholic solace for hard labour and hard times but it also features games and recreation, conviviality and association—both association for its own sake and for a multiplicity of purposes lawful and unlawful. It is not by chance that pubs feature prominently in the longest running radio soap opera and the two best-known television soap operas. Radio's 'The Archers', set in Ambridge, a fictional village in the Midlands, has The Bull; television's 'Coronation Street', set in a working-class Salford that no longer exists, has the Rovers Return, whilst EastEnders, set in multicultural east London, has The Queen Vic. With affluence pubs have become more comfortable, more attractive to the middle class, less of a male preserve, and more likely to serve food. In some ways they have also been sentimentalized in representations of England. The wonderful fittings of Victorian city pubs, for example, have mostly long since been stripped out where the pubs have survived at all (Girouard 1975). The best pubs are now deemed worthy of conservation. The National Trust owns The Fleece Inn near Evesham which started life as a farmhouse and whose interior is unaltered since the pub was first licensed in 1848, and The George Inn in Southwark, the last remaining galleried coaching inn in London, which dates from the seventeenth century and is mentioned in Dickens' *Little Dorrit*.

The fourth of the peculiarities, cricket, dates from the early seventeenth century and has long been part of the fabric of English life (Birley 1999). First-class cricket is also played in Wales and a Welshman—or for that matter a Scot or an Irishman who happens upon the game and proves good at it—can only play test cricket, the highest level international contest, for England. The fortunes of the national team (seldom glorious) are still widely followed. Interestingly so are the fortunes of the county sides even though gates for anything but one-day matches are pitiful. Cricket's historic notions of fair play and acceptance of the umpire's decision even when the latter is believed to be wrong have passed into the language. The complaint 'it is not cricket' refers to not playing by the rules whatever the activity.

The fifth of the peculiarities, foxhunting, has also taken place in Scotland and Wales but it is its devotees in England who regard it as essential to the fabric of rural life. It was included in 1932 in an official pamphlet on 'The Projection of England' (Lunn 1996: 91–2). It has always had its critics, of which Oscar Wilde—'The English country gentleman galloping after a fox—the unspeakable in full pursuit of the uneatable' (1893)—was the wittiest. The common call for the banning of a cruel sport finally succeeded in 2004, despite huge and continuing opposition from the Countryside Alliance in the name of rural resistance to a government and urban populace unsympathetic to country ways (see Clayton 2004). For Scruton, author of an elegy for England and a keen foxhunter, the ban would have been drearily predictable.

There have been countless contributors to the cultural construction of an English nation. Some have been painters of English scenes and figures—most notably Gainsborough, Constable, Turner, Nash, Piper, and, for today's English public, Lowry. (Art historians have long debated what makes English art English with the depiction of landscape at the heart of the argument (see Corbett, Holt, and Russell 2002), and William Vaughan (2002) has pointed out that it was Nikolaus Pevsner (1956) who first used 'Englishness' in the title of a book.) A few have been classical composers inspired by the English landscape, the English love of the oratorio, or other English themes, of which Elgar, Delius, Vaughan Williams, Holst, and Britten are the most celebrated; others have been devoted to popular music and entertainment; but most have been writers. There have been so many of these from Shakespeare and Milton to Orwell and Betjeman—leaving aside living writers—that it is impossible to examine them properly. In any case the job has already been done for different periods and selections of writers, and in very different ways, by Godfrey Smith (1988), David Gervais (1993), Judy Giles and Tim Middleton (1995), Anthony Easthope (1999), and Peter Ackroyd (2002). The writers include not only novelists, poets, and playwrights, but travel writers (such as, famously, H. V. Morton (1927), J. B. Priestley (1934), and Arthur Mee (1936–42) and politicians (such as, equally famously, Stanley Baldwin (1926) who was three times prime minister in the 1920s and 1930s). Instead I want to highlight just a few themes, and then make a serious point about the very exercise of characterizing Englishness.

Rupert Brooke's First World War sonnet 'The Soldier' (in Keynes 1946: 23) contains lines known to generations of the English for whom the war poets have been very much part of the English literature school syllabus. The lines, first published in 1915, are these:

> If I should die, think only this of me:
> That there is some corner of a foreign field,
> That is for ever England.

Brooke's poem is almost unbearably poignant because later in 1915 he died a painful death on his way to the Dardanelles and the war against the Ottoman Turks.[7] Even so, for many English readers, it is not Brooke's Englishness but their own that his poem calls to mind: 'What makes me English, what is it about England I would miss if I were separated from it, and what is there about my country I would die for?' In other words it is about patriotism, love of country. Lots of writers have told us what it is for them. Some, like George Orwell, in his 1941 essay 'England, Your England' (discussed below), have moved uncertainly between England and Britain but this is something most of the English do on occasions. John Betjeman (1843: 137), descendant of a Dutch immigrant and British press attaché in Dublin from 1941 to 1943, on coming home, told radio listeners how 'Exile from England [had] uncorked the bottle of sentiment'. For him

England stands for the Church of England, eccentric incumbents, oil-lit churches, Women's Institutes, modest village inns, arguments about cow parsley on the altar, the noise of mowing machines on Saturday afternoons, local newspapers, local auctions, the poetry of Tennyson, Crabbe, Hardy and Matthew Arnold, local talent, local concerts, a visit to the cinema, branch-line trains, light railways, leaning on gates and looking across fields. (Betjeman [1943] in 1993: 141)

Robert Winder (2004: 354) calls this a 'Sunday afternoon utopia'. After the war another poet, T. S. Eliot (1948: 31), an American Anglophile, published a famous essay on three senses of culture, one of which 'includes all the characteristic activities and interests of a people'. In the English case he offered 'Derby Day, Henley Regatta, Cowes, the twelfth of August, a cup final, the dog races, the pin table, the dart board, Wensleydale cheese, boiled cabbage cut into sections, beetroot in vinegar, nineteenth-century Gothic churches and the music of Elgar' before adding, 'The reader can make his own list'.

And, then and now, so they can. No wonder others, such as Julian Barnes, in his 1998 novel *England, England*, have satirized the whole genre. Barnes imagines the ultimate English heritage theme park of the future in which everything attractive the tourist expects in England is relocated or recreated on the Isle of Wight, deviations are forbidden, and the rest of the country is abandoned to its unkempt and misguided ways.

One of the most persistent themes in writing about England is 'the green and pleasant land'. The expression is from a poem of William Blake's written in 1804, which was set to magnificent music by Hubert Parry in, significantly, 1916 (Blake 1927: 109–10). Words and music are known to generations of the English as the hymn 'Jerusalem', and there are many who would like it to be England's national anthem.

> And did those feet in ancient time
> Walk upon England's mountains green:
> And was the holy Lamb of God
> On England's pleasant pastures seen!
>
> And did the Countenance Divine
> Shine forth upon our clouded hills?
> And was Jerusalem builded here
> Among these dark Satanic Mills?
>
> Bring me my Bow of burning gold:
> Bring me my Arrows of desire:
> Bring me my Spear: O clouds unfold!
> Bring me my Chariots of Fire!
>
> I will not cease from Mental Fight,
> Nor shall my Sword sleep in my hand
> Till we have built Jerusalem
> In England's green and pleasant Land.

The first two verses refer to the legend that Jesus when a boy visited Glastonbury (see Wood 1999: ch. 3). 'Jerusalem' would thus make an unusual national anthem in so far as it begins with four questions the answer to all of which is 'no'. The 'clouded hills' is taken as an all-too-familiar reference to English weather. The Satanic mills are invariably thought by those who sing or hear the hymn to be a reference to the mills of the industrial revolution with their smoking chimneys and wretched working conditions. There is thus a contrast between the evils of materialism and early industrial capitalism and the organic green and pleasant land of the countryside in which

Blake wanted to build a Christian new Jerusalem. Many since have substituted their socialist new Jerusalem for Blake's spiritual one. But for Blake, very much a Londoner, the new Jerusalem is still a city, not some romantic return to the land (cf. Lucas 1990: ch. 4). The hymn thus has broad appeal. The 'chariots of fire' provided the title of an Oscar-winning film about the triumphs of two British athletes at the Paris Olympics of 1924, Harold Abrahams, an English Jew of Lithuanian descent, and Eric Liddell, a Scot. In a brilliant review of the film Sheila Johnston notes how its narrative is organized around Abrahams' social exclusion and then acceptance by guardians of Englishness initially offended by the pretensions of a parvenu who pays for a trainer, and an Arab at that (in Osmond 1988: 178–80).

Like Martin Wiener (1981), Paxman has described 'how the English mind kept alive the idea that the soul of England lay in the countryside' and this in the country that not only industrialized but also urbanized before all others (1998: 147)—but he is less sure that he deplores it. There seem to me good reasons for this predilection. Rural England is green, and often lush, thanks to the rain, and it is also accessible thanks to a dense network of footpaths that are public 'rights of way' even though they cross private land; a lot of the English countryside looks attractive and it promises the space the cities deny. Its topography, vegetation, and patterns of settlement are also distinctive (Hoskins 1955). Scotland and Wales are predominantly mountainous, but England is not; the English may often be unclear whether they are English or British, but when they are in the English countryside they do know it is an English countryside that appeals to them. Connected with this attachment to the countryside is the well-known English love of gardens and gardening. It is also notable that the voluntary association with the biggest membership in England—3.3 million in 2004—is the National Trust, which conserves stately homes, country houses and their gardens, and areas of outstanding natural beauty.

In choosing what to conserve, the National Trust gives form to what Ian Ousby calls *The Englishman's England* (1990). Ousby is interested in 'how the tourist map of England has been created' (p. 4). The process begins with taste which indicates what is of value and what is not. Travel then identifies objects of taste and turns them into sights to be seen, and tourism classifies and ranks sights and guides the sightseeing of us all. The English cannot be other than tourists in their own land. 'Our communal sense of England has been codified into the familiar images of the travel poster and the accompanying rhetoric of the guidebook far more than we care to admit' (ibid.). Ousby's Englishman (*sic*) is not without discernment but he can never see for himself without any mediation by those (entrepreneurs) who would tell us what to see and how to see it. Ousby's particular interests are literary shrines, country houses, ruins, and nature, but his approach has a general application. In other words, regard for the green and pleasant land is not untutored. To use a term he does not, Ousby throws light on the construction of 'heritage'. Here it is notable how the National Trust has in recent times broadened the range of properties it conserves to include a cotton mill (Styal in Cheshire), a workhouse (Newark), back-to-back houses (Birmingham), and a 1930s semi-detached house, albeit the one John Lennon grew up in, and a 1950s council terraced house, albeit the one Paul McCartney grew up in (both Liverpool).

So much for the green land, what of the pleasant? For Blake the reference would still be to the countryside but the notion of the pleasant has its own resonance. What makes England pleasant? Historic answers have had to do with many different practices and traits from the lofty—respect for individual liberties, respect for privacy ('the Englishman's home is his castle'), religious toleration, etc.—to the mundane—the sense of humour, queueing not pushing and shoving, relatively good road manners (road death rates are low compared with many Continental countries), etc. Orwell (1941) associated much of this with 'common decency' and 'the gentleness of English civilisation'. Barker (1947, 1948) discussed it at some length as civility— a civility more evident to him during Labour's post-war reconstruction than any class antagonism. Much more recently Bernard Crick (1991: 94–5) has written about the influence of the ideal of the gentleman on those who were not.

It encapsulated many clichés about the English character: love of property but respect for persons; a certain *savoir faire* going with no great intellectuality; wanting to know what's going on but distrust of ideas and of aesthetic (as much as of religious) enthusiasm; a love of style but a dislike of ostentation; a refusal to let experts decide but willingness to take advice; a certain respect for amateurishness; a love of leisure and sport and thus a limited capacity for sustained work; a cult of good manners—which, after all, has implications for the parliament house not simply the private house; a social tolerance of the upwardly mobile from trade or industry, but aversion to any obsessive commitment to making money; not to forget, something genuinely and oddly English, a belief that a good life moves back and forth from town to country, country to town; and from all this a conscious cultivation of a somewhat conformist code of behaviour, but resulting in a self-satisfied inner-security that allows for a great deal of cynical toleration of eccentricity or even of verbally threatening behaviour.

Gentlemanliness was cultivated in the public schools, which grew greatly in number in the Victorian era, and aspects of it, transmuted as respectability, were diffused to other classes via board schools, churches, chapels, newspapers, and the Labour movement. Julia Stapleton (1994), writing about Barker, has noted, like critics before her, the missing England of industrial toil, and Philip Dodd (1986) has pointed up the absence of women—even ladies were largely confined to domesticity—but in so far as there has been a gentling of behaviour, and a growing regard for civility, throughout English society from the late nineteenth century onwards, it is hard to deny that it is more pleasant than the alternatives. (Jane Mackay and Pat Thane (1986), incidentally, question whether there was anything distinctively English about the ideal of the Englishwoman that accompanied the idealization of the distinctively English gentleman.)

Attachment to the green and pleasant land, moreover, seems strong enough to overcome evidence that all too often the land is neither green nor pleasant. Industrialized farming (with its battery hen sheds, factory piggeries, and very large fields with hedgerows and copses removed), BSE, foot-and-mouth disease, and (a pet hate) power pylons may have disfigured the countryside, but they have not extinguished idealization of the green and pleasant land. As David Matless (1998: 10) says, 'if landscape is a site of value, it is also a site of anger; at buildings, against authorities, developers, different pleasures'. He refers, tellingly, to 'moral landscapes', and gives as one example the Norfolk Broads whose Broads Authority determined, *circa* 1989, to save 'the last enchanted land' from ugly developments and visitors who come to it 'for the wrong reasons' (p. 9). Likewise incivilities from race riots and football hooliganism to the excesses of the tabloid press, vandalism, binge drinking and public drunkenness on Saturday nights, and graffiti and littering ('our England is a litter bin') have disfigured towns and prompted condemnation from home secretaries to indignant local citizens. There are moral townscapes too. There are also, significantly, many vocal voluntary associations dedicated to conservation and sensitive development from the Council for the Preservation (now Protection) of Rural England (founded in 1926) to local civic trusts.

Robert Colls (2002) notes how many commentators from the late nineteenth century onwards have regarded suburbia as neither homeland nor pleasant land but rather as a spiritual wasteland (alongside other wastelands such as city slums and depopulated uplands). In an extraordinary variation on the green and pleasant land theme, Michael Bracewell (1998) contrasts the refined Arcadian idyll of Englishness celebrated by the literary establishment of old with suburban and working-class English reality as expressed with perception and verve in popular music. His title, *England is Mine*, celebrates the appropriation of England by youth for whom the Arcadian dream has little appeal and cannot come true but it does so without offering an alternative English dream. Prescriptive Arcadianism gives way to reactive suburbanism. This may be thought an uninspiring message but what it says is important. Do not underestimate suburbia. After all, what sort of 'wasteland' is it that has given us the Beatles and the Rolling Stones?

It would be easy to continue at length a discussion of the representations of England and Englishness that figure in literature and recur in the understandings of ordinary Englishmen and women but I would rather close by making four quite different points. First, depictions of England are often made for a political purpose. Orwell in 'England, Your England' (1941) illustrates this particularly well. He claimed that these 'are not only fragments, but characteristic fragments, of the English scene': 'The clatter of clogs in the Lancashire mill towns, the to-and-fro of the lorries on the Great North Road, the queues outside the Labour Exchanges, the rattle of pin-tables in the Soho pubs, the old maids biking to Holy Communion through the mists of the autumn mornings' (p. 10). He then says of 'English civilization': 'It is somehow bound up with solid breakfasts and gloomy Sundays, smoky towns and winding roads, green fields and red pillar-boxes' (p. 11). As for the English themselves, they 'are not gifted artistically', 'are not intellectual', 'feel no need of any systematic "world-view" and are nothing like as practical as they care to imagine (look at their unreformed spelling and their unintelligible weights and measures)'. But they do 'have a certain power of acting without taking thought. Their world-famed hypocrisy—their double-faced attitude towards the Empire, for instance—is bound up with this' (pp. 12–13), double-faced because they are anti-militaristic at home but rely on (the threat of) force in the Empire. Orwell then notes that 'in moments of supreme crisis the whole nation can suddenly draw together and act upon a species of instinct, really a code of conduct which is understood by almost everyone, though never formulated' (p. 13). His political purpose is now transparent. He wants to help draw the nation together in the dark days of 1941 by evoking what the English value most from familiar sights and sounds to more profound matters of conduct. These latter have to do with 'the *privateness* of English life'.

We are a nation of flower-lovers, but also a nation of stamp-collectors, pigeon-fanciers, amateur carpenters, coupon snippers, darts players, crossword-puzzle fans. All the culture that is most truly native centres round things which even when they are communal are not official—the pub, the football match, the back garden, the fireside and the 'nice cup of tea'. (ibid.)

There is no pomp and circumstance here, no display of the high and mighty with the masses looking on. Instead ordinary men and women reproduce the nation by doing ordinary things. But there is a big conclusion. 'The liberty of the individual is still believed in, almost as in the nineteenth century' (ibid.). This is not economic liberty, 'the right to exploit others for profit', but rather 'the liberty to have a home of your own, to do what you like in your spare time, to choose your own amusements instead of having them chosen for you and from above' (pp. 13–14). 'The gentleness of the English civilization is perhaps its most marked characteristic' (p. 15). In time of war there would have to be regimentation, but it would go against the English grain. Even then another 'all-important English trait' would still apply: 'The respect for constitutionalism and legality, the belief in "the law" as something above the State and above the individual, something which is cruel and stupid, of course, but at any rate incorruptible' (p. 19). The law may favour the rich, but the people know that the *rule* of law is in their interest too.

Orwell's period piece still has its appeal. On St George's Day 1993 the Conservative prime minister John Major invoked it for his own political purpose, reassurance of the Eurosceptics in his party who were fearful of the European Union's Treaty of Maastricht.

Fifty years from now Britain will still be the country of long shadows on county [cricket] grounds, warm beer, invincible green suburbs, dog lovers and pools fillers and—as George Orwell said—'old maids bicycling to Holy Communion through the morning mist' and—if we get our way—Shakespeare still read in school. Britain will survive unamendable in all essentials. (Major 1993, quoted in Weight 2002: 666)

Major's use of English emblems such as county cricket and Anglican communion to represent Britain was not well received in Scotland.

Second, even the briefest reflection on the English people, language, literature, and culture indicates how many and varied have been the contributors to the formation of each. In his satirical poem, 'The True-Born Englishman', written in 1701 (see 1997), Daniel Defoe refers to 'Your Roman-Saxon-Danish-Norman English'. Plenty more ethnic infusions before and since justify Philip Dodd's (1995) reference to a 'mongrel nation'. English is a Germanic language with a large vocabulary and some grammar derived from the Norman French. English literature has long been enriched by Scottish, Welsh, Irish, and American writers as well as those from the former Empire, Europe and elsewhere. Other components of English culture have equally long been enriched by an incredible diversity of sources whether one looks to religion, architecture, fashion, popular music, or whatever. In other words, there is no reason why the English should not prize many of their peculiarities but there is also no historical justification for relating them to any idea of ethnic purity or cultural exclusiveness.

Third, attitudes towards this English past range from the elegiac, as in Roger Scruton (2000), to the bracing, as in Simon Heffer (1999). Scruton describes England as a place 'consecrated by custom' (2000: 7) and 'domesticated by its indigenous law' (p. 234), the last a sentiment similar to Colls's 'the law becomes you' (2002: ch. 1). Scruton's veneration of the land, the common law, and the measured ways of the English is of a world increasingly lost. It can go to surprising lengths, as in this singular praise (assuming it is not a joke) of the 'triumph' of the English cooking of the nursery, public schools, Oxbridge, and gentlemen's clubs: 'a cuisine in which ingredients were systematically deprived of their flavour, so that everything tasted roughly the same and manly stoicism prevailed over sensory enjoyment' (p. 51). Heffer, by contrast, sword in hand, is confident that the English, freed from union with the Scots, can build a new Jerusalem which will combine recovery of the best of English traditions with the apotheosis of Margaret Thatcher. It is easy to criticize Heffer, but, unlike Scruton, at least the England he holds dear still has a future. English England has its historical continuities but it is also layered, variegated, and ever-changing as each generation, and each new source of people and ideas, engages with the peculiar mix of what has gone before. It is this thought that allows Colls, more knowledgeable about England's past than Scruton or Heffer, to look confidently to the Cosmopolitan England of the future.

Finally, at least since J. B. Priestley's *English Journey* (1934) there have been those who view with distaste what Stephen Haseler (1996) has called the 'Americanisation of Englishness'. But talk of Americanization, now globalization, can easily overlook that each nation varies in its engagement with American or global influences in more or less subtle ways. To take an obvious example, many American pop and rock musicians have sold records, CDs, and concert tickets all over the world, but each country's popular music scene still differs. There is no reason to suppose that there will not continue to be some peculiarly English responses to American culture and global trends.

2 Anglo-British England

My construction of the Anglo-British is different from those of John Osmond (1988) and Peter Taylor (1991). Their reference is to a hegemonic establishment in London and the tellingly named 'Home Counties' who have benefited from association with crown, state, and the City of London, and the part each played in the Empire, and who assume, sometimes with justification, that their ideas of Britain, its people and culture are the ruling ideas. This assumption is reinforced by their belief that the talented migrate from all over Britain to London because that is where power, influence, wealth, and opportunity lie. Location in London and the Home Counties, at a maximum distance from Scotland and Wales, confirms to them just how peripheral the Celtic periphery is. Their Britain is in all significant matters Anglo-Britain, and Anglo-Britain is not all England writ larger but rather London and the South-East writ larger.

I prefer to associate the Anglo-British not with an Anglocentrism whose epicentre is London, but rather with those in all regions and all classes in England for whom the difference between being English and being British, is, for the most part, unclear, unimportant, and/or irrelevant. Many of them would see nothing amiss in the title of Clive Aslet's *Anyone for England? A Search for British Identity* (1997). They inhabit an Anglo-British England. I know of no evidence that there are proportionately fewer of them outside London and the Home Counties. Second, whereas Anglo-Britain refers to an Anglicized Britain (whether dominated by London and the South-East or not), Anglo-British England refers to an England whose development owes much to being a part of Britain and the British Empire. It acknowledges that migrants from Scotland, Wales, and Ireland, and distinctively British projects such as Empire, have made their mark on England.

The Anglo-British do not notice when an institution or person associated with England performs a British function. For example, it goes unremarked that the Bank of England is the central bank for all Britain, or that the archbishop of Canterbury, the primate of the Church of England, crowns the sovereign of the United Kingdom of Great Britain and Northern Ireland. Nor do countless references to 'England' that should have been to 'Britain' grate on the English ear. Nelson's famous signal at the Battle of Trafalgar in 1813, 'England expects that every man shall do his duty', seems natural enough to those taught that the Royal Navy originated with the English king Henry VIII in the sixteenth century. Similarly Walter Bagehot's famous *The English Constitution* (1867) does not strike the Anglo-British as mistitled. (But then it is the near 800-year continuity of the parliament at Westminster—originally English, later British—that enables Rebecca Langlands (1999) to speak of the English core of the British state.) Even when inclusiveness is at an absolute premium the Anglo-British can blunder. The supporter of Empire and anti-appeasement Conservative, Leo Amery, born in India of Hungarian Jewish parents, famously called across the Commons on 2 September 1939, the day after Germany had invaded Poland, 'Speak for England, Arthur', as the deputy Labour leader, Arthur Greenwood, challenged the prevarication of a prime minister, Neville Chamberlain, still hoping to avoid war. If the English so often get it wrong, one can hardly be surprised that foreigners do too. To give just one example, panels listing Polish battle honours at the tomb of the unknown soldier in Warsaw include the Battle of England in memory of the many Polish pilots killed fighting the *Luftwaffe* in the Battle of Britain in 1940–1.

Kumar (2000 and 2003) has argued that 'English nationalism, past and present, is the nationalism of an imperial state—one that carries the stamp of its imperial past even when the empire has gone' (2000: 577; see also Wellings 2002). Empires have typically been opposed to nationalisms because nation-states threaten their break-up, but they can also 'be the carriers of a certain kind of national identity that gives to the dominant groups a special sense of themselves and their destiny' (2000: 579). These core 'state-bearing' peoples take care not to stress their ethnic identity; instead they identify with 'a state entity that conceives itself as dedicated to some large cause or purpose, religious, cultural, or political' (p. 580). 'The enigma of English nationalism—the puzzling fact that the English do not think they have nationalism, the confusions of English/British, the current difficulties in trying to define or redefine Englishness and English national identity—can best be approached by considering it the nationalism of an imperial state' (Kumar 2003: 34). The mission of the English/British, at least by the nineteenth century, was to civilize and liberalize. This 'missionary nationalism' of British imperialism obscured the national identity of the English. What Kumar underestimates are the consequences of the union with Scotland in 1707. The subduing of English nationalism began in the eighteenth century for without it the union might have broken up. It then continued in the nineteenth century, when the union was secure, partly because the British Empire was always more than the expansion of England (the Scottish participation, in particular, was immense—so much so Michael Fry has recently written of *The Scottish Empire* (2001) and Tom Devine of *Scotland's Empire 1600–1815* (2003)) and partly for the reason Kumar gives, the need to invest Empire with lofty motives. Kumar's notion of a 'dominant group', however, presents difficulties. In the British case, is it just members of the political nation, the English enfranchised and their allies, who have this special sense of the nation and its destiny or does it go beyond them to most, or even all, of the people?

The English case is complicated because there were three phases of empire building. On land, the English domination of Britain began with the incorporation of Cornwall, continued with the incorporation of Wales, and progressed to a union with Scotland in 1707 in which the latter was the junior partner, much less populous, and significantly poorer. Protestantism was the cause that cemented the union with Scotland. 'As against the autocracy and "despotism" of the Catholic monarchies' which led to decay and ruin in Spain and bloody revolution in France, 'the British saw themselves as the people of parliamentary government and peaceful progress ("the Whig interpretation of history")' (Kumar 2000: 589). The union with Ireland in 1801, however, was the prelude to Catholic emancipation in Britain, and the willing incorporation of all Ireland within Britain was never achieved. Instead British overreach led to a process of separation beginning with the establishment of the Irish Free State in 1922.

Overseas the first empire proper in North America and the Caribbean was begun by the English in the sixteenth century and reinforced by Scottish participation after 1707, but suffered a mighty reverse with the loss of America after 1776. The second empire built up in the nineteenth century concentrated on the Antipodes, India, and finally Africa. By the 1920s, this empire covered a fifth of the globe and included a quarter of its people. The Industrial Revolution had made Britain the world's first industrial society, and the Empire enabled Britons to consider themselves the bearers of civilization ('the white man's burden'), the bringers of law and industry, and the teachers of liberty to the backward peoples of Asia and Africa.

Niall Ferguson (2003) argues that the Empire all too often did not civilize and liberalize—its mission according to Kumar—especially early on, but in the nineteenth century it did pioneer global free trade and liberal capitalism, it did spread the idea of parliamentary democracy around the globe, it did give the world English as a lingua franca, and it did invest heavily in a global communications network. Ferguson, a Scot, refers to all this as anglobalization (with gunboats). Fry and Devine would argue that this belittles the non-English part in it, but it is consistent with an expansion-of-England view of Empire that has always found expression. In 1788 Edmund Burke, an Irishman, for example, opened the trial for misrule of Warren Hastings, the first governor-general of India, and a Scot, with the words, 'I impeach him in the name of the English nation, whose ancient honour he has corrupted' (ibid. 55); and in 1858 David Livingstone, the Scottish missionary, wrote that he hoped to see the establishment of 'an English colony in the healthy highlands of Central Africa' (ibid. 157). The missionary nationalism of the British Empire may have veiled English national identity but it resulted in anglobalization.

By the end of the nineteenth century, the veil was slipping. Kumar describes 'the moment of Englishness' from the mid-nineteenth century to the Great War when a number of developments combined to concentrate attention on specifically English matters of language, literature, and landscape. One was romantic nationalism in Europe. Another was the Whig version of English history that started with the lauding of Saxon liberties and culminated in celebration of the civilizing mission of the largest empire the world had ever seen. A third, conversely, was the refocus on England of little Englanders dismayed by imperial overreach, the costs of Empire, and, in particular, the Boer War. This is the moment when English England secured much of its articulation in literature, music, arts and crafts, and love of the countryside and historic towns. The triumph of the Empire, however, ensured that the stirrings of an English cultural nationalism never spilled over into political demands. What need had the English of an English state when they were the core of the United Kingdom and thus of the British Empire, and when too, as Ben Wellings (2002) has added, the British state continued to be seen as the protector of English liberties?

Anglo-Britain, it is important to stress, has always accommodated large numbers of non-English at all levels of society. Starting with English and Scots — and Welsh whose incorporation within an expanded England never extinguished their Welshness — Britain has always accommodated different ethnicities. There has always been more than one way of being British. The British nation whose formation Colley (1992) describes so brilliantly has always been a civic, not an ethnic, nation. In particular English origins have never mattered much to the English establishment. What has mattered is fitting in. The motto of Winchester School, 'manners maketh man', says it all; learn to behave like a British gentleman and you will be accepted as one. This displacement of English nationalism continued until the last third of the twentieth century. Then, with the Empire finally gone, and industrial supremacy long gone, the development of the Common Market posed the biggest challenge to British self-understanding. This is the context in which Scottish and Welsh nationalisms have grown, but what of the English? Can they remain British — and proud of it? Or will they construct an English ethnicity for the first time? Kumar (2000: 593) wondered whether 'England for the English' might prove a rallying cry, and noted how the Conservative Party of Margaret Thatcher and John Major 'has been beating the English drum, defying Scots nationalists, Europeanists, and multi-culturalists', but acknowledged it was only one possibility. Subsequently, William Hague, successor as Conservative leader to John Major, suggested that only MPs for English constituencies should vote on English laws, and in 2001, Sir Richard Body, a Conservative backbencher, published a book with the very title *England for the English*. Beating the English drum cannot be said, however, to have served the Conservatives well; in the 1997 and 2001 general elections they suffered the two biggest defeats in their history. Significantly the 1999 BSA survey found that only 18 per cent of respondents in England favoured an English parliament (Curtice and Heath 2000: 166).

Kumar's analysis explains why an attachment to Britain might persist longer in England than in Scotland or Wales. The development of British culture has never jarred English sensibilities (as it did the Welsh when threatened with the loss of their language) and the government of Britain has never offended majority political opinion in England (as it did the Scots and the Welsh who never gave majority support to Margaret Thatcher and who found themselves governed between 1979 and 1997 by a Conservative party they massively rejected). In short it has been easier for the English to be British and it is not surprising that many of them still share a construction of England that is Anglo-British.

In their embrace of Britishness, the English have denied themselves many of the signs of Englishness one might otherwise have expected. Very many firms, state organizations, and voluntary associations have been called British, national, or, and this is highly significant, royal. Examples are the British Council, British Airways, the National Health Service, the National Trust, the Royal Mail, and the Royal Society. Interestingly some, like the National Trust, do not operate in Scotland, there being instead a separate National Trust for Scotland. There is also a National Library of Wales, but no English national library, just the British Library; similarly there is a Scottish National Gallery but not an English national gallery, just the National Gallery; and a Museum of Scotland but not an English national museum, just the British Museum. There are also national anthems for Wales (late nineteenth century) and Scotland (recently adopted), but not England; instead the national anthem of the United Kingdom ('God save the Queen') is played. The saints days of Andrew and David are celebrated in Scotland and Wales respectively, but not St George's day in England (despite it also being Shakespeare's birthday); and national flags are commonly flown in Scotland and Wales but, at least before the mid-1990s, the English flag was rarely seen in England except on Anglican churches. (There are, of course, exceptions to the general absence of 'English' organizations—English Heritage, which looks after historic sites, and the English National Opera are two of the most obvious—but the exceptions are relatively few.)

The Empire was fundamental to the formation of Anglo-British England but it should not be supposed that the end of Empire necessarily favours the repudiation of Britishness. The half-century of decolonization from the independence of India in 1948 to the return of Hong Kong to China in 1997 inevitably led to a reassessment of Empire, and that reassessment equally inevitably emphasized the negatives from subjugation and racism to exploitation and plunder. For younger generations, in particular, pride in the Empire has been replaced by shame, distaste, or, perhaps most often, indifference. But the Empire did occasion extraordinary feats of exploration, public administration, civil engineering, and knowledge transfer. The Anglo-British like to think of the Empire as a great undertaking with many commendable features. There are black and Asian British writers who have had positive things to say about it. The sociologist, Harry Goulbourne (1998: 33), says of India for example: 'The massive work the British undertook of laying rails, telegraph poles, and building new institutions for governance must be seen as meaningful achievements once the just anger over colonialism is set aside.' And the achievements were not only infrastructural and governmental. The film director, Hanif Kureishi, tells how, on a visit to Karachi, he met rich and well-educated Pakistanis who were dismayed by the Islamization of their country. For them the positive legacy of the British was not material but

the idea of secular institutions based on reason, not revelation or scripture; the idea that there were no final solutions to human problems; and the idea that the health and vigour of a society was bound up with its ability to tolerate and express a plurality of views on all issues, and that these views would be welcomed. (Kureishi 1989: 281)

How ironic these words are given the experience of many Pakistanis in Britain. It is possible that with decolonization completed, the achievements will again win attention and a more balanced view of Empire prevail. Anglo-Britain is still a construction many people can be expected to remain proud of.

3 Little England

Anglo-British England has always looked beyond itself to the Empire, to world trade, and to power and influence abroad—to ventures in which the British rule, lead, or are at least among the select powers who set the terms. From the late eighteenth century onwards, however, there have also always been supporters of another England that turns her back on these imperial and imperious ambitions. The terms 'little England' and 'little Englanders' date, according to the *Oxford Dictionary*, only from 1884 and 1895 respectively, and they referred originally to the anti-imperialism of those opposed to the scramble for Africa. Critics of the Boer War were soon to express similar sentiments: G. K. Chesterton, for example, asked, in a volume entitled *England: A Nation*, 'Is there anyone today who can reasonably doubt that what led us into error in our recent South African politics was precisely our Imperialism, and not our Nationalism?' (in Oldershaw 1904: 38). There is a similar claim to know the will of the silent majority in Chesterton's *The Secret People* (1915):

> Smile at us, pay us, pass us; but do not quite forget.
> For we are the people of England, that have never spoken yet.

But anti-imperialism in Britain is, as the historian A. J. P. Taylor (1954) documented, as old as the British Empire itself. One reason for this is, in Richard Gott's (1989: 91) words, 'the ancestral belief that foreign adventures tend to stifle the spirit of domestic reform'. Another, articulated by J. A. Hobson, is that imperialism leads to under-investment at home and wars to protect investments abroad; in both respects, workers at home pay the price (cf. Green and Taylor 1989). A third is repugnance at the presumption of those who dictate to others. The playwright J. B. Priestley (1934), for example, declared his love for 'little England' and his dislike of 'Big Englanders' whom he saw as 'red-faced, loud-voiced fellows, wanting to go and boss everybody about all over the world' (in Giles and Middleton 1995: 26). A fourth is the reluctance of mothers to lose their sons to foreign wars.

From the late 1960s onwards, what had historically been a left-radical stance found favour with the radical right. The first object of dismay and unease, fear and loathing, was not the Empire but the Empire striking back in the guise of 'coloured' immigration. The England of white Britons hostile to black and Asian Britons and now to economic migrants and asylum seekers is also a Little England. It is intolerant of cultural difference and resentful of black and Asian Britons who it accuses of taking jobs, housing, and welfare benefits which should have gone to whites and of not assimilating to (a supposedly homogenous) white British culture. Not all little Englanders are racists but most racists are little Englanders. The second object of distaste and resentment was the project that succeeded Empire, known first as the Common Market, then the European Community, and latterly the European

190 | SPEAKING FOR ENGLAND

Union. The main problem with Europe was that it was run by Continentals, principally an alliance of French and Germans. It could not be bent to Britain's will and, though the single market was welcome to Margaret Thatcher, the ever-closer union proclaimed by the founding Treaty of Rome was not. There have been two responses to this on the right. One is to look west to America. The other is to look inwards and seek disengagement from grand and expensive international ventures which, the complaint goes, compromise Britain's sovereignty and do not serve its interests. These retreatists have repeatedly been condemned as little Englanders.

In December 1989, the former Conservative cabinet minister Norman Tebbit declared that 'most people in Britain did not want to live in a multicultural, multiracial society, but it has been foisted on them' (*Evening Standard*, 21 December 1989). In April the following year he proposed a cricket test to establish the loyalty to Britain of black and Asian immigrants of whatever generation. They should, Tebbit argued, support England, not their family's country of origin, when England played test cricket and one-day internationals against the West Indies, India, or Pakistan. Few did. A month later he combined opposition to immigrants with hostility to the European Community.

In recent years our sense of insularity and nationality has been bruised by large waves of immigrants resistant to absorption, some defiantly claiming a right to superimpose their culture, even their law, upon the host community. All this in the era when the great Euro legal and cultural magimixer of Brussels is trying to blend us into a Continental culture, abusing our linguistic heritage with crude Eurospeak ... (Tebbit, in *The Field*, May 1990, quoted in J. Solomos 2004: 219)

As for moves towards monetary union and a common currency, he continued, they revealed the Deutsches Bundesbank to be the peacetime successor to the wartime Panzer. Out of office following the general election of 1997, Tebbit returned to the attack on multiculturalism.

Multiculturalism is a divisive force. One cannot uphold two sets of ethics or be loyal to two nations, any more than a man can have two masters. It perpetuates ethnic divisions because nationality is in the long-term more about culture than about ethnics. Youngsters of all races born here should be taught that British history is their history, or they will forever be foreigners holding British passports and this kingdom will become a Yugoslavia. (Tebbit, reported in *The Guardian*, 8 October 1997; quoted in Solomos 2004: 219)

Commenting on immigration in 1968 Enoch Powell, classicist and more an Anglo-Briton than a Little Englander, had looked ahead to a chilling prospect; 'I seem to see "the River Tiber foaming with much blood" ' (*The Observer*, 21 April 1968). Three decades on Norman Tebbit summoned up a prospect more contemporary but equally dreadful—another Yugoslavia.

'Little England' and 'little Englanders' have mostly been pejorative terms, but the denial of foreign engagements to which they refer still often has its appeal. Eurobarometers, for example, repeatedly reveal that the people of Britain are the least likely to identify with the European Union and the most opposed to adoption of the euro of all the citizenries of the member states (see Ch. 7).[8] The reluctance of so many in Britain to accept the pooling of sovereignty is reinforced by their perception of the EU's democratic deficit. Globalization is also more often seen as a threat than an opportunity. Additionally, there are those who reject Britain's international military pretensions as exemplified in Kuwait, the Balkans, Afghanistan, and now Iraq. Little England can be smugly self-regarding, suspicious of foreigners, hostile to immigrants, even downright racist, but it can also display more positive qualities such as humility and humanity, rather than presumption and domination ('who are we to tell others?'), and contentment and reliability. There is a recurrent expression of Little Englandism, both nostalgic and mocking as Michael Frayn has pointed out, in the writings of Alan Bennett (see Edemariam 2004). In *Forty Years On* (1969), for example, a minor southern public school serves, the playright says, as 'a loose metaphor for England'. In one scene, its headmaster posts this notice about England. 'To let: A valuable site at the cross-roads of the world. At present on offer to European clients. Outlying portions of the estate already disposed of to sitting tenants. Of some historical and period interest. Some alterations and improvements necessary.'

4 Cosmopolitan England

Having interviewed seven women plucked from *Who's Who?*, June Edmunds and Bryan Turner (2001: 83) claim to have identified a cosmopolitan English nationalism among 'the post-war elite generation of women'. This nationalism is said to be benign in that it is open (e.g. tolerant of Welsh/Scottish nationalism), cosmopolitan (e.g open to European integration), ironic (e.g. aware of the contingency of national identity), feminine (e.g. pacifist), and creative (Englishness is to be rebuilt around values of openness). By contrast malign Englishness is closed (e.g. resentful of Scottish/Welsh nationalism), insular (e.g. threatened by European identity), earnest (e.g. sees national identity as 'sacred'/in the blood), masculine (e.g. aggressive), and reactive (nostalgically defends traditional Englishness) (p. 93). Few studies could be more tendentious—Curtice and Heath's (2000) survey evidence shows, for example, that there is little resentment at Scottish and Welsh devolution in England—but it would be a pity if it discredited the idea of a cosmopolitan Englishness. My construction of a cosmopolitan England is also open and arguably ironic but it is ungendered and, like the other three Englands, it has both light and dark, benign and malign, sides.

Where English England is inward- and backward-looking, and Little England is contemporary but inward, cosmopolitan England is outward-looking and contemporary in its orientation. It acknowledges not just the diversification of the people—particularly that legacy of the Empire, citizens (whose forebears are) of black or Asian origin—but also the enrichment of its economy and culture from sources abroad whether carried by immigrants or transmitted by trade or the media. It looks out not just to the former Empire but crucially to Europe, America, and the world. It thus represents a new version of an old story. Winder (2004) recalls how Britain, most often England, has for centuries benefited from the rich talents, scarce skills, and cheap labour of successive immigrations even though there are typically many English at the time who have deplored them as threats to English culture and to the profits and jobs of English men and women, and there are many immigrants who have met with racist prejudice and discrimination and some who have suffered physical violence. French Huguenots, Germans, Jews, Italians, Irish, Chinese, Poles, and others in the past, West Indians, Indians, Pakistanis, Bengalis, East African Asians, West Africans, and others since the Second World War are all part of the same story of entry into the fabric of English life whatever the odds. Those comfortable in Cosmopolitan England are quite capable of recognizing this and will find Winder's title, *Bloody Foreigners*, indiscriminate and anachronistic. Too many of who they value, too much of what they value, are of foreign provenance for it to ring true. But this is not to say that all who are foreign and all that is foreign is valued. It is to say that Cosmopolitan England is capable of making relatively sophisticated choices.

That many black and Asian *British* identify themselves as such diverts attention from the very different ethnic compositions of England, Scotland, and Wales. The 2001 census recorded the non-white population of England as 9.0 per cent of the whole compared with 2.1 per cent of the population of Wales, and 2.0 per cent of the population of Scotland.[9] The English figure covered the very big variations from 28.8 per cent in Greater London to 0.7 per cent in Cumbria discussed in Ch. 2. This uneven distribution of the ethnic minority population of England is significant in so far as multiculturalism is consistent with the daily experience of most people in Inner London, but not that of most people in, say, Devon and Cornwall or Norfolk (cf. Younge 2000). Politicians and media commentators based in London—now, it is claimed, the most ethnically diverse city in Europe—do not always remember that. Mike Phillips and Trevor Phillips (1998) have subtitled their book *Windrush* about the post-war migration and settlement of West Indians *The Irresistible Rise of Multi-Racial Britain*, but the story as they tell it is very much a London one. Cosmopolitan England is ethnically diverse but it is not equally diverse everywhere.

Cosmopolitan England is culturally diverse. It endorses multiculturalism in principle, but it acknowledges that there are necessarily limits to it in practice. Everyone needs to be able to speak English as the common language, must respect the law, and acknowledge the equal rights of men and women. The diversity of cultures has thus to be accommodated within a common culture. Recognizing this Bhikhu Parekh (2000*b*) refers to Britain as a community of communities. This implies that everyone is a member of one or more sub-communities of Britain, but the attachment of individuals to the particular cultural and religious communities in which they were more or less tightly brought up varies greatly. Hybridity and cultural exchange are also commonplace. It would thus be better to say simply that Britain is a community within which there are many differences of culture, that these differences are sometimes themselves community-based, and that England is more diverse in terms of the recent origins and current cultures of its people than Scotland or Wales. There is also nothing new in dual loyalties. Neither official Britain nor Cosmopolitan England expects its citizens to have loyalties exclusively to Britain or England. Britain, significantly, has long allowed dual citizenship when many other countries have not.

Multiculturalism is not easy to achieve and sustain. In requiring integration, it rejects both assimilation ('they' must become like 'us') and separation ('we' have nothing to do with 'them'). The history of immigration and 'race relations' in England is much too big, complex and multi-faceted a subject to review in a few paragraphs here.[10] It is, however, salutary to remember that it has been punctuated by riots including those in Nottingham (1958), Notting Hill in London (1958), St Paul's in Bristol (1980), Brixton in London (1981), Toxteth in Liverpool (1981), Handsworth in Birmingham (1985), Brixton (1985), Broadwater Farm Estate in Tottenham, London (1985), Bradford (1995, 2001), Burnley (2001), Leeds (2001), and Oldham (2001), and that a recurrent theme has been the tensions generated by the activities of political parties of the extreme right such as the National Front and the British National Party. There has been racism and discrimination on a large scale, though most commentators agree that over the decades both have reduced significantly and that enough black and Asian Britons have now made conspicuous successes of their business, professional, and local community lives to inspire others to follow them. Does this augur well for the future of Britain in general and England in particular?

The Parekh Report (2000a) on *The Future of Multi-Ethnic Britain* has very many well-considered things to say about ethnic relations in Britain but it is never entirely sure what Britain is. In particular it seems to say that the imperial and colonial associations of 'Britain' make any conception of a post-imperial Britain a non-starter. 'Britishness, as much as Englishness, has systematic, largely unspoken, racial connotations. Whiteness nowhere features as an explicit condition of being British, but it is widely understood that Englishness, and therefore by extension Britishness, is racially coded. "There ain't no black in the Union Jack", it has been said' (Parekh et al. 2000a: 38). If this were the whole story it is hard to see why black and Asian citizens should think of themselves as Black British, Indian British, or British Muslims when as, the report concedes (in the previous paragraph!), many do. It leaves those white British who cannot identify with Scotland or Wales without a national identity untainted by racial coding (even though only 12 per cent of Curtice and Heath's respondents said that to be English it matters a great deal to be white.) Both British and English seem to be ruled out. No wonder the press criticisms were fierce. No one argues that the French, Spanish, Portuguese, and Dutch can no longer embrace their identities because of their countries' imperial histories. No one says Americans should no longer be American in view of their forebears' extermination of native peoples and enslavement of blacks, or that Germans cannot be Germans because there cannot be a post-Nazi Germany. The reason why many black and Asian Britons increasingly think of themselves as British, often hyphenated British but nonetheless British, is that it means something to them. Their families would not be in Britain—usually England—had it not been for the *British* Empire. West Indians, for example, arrived after the Second World War already thinking of themselves as British because that is what they had been taught in school and that is where many volunteers had served in the armed forces during the war (Phillips and Phillips 1998). Some black and Asian British can and will identify with elements of England and Englishness—black and Asian successes in English contexts, footballers and cricketers playing for England for example, will ensure that—but Britain from its beginnings in 1707 has always accommodated alternative ways of being British and British is likely to remain a more capacious and accommodating identity (cf. Colley, 1999). Parekh et al. offer the white English nothing and, by repeating the Paul Gilroy (1987) quip that 'there ain't no black in the Union Jack', they give black and Asian fellow citizens the wrong steer. Imagining a new Britain, as Yasmin Alibhai-Brown (2000) urges her readers to, would seem a more realistic and constructive option.

It is significant that most Muslims in Britain prefer to describe themselves as British Muslims rather than Muslim British. 'Muslim' is then the primary identity and 'British' the qualifier. It is a reminder that the salience of national identity compared with other identities is not the same for everyone. The question has also arisen whether all Muslims in Britain want integration and whether all those who do want it can secure it. It is a question prompted by 9/11 and the fear in some quarters that there are Muslims in Britain who have nothing but disgust and hatred for a country they believe morally corrupt, a people they regard as worthless infidels, and a government they see bent on wars against Islam. It is also a question raised more temperately by reports on the 2001 riots in northern towns which suggested that Muslim communities were effectively segregated in particular localities with very poor housing and that this separated world made it hard for those who wanted to move out and broaden their horizons to do so and easy for those who did not, and who did not want others to either, to succeed.

In this connection it is instructive to consider the case of Oldham, not because it saw the worst rioting in 2001—it did not—but because the 1991 census had indicated that it was the most ethnically segregated borough in the UK. It also had the second largest percentage of pre-Second World War houses (after Liverpool) and some of the most deprived wards in Britain. The report of the independent local inquiry on the May 2001 riot in Oldham, the council and police response, and later work on the future of the town, all recognize the segregation, the complex combination of general and local factors responsible for it, and the need to counter it.[11] Immigrants from Pakistan and Bangladesh who came over in the 1960s and early 1970s to work the unwanted night shift in the cotton mills had bought cheap, old, small houses, turning some localities into Pakistani and Bangladeshi enclaves, rather than wait for council housing. When the mills closed Pakistani unemployment rose dramatically but it was very hard for the Pakistanis and Bangladeshis to sell up and move on as there was not much of a market for their houses, they did not have skills in demand elsewhere, and those who spoke little or no English—often wives brought over from the subcontinent in arranged marriages—did not want to leave the ethnic enclave. There have been publicly funded initiatives to upgrade housing in particular localities—sometimes the result of successful bids to competitive government schemes—but poor whites on run-down council estates have resented them when it has been an Asian locality and not their own that has benefited. The post-riot reports advocate the need to respect and value cultural diversity but reject multiculturalism without interaction. The far-right British National Party had been vocal and visible in the town. It insisted multiculturalism could never work and won 13.6 per cent of the vote in the two Oldham constituencies in the May 2001 general election. By contrast the reports are confident that multiculturalism can and does work—but only in so far as it takes the form, not of self-segregation and separate development as has evolved in Oldham, but of an interculturalism that affords members of different communities opportunities to interact and learn from each other. To this end, efforts are being made to extend mixed housing, twin schools, facilitate mixed further education and vocational training, and regenerate shopping and leisure facilities to make them attractive to all. The minimum requirement for these to succeed is that everyone be able to speak English well and that those Oldhamers of Pakistani and Bangladeshi origin who cannot, more often women, be enabled to do so by the provision of classes and family support.

In 2004 multiculturalism was questioned from the left and from the Commission for Racial Equality as never before. The debate began in late

February when David Goodhart (2004: 24) argued that progressives want 'plenty of both solidarity (high social cohesion and generous welfare paid out of a progressive tax system) and diversity (equal respect for a wide range of peoples, values and ways of life)' but there comes a point beyond which these are inversely related. The volume of asylum seekers threatened to take us beyond that point. Newspapers picked up on Goodhart, for and against, and the gloves were off. Then Trevor Philips, the co-author of *Windrush* and head of the Commission for Racial Equality, who had called Goodhart 'racist', changed sides in an interview in *The Times*, 3 April 2004, and argued that multiculturalism was out of date. It encouraged separateness when the need now was to re-emphasize 'common values . . . the common currency of the English language, honouring the culture of these islands, like Shakespeare and Dickens'. He continued the unity-in-diversity theme in a speech reprinted in the Commission's magazine, the appropriately named *Connections* (Phillips 2004), which also mentioned devolution. Again debate was fierce and Muslims bridled at any suggestion that they were the separatists. Both Goodhart and Tebbit commended Phillips's change of course. The view seemed to prevail that multiculturalism could issue in a dangerous separateness though it need not, that all responsible citizens should guard against this, that more attention to common values and practices was overdue, that the problem of the radicalized minority of young Muslims who rejected Britishness could no longer be ignored, that the ceremonies to mark the award of British citizenship recently introduced by the Home Secretary, David Blunkett, were a good idea, and that it was time to take forward a Britain of which all citizens would be proud. Some rebalancing was in order.

What impact has the debate had on Muslims in Britain? There is a partial answer in an ICM survey of 500 randomly selected Muslims reported in *The Guardian*, 30 November 2004. In answer to the question about the integration of the Muslim community into mainstream British culture, 40 per cent replied that it needed to do more, 32 per cent that it had got it about right, 20 per cent that it had integrated too much already, and 8 per cent did not know. Forty-four per cent thought their position and that of their family would get better, 20 per cent thought it would stay the same, 33 per cent that it would get worse, and 3 per cent did not know. Only 6 per cent said they had no non-Muslim close friends. Fifty-three per cent of men, but only 14 per cent of women, said they would consider marrying a non-Muslim. Only 11 per cent agreed that it is acceptable for religious or political groups to use violence for political ends, whilst 69 per cent agreed with the mosques that Muslims should inform on people who are involved or connected with terrorist activities. This is particularly significant in that only 37 per cent agreed that the Muslim Council of Britain generally reflected their views. Sixty-one per cent supported the introduction of Shariah courts in Britain to resolve civil cases within the Muslim community so long as the penalties do not contravene British law, 88 per cent agreed that schools and workplaces should accommodate Muslim prayer times as part of their normal working day, and 46 per cent of men and 58 per cent of women said they prayed five times a day, and 81 per cent wanted a new law to make incitement to religious hatred a criminal offence. With respect to integration the overall picture is mixed. The 40 per cent who would like more integration is greater than the 20 per cent who would prefer less, and the 44 per cent who thought their family's prospects would get better is greater than the 33 per cent who thought they would worsen. But the majority support for Sharia courts for civil offences within the Muslim community is separatist and that for a new law against religious hatred is defensive. For the rest the exceptional religiosity of Muslims is obvious. In sum, the evidence for integration and accommodatability is greater than the opposite.

The rediscovery of the English flag is interesting for its connection with events in which large-scale black participation was very visible. In 1999 a MORI poll reported that 'In England, 88% identify with the Union Jack and only 38% with St George's Cross; but in Wales the dragon outscores the Union Jack by 85% to 55%, and while 75% of Scots identify with the Saltire only 49% do with the Union Jack' (MORI 2000). This may be changing. In the summer of 2002 the Queen's Golden Jubilee was quickly followed by the football World Cup and then the Commonwealth Games in Manchester. There was more enthusiasm for the jubilee celebrations in England than elsewhere in Britain and much flying of the union flag. But there was also huge interest in the fortunes of the English football team and English flags appeared on homes, shops, and vehicles on a scale not remotely seen before. Interest in a Commonwealth Games in England, the first since 1932, and the success of the English team there, maintained the focus on England as distinct from Britain. And in the World Cup and the Commonwealth Games the proportion of blacks in the English teams was large. In the Manchester games, black English winner after black English winner in the athletics was roared on by a capacity crowd in party mood. Michael Billig (1995) has argued that the banal nationalism of flags and symbols serves to reinforce a national consciousness regardless of the commitments of citizens exposed to them. There is still much more banal Scottish nationalism in Edinburgh than there is banal English nationalism in London, but the banal English nationalism of the Cross of St George was much more evident throughout England in 2002 than anyone I have asked can remember in his or her lifetime, and in circumstances that included enthusiastic white celebration of black success. Flying the English flag is becoming commonplace.

Asian Britons, in contrast to black Britons, were conspicuous by their absence in the England football team and the England teams in many of the biggest spectator sports in the Commonwealth games, which is why the celebrations which greeted the success of Amir Khan, the 17-year-old boxer from Bolton who won a silver medal at the 2004 Olympics in Athens, and whose father supports him always wearing a union-flag jacket, are worth noting. It is not just black and Asian Britons who have made England more cosmopolitan, however. There are also increasing numbers of citizens of other EU countries as well as Americans, Australians, and numerous others—some of them managers of the vast number of firms that are foreign-owned. The cosmopolitanism of England shows in the restaurants in every town, in popular culture from television to music, even in its domesticity—showers now, not baths; duvets, not blankets. Its top football teams used to have lots of Scots, now they have Continentals and Latin Americans; and even so traditional a competition as the FA Cup is regarded by all fans these days as of less significance than the European Champions League. The English also holiday abroad in huge numbers, though most are still monoglot.

In *The Guardian* article with which I began this chapter Hunt complained that no one in Labour government circles was speaking for England with the clarity and confidence needed to extinguish 'white van man xenophobia'. This is a serious omission which the former home secretary, David Blunkett (2005) is beginning to remedy by drawing upon the work of academics who have pointed the way to a progressive articulation of English national identity. Though still potent, the residues of the late-Victorian and Edwardian moment of Englishness are not enough to define today's England—urban and suburban, post-industrial, and multicultural—whether the United Kingdom continues or not. After casting a critical eye on recent debates, Kumar opts for a Cosmopolitan England as both the likeliest and the most desirable possibility. England has always benefited from the diversity of its people and has, over the centuries, been remarkably open to infusions of new talents and sensibilities. It might yet 'show what a truly civic nationalism can look like' (2003: 273). The social historian Robert Colls in his book *Identity of England* (2002) expresses a similar hope. Colls reaches four main conclusions. First, the crown in parliament can no longer represent the nation, the state is too centralized, and the old party politics is failing. Second, the nation is diverse and plural. Third, popular historical memory of who we were impedes adaptation to the European Union, globalization, multiculturalism, and who we must become. Fourth, English England is no longer sufficient, but 'the English have never only been right, tight little islanders' and can repeat that 'extraordinary openness to the cultures of other peoples' that Kumar also lauds (2002: 380). What Colls does not remind us is that the right, tight little islanders gibe was made by the Scottish nationalist poet Hugh MacDiarmid in 1949. England, he said, was finished as a world power and the English oppressors of the colonies and of Scotland 'must be forced back upon their own "right little, tight little island"—or rather that part of it which is their own ...' (p. 205). The gibe is bound to be a sore point with Colls, a good citizen of Leicester. Scotland is 98.0 per cent white; Leicester is 36.1 per cent non-white and is projected to become the first major city in Europe with a non-white majority by 2012.[12]

A cosmopolitan England could accumulate more differences than are accommodatable, more communities than could learn how to live together. It could be so open to new cultural influences as to be disorienting to its citizens and unsure what it values. It is more likely, however, that its future vibrancy will depend on the combination of (1) its understanding of its own past, (2) the legacy of Empire, (3) its tradition of looking to America, and (4) recognition that its future must lie within the European Union.

Conclusions

It is not easy to address the English question because there are available to us different representations of England and Englishness. Two of the four distinguished in this chapter also blur the distinction between England and Britain. Different citizens will, collectively and individually, reproduce and transform different combinations of all four of them in different parts of the country at different times. No one can predict quite how this will work out, but I do expect more of the English to remain more British than English than I expect the Welsh to remain more British than Welsh and, especially, the Scots to remain more British than Scottish, I do expect further constitutional evolution in Britain to generate more searches for Englishness but the more sophisticated the searches the less likely they are to prompt claims for ethnic purity or cultural exclusiveness, and I do think identification with the cosmopolitanism of England will increase but the very uneven cosmopolitanization of the regions will continue to complicate the collective representation of England.

NOTES

1 The question of the English regions is discussed in the next chapter.

2 Others include Giles and Middleton (1995); Haseler (1996); Aslet (1997); Hastings (1997); Matless (1998); Paxman (1998); Davey (1999): Easthope (1999); Heffer (1999); Langlands (1999); Wood (1999); Chen and Wright (2000); Curtice and Heath (2000); Kumar (2000); Wadham-Smith and Clift (2000); Body (2001); Edmunds and Turner (2001); Linsell (2001); Ackroyd (2002); Corbett, Holt, and Russell (2002) and Wellings (2002).

3 On the Moreno question, see the first section of Ch. 1.

4 On the early history of England, I have made use of Morgan (1984); Elton (1992); Strong (1996); Davies (1999); Schama (2000); and Cunliffe et al. (2001). On the early history of English, I have used mainly Crystal (1995), but also Bragg (2003).

5 King Harold of England and William of Normandy were distantly related, each descendants of a family from Denmark. Normandy had been invaded and settled by Vikings led by William's grandfather; the

name they gave their new land reflects their northern origins. That the Normans had had less cultural impact on the land they settled than their counterparts across the Channel is indicated by language. Harold spoke English; Guillaume spoke French.

6 I have often wondered, for example, where the expression 'the peculiarities of the English' comes from. E. P. Thompson's (1965) well-known essay of that title does not enquire. Kumar (2003: 107) might have supplied the answer when quoting the sixteenth century dramatist, John Lyly: 'so tender a care hath [God] always had of England, as of a new Israel, his chosen and peculiar people'.

7 The life and death of Brooke and other war poets is often taken to stand for the vibrant promise and appalling waste of the generation that died in the trenches of the Western Front. Nigel Jones (1999) argues that in the process the real Brooke, sometimes attractive, sometimes less so, has been mythologized.

8 British attitudes to Europe are discussed more fully in the next chapter.

9 All 2001 census figures have been obtained via the websites of National Statistics (www.statistics.gov.uk/census2001) and the General Register Office for Scotland (www.gro-scotland.gov.uk/census2001), accessed 1 June 2005.

10 A vast literature on migrants and race relations in Britain includes Rex and Moore (1967), Deakin (1970), Rex and Tomlinson (1979), Banton (1983: ch. 11), Husband (1987), Skellington (1996), Spencer (1997), Blackstone, Parekh, and Sanders (1998), Goulbourne (1998), Phillips and Phillips (1998), Alibhai-Brown (2000), Parekh (2000*a*, *b*), Pilkington (2003), Solomos (2004), and Winder (2004).

11 Oldham Metropolitan Borough Council, Greater Manchester Police, and the Greater Manchester Police Authority set up an independent panel to report on the riot and make recommendations. The panel produced the *Oldham Independent Review:*

One Oldham One Future in December 2001. The council and police response to this and to national reports on all the 2001 riots, entitled *Oldham Together: The Outlook's Bright*, was published in June 2002. The council and the North-West Development Agency commissioned further work on the future of Oldham, which led to *Oldham Beyond: A Vision for the Borough* of Oldham in April 2004. I am grateful to Oldham Metropolitan Borough Council for making all these documents available to me.

12 The projection is mentioned in 'All Together', an article by Michelle Obasi in a promotional supplement to *The Guardian*, 14 November 2003, entitled 'Revealing Leicester'. Madeleine Redway, public relations manager for Leicester City Council, informs me that it originated within the council and was first published in an article by Jonathan Guthrie in *The Financial Times*, 7 December 2000.

REFERENCES

ACKROYD, PETER (2002), *Albion: The Origins of the English Imagination* (London: Chatto & Windus).

ALIBHAI-BROWN, YASMIN (2000), *Who Do We Think We Are? Imagining the New Britain* (London: Allen Lane).

ASLET, CLIVE (1997), *Anyone for England: A Search for British Identity* (London: Little, Brown (UK)).

BAGEHOT, WALTER (1867), *The English Constitution* (London: Watts, 1964).

BALDWIN, STANLEY (1926), *On England and Other Addresses* (London: Hodder & Stoughton).

BANTON, MICHAEL (1983), *Racial and Ethnic Competition* (Cambridge: Cambridge University Press), ch. 11.

BARKER, ERNEST (1947)(ed.), *The Character of England* (Oxford: Clarendon).

—— (1948), *Traditions of Civility: Eight Lectures* (Cambridge: Cambridge University Press).

BARNES, JULIAN (1998), *England, England* (London: Cape).

BATES, STEPHEN (2004), *A Church at War: Anglicans and Homosexuality* (London: IB Tauris).

BEDE, The Venerable (731), *The Ecclesiastical History of the English People*, ed. JUDITH MCCLURE and ROGER COLLINS (Oxford: Oxford University Press, 1994).

BETJEMAN, JOHN [1943], 'Coming home', talk broadcast on BBC Home Service, 25

February 1943, and published in *The Listener*, 11 March 1943, as 'Oh to be in England . . . '. Reprinted in *John Betjeman: Coming Home: An Anthology of His Prose 1920–1977*, ed. CANDIDA LYCETT GREEN (London: Methuen), 137–41.

BILLIG, MICHAEL (1995), *Banal Nationalism* (London: Sage).

BIRLEY, DEREK (1999), *A Social History of English Cricket* (London: Aurum).

BLACKSTONE, TESSA; PAREKH, BHIKHU, and SANDERS, PETER (1998) (eds.), *Race Relations in Britain: A Developing Agenda* (London: Routledge).

BLAKE, WILLIAM (1927), *Blake's Poems and Prophecies* (London: Dent).

BLUNKETT, DAVID (2005) 'A new England: an English identity within Britain', speech to the Institute for Public Policy Research, London, 14 March 2005.

BODY, RICHARD (2001), *England for the English* (London: NEP).

BRACEWELL, MICHAEL (1998), *England is Mine: Pop Life in Albion from Wilde to Goldie* (London: Flamingo).

BRAGG, MELVYN (2003), *The Adventure of English 500AD to 2000: The Biography of a Language* (London: Hodder & Stoughton).

CHANDOS, JOHN (1984), *Boys Together: English Public Schools 1800–1864* (London: Hutchinson).

CHEN, SELINA, and WRIGHT, TONY (2000) (eds.), *The English Question* (London: Fabian Society).

CLAYTON, MICHAEL (2004), *Endangered Species: Foxhunting — The History, the Passion and the Fight for Survival* (Shrewsbury: Swan Hill Press).

COLLEY, LINDA (1992), *Britons: Forging the Nation 1707–1837* (New Haven Conn.: Yale University Press).

_____ (1999), 'Britishness in the 21st Century', Millenium Lecture delivered at 10 Downing Street, 8 December 1999, <www.number-10.gov.uk/output/Page 3049.asp>, accessed 1 June 2005.

COLLS, ROBERT (2002), *The Identity of England* (Oxford: Oxford University Press).

COLLS, ROBERT, and DODD, PHILIP (1986) (eds.), *Englishness: Politics and Culture 1880–1920* (Beckenham: Croom Helm).

CORBETT, DAVID P.; HOLT, YSANNE; and RUSSELL, FIONA (2002) (eds.), *The Geographies of Englishness: Landscape and the National Past 1880–1940* (New Haven Conn.: Yale University Press).

CRICK, BERNARD (1991), 'The English and the British', in B. CRICK (ed.), *National Identities: the Constitution of the United Kingdom* (Oxford: Blackwell), 90–104.

CRYSTAL, DAVID (1995), *The Cambridge Encyclopedia of the English Language* (Cambridge: Cambridge University Press).

CUNLIFFE, BARRY; BARTLETT, ROBERT; MORRILL, JOHN; BRIGGS, ASA; and BOURKE, JOANNA (2001) (eds.), *The Penguin Atlas of British and Irish History* (London: Penguin).

CURTICE, JOHN, and HEATH, ANTHONY (2000), 'Is the English lion about to roar? National identity after devolution', in R. JOWELL et al. (eds.), *British Social Attitudes, 17th Report: Focusing on Diversity* (London: Sage), 155–74.

DAVEY, KEVIN (1999), *English Imaginaries: Six Studies in Anglo-British Modernity* (London: Lawrence & Wishart).

DAVIES, NORMAN (1999), *The Isles: A History* (London: Macmillan).

DAVIES, REES R. (1999), *The First English Empire: Power and Identities in the British*

Isles 1093–1343 (Oxford: Oxford University Press).

DEAKIN, NICHOLAS (1970), *Colour, Citizenship and British Society* (London: Panther).

DEFOE, DANIEL (1997), *The True-Born Englishman and Other Writings* (London: Penguin).

DE-LA-NOY, MICHAEL (1993), *The Church of England: A Portrait* (London: Simon & Schuster).

DEVINE, T. M. (2003), *Scotland's Empire 1600–1815* (London: Penguin—Allen Lane).

DODD, PHILIP (1986), 'Englishness and the national culture', in Colls and Dodd (eds.) 1–28.

—— (1995), 'A mongrel nation', *New Statesman*, 24 February, 26–7.

EASTHOPE, ANTHONY (1999), *Englishness and National Culture* (London: Routledge).

EDEMARIAM, AIDA (2004), 'The Guardian profile: Alan Bennett', *The Guardian*, 14 May 2004.

EDMUNDS, JUNE, and TURNER, BRYAN S. (2001), 'The re-invention of England? Women and "cosmopolitan" Englishness', *Ethnicities*, 1: 83–108.

ELIOT, T. S. (1948), *Notes towards the Definition of Culture* (London: Faber).

ELTON, GEOFFREY (1992), *The English* (Oxford: Blackwell).

FERGUSON, NIALL (2003), *Empire: How Britain Made the Modern World* (London: Allen Lane).

FRY, MICHAEL (2001), *The Scottish Empire* (Phantassie, East Lothian: Tuckwell, and Edinburgh: Birlinn).

GERVAIS, DAVID (1993), *Literary Englands: Versions of 'Englishness' in Modern Writing* (Cambridge: Cambridge University Press).

GILES, JUDY, and MIDDLETON, TIM (1995) (eds.), *Writing Englishness 1900–1950: An Introductory Sourcebook on National Identity* (London: Routledge).

GILROY, PAUL (1987), *There Ain't No Black in the Union Jack: The Cultural Politics of Race and Nation* (London: Hutchinson).

GIROUARD, MARK (1975), *Victorian Pubs* (London: Studio Vista).

GOTT, RICHARD (1989), 'Little Englanders', in R. SAMUEL (ed.), *Patriotism: The Making and Unmaking of British National Identity*, i. *History and Politics* (London: Routledge), 90–102.

GOULBOURNE, HARRY (1998), *Race Relations in Britain since 1945* (Basingstoke: Macmillan).

GREEN, E., and TAYLOR, M. (1989), 'Further thoughts on Little Englandism', in R. SAMUEL (ed.), *Patriotism: The Making and Unmaking of British National Identity*, i. *History and Politics* (London: Routledge), 103–9.

GOODHART, DAVID (2004), 'Discomfort of strangers', *The Guardian*, 24 February. Reprinted in full from the February 2004 number of *Prospect* Magazine.

HARDING, ALAN (2000), *Is There a 'Missing Middle' in English Governance?* (London: New Local Government Network).

HARVIE, CHRISTOPHER (1991), 'English regionalism: the dog that never barked', in B. CRICK (ed.), *National Identities: the Constitution of the United Kingdom* (Oxford: Blackwell), 105–18.

HASELER, STEPHEN (1996), *The English Tribe: Identity, Nation and Europe* (Basingstoke: Macmillan).

HASTINGS, ADRIAN (1997), *The Construction of Nationhood: Ethnicity, Religion and Nationalism* (Cambridge: Cambridge University Press).

HEFFER, SIMON (1999), *Nor Shall My Sword: The Reinvention of England* (London: Weidenfeld & Nicolson).

HOSKINS, W. G. (1955), *The Making of the English Landscape* (London: Hodder & Stoughton).

HUSBAND, CHRISTOPHER (1987) (ed.), *'Race' in Britain*, 2nd edn. (London: Hutchinson).

INGRAMS, RICHARD (1989) (ed.), *England: An Anthology* (London: Collins).

JOHNSON, PAUL (1977), 'Education of the establishment', in G. MACDONALD FRASER (ed.), *The World of the Public School* (London: Weidenfeld & Nicolson).

JONES, NIGEL (1999), *Rupert Brooke: Life, Death and Myth* (London: Richard Cohen).

KEYNES, GEOFFREY (1946) (ed.), *The Poetical Works of Rupert Brooke* (London: Faber & Faber).

KUMAR, KRISHAN (2000), 'Nation and Empire: English and British national identity in comparative perspective', *Theory and Society*, 29: 575–608.

——— (2003), *The Making of English National Identity* (Cambridge: Cambridge University Press).

KUREISHI, HANIF (1989), 'London and Karachi', in R. SAMUEL (ed.), *Patriotism: The Making and Unmaking of British National Identity*, ii. *Minorities and Outsiders* (London: Routledge), 270–87.

LANGLANDS, REBECCA (1999), 'Britishness or Englishness? The historical problem of national identity in Britain', *Nations and Nationalism*, 5: 53–69.

LINSELL, T. (2001), *An English Nationalism* (London: Athelney).

LUCAS, JOHN (1990), *England and Englishness: Ideas of Nationhood in English Poetry 1688–1900* (London: Hogarth).

LUNN, KENNETH (1996), 'Reconsidering "Britishness": the construction and significance of national identity in twentieth century Britain', in B. JENKINS and S. SOFOS (eds.), *Nation and Identity in Contemporary Europe* (London: Routledge).

MACDIARMID, HUGH (1949), 'Two Scots who like the English', in A. CALDER, G. MURRAY, and A. RIACH (eds.), *Hugh MacDiarmid, The Raucle Tongue: Hitherto Uncollected Prose* (Manchester: Carcanet, 1998), iii. 202–6.

MACKAY, JANE, and THANE, PAT (1986), 'The Englishwoman', in Colls and Dodd (eds.), 191–229.

MARR, ANDREW (2000), *The Day Britain Died* (London: Profile Books).

MATLESS, DAVID (1998), *Landscape and Englishness* (London: Reaktion Books).

MEDHURST, KENNETH, and MOYSER, GEORGE (1988), *Church and Politics in a Secular Age* (Oxford: Clarendon).

MEE, ARTHUR (1936–42) (ed.), *The King's England*, 41 vols. (London: Hodder & Stoughton).

MORGAN, KENNETH O. (1984) (ed.), *The Oxford Illustrated History of Britain* (London: Oxford University Press).

MORI (2000), 'What is Britishness?', 31 March, <www.mori.com/mrr/2000/c000331.shtml>, accessed 21 June 2005.

MORTON, H. V. (1927), *In Search of England* (London: Methuen).

NAIRN, TOM (1977), *The Break-Up of Britain* (London: Verso).

OLDERSHAW, L. (1904) (ed.), *England: A Nation* (London: R. B. Johnson).

ORWELL, GEORGE (1941), 'England, Your England', in his *The Lion and the Unicorn* (London: Secker & Warburg).

OSMOND, JOHN (1988), *The Divided Kingdom* (London: Constable).

OUSBY, IAN (1990), *The Englishman's England: Taste, Travel and the Rise of Tourism* (Cambridge: Cambridge University Press).

PAREKH, BHIKHU, et al. (2000*a*) *The Future of Multi-Ethnic Britain: The Parekh Report* (London: Profile).

―――― (2000*b*), *Rethinking Multiculturalism: Cultural Diversity and Political Theory* (Basingstoke: Macmillan).

PAXMAN, JEREMY (1998), *The English: A Portrait of a People* (London: Michael Joseph).

PEVSNER, NIKOLAUS (1956), *The Englishness of English Art* (London: The Architectural Press).

PHILLIPS, MIKE, and PHILLIPS, TREVOR (1998), *Windrush: The Irresistible Rise of Multi-Racial Britain* (London: HarperCollins).

PHILLIPS, TREVOR (2004), 'Britishness and the "M" Word', *Connections*, Spring 2004. Accessible on line at <http://www.cre.gov.uk/publs/connections/con_04sp_britishness.html>, accessed 1 June 2005.

PILKINGTON, ANDREW (2003), *Racial Disadvantage and Ethnic Diversity in Britain* (Basingstoke: Palgrave).

PRIESTLEY, J. B. (1934), *English Journey: Being a Rambling but Truthful Account of what One Man Saw* (London: Heinemann).

REX, JOHN, and MOORE, ROBERT (1967), *Race, Community and Conflict: A Study of Sparkbrook* (London: Oxford University Press for the Institute of Race Relations).

―――― and TOMLINSON, SALLY, with HEARNDEN, DAVID, and RATCLIFFE, PETER (1979), *Colonial Immigrants in a British City—A Class Study* (London: Routledge & Kegan Paul).

SCHAMA, SIMON (2000), *A History of Britain, i. At the Edge of the World? 3000BC–AD1603* (London: BBC).

SCHWARZ, BILL (1996) (ed.), *The Expansion of England: Race, Ethnicity and Cultural History* (London: Routledge).

SCRUTON, ROGER (2000), *England: An Elegy* (London: Chatto & Windus).

SEELEY, JOHN R. (1883), *The Expansion of England: Two Courses of Lectures* (London: Macmillan).

SKELLINGTON, RICHARD (1996), *'Race' in Britain Today*, 2nd edn. (London: Sage).

SMITH, GODFREY (1988) (ed.), *The English Reader: An Anthology* (London: Pavilion).

SMITH, MICHAEL A. (1983), 'Social usages of the public drinking house', *British Journal of Sociology*, 34: 367–85.

SOLOMOS, JOHN (2003), *Race and Racism in Britain*, 3rd edn. (Basingstoke: Palgrave).

SPENCER, IAN R. G. (1997), *British Immigration Policy since 1939: The Making of Multi-Racial Britain* (London: Routledge).

STAPLETON, JULIA (1994), *Englishness and the Study of Politics: The Social and Political Thought of Ernest Barker* (Cambridge: Cambridge University Press).

STAUNTON, HOWARD (1865), *The Great Schools of England* (London: Sampson Low, Son, and Marston).

STOKER, GERRY (2000), 'Is regional government the answer to the English question?', in Chen and Wright (eds.), 63–79.

STRICKLAND, PAT, and WOOD, EDWARD (2002) 'The *Regional Assemblies (Preparations) Bill*', House of Commons Research Papers, 02/62.

STRONG, ROY (1996), *The Story of Britain* (London: Hutchinson).

TAYLOR, A. J. P (1954), *The Trouble Makers: Dissent over Foreign Policy 1792–1939* (London: Hamish Hamilton).

TAYLOR, PETER J. (1991), 'The English and their Englishness: "a curiously mysterious, elusive and little understood people" ', *Scottish Geographical Magazine*, 107: 146–61.

THOMPSON, E. P. (1965), 'The Peculiarities of the English', in R. MILIBAND and J. SAVILLE (eds.) *The Socialist Register: 1965* (London: Merlin).

TOMLINSON, B. R. (1982), 'The contraction of England: national decline and the loss of empire', *Journal of Imperial and Commonwealth History*, 11: 58–73.

VAUGHAN, WILLIAM (2002), 'Behind Pevsner: Englishness as an art historical category', in D. CORBETT, P. DAVID, Y. HOLT, and F. RUSSELL (eds.), *The Geographies of Englishness: Landscape and the National Past 1880–1940* (New Haven Conn.: Yale University Press), 347–68.

WADHAM-SMITH, NICK, and CLIFT, NAOMI (2000) (eds.), 'Looking into England', *British Studies Now*, 13 (London: British Council).

WEIGHT, RICHARD (2002), *Patriots: National Identity in Britain 1940–2000* (London: Macmillan).

WELLINGS, BEN (2002), 'Empire-nation: national and imperial discourses in England', *Nations and Nationalism*, 8: 95–109.

WIENER, MARTIN J. (1981), *English Culture and the Decline of the Industrial Spirit 1850–1980* (Cambridge: Cambridge University Press).

WINDER, ROBERT (2004), *Bloody Foreigners: The Story of Immigration to Britain* (London: Little, Brown).

WOOD, MICHAEL (1999), *In Search of England: Journeys into the English Past* (London: Viking).

YOUNG, G. M. (1947), 'Government', in Barker (1947: 85–111).

YOUNGE, GARY (2000), 'On race and Englishness', in Chen and Wright (eds.), 111–16.

| MAP 6.1 | **The English regions** |

NORTH-
EAST

NORTH-
WEST

YORKSHIRE &
THE HUMBER

EAST MIDLANDS

WEST MIDLANDS

EAST OF ENGLAND

LONDON

SOUTH-EAST

SOUTH-WEST

6

The English Regions: Who Cares?

Introduction

This is a book about nations and national identities in Britain, not regions and regional identities in England, but a chapter on the regions of England is in order for three reasons. First, there are some who argue that many who live in England have a weak identification with England the nation because they have a strong identification with their English region of origin or residence (and sometimes, too, a strong identification with Britain). Second, new Labour constitutional reformers viewed elected regional assemblies for England as a necessary complement to devolution to Scotland and Wales. Robert Hazell (2000: 29) agreed with them. 'England is the hole in the devolution settlement. Scotland, Wales and Northern Ireland are to have a stronger political voice, thanks to their new assemblies. The English regions risk losing out in the distribution of government funds, the bids for European funding programmes and the competition for inward investment.' But Hazell also added, 'Do the English care?' (ibid.). The rejection of an elected assembly in the North-East in a referendum in November 2004 suggests perhaps not. Some Scottish and Welsh commentators also favoured assemblies for the English regions not for fear that otherwise the English would lose out economically but for fear that without them Britain would still be Anglo-Britain and Scotland and Wales would lose out politically. Third, new Labour had already established an elected assembly for one region, Greater London, thereby confirming how different London is from the rest of England, and indeed the rest of Britain. The difficulty for the government is that the regions for which it proposed to roll out elected regional assemblies if the voters wanted them do not necessarily mean much to the voters, and, even where they do, voters were hardly clamouring that they be given a political form—with one possible exception, the North-East.

In the last chapter I noted a letter from Simon Partridge to *The Guardian*, published on 27 April 2003, three days after St George's Day, in which he claimed that 'The bad news for aspiring English nationalists ... is that not feeling very English seems to be the predominant aspect of living in England,' the implication being that for English residents regional identities mattered more. But then Partridge is a vigorous advocate of regional assemblies for England (as in his *The British Union State*, 1999). No doubt he would draw comfort from Mike Storry and Peter Childs's (1997: 6) claim that 'Regional and local identities are extremely strong'. It is a line supported by John Prescott, the Deputy Prime Minister and Hull MP and prime mover behind Labour proposals for English regional assemblies. It is also endorsed by Austin Mitchell, the Grimsby MP and journalist, in this encomium for the North.

The North of England is in England, but never quite of it. There is a northern identity, a northern difference and little solidarity with "Englishness"—a Home Counties, R.P. speaking, service-centred, rentier-ruled, elitist identity focussing on, and dominated by the Great Wen. The North feels itself different but defines itself by more than just reacting against the South or by London and effete assumptions of Englishness, such as those offered by John Major's elegiac vision. . . .

If the North were an independent state it could have managed its currency to sustain its economy and make its industry competitive with the opportunity to become a small, dynamic, hardworking, single-minded powerhouse like Singapore, Taiwan or Hong Kong. (Mitchell 2000: 46)

Mitchell's North embraces 'Tykes, Lancastrians and the "Geordie Nation"'. Its positive identifiers are basic industries and the needs left by a decline attributed to Westminster and Whitehall misgovernment and City of London financial mismanagement. The second of the quoted paragraphs is an extraordinary example of wishful thinking.

For others English regional identities are notable not for their strength but their weakness. In the section on the English and the Lowland Scots in *The Times Guide to the Peoples of Europe* (1994: 42), Felipe Fernández-Armesto concedes that there is some substance to the North–South divide, that Yorkshire men and women have a strong attachment to their county, and that the people of Tyneside evince a 'fierce local chauvinism', but he still deems provincial identity in England slight by Continental standards: 'All in all, the English are, for their size, among the most consistent of European peoples' (ibid.). Vernon Bogdanor (1999: 271) goes further: 'Devolution in England has to confront the problem that the regions are in large degree simply ghosts.'

There are, of course, private companies with regional responsibilities and sometimes regional names—television and utilities companies are only the most visible—as well as the countless variations on regional divisions adopted by different firms operating across England or Britain. There are also numerous regional structures operated by ministries and quangos. Brian Hogwood (1996) counted nearly a hundred, 'ranging from the six regional crime squads covering England and Wales to the nine Bee Health Inspection regions of the Ministry of Agriculture, Fisheries and Food' (Bogdanor 1999: 269). This profusion of regional structures has made the generation of a popular consensus on a regional structure for England even more elusive, but the 1990s did see considerable rationalization. In 1994 the Conservative Government of John Major established Government Offices (GOs) for the regions as defined in Map 6.1 (Mawson 1997); and in 1999 the Labour Government of Tony Blair established Regional Development Agencies (RDAs) in these same regions with unelected regional chambers to hold them to account. Many public and private bodies have now adjusted their regional structures to coincide with these regions.

The sections that follow deal first with the eight regions beyond the capital as now officially constituted; then with the North-East, the only one to vote on whether it wanted an elected regional assembly; and then with the two special cases, London, which is similar to the other eight regions in some respects but different in so far as it has a directly elected mayor that they would not have even if they were to acquire an elected assembly, and Cornwall, which is not only not an English region but also, in the eyes of some Cornish men and women, not English at all. A concluding section deals with prospects for the English regions and their implications for devolution.

Regions, regional development agencies, and regional assemblies

In 1997 the Minister for the Regions, Richard Caborn, said that the new English regions needed populations of around 5–6 million if they were to be 'in line with European regional spatial plans' and the 1997 white paper dismissed the 'traditional regions' as unsuitable (see Partridge 1999: 17). This revealed that government thinking on regional size and boundaries was driven by an administrative convenience—conformity with a supposed EU norm—not popular sentiment. Thus the North is disqualified as a region—to Austin Mitchell's chagrin?—because, with a population of 14 million in 2001, it is too big (and potentially too hard to ignore for London's taste?). And Cornwall, where a nationalist movement seeks, at a minimum, more than county status, is ruled out because with a population of only half a million it is too small.

There are many ways in which these regions often do not seem entirely right to the people who live there. Here are just three examples. (1) The Home Counties are split between the South-East and the East of England when it is proximity to London that most determines all their fortunes. Prior to 1994 they were all part of the South-East standard (economic planning) region. When the GO regions were established, Essex, Hertfordshire, and Bedfordshire from the South-East standard region were merged with the East Anglia standard region to form the East of England region. East Anglia (Norfolk, Suffolk, and Cambridgeshire) does have an identity that is widely acknowledged. The hybrid East of England does not. Watford in Hertfordshire, for example, is more akin to an outer London borough than it is to East Anglia. (2) Cumbria is included in the North-West. For twenty years prior to 1994 it was part of the North standard region along with Northumberland, Tyne and Wear, Durham, and Cleveland. Furness, part of Lancashire until local government reform in 1974, and Windermere with its railway connection to Manchester, do have historic associations with the North-West, but Carlisle has as often looked east to the English borderlands and Newcastle. North Cumbria seems like an ill-fitting add-on to the North-West. (3) South Hampshire and the Isle of White is in the South-East Region, just as it was in the South-East standard region, but it is arguably South rather than South-East or South-West—the only two possibilities allowed before and after 1994.

Ross Bond (2003: 99) notes that some of the English regions are 'identity-rich' whilst others are 'identity poor'. Identification with the regions is usually discussed in terms of circumstantial evidence, but in 1999 MORI conducted a poll for *The Economist* that included a question on geopolitical identification (see Table 6.1). In 38 sampling points across Britain 923 adults were offered eight possibilities from the local to the global community and asked which two or three they most identified with and which two or three the least. The 50 per cent of respondents across Britain who included their GO region in their most favoured choices masked huge regional variations from 83 per cent in the North-East to 17 per cent in the East of England. Two caveats are necessary. First, MORI did not themselves publish the English regional breakdowns but Neil Ward and John Tomaney (2002: 112) have done so without warning that sample sizes for individual regions were small. Second, comparisons between English regions and Scotland and Wales are problematic in so far as MORI did not indicate what analogues for GO regions they used in Scotland and Wales. Having noted the caveats, the hierarchy in Table 6.1 mostly rings true. One might have expected the figure

| TABLE 6.1 | Identification with the regional level in British regions |

Q: Which two or three of these, if any, would you say you most identify and least identify with?

	% identifying with (GOR) region	
	Most	Least
All	50	9
North-East	83	0
North-West	70	2
Scotland	62	1
South-West	58	7
West Midlands	55	7
Yorkshire and Humberside	52	7
Wales	50	0
London	43	10
South-East	41	18
East Midlands	31	9
East of England	17	29

Base: 923 British adults aged 18+ (24–7 September 1999).
Source: MORI/*The Economist*: 'British Identity' as in Ward and Tomaney (2002), table 8.2, p. 112.

for Yorkshire and Humberside to be higher—more like that for the North-West—but it is possible some Yorkshire men and women objected to the GO region contrivance of Yorkshire minus south Teeside plus south Humberside. One might also have expected identification with London to be greater, but some respondents in London may have had difficulty identifying it as a region rather than a city. But even if identification with some regions was lower than might have been expected only identification with the East of England was negligible. The general indication that regional identification increases with distance from London and is strongest in the North-East is both unambiguous and politically significant.

The Government Offices in the Regions were established in 1994 to co-ordinate the regional implementation of government policies, or more precisely the policies of nine 'sponsoring' ministries. This they still do, indeed they have grown in size and importance. According to the 2003 white paper *Your Region, Your Choice* (on proposals for elected regional assemblies), there are over 3,000 civil servants in the offices themselves and nearly 400,000 in the regional networks of the sponsoring ministries (para 2.29 and box 2.6). The Government Offices in the Regions thus constitute a measure of administrative devolution without any political devolution or regional accountability. The Regional Development Agencies (RDAs) were established in 1999. They are quangos with leaderships appointed by the government. The 2003 white paper (box 2.1) describes them thus:

> Regional Development Agencies are business-led and are strategic drivers of regional economic development. Their aims are to:
>
> - further the economic development and the regeneration of their area;
> - promote business efficiency, investment and competitiveness in their area;
> - promote employment in their area;
> - enhance the development and application of skills relevant to employment in their area; and
> - contribute to the achievement of sustainable development in the United Kingdom, where it is relevant to their area to do so.

The government also encouraged the establishment of regional chambers 'to scrutinise the works of the RDAs' (ibid.). Tomaney (2002a: 33) gives their three roles as 'holding RDAs to account', 'representing regions in conflicts with central government', and 'policy integration'. All eight chambers have now chosen to style themselves as regional assemblies. They range in size from thirty-five members (Yorkshire and the Humber) to 117 (South-West). The majority of members are local authority councillor nominees, ranging from 63 per cent in the East Midlands and Yorkshire and the Humber to 75 per cent in the South-West (p. 34). The rest represent stakeholders, with businessmen to the fore.

In its 1997 manifesto the new Labour Government committed itself to establishing elected regional assemblies where there was a regional demand for them. The 2003 white paper (ch. 4) summarized the proposed functions of regional assemblies thus:

- Elected assemblies will improve the quality of life for people in their regions, particularly by improving regional economic performance.

- Assemblies will be given the lead role in developing strategies to achieve this. They will drive the implementation of their strategies, monitor progress and revise strategies when appropriate.

- Assemblies will be given a range of powers to help them to deliver these strategies. These will include executive functions such as responsibility for resources and influence to promote results that will benefit the region.

- Specific responsibilities include economic development and regeneration, spatial development, housing, transport, skills, and culture.

- Regional Development Agencies will be accountable to their elected assembly, which will appoint the Chair and Board members.

Other responsibilities included public health, the environment, and crime reduction. It was stressed that the assemblies would have a mainly strategic function and that they would work with RDAs, GOs, local authorities, and partnerships with stakeholders to deliver their goals. They would primarily be funded by a block grant from central government but would also be able to add a small precept to the local authority council tax and borrow money up to a prescribed limit. They would also be much smaller than the current unelected regional assemblies, and much smaller than the Scottish Parliament (129 members) and the Welsh Assembly (60 members) with a range of 25–35 members elected using the additional member system as in Scotland, Wales, and London. Their executives would have up to six members. They would thus be much less powerful not only than the Scottish Parliament with its primary legislation and tax-raising powers but also than the

Welsh Assembly with its secondary legislation powers. In Wales the Welsh Assembly Government determines how the block grant to Wales is spent. That grant covers both the relatively small expenditure of the assembly itself and the enormously larger expenditure of the Wales Office which discharges most of the responsibilities of the nine sponsoring ministries of the Government Offices in the regions in England and which is accountable to the assembly. By contrast, each English regional assembly would determine how the relatively small block grant it receives for its own purposes would be spent, but not the enormously larger expenditure of the Government Office and the regional networks of the sponsoring ministries which would not be accountable to it but rather remain accountable to central government. Using London as a guide, Paul McQuail and Mark Sandford (2002: 178–9) estimated that a regional assembly with the limited strategic/coordination function envisaged could have expected a block grant of about £20 million, whereas an assembly with powers comparable to the Welsh Assembly could have expected £1.1–2.5 billion depending on the population of the region. In its small assembly and budget, each English region would be more like the Greater London Authority—but would not have a directly elected mayor, the position Ken Livingstone has filled so visibly and skilfully in London.

In 2002–3 the Office of the Deputy Prime Minister conducted soundings to estimate demand for regional assemblies. The methodology was risible. Basically it invited representations from bodies and individuals, totalled them, and then announced percentages for and against. The percentages 'for' exceeded 50 per cent in the three northern regions (North-East, Yorkshire and the Humber, and the North-West) and the government committed itself to holding referendums in those regions on 4 November 2004 using all-postal ballots. In July it 'postponed' the ballots in Yorkshire and the Humber and the North-West. The official reason was that it needed to await the results of an inquiry into alleged abuses of all-postal ballots in the local authority elections in the two regions the previous May. The unofficial reason was that the 'fors' were expected to lose the referendums. The official reason for going ahead with the referendum in the North-East was that there had not been comparable allegations in that region of abuse of all-postal ballots in the May local authority elections. The unofficial reason was that there seemed a real prospect of the 'fors' winning and John Prescott achieving the breakthrough for regional government he craved. The precedent of political devolution to complement administrative devolution and provide regional democratic accountability would then have been set. But it was not to be.

The North-East: a region conscious of itself

There are a number of reasons why popular identification with the North-East is strong and support for an elected assembly appeared greater than in any other region. First, the regional boundaries make sense to those who live there. To the north there is Scotland, to the east the North Sea, to the south the Cleveland Hills, and to the west the Pennines. The region has always had a strong geographical identity based not just on remoteness from London, but on being England beyond Yorkshire, a county with a strong identity of its own. It also has an obvious regional capital in Newcastle (see Lancaster 1992), even if the RDA is based in Durham. Second, it has a strong historical identity, the legacy of Northumbria, of the early church in Durham, Jarrow, and Lindisfarne and of the powers and privileges of the medieval see of Durham, which the tourist board now markets as the Land of the Prince-Bishops. The idea of a land beyond the immediate control of the English state is confirmed by the Norman Domesday Book whose coverage stopped at the Tees and by the dependence of Norman and Angevin kings on the northern earls to defend their kingdom from the Scots. Henry VIII's suppression of the Pilgrimage of Grace in 1536 in Yorkshire signalled the tightening of central control over the north,[1] but Tomaney and Ward (2000: 477) suggest that the 'semi-detachment' of the North-East from the rest of England came to an end only with the union of the English and Scottish crowns in 1603 and states in 1707, and that 'it may be more accurate to think of the North-East as a "British" region, whose final incorporation into the English polity occurred alongside the formation of British identity'. Second, the region has had a strong economic identity based on heavy industry—mining, steel, ship-building and repair, engineering, and chemicals, even if only the last still flourishes—and now has a need comparable to Strathclyde's to construct a successful post-industrial service-based economy. Newcastle, like Glasgow, is reinventing itself (see Colls 1992). Third, the North-East has a strong cultural identity. In the past this revolved around Methodism and the Labour movement (cf. Moore 1974; Williamson, 1992; Beynon and Austrin 1994). It is still marked by distinctive accents (Geordie, the Newcastle accent is only the best known), and a passion for football (and the fortunes of Newcastle United, Sunderland, and Middlesbrough (cf. Taylor 1992)). The North-East is also the most ethnically homogenous region in England with a population that was 96.4 per cent white British at the time of the 2001 census.

The North-East is the poorest region in England. It is also poorer than Scotland where per capita public expenditure is higher. The argument about the relative treatment of the North-East compared with Scotland and other English regions is, however, a complicated one. Table 2.2 in Ch. 2 shows that: in 2001 gross value-added per head and gross disposable income per head in the North-East were the lowest of any English region, and, crucially, lower than in Scotland; in 2003 the unemployment rate was higher than in any other English region except London, and, crucially, higher than in Scotland; and in 2002 the unemployment claimant rate was the highest of any English region, and, crucially, higher than in Scotland. On the other hand, Table 2.3 shows that by 2002–3 total identifiable expenditure on services by nation and region was higher in the North-East than in any other English region except London, but still a little less than in Scotland, the gap having grown smaller since 1998–9. By these measures the North-East still gets an inferior deal to Scotland's but the North-East's disadvantage is not as great as it once was, and is still often imagined to be—not least in the North-East itself.

There are other measures that confirm the disadvantage of the North-East, but it is interesting that Peter Jones (2002: 201) has calculated on the basis of 2000 Treasury figures that in any redistribution of public spending to match a UK per capita average, the North-East would be by far the smallest gainer, the North-West the next smallest, and the South-East the biggest, with London a much bigger loser than Scotland. 'This', he adds, 'may be why John Prescott said there would be "blood on the carpet" in any review of Barnett' (ibid.). Indeed there may be, but a review of Barnett would hinge not on redistribution to a UK average but rather on reassessment of need and it would have to take account of the English regions. The Barnett formula, after all, was never meant to deal with the English regions and it was certainly never meant to deal with equity in spending between Scotland and the North-East. Given the adoption in 1974 of standard regions that included both Scotland and, then, the North (North-East and Cumbria), however, politicians, commentators, academics, and citizens in the North-East were bound to start making invidious comparisons with their northern neighbours. The increase in prosperity in Scotland has been greater than that in the North-East but, in north-eastern eyes, Scotland continues to get more favourable treatment. This perception of relative disadvantage has long fuelled demand for a North-East assembly. Having reviewed the evidence for six decades, however, both Kevin Morgan (2002) and Robert Colls (2002) concluded that regional economic planning has never delivered benefits on the scale its proponents anticipated. Morgan nevertheless supported development agencies for the English regions while pointing out that if the Welsh precedent of twenty-three years standing was any guide their achievements would prove modest. He also favoured elected regional assemblies but cautioned that the economic dividends expected of them were, quite literally, unproven.

Higher public spending in Scotland has long been attributed to the British political desire to moderate Scottish nationalism and to the effectiveness of Scottish political representation—an effectiveness now rewarded and enhanced by a devolved parliament in Edinburgh. Back in the 1970s politicians in the North-East were suspicious of the unfair advantage a Scottish assembly would give the Scots in the competition for public funding and inward investment. In the 1990s this turned to admiration for the way the Scots obtained their parliament, and a simple judgement: if you can't beat them, join them. The change was a product of what Colls (1992) called 'born-again Geordies' determined to harness the region's independence of spirit in its remaking. The North-East now needed, the regional media and many other voices concluded, a stronger regional voice which London would have to reckon with, and that meant regional politicians and an elected assembly of its own.

The Campaign for a North East Assembly was started in 1992, seven years before equivalents in any other region (see Byrne 1992; Tomaney 2002a: 38). The North-East Constitutional Convention was formed in 1999. Media interest in the issue had long been much greater than in any other region. In the years leading to the 2004 referendum, the campaigners were headed by the sociologist, John Tomaney. Tomaney (1999a: 64) argued that 'North-East England has had a marked political identity for centuries' and he presented 'contemporary North-East regionalism' as only its latest manifestation. His basic message had a simple appeal. 'If we had a decent structure of governance and decent leaders we could produce a better strategy for the development of our society, economy and culture than that handed down from London' (Tomaney 2004: 37). The campaign did not have to counter much organized opposition until the last three months before the vote. Most regional MPs were in favour as were Northumberland and Durham County Councils. The county councils' support was significant because the government had ruled that three-tier subnational government (region, county, and district) was unacceptable and in those parts of the North-East where there were still two tiers (counties and districts) unitary authorities would have to supersede them. In effect the county councils would have to support their own demise, which they did.

In the referendum on 4 November 2004 voters rejected an assembly by 77.9 per cent to 22.1 per cent on a 47.7 per cent turnout. The regional establishment had favoured an assembly for a decade but opinion polls in the lead-up to the vote indicated that proponents of the assembly were likely to lose. Even so the scale of their defeat was a surprise. On reflection a number of reasons for it can be given. First, a strong historical and cultural identity in a region does not necessarily translate into a strong popular demand for a regional assembly. Second, an assembly with few powers and a small budget is particularly unattractive when it is unaccompanied by any directly elected leader who could become the voice of the region. The government intimated that small beginnings could lead to more substantial powers later, but intimations are not enough and some beginnings are too small. Third, insertion of a level of regional government between existing unitary authorities and Westminster and Whitehall can be construed as an extra level of bureaucracy, which is particularly unwelcome when it is suspected, rightly or wrongly, that more powers will pass up to it from local government than will pass down to it from national government and thereby make government on balance more, not less, remote. Fourth, tying introduction of a regional assembly to a reform of local government with more than one option in the areas concerned is too complicated a proposition. Fifth, more ministers need to campaign for elected regional assemblies with more conviction than was the case in the North-East in the autumn of 2004 where only the deputy prime minister, John Prescott, seemed really to care about the outcome. Sixth, it is hard to secure consent for new government structures when politicians are as widely distrusted as was the case in Britain in the autumn of 2004. The proposed assembly was attacked for both having too small a budget to do anything worthwhile and costing too much, and for adding to the number of politicians and bureaucrats in the region when it would have added fewer than were lost in the accompanying introduction of unitary authorities where they did not already exist. Distrust nullified attempts by ministers to counter the misrepresentations of the 'no' campaign.

Colin Rallings and Michael Thrasher (2005) have reported polling since the referendum that shows that those opposed to an assembly were more motivated to turn out and vote than those in favour. Most opponents believed taxes would go up and that the assembly would be a waste of money and more of them 'almost never' trust politicians. In terms of party identification, only 4 per cent of Conservatives (14% of the sample) voted yes, compared with 17 per cent of Liberal Democrats (11% of the sample) (ibid. table 4). But the killer for those in favour was that only 23 per cent of Labour supporters (53% of the sample) voted 'yes'.

Writing before the North-East referendum, Tomaney and Hetherington (2004) referred to the 'quiet regionalisation' of England and suggested RDAs would survive the election of a Conservative government because they have come to be regarded by all parties as useful. Maybe so, but quiet regionalization did not lead to a quiet revolution in the North-East. And without an elected regional assembly in the North-East to press the case, an early reform of the Barnett Formula to take account of both changes in the relative needs of the constituent parts of the United Kingdom and, for the first time, the relative needs of the regions of England is less likely.

London: world city, metropolis, and region

There are many things that mark London out from the rest of Britain. First, it has a population nearly three times larger than the next conurbation. The 2001 census recorded the population of Greater London at 7.17 million compared with 2.48 million in Greater Manchester. The population is projected to grow by another 800,000 by 2016 (Mayor of London (MoL) 2004b: 2). London is the largest city in the European Union. Second, London alone of British cities is a world city. It is one of the three top financial centres (with New York and Tokyo) and a big centre of international commerce; it is the seat of government of a permanent member of the United Nations Security Council and of a member of G7 (and G8), the countries with the world's largest economies (plus Russia); it is one of the top three

English-speaking cultural, media, and creative centres (alongside New York and Los Angeles), with world-class cultural and academic institutions, and this in an age in which English is the nearest we have to a global language; and it is one of the world's top tourist destinations. Third, the Mayor of London (2004a: 1) claims that it is the most culturally diverse city in the world. (The same is sometimes said of New York.) One-third of its population is not white British, and most of that third is not white. The percentage of the total population of London in all but one of the 2001 census categories other than white British was the highest of any English region (the exception being Pakistani for which the highest was Yorkshire and the Humber). Yasmin Alibhai-Brown (2000: 271) notes the currency now given to the four-homelands version of Britain and asks wryly where black Britons are to go. 'Perhaps we can put in a bid for London, please?' I argued in the last chapter that politicians and pundits in London can and do sometimes forget how much more multicultural London is than anywhere else in England (or Britain).

Fourth, London has the greatest extremes of wealth and poverty. Higher percentages of the population of London are very rich and very poor than in any other part of Britain. Of Greater London's children, 35 per cent live in poverty (that is in households with incomes less than half the national mean), a higher percentage than in any other English region or in Scotland or Wales (MoL 2004b: 17). Fifth, London has by far the highest cost of living, with very high housing costs. Housing is a particular problem for public service workers with low London weightings or salary or wage premiums. Both nurses and primary school teachers in the capital on average earn 9 per cent more than their counterparts elsewhere in England, compared with a 31 per cent differential for all employees (p. 27). London also has the dearest and most heavily used public transport in Britain as well as the most congested roads (though the introduction in February 2003 of a congestion charge, a daily toll to drive, in the City of London and the West End has brought the first reduction in traffic since the Second World War). Sixth, London has the most buoyant economy in Britain. It is often forgotten that London was until the 1970s a major centre of manufacturing and it has since suffered a large-scale loss of manufacturing jobs—750,000 between 1973 and 1999—as have other such centres (p. 6). Only the North-East has higher unemployment. But London also has the biggest post-industrial economy in Britain and it houses the head offices of most big British firms and many transnationals with major British components. One indicator of both the buoyancy of the London economy, and the Mayor's complaint that London gets an unfair deal in terms of public spending, is the claim that it 'contributes between £9–£15 billion more in taxes to central government than it receives in spending' (p. 5).[2] In sum, London is big, crowded, expensive, cosmopolitan, vibrant, and trend-setting. Its streets are not paved with gold but it continues to offer new opportunities and career advancement to people from all over Britain, the European Union, and beyond. Just about the only thing promoters of London do not emphasize is that it is also the capital of England.

The poet de Quincey, Wordsworth's contemporary, wrote an essay entitled 'The Nation of London' (see Ackroyd 2000: 589). The Scot, Andrew Marr, now the BBC's chief political correspondent, does not go that far but he does say this. 'Friends from Scotland sometimes ask what it feels like, living for so long in England, and I say I do not live in England I live in London' (Marr, 2000: p. xiii). All Britons know where London is and that it is much bigger than any other city. They also know enough about some of the things that mark it out from the rest of Britain not to contest that it is indeed a place apart. In many respects, then, it is identity-rich; in others, however, it is less so. One issue has to do with its boundaries. Its suburbs spread beyond those of the Greater London Authority and its travel-to-work area extends to the whole south-east. Another has to do with its political status. The square mile of the City of London, with its lord mayor chosen by the guilds and its huge working and tiny residential population, is a political anomaly. London acquired city-wide administration only with the creation of the Metropolitan Board of Works in 1855 and elected city-wide government with the creation of the London County Council in 1889. It lost city-wide government again in 1986 with Margaret Thatcher's abolition of the Greater London Council. Following abolition all services except education in Inner London were delivered by the thirty-two London boroughs (and the City). Abolition of the Inner London Education Authority followed in 1990. The restoration of greater London government in 2000 has taken the novel form of the Greater London Authority discussed below. Most services are still delivered by the London boroughs. London is still politically fragmented and who is to say where it begins and ends. There are so many Londons. The City of London, the London Borough of the City of Westminster, Inner London, Outer London, Greater London, the London metropolitan area,

London as a city-region in official terms and in the unofficial discourses of commentators and academics, likewise London as a planning region.

So who is a Londoner in all this and who not? What do the residents and the voters of these various Londons identify with in terms of place? What form do the residents and voters of these Londons think the government of London should take? It is notable that the social science literature on London never seems to ask these questions. Susan Fainstein, Ian Gordon, and Michael Harloe (1992), for example, edited a volume comparing New York and London which begins by discussing the boundary question. It then examines each city in terms of its economy, labour markets, income inequality, migration patterns, and ethnic division of labour, housing, politics, and economic restructuring policy. It emphasizes that London has always been hard to govern but treats the issue as a technical one, essentially a matter of finding the best way of delivering services. A decade later Nick Buck et al. (2002) published *Working Capital: Life and Labour in Contemporary London*. It includes detailed study of six inner and outer London districts and is by far the best treatment of life and labour in London since that of Charles Booth a century before. It covers the ground of Fainstein et al. with greater thoroughness and adds discussion of education and the modernization of government. But it still does not (aim to) connect life and labour to government in a way that takes account of what residents and voters identify with in terms of place, and what structure of government residents and voters might want. It is still all about experts assessing the best way of securing jobs, prosperity, and the delivery of services.

Jonathan Glancey (2001) would endorse these laudable ambitions and finds much to criticize in new Labour's London. He dedicates his book *London: Bread and Circuses* to the memory of Frank Pick who worked for the London Passenger Transport Board, becoming chief executive in 1933. Pick greatly extended the London Underground and did much to improve the buses and trams not only in terms of routes but also in terms of design. He contrasts Pick's era with subsequent under-investment in, and fragmentation and privatization of, London transport. More generally he presents 'the old London County Council's stuffy, patronizing, intelligent-design-and-public-services-are-good-for-you approach when London was run by socialists and liberals' as a an interlude in the much longer story of London as a vibrant city of traders, moneymakers, and buccaneers (p. 12). It has never been amenable to overall planning and control; he does not expect that to change and he is unsure he wants it to in so far as it is responsible for the best as well as the worst of London.

Given that London is in many ways a city of extremes, the subtitle of Tony Travers's (2004) book on London's politics, *Governing the Ungovernable City*, does not surprise even if it is a rhetorical excess. As Travers shows, governing London has always been controversial and never been easy for two main reasons. First, British governments have never wanted a powerful rival in the capital city. Second, London has always presented problems of scale for which solutions do not come easily. This is still the case. The thirty-two London boroughs created in 1964 deliver most services. Margaret Thatcher abolished the Greater London Council in 1986 having found it impossible to defeat Ken Livingstone's left-wing Labour administration at the ballot box. Thereafter London-wide services and planning were the responsibility of a motley collection of bodies that linked London boroughs for particular purposes, sometimes alongside wider south-eastern representation, and of various quangos, development corporations, and public–private partnerships. These arrangements were convoluted, opaque, undemocratic, and, as was finally acknowledged even by many Conservatives, unequal to the task of providing strategic direction for the development of London. In 1994 John Major's Conservative Government broke new ground. Major appointed a Minister for London. When establishing government offices in the regions, his government also included a Government Office for London. Following victory in the 1997 general election, Labour honoured its commitment to establish a new all-London authority. In 1998 it published a white paper on the government of London and put its proposals to a referendum. The electorate was asked, 'Are you in favour of the government's proposals for a Greater London Authority, made up of an elected mayor and separately elected authority?' Seventy-two per cent voted 'yes', though the turnout was only 34 per cent (B. Morgan 1998: 3).

Following complex legislation, elections for mayor and the assembly were held in 2000 and the GLA came into being. Ken Livingstone, having failed to get the Labour nomination for mayor, ran as an independent and won. The turnout was 33.7 per cent. Travers (2004: 65) emphasizes how untried the GLA mode of governance is.

The GLA represented a new form of governance in Britain, with an attempt at a separation of powers between the directly elected mayor and a small London assembly of 25 members. The mayor was made responsible for developing the GLA's strategies for transport, planning, the environment . . . economic development and culture. The mayor was also given responsibility for setting a budget for the GLA and its four functional bodies: Transport for London (TfL); the London Development Agency (LDA); the London Fire and Emergency Planning Authority; and the Metropolitan Police Authority.

The mayor has to consult the assembly during the preparation of each of the GLA's strategies, and the assembly can veto the mayor's budget by mustering a two-thirds majority for an alternative. The powers of the mayor are largely those of 'patronage, persuasion and publicity' (p. 68). Ken Livingstone, an ultra-confident self-publicist with the common touch, has proved able to do quite a lot with them and was re-elected in 2004, this time running as the Labour candidate. The turnout was slightly improved at 35.9 per cent.

The Mayor of London is an executive organization, a position, and a person. The use of the same name for the organization and the position is odd. It is equivalent to calling both the government and the prime minister the prime minister. It would seem to invite a cult of the personality not uncongenial to the present mayor. *The London Plan* (MoL 2004a), for example, is an impressive document. It provides a comprehensive overview of the present condition of London and a strategy for its future development—the first for thirty-five years. But it is also disconcerting to find throughout dozens of seemingly personalized references to the mayor's vision and the mayor's conclusions. If the mayor is larger than life, however, the assembly is barely visible. Travers (2004: 113) refers to '25 members in search of a role?'

The government intended that elected assemblies in the English regions be small and have limited powers broadly comparable to those of the GLA. In London, however, it is not the assembly but the directly elected executive mayor that has made the impact. There would be no equivalent to the Mayor of London in the regions.

Cornwall: nation, region, or county?

There is one part of England where there is significant support for a special constitutional status. That part is Cornwall and that support is associated with a claim that Cornwall is not part of England. In the rest of what became England invading Angles, Saxons, Norsemen, and Danes displaced or absorbed the Celts. In the far south-west they did not. In 936, after driving the Celts out of Exeter, King Athelstan of Wessex resolved to leave Cornwall—the land beyond the River Tamar—to the Cornish, and not settle any more Saxons there, in return for Cornish tribute. Later Cornwall became a shire but it was not like other English counties in so far as its people remained mostly Celts and spoke Cornish. Two constitutional devices also allowed Cornwall some measure of autonomy. The customary rights of tinners (tin miners), conceded in 1198 and 1201, developed into the special, if limited, local jurisdiction of the Stannary courts and parliament; and the Duchy of Cornwall, established in 1337, acquired prerogatives that led it to claim as late as 1855 that Cornwall was separate from England. These enabled Philip Payton (1996b: 402) to conclude that 'At the very least . . . the constitutional history of Cornwall is singular and . . . the territory is, in that sense, one of the distinctive components that came to comprise the United Kingdom'. Over the centuries there were uprisings in Cornwall as there were in many other parts of England but they always had an extra edge in so far as they were mounted by people who did not consider themselves English and who spoke English as a second language if at all (see Stoyle 1999). The most famous was in 1497; in that year Cornish protesters marched to Blackheath on the outskirts of London before they were routed. The 500th anniversary of the protest was marked by a new march which enjoyed strong popular support and media interest as it crossed the Tamar 'into England'.

In their book on Cornish nationalism Bernard Deacon, Dick Cole, and Garry Tregidga (2003: 6) recall how the ambiguous status of Cornwall—'politically incorporated into the English realm but culturally regarded as a distinct nation—was fatally compromised by the religious Reformation of the 16th century and the centralising tendencies of the Tudor state'. In the short term these prompted the Cornish uprising in 1549 in which large numbers died. In the longer term they 'led to closer political oversight and, crucially, guaranteed the decline of the Cornish language' because 'Unlike Welsh, no literate lay class of Celtic language speakers had emerged before the 1550s. The gentry had deserted Cornish well before then and, in consequence, the Cornish did not follow the Welsh in translating the Bible into the local tongue in the 1560s. Cornish as a community language was doomed' (ibid.). There are a number of contenders for the distinction of last Cornish-speaker. The most famous, Dolly Pentreath, died in 1777. A handful of others are said to have spoken some Cornish (but with whom?) well into the nineteenth century. Early in the twentieth century enthusiasts began a revival of the language. Kesva an Tavas Kernewek (The Cornish Language Board) was established in 1967 and Payton (2000: 117) estimates that there were about forty fluent speakers by 1981. Cowethas an Yeth Kernewek (The Cornish Language Society) was founded in 1979. In 2000 the Government Office South-West published a report on Cornish that estimated that there were approaching 300 effective speakers and about 750 people learning the language at adult education centres or by correspondence classes. There is some teaching in twelve primary and four secondary schools.

Mark Stoyle (1999: 441) has argued that the Cornish as a separate people came to an end in the sixteenth century and by 1750 'the spark of Cornish ethnicity' had been practically extinguished. Deacon, Cole, and Tregidga disagree. What matters, they contend, are not just the facts of history but how history is remembered. From the nineteenth century onwards there has been a movement to recreate the Celt, retell Cornish history, and reimagine Cornwall. It may have had small beginnings but now has a presence that none can ignore, aided by such works as Payton's *Cornwall: A History* (1996*a*, rev. 2004) which speaks of reinventing Kernow. How robust the evidential basis for this reworking is remains a matter of dispute, but it draws upon the history of hard-rock mining, the rights of the tinners, and the early industrialization of Cornwall, as well as the Cornish language and folk culture, Methodism, and rugby. What resonance this has for 'English' in-migrants is an open question. Latterly the reimagining of Cornwall has extended beyond (re)generation of a cultural nation to claims for political nationhood. In particular Mebyon Kernow (Sons of Cornwall) was founded in 1951 (in a less gender-sensitive age) as a cultural movement but grew into a political party, first contesting elections in the late 1960s. The party gets only a few per cent of the vote in parliamentary elections (2.3 per cent in its best two constituencies in the 2001 general election) but has had a few successes in council elections. What percentages of the population of Cornwall consider themselves (1) Cornish only, (2) more Cornish than English, (3) equally Cornish and English, (4) more English than Cornish, and (5) English only has not been put to a Moreno-style test, but much of the population are in-migrants, including retirees, or the descendents of in-migrants. (My guess is that the first two categories would total less than 10 per cent.)

Some native Cornish have on occasions questioned the loyalty of English in-migrants to Cornwall and have opposed initiatives that would bring in more of them, but in practice there is a widespread sentiment that Cornwall needs a stronger voice to ensure that its particular needs are heard and that it gets a better economic deal from London and Brussels. Cornwall's tin mining is a thing of the past (the last mine, South Crofty, having closed in 1997), the viability of its fishing is continually threatened by European over-fishing, its agriculture no longer provides secure incomes, and much of the employment in its biggest industry, tourism, is seasonal. It is also one of the poorest counties in England. By 1997 'Cornwall's GDP had plummeted to less than 75 per cent of the EU average, [and] male wages were the lowest in Britain at just 77 per cent of the average' (Deacon, Cole, and Tregidga 2003: 95). There is much dislike of the hybrid 'Devon and Cornwall' because the centres of decision-making in 'Devonwall' are always in Devon, linkage with more prosperous Devon delayed the acquisition of EU Objective One aid status, and the very idea of Devon and Cornwall supposes they are equivalent when Cornish activists insist Cornwall is more than a county. At a minimum, Cornish nationalists and Mebyon Kernow, in effect a ginger party, are visible and vocal enough to ensure that all parties in Cornwall pay growing attention to distinctive Cornish interests and growing respect to the regeneration of Cornishness. In Penwith district (in the far west of Cornwall) there are now bilingual road signs and, following a campaign of overpainting in 2001 by Cornish nationalists, the names of English Heritage sites on brown tourist road signs throughout Cornwall are no longer accompanied by red English roses, as they are everywhere east of the Tamar, but by black Cornish choughs (birds of the crow family). The Cornish flag of St Piran, a white cross on a black field, is also now widely seen and is flown by the county council.

On 5 March, St Piran's Day, 2000 Mebyon Kernow marked the new millennium by declaring that 'Cornwall is a nation with its own identity, culture, traditions and history' and it called for a 'Cornish assembly that could set the right democratic priorities for Cornwall and provide a stronger voice for our communities in Britain, Europe and throughout the wider world' (quoted in Deacon, Cole, and Tregidga 2003: 107). The declaration caught the mood and led to a petition for a referendum on a Cornish Assembly that had gathered 50,000 signatures (a tenth of the population) by the time it was presented to 10 Downing Street in mid-2001. The government ignored it, but in 2002 it did designate Cornish as an indigenous language in terms of the Council of Europe's Charter on Regional and Minority Languages whilst refusing to recognize Cornish as an ethnicity in terms of the Council's Framework Convention for the Protection of National Minorities. Having fought off proposals for unitary authorities in 1994–5, Cornwall retains a county council. Cornwall is included in the South-West Region, being too small by the Caborn standard to be a region in its own right. As elections to the European Parliament are based on regional lists of candidates, inclusion in the South-West precludes election of an MEP for Cornwall—another grievance. Cornwall thus remains a county, though many of the most vocal Cornish claim that it is a nation and significantly more would accept the status of a region if that would bring with it a regional assembly. Mebyon Kernow, however, envisages an assembly along the lines of the National Assembly for Wales.[3] The proposed assemblies for English regions would be much weaker. Payton (1996*b*) describes Cornwall as part of the 'inconvenient periphery', along with Northern Ireland, of the United Kingdom state. This is an exaggeration. Its inconvenience to British governments has been as nothing compared with Northern Ireland's, but the peculiarities of the Cornish are sufficiently inconvenient to call in question whether the integrity of the South-West region as presently constituted can ever be established.

Conclusions: our regions, your choice

There are two different sets of reasons why English regional government is currently under consideration. The first, not examined here, has to do with rectification of what Alan Harding (2000: 4, 48) calls the 'missing middle' and the 'chaotic middle' in English governance. Regional governments, it is claimed, would ensure more effective governance, public administration, and economic development in the regions including better exploitation of the possibilities afforded by structural funds and other European Union initiatives than government of the regions from London.[4] For this purpose the government has prejudged that the eight regions plus London created in 1994 (perhaps with minor adjustments) are the most suitable. In the North-East referendum campaign it never became clear how much regional assemblies would assume powers and responsibilities devolved from London rather than taken up from local authorities, but it is certainly possible that the former would outweigh the latter. The objection that regional assemblies would add another level of bureaucracy is partly met by the insistence that their introduction be accompanied by the establishment of unitary authorities in those parts of each region where they do not already exist. It could also be met by demonstration that much of the supposedly additional bureaucracy already exists in connection with a chaotic plethora of multi-council authorities, quangos, networks, and public–private partnerships, and that the establishment of regional assemblies could be accompanied by a rationalization that actually reduces the volume of bureaucracy as well as making the working of what remains more visible and democratically accountable.[5] In other words, a case can be made that regional assemblies would bring a political dividend in terms of reducing the regional democratic deficit and an economic dividend in terms of increasing sustainable economic growth beyond what otherwise would have happened. Citizens could expect more effective government, better value for money, and greater sensitivity to regional needs and *sentiments*. Take, for example, the case of the Manchester Metro. In July 2004 the government indefinitely postponed the referendums on regional assemblies for the North-West and Yorkshire and the Humber. The next day it announced it was not providing funding for the expansion of the Greater Manchester Metro tram system as the cost had gone up too much. This decision was greeted with incredulity by politicians, business, the media, and the public. There was hardly a voice suggesting the government had made the right decision. It is very hard to believe a North-West regional assembly with any influence over the use of funds available for investment in infrastructure would have made such a decision and the Northwest Regional Development Agency made its determination to overturn it absolutely clear at its annual general meeting in September 2004.

The second reason for introducing regional government in England is as a complement to devolution to Scotland and Wales. Without it, there are fears that the English could both come to resent the advantages devolution is perceived to have given the Scots and Welsh (though there is no evidence yet that this is happening except, fitfully, in the North-East) and find themselves losing out in competitive bidding for funding from London and Brussels and in attracting inward investment. Regional government in England would further weaken the London-knows-best culture that has so grated in Scotland and Wales (and the north of England). In some Scottish and Welsh eyes it would also serve further to diversify modes of Englishness and reduce the domination of England within Britain. Kevin Morgan (2002: 798), writing from Cardiff about England as a 'fractured nation', provides an interesting example: 'If the renaissance of national identity in Celtic Britain is incompatible with the traditional London-centric notion of Britishness, it is not necessarily inimical to a devolved and pluralistic British polity.' The time is ripe for an alternative to 'received notions of Britishness'.

If Britain is to have a viable and progressive future . . . Anglocentric notions of Britishness have to be jettisoned in favour of a notion of Britishness which is synonymous with a devolved and multicultural polity. . . . [T]he richer political diversity of the Isles makes a devolved Britain a more congenial context for the English regions which opt for devolution that a resurgent England.

Morgan argues that English regionalism offers a better prospect for progressive civic politics than 'an English parliament sporting the banner of St George' (p. 806) and that 'some English regions seem to be more closely attuned to the idea of a regionally devolved Britain than a nationally resurgent England' (p. 807). He reserves his deepest scorn for 'dessicated, mono-cultural conceptions of identity which populate Anglocentric narratives of "Britishness" ' (ibid.), the Anglo-British England discussed in the last chapter, without acknowledging that today's London is the home not of monoculturalism but of the most diversified multiculturalism in Britain. He also assumes that an England reasserting its identity will be the England of the anti-immigrant right. The banner of St George has some interesting carriers these days—Asian taxi drivers in Rochdale during the European Football Championships in Portugal in the summer of 2004, for example. An alternative England, Cosmopolitan England, is reclaiming traditional English emblems purloined by the far right.

Sentiments, that is the problem. As Colls and Lancaster (1992: p. xii) say, 'regions, no less than nations, are imagined communities'—except that most of them are not. In the North-East there is a population with loyalty to a well-defined region. In this it is exceptional. Elsewhere loyalty is weaker, sometimes very much so. The government recognized this in its commitment to the rolling out of regional assemblies only as regional electorates vote in favour of them, but it deluded itself if it ever believed the title of its own white paper, *Your Regions, Your Choice*. A more accurate, but politically provocative, title would have been *Our Regions, Your Choice*. The unwillingness to attend to popular sentiment with respect to the formation of regions and the definition of regional boundaries is understandable in one way but anomalous in another. Nations exist where a people claim to be one and that claim is accepted by other nations and by nation-states and multinational states. Sometimes states precede nations and then engage in state nationalization. Regions are also about the making and accepting of claims. Sometimes the claims reflect popular sentiment, but sometimes, too, states create regions for their own purposes in advance of regional sentiment. Germany, France, Italy, and Spain all have systems of regional government in which different regions owe their existence to very varying combinations of historical provenance, political contrivance, and administrative convenience. Why, amid talk of a Europe of the Regions, should England be any different? One answer would be that the successful introduction of regional assemblies in a country that has known only centralized power since the Tudors needs the best start it can get, and that includes regions its people can identify with. Another answer is that regions that are expected to serve as analogues of nations in a new British constitutional settlement cannot do so if people do not feel any attachment to them.

The unwillingness to attend to popular sentiment is also anomalous. Britain has constituent nations of very different sizes and has made different arrangements for the government of England, Scotland, and Wales, including different degrees of devolution to Scotland and Wales. England also has an asymmetrical localism—a system of local government with two tiers, counties and districts, in some areas and one tier only, unitary authorities, in others. Unitary authorities varied in population from 381,000 in Bristol to 35,000 in Rutland in the 2001 census, and some counties, such as Cheshire and Cornwall, are upper-tier local authorities, while others, such as Herefordshire, are unitary authorities, another, Huntingdonshire, is now a district, and still others, such as Berkshire, no longer exist in terms of local government. On top of all this, some local authorities have directly elected mayors, though most do not. It is against this background that the government demanded consistency with respect to the dimensions of the regions (the Caborn standard), while tolerating variation in their government (an elected regional assembly here, an unelected one there). In the British context, consistency would have been the surprise. Why should regions be the exception to the principle of asymmetry (pragmatic accommodation of spatial differences of sentiment and will)?

Having applied the Caborn standard, the government is itself now also disregarding it when it chooses to. In February 2004 the deputy prime minister, John Prescott, launched a programme called The Northern Way in which the three northern RDAs will combine to promote initiatives intended to close the productivity gap between the north and the south—initiatives centred on sustainable economic development, urban regeneration, reskilling and enskilling labour, knowledge and technology transfer, and improved communications (OPDM 2004). Then in September 2004 the Northern Way Steering Group published *Moving Forward: The Northern Way* which, it transpires, revolves around proposals for eight city-regions of varying familiarity in terms of names and boundaries. However worthy the initiative, it is hard to see how the new discourse about the north as a whole on the one hand and sub-regions on the other could have done anything but dilute attention to the regions when identification with two of the northern regions was not even strong enough for the government to go through with the proposed referendums on regional assemblies.

Vernon Bogdanor (1999: 265) argued that 'England is, in many respects, the key to the success of devolution'. It is early days yet, but the evidence so far is that it is not. There has been no English backlash following the establishment of a parliament in Edinburgh and an assembly in Cardiff, and no groundswell in support of the proposition that devolution to Scotland and Wales now necessitates change to the government of England, let alone change in the form of elected regional assemblies. Tomaney (1999*b*: 75) called English regional government 'the Cinderella of New Labour's constitutional reform plans', but there seems little popular conviction in most regions that the Scots and Welsh are having a ball while the English remain the drudges. Having said that, some sense of the existence of the official regions can be expected to register with growth in the activity and visibility of the regional development agencies.

In the previous chapter I suggested that English regionalism largely remains what Christopher Harvie (1991) called it a decade and a half ago—'the dog that never barked'—even though regional loyalties can still be strong enough to dilute interest in the identification of any common

Englishness.[6] This chapter has indicated that the dog is stirring slowly; it has pricked one ear, prowls a bit, and barked enough in one corner of its patch to attract attention for a while. There is also a dog in London that has proved quite frisky, though with a bark more notable than its bite. And that is where matters will lie for a generation or so, but, if the Welsh example is any guide, not forever. In 1979 in the first Welsh referendum only 20.9 per cent voted in favour of an assembly with few powers. In the second in 1997 50.3 per cent voted in favour of an assembly with much more substantial powers. In 2004 in the first North-East referendum only 22.1 per cent voted in favour of an assembly with very few powers. In the second in . . . well who knows?

NOTES

1 In 1534 Henry VIII broke with Rome and continued his consolidation of the power of the English state. The Pilgrimage of Grace combined a defence of both the Catholic faith in the north and the powers and privileges of the great landed families of the north. Henry's need to enforce the break with Rome and the desire to centralize power also prompted the annexation of Wales to England in 1536. It is not often remembered that the full incorporation of the north in the English state system came as late as the annexation of Wales.

2 The claim is contested by Iain McLean and colleagues at Nuffield College, Oxford, who argue that official figures are distorted by Home Office and Department of Education and Skills understatement of spending in London. McLean was reported in *The Guardian*, 12 September 2003, as saying, 'If politicians in London think they are getting too little, they are not getting as little as they think they are.'

3 For a Welsh comparison of Wales and Cornwall which is sympathetic to Cornish

aspirations but also realistic about their practicality, see Alys Thomas (1997).

4 Regions and regional assemblies are not the only contenders for reform of sub-national government in England. Gerry Stoker (2000) argues that city regions and elected mayors offer a better way forward for England which should not be discounted just because they are not the counterparts to the Scottish Parliament and Welsh Assembly sought by advocates of devolution for all parts of Britain. RDAs have also been allowed to define their own sub-regions. In some cases—greater Manchester and greater Liverpool in the North-West for example—these amount to city regions. In early 2005 the Labour government is reported to be returning to regeneration of local government.

5 For an illustrative diagram of the current bewildering complexity of regional governance, see Tomaney (2002b: Fig. 12.1) on the North-East.

6 For a historical account of the faltering debate about English regionalism, see Mawson (1997).

REFERENCES

ACKROYD, PETER (2000), *London: The Biography* (London: Chatto & Windus).

ALIBHAI-BROWN, YASMIN (2000), *Who Do We Think We Are? Imagining the New Britain* (London: Allen Lane).

BENNEWORTH, PAUL, and TOMANEY, JOHN (2002), 'Regionalism in North East England', in Tomaney and Mawson (eds.), ch. 10.

BEYNON, HUW, and AUSTRIN, TERRY (1994), *Masters and Servants: Class and Patronage in the Making of a Labour Organization. The Durham Miners and the English Political Tradition* (London: River Oram Press).

BOGDANOR, VERNON (1999), *Devolution in the United Kingdom* (Oxford: Oxford University Press).

BOND, ROSS (2003), 'English regions', *Scottish Affairs*, 44: 98–102. Review of Tomaney and Mawson (2002).

BYRNE, DAVID (1992), 'What sort of future?', in Colls and Lancaster (eds.), ch. 2.

BUCK, NICK; GORDON, IAN; HALL, PETER; HARLOE, MICHAEL; and KLEINMAN, MARK (2002), *Working Capital: Life and Labour in Contemporary London* (London: Routledge).

Cabinet Office/DTLR (2002), *Your Region, Your Choice: Revitalising the English Regions* (white paper), <www.regions.odpm.gov.uk/governance /whitepaper/>, accessed 1 June 2005.

CHEN, SELINA, and WRIGHT, TONY (2000) (eds.), *The English Question* (London: Fabian Society).

COLLS, ROBERT (1992), 'Born-again Geordies', in Colls and Lancaster (eds.), ch. 1.

—— (2002), *Identity of England* (Oxford: Oxford University Press).

—— and LANCASTER, BILL (1992) (eds.), *Geordies: Roots of Regionalism* (Edinburgh: Edinburgh University Press). Includes Editors' Foreword.

DEACON, BERNARD; COLE, DICK; and TREGIDGA, GARRY (2003), *Mebyon Kernow and Cornish Nationalism* (Cardiff: Welsh Academic Press).

FAINSTEIN, SUSAN S.; GORDON, IAN; and HARLOE, MICHAEL (1992), *Divided Cities: New York and London in the Contemporary World* (Oxford: Blackwell).

FERNÁNDEZ-ARMESTO, FELIPE (1994) (ed.), *The Times Guide to the Peoples of Europe* (London: Times Books).

GLANCEY, JONATHAN (2001), *London: Bread and Circuses* (London: Verso).

Government Office South West (2000), *Cornish Language Study*, report by K. McKinnon, <www.cornwall.gov.uk /cornish/GOSW/>, accessed 1 June 2005.

HARDING, ALAN (2000), *Is There a 'Missing Middle' in English Governance?* (London: New Local Government Network).

HARVIE, CHRISTOPHER (1991), 'English regionalism: the dog that never barked', in B. CRICK (ed.), *National Identities: The Constitution of the United Kingdom* (Oxford: Blackwell), 105–18.

HAZELL, ROBERT (2002), 'Regional government in England: three policies in search of a strategy', in Chen and Wright (2000: ch. 3).

HOGWOOD, BRIAN (1996), *Mapping the Regions: Boundaries, Coordination and Government* (Bristol: Policy Press), report to the Joseph Rowntree Foundation.

JONES, PETER (2002), 'Barnett plus needs: the regional spending challenge in Britain', in Tomaney and Mawson (eds.), ch. 14.

LANCASTER, BILL (1992), 'Newcastle—capital of what?', in Colls and Lancaster (eds.), ch. 3.

MCQUAIL, PAUL, and SANDFORD, MARK (2002), 'Elected regional government: the issues', in Tomaney and Mawson (eds.), ch. 13.

MARR, ANDREW (2000), The Day Britain Died (London: Profile).

MAWSON, JOHN (1997), 'The English regional debate: towards regional governance or government?', in J. BRADBURY and J. MAWSON (eds.), British Regionalism and Devolution: The Challenges of State Reform and European Integration (London: Jessica Kingsley).

Mayor of London (2004a), The London Plan: Spatial Development Strategy for Greater London (London: Greater London Authority).

_____ (2004b), The Mayor's Submission to Spending Review 2004 (London: Greater London Authority).

MITCHELL, AUSTIN (2002), 'A manifesto for the North', in Chen and Wright (eds.), ch. 4.

MOORE, ROBERT (1974), Pitmen, Preachers and Politics: The Effects of Methodism in Durham Mining Community (Cambridge: Cambridge University Press).

MORGAN, BRYN (1998), 'The local elections of 7 May 1998 and the London referendum', House of Commons Library Research Papers, 98/59.

MORGAN, KEVIN (2002), 'The English question: regional perspectives on a fractured nation', Regional Studies, 36: 797–810.

Northern Way Steering Group (2004), Moving Forward: The Northern Way—First Growth Strategy Report <www.thenorthernway.co.uk>, accessed 1 June 2005.

Office of the Deputy Prime Minister (2004), Making it Happen: The Northern Way, <www.odpm.gov.uk>, accessed 1 June 2005.

PARTRIDGE, SIMON (1999), 'The British union state: imperial hangover or flexible citizens' home', Catalyst Papers, 4 (London: The Catalyst Trust.)

PAYTON, PHILIP (1996a), Cornwall: A History (Fowey: Cornwall Editions), rev. edn. 2004.

_____ (1996b), 'Inconvenient peripheries: ethnic identity and the "United Kingdom estate"—the cases of "Protestant Ulster" and Cornwall', in I. HAMPSHER-MONK and J. STANYER (eds.), Contemporary Political Studies (Belfast: Political Studies Association), 395–407.

_____ (2000), 'Cornish', in G. PRICE (ed.), Languages in Britain and Ireland (Oxford: Blackwell), ch. 8.

RALLINGS, COLIN, and THRASHER, MICHAEL (2005), 'Why the North East said "no": the 2004 referendum on an elected regional assembly', ESCR Research Programme on Devolution and Constitutional Change, Devolution Briefings, 19 (February).

STOKER, GERRY (2000), 'Is regional government the answer to the English question?', in Chen and Wright (eds.), ch. 5.

STORRY, MIKE, and CHILDS, PETER (1997) (eds.), British Cultural Identities (London: Routledge).

STOYLE, MARK (1999), 'The dissidence of despair: rebellion and identity in early modern Cornwall', Journal of British Studies, 38: 423–44.

TAYLOR, HARVEY (1992), 'Sporting heroes', in Colls and Lancaster (eds.), ch. 7.

THOMAS, ALYS (1997), 'Region, culture and function on the Celtic periphery: Wales, Cornwall and the EU', *Contemporary Wales*, 10: 7–31.

TOMANEY, JOHN (1999*a*), 'In search of English regionalism: the case of the North East', *Scottish Affairs*, 28: 62–82.

—— (1999*b*), 'New Labour and the English question', *Political Quarterly*, 70: 74–82.

—— (2002*a*), 'New Labour and the evolution of regionalism in England', in Tomaney and Mawson (eds.), ch. 3.

—— (2002*b*), 'The problem of regional governance', in Tomaney and Mawson (eds.), ch. 12.

—— (2004), 'The sociological drive for a North East assembly, interview by M. Cieslek, *Network: Newsletter of the British Sociological Association*, 86: 35–8.

—— and HETHERINGTON, PETER (2004), 'English regions: the quiet regional revolution?', in A. TENCH (ed.), *Has Devolution Made a Difference? The State of the Nations* (London: Imprint Academic and The Constitution Unit), ch. 3.

—— and MAWSON, JOHN (2002) (eds.), *England: The State of the Regions* (Bristol: Policy Press).

—— and WARD, NEIL (2000), 'England and the "new regionalism"', *Regional Studies*, 34: 471–8.

TRAVERS, TONY (2004), *The Politics of London: Governing the Ungovernable City* (Basingstoke: Palgrave).

WARD, NEIL, and TOMANEY, JOHN (2002), 'Regionalism in the East of England', in Tomaney and Mawson (eds.), ch. 10.

WILLIAMSON, BILL (1992), 'Living the past differently: historical memory in the North-East', in Colls and Lancaster (eds.), ch. 9.

7

Britain: Relating to Others

Introduction

Anyone considering constructions and representations of Britain and its constituents today has to take into account relations between Britain and significant Others. Two sets of relations would seem especially pertinent, those with the Commonwealth and with Europe. A third set of relations, that with Ireland, is the culmination of more than eight hundred years of contact, and it is with Ireland that this the chapter begins. Attention to Ireland, the Commonwealth, and Europe provides a lead in to the discussion of British citizenship with which the chapter ends.

Ireland

Symbols of Britain's connection with Ireland are still evident. The concocted cross of St Patrick (he was not a martyr) added to the union flag on the union of Great Britain and Ireland in 1801 still remains—as does the Irish harp in the third quarter of the royal standard. Some pound coins also bear the Irish emblem of a Celtic cross. But symbols retained because Northern Ireland remains within the United Kingdom cannot conceal the irrelevance of Ireland to most Britons and their understanding of Britishness today. That more than eight hundred years of contact between 'England' and Ireland have come to this deserves some comment. The discussion that follows begins with Ireland before partition, continues with the Irish Free State and the Republic of Ireland and then turns to Northern Ireland.

Ireland before partition

The Normans who invaded England in 1066 extended their land-grabbing to Ireland in 1169. Norman invaders in English historiography become Anglo-Norman invaders in Irish historiography. For Norman Davies (1999) the invasion of Ireland belongs to the period of the Isles of *Outremer*, the Isles Beyond the Sea, which are such only from the perspective of 'France', and responsibility for it is Norman not English. He adds that 'Punctilious historians call [the invaders] "Cambro-Normans" ', as the particular Normans concerned had, or had had, estates in Wales (p. 366). Punctiliousness is not a constant feature in writing about Ireland. Reference to the invaders as 'English' began at the time. An Irish eyewitness, writing in French, called these Cambro-Normans 'English'. What is unambiguous is that Henry II (Davies's Henri II, who, if one is to be punctilious, was Angevin, not Norman) bestowed on his youngest son, Prince John (Jean), the Lordship of Ireland that Pope Adrian IV had granted him in advance of conquest in 1155. John/Jean was not expected to succeed to the throne but in 1199 he did. Thereafter his successors as king also acquired the Lordship of Ireland. Neither the Normans (and Angevins), nor the English after them, ever succeeded in bringing all of Ireland beyond the pale—Dublin, its hinterland, and sometimes the east coast to the north and south—under their direct control, but in 1541, Henry VIII, having broken with Rome in 1534, signalled the tightening of his grip on Ireland by elevating the lordship to a kingdom. The Gaelic Irish for the most part remained loyal to Rome and, abetted by Catholic Spain and France, they could have posed a threat to Henry's Anglo-Catholic cum Protestantizing kingdom. But the Tudor and later Stuart reinforcement of the central English state still met resistance in Ireland for the reason summarized by Patrick O'Mahoney and Gerard Delanty (2001:36).

The incomplete extension of the Tudor and Stuart state to Ireland goes back to the failure of the medieval state to engage in full-scale conquest. When the Anglo-Norman elite extended their rule over Ireland they had to rely on making allies in Ireland and on papal support. Ever since Pope Adrian granted Henry II a bull giving him the Lordship of Ireland the papacy was an ally of monarchical supremacism. By relying on alliances with magnate power, the English state paradoxically strengthened the Gaelic order. The determined Tudor attempt to extend the centralized English state led to an impasse as the Gaelic magnates rejected a form of government that was incompatible with the liberties they had been granted under the polity of the Lordship of Ireland.

In short the English had to work with the local lords to impose their will and reward them accordingly but they could never entirely rely on lords whose language and culture was mostly different from their own, as, after 1534, was their religion. After 1534 English, and after 1603 English and Scottish, and after 1707 British, interest in Ireland of necessity always mixed the religious with the political and economic.

In 1607, two years after Guy Fawkes and the Catholic Gunpowder Plot, James VI and I resolved that Ulster, the most Gaelic, Catholic, and traditional province in Ireland, and the home of the O'Neill clan that had just waged war on English garrisons, should never again be a threat to his crown. He expropriated the rebels and settled Scots and English on their lands (Devine 2003). The Tudors before him had encouraged trusted landowners to establish the first 'plantations' but they were not state enterprises and the settlers were Anglicans. The new Scottish Presbyterian settlers proved to have little regard for the English in Ireland, old or new, and even less for the Catholic Irish. They built new towns and developed major trades in timber, cattle, and flax. Davies (1999: 569) comments that 'Their self-reliance and truculence were legendary: their devotion to the Protestant cause, unshakeable.' Other plantations, new and revived, brought in further English and Scottish settlers. Needless to say the dispossessed Catholic Irish were never reconciled to their dispossession. The Ulster plantation, in particular, was an economic success but the plantations also ensured that the Catholic Irish would never regard English or British rule as just.

In the War of the Three Kingdoms, 1639–51, Irish combatants, Catholic and Protestant, sided with the royalists.[1] In the turmoil Catholic rebels massacred Protestants in 1641. Royalists and rebels paid a high price when Oliver Cromwell wreaked his revenge in 1649–52. When James VII of Scotland and II of England, a Catholic, was deposed in 1688 there was strong support in Ireland for his restoration. His usurper, the Dutch Protestant William of Orange, was crowned joint sovereign with his wife Mary, James's Protestant daughter, in 1689, and had soon to contend with armed rebellion in Ireland. The Jacobites were about to take Londonderry, but the Protestant Apprentice Boys closed the city gates, vowed 'no surrender' and held out till the siege was lifted. William's victory over the Jacobites at the Battle of the Boyne in 1690 has been celebrated by Ulster Protestants ever since (Lucy and McClure 1997), though William's motivation was not so much anti-Catholic—he had no personal animus against Catholics—as anti-French. The attempted restoration of James VII and II was supported politically and financially by Louis XIV of France, who also had imperial ambitions in the Low Countries and the Papal States in Italy—which was why King Billy, that Ulster Protestant hero, received the congratulations of the Vatican for his victory at the Boyne. Following William's triumph, many Catholics forfeited their land. Other penal laws reinforced the Protestant ascendancy.

The first known Irish parliament met in 1264. It and its successors legislated only for the pale, but the Anglo-Irish soon made it evident that their loyalty to the king could not be taken for granted. A succession of measures were aimed at deterring the Anglo-Irish from going native, often an indicator of Anglo-Irish weakness rather than strength. In 1495 Henry VII's commissioner, Sir Edward Poynings, required the parliament to approve a statute that rendered invalid any legislation that had not previously been approved by the king and Privy Council in England. This made plain that the kingdom of Ireland was a lesser kingdom subordinate to England. Poynings' Law continued to apply after 1707. Fearing that Ireland might otherwise go the way America had in 1776, Westminster dispensed with Poynings' Law in 1782. Henry Grattan, a Protestant lawyer and Irish patriot, responded by demanding more powers for the parliament and Catholic emancipation. The new dispensation did not last long. Theobald Wolfe Tone, a Protestant Dubliner, and the leader of the United Irishmen, a radical society with Presbyterian members in Belfast and Anglican and Catholic members in Dublin, urged Protestants and Catholics to unite to put an end to British domination in Ireland. He worked with the Catholic Convention of 1792 to get the British government to repeal the penal laws; then, having failed, he sought help from France. Following the French Revolution of 1789 the British government feared revolutionary sentiment at home and the designs on Britain of revolutionaries abroad. Wolfe Tone twice moved the French to mount invasions of Ireland. Both attempts failed miserably and after the second, in 1798, in support of rebellion on a significant scale, he was captured, tried, and executed. In the light of this experience, the British government decided that rather than freeing the Irish parliament the safer course was to close it and to end the semi-detached status of Ireland. Accordingly the United Kingdom of Great Britain and Ireland came into being in 1801 with Irish membership of the parliament at Westminster. This union differed from the union of 1707, however, in that Irish ministries separate from British ministries were retained in Dublin and a lieutenant-governor served there as representative of the king.

Nineteenth century Ireland is forever associated with rural poverty and the famine of 1845–51 in which a million died with a million more emigrating within a decade, but it also experienced considerable development. By the end of the century Ireland may have been less developed than Britain but in terms of transport, banking, higher education, the professions, and much else it was more developed than many countries elsewhere in Europe that had by then obtained their independence. The Young Ireland movement in the 1840s had given a significant boost to Irish nationalism and the century had seen a succession of eloquent Irish political leaders—Daniel O'Connell, Charles Parnell, and John Redmond—use the Westminster parliament to press the case for Catholic emancipation, repeal of the union, land reform, and home rule, the first and third successfully, the fourth less so, and the second not at all. Redmond was notably conciliatory, emphasizing the huge Irish contributions to the successes of Victorian Britain and the Empire. William Gladstone tried unsuccessfully to legislate for Irish home rule in 1886 and 1893. Another Liberal premier, Herbert Asquith, got a home rule bill through the Commons in 1913 but not the Lords. The bitterly contested bill was reintroduced in 1914 but with the outbreak of war further discussion was shelved (Kee 1972).

Jim Mac Laughlin (2001) argues that when the English, the Scots, and later the British, came to Ireland they did so believing themselves to be superior peoples with an opportunity to exploit and a mission to civilize the Celtic Irish. The Irish were savage and poor beyond necessity, they thought, failing even to manage the land productively. But the social and economic gap between the stubbornly Catholic Irish and their Protestant settler neighbours and political masters closed only slowly. Additionally, the cultural gap did not so much close as change. 'Civilizing' the Irish turned out to be only partly a story of the Irish adopting the manners of the invaders; it was also a story of the Irish resisting by recovering and promoting their rich Celtic cultural inheritance. The barbarians had a history after all. Instead of the cultured and the cultureless, the polished and the rude of the Enlightenment (including very much the Scottish Enlightenment), there were two cultures, the Celtic and Catholic Irish and the Protestant British. O'Mahoney and Delanty (2001: 54) emphasize how following land reform, 'The Irish path to modernity was undertaken neither by ruling elites nor by the working class but by a rural bourgeoisie in alliance with a nationalist intelligentsia and Church', and Mac Laughlin describes how the larger farmers, the petty bourgeoisie, and the Catholic priesthood played key parts in the formation of an Irish ethno-nation in the nineteenth century. Irish ethno-nationalism then and since has necessarily excluded the Other—the Protestants, the Anglo-Irish, and especially the Ulster unionists. The Ulster unionists in turn have refused to 'surrender' to the papists in the republic. The Irish ethno-nation did not have sole claim to the territory of Ireland. The unionists imagined a bigger progressive, and imperial, British nation of which Ireland was but a part and they noted how often Irish men and women took advantage of the opportunities for individual betterment it offered.

The Irish Free State and the Republic of Ireland

The Irish Republican Army's Easter Rising of 1916 in Dublin was put down with great force by the British army. The British government had been alarmed by rebellion at 'home' in the middle of the First World War but it miscalculated in executing the leaders of the rising, turning republicans such as Pádraic Pearse and James Connolly, who hitherto had had only minority support, into national heroes and martyrs, and prompting a shift in public preference from home rule to independence (Kee 1972). After the 1918 general election seventy-three newly elected republican Sinn Féin MPs refused to take their seats at Westminster and instead established their own parliament, the Dáil, in Dublin. Between 1919 and 1921 republicans fought a War of Independence against the British. In response the 1920 Government of Ireland Act provided for the partition of Ireland and the establishment of two home-rule parliaments in Dublin and Belfast (though few in Britain or Ireland expected partition to be permanent). In 1921 the Anglo-Irish Treaty agreed on implementation of the act, and in 1922 the Irish Free State came into being with the same dominion status as Canada, Australia, New Zealand, and South Africa. Partition split the republicans. Some accepted the treaty, others did not. The result was the civil war of 1922–3 during which Michael Collins, who had negotiated the treaty, was assassinated. The pro-treaty forces prevailed. The leader of the anti-treaty republicans, Éamon de Valera, entered the Dáil in 1927 as head of a new party opposed to the treaty, Fianna Fáil, and became taoiseach (prime minister) in 1932. In office de Valera accepted the treaty de facto and concentrated on ensuring that

Ireland developed the very distinctive national identity discussed below. He declared Ireland to be a Catholic state, prompting James Craig, the prime minister of Northern Ireland, to respond in 1933 that he was glad to preside over a Protestant parliament and a Protestant state (Aughey 2001: 130). In 1937 the Irish Free State adopted a new constitution in which it renamed itself Éire (Irish for Ireland) in both the English and Irish texts, claimed all Ireland as its territory, and, in contrast to the strictly secular constitution of 1922, formalized the privileged status of the Roman Catholic Church. Alone of the dominions, Éire remained neutral during the Second World War although many citizens of the Free State volunteered to join the British forces.[2] In 1949 Éire declared itself a republic and left the Commonwealth.

O'Mahoney and Delanty (2001: 58) argue that the 'petit-bourgeois class of medium-to-large farmers, rural, small-town and urban service providers including clerics, shopkeepers, publicans, doctors, solicitors, clerks, accountants, were the dominant force in twentieth century Ireland' and they were 'triumphant in defining what constituted national identity'. They were committed to a Catholic church for a Catholic people, to the Catholicization of culture, and to a state which would 'enshrine a Catholic ethical code in its laws and practices' (p. 66). The church 'sought to retain control of socialisation . . . by establishing a firm grip on education as well as by its doctrine of familism with its chief tenet, the subordination of women and control of their sexuality through the doctrine of "the home" ' (ibid.). This was not the only vein of Irish nationalism in pre-partition Ireland—there had also been liberal democratic, revolutionary, and radical veins—but it was the most prominent and it was the one the governments of de Valera sought to institutionalize by embracing the church, reviving the Irish language and Gaelic culture, adopting a Catholicized constitution, favouring protectionism and autarchy, and resisting economic developments that threatened petit-bourgeois ascendancy in an Irish Ireland. Better poor and pure than rich, worldly, and sullied. Better the small world of Ireland than a wider world in which Britain loomed large. According to O'Mahoney and Delanty (2001: 155), 'The first twenty years of Independence therefore saw a society endeavouring to roll back the threat of modernity.' The Protestant population of the Free State, initially 10 per cent, halved and the economy languished. It was not until the 1960s that the idea of a more modern Ireland began to win favour.

It is notable that the proclamation of the 'The Provisional Government of Ireland to the People of Ireland' made during the Easter Rising in 1916 refers to 'the whole people of Ireland' in the singular and ascribes to an 'alien [British] government' responsibility for the differences 'which have divided a minority from the majority in the past'. It does not allow that there might be two peoples in Ireland or that there might be differences not fostered by the British. John Coakley (1999: 49) describes Irish nationalism after 1922 as irredentist, but it was irredentist only in aspiration; for example, as Coakley himself says, the main Irish political parties did not attempt to organize on an all-Ireland basis. The 1937 constitution is extraordinary for granting a special status to the Catholic church *and* laying claim to all Ireland. Was it supposed that a million Protestants in the north with Presbyterians to the fore would submit to a Catholic order, or 'return' to Scotland and England three centuries after their forebears had left them? After all, the imagined community of Ireland in the 1930s had no place for them. Or was it a charade? Lay claim to all Ireland in honour of the Irish republican tradition but do nothing to act upon it. It would seem the latter; neither the Irish government nor the people of the Free State showed much concern for Catholics in the north and the discrimination they suffered (Elliot 2000). But if a charade, it was a dangerous one. It intensified the suspicions of Protestants in the north and left an opening for the IRA who were prepared to act upon it.

Bit by bit through the second half of the twentieth century the Republic of Ireland has been transformed. The questioning began in the late 1940s, as the post-war Labour government in Britain put in place the welfare state and extended the public sector. Why was welfare in Ireland left to a church with its own priorities? Were the values of rural Ireland appropriate to an urbanizing society? Did Ireland have to be so poor? Why should not women have aspirations outside the home? Had not economic self-sufficiency held the country back? Would not participation in the international economy be better? The questioning led to initiatives in health and housing from the late 1940s but it was in the 1960s that the old Catholicized order began seriously to lose its hold on Irish society. The state, not the church, expanded health services and secondary and tertiary education. Television and youth culture overcame Irish isolation. Censorship eased. Contraception was legalized in the 1970s. Irish Ireland did not disappear but it was no longer all pervasive and national identity, like other identities, increasingly became a matter of choice and individual lifestyle. The reference to the special position of the Catholic church was dropped from the constitution in 1972. The following year Ireland entered the European Economic Community and never looked back. Entry committed Ireland to the internationalization of its economy. The republic benefited massively from EEC payments and from inward investment. It opened up to Continental trends and cultures and gained access to an international stage on which Britain did not play a leading role. Restrictions on the sale of contraceptives were lifted in 1993, the same year that homosexuality was decriminalized. Divorce was permitted following a referendum vote in favour in 1995, itself an interesting development in so far as the intervention of the church had defeated those in favour in a previous vote in 1980. In the 1990s the lowest corporation tax in the European Union attracted huge inward investment especially from the United States. From 1994 the economy grew rapidly and prompted talk of a Celtic tiger. By the end of the century the once impoverished south was richer not only than Northern Ireland but also, on some measures, Britain. Weakened by repeated revelations of the sexual misconduct of its priests and by the big fall in vocations, the once ubiquitous Roman Catholic Church was on the back foot, no longer the biggest influence on welfare and culture.

Cathair Ó Dochartaigh (2000: 32) notes that 'Although the Irish constitution adopted in 1937 speaks of Irish as the first official language, no policies were devised to support this statement and it has taken on the iconization of an aspiration, with no relevance for the everyday life of the country.' Native Irish speakers in the Gaeltacht (the three small areas in the west of Ireland where Irish was officially supported as a first language) are estimated at less than 20,000. Following second language acquisition in school, more than a million claimed to speak Irish in the Irish census of 1991, but very few were fluent (pp. 10–11).

The modernization of Ireland has been uneven across the republic and some of the successes of the Celtic tiger have been the product of creative accounting by transnational companies who choose to declare profits in Ireland where they are taxed less (Coulter and Coleman 2003). The new import of labour and reception of asylum seekers has also been accompanied by racism (Loyal 2003; Devereux and Breen 2003). The republic, almost entirely Catholic (the Protestant population is now down to 3 per cent) and white, is not a notably plural society. These qualifications, however, do not alter the basic conclusion that the modernization of Ireland has been remarkable.

Neil Collins and Terry Cradden (2001: 150) comment that 'For Ireland, nationalism is the dominant ideology. It binds diverse individuals into a "people", acts as a motive for economic, cultural and sporting achievement, and provides a source of genuine pride and sympathy. The nation has become the highest affiliation and obligation of the individual, and through it a significant part of personal identity is formed.' But how diverse are the people it binds? In his account of nationalism in Ireland from medieval to modern times, George Boyce (1995) examines developments over eight centuries which are complex in terms of the ethnic origins, languages, cultures, and religions of the contributors. But in the nineteenth century it is the Catholic nation emphasizing its Celtic heritage that comes to the fore and this development culminates in de Valera's Ireland, an exclusive Irish Ireland. Boyce's is an account of how past centuries of heterogeneity gave way in the Free State and the Republic to the most homogenous society Ireland has known for a millennium or more. There is developing in today's Ireland, however, a very different nationalism. James Goodman (1998) refers to official advocacy of a more secular, civic, and inclusive Ireland comfortable with the wider world represented by free trade and inward investment, the European Union, and the support of the American government for a power-sharing settlement in the north. He refers to a cosmopolitan nationalism but cosmopolitan suggests a population of Ireland more varied than it is. It is an open question how heterogenous a society the Irish will prove willing to accept. It would be better for the moment to speak of a pro-European liberal nationalism.

However it is characterized, northern Protestants do not imagine this new Irish community includes them. But then many citizens in the south remain unsure they want them. Surveys suggest opinion in the republic has long been ambivalent about reunification (Davis 2003). On the one hand Eurobarometers indicate that the Irish have much greater pride in their nation than do the citizens of any of the other pre-2004 EU members except the Greeks, and Bernadette Hayes and Ian McAllister (1996: 78) note how 82 per cent of the Irish in 1991 agreed a united Ireland was 'something to be hoped for'. But Harvey Cox (1985: 37) reported that according to a survey in 1983 only 41 per cent of the Irish considered the people of Northern Ireland to be Irish compared with 3 per cent who thought them Irish and British, and 13 per cent who thought them British; Hayes and McAllister noted (1996: 76) that a survey in 1991 indicated that only 41 per cent still thought Irish unity was a solution to the problems in Northern Ireland compared with 72 per cent in 1984; and Thomas Davis (2003: 32) cites a survey for the *Irish Times* in 1996 that found that only 30 per cent of respondents wanted Northern Ireland incorporated in a united Ireland compared with 29 per cent who wanted it linked to both the republic and the United Kingdom, and 22 per cent who wanted it to become independent. It was thus no surprise that in the referendum following the 1998 Good Friday Agreement 94 per cent approved an amendment to remove the republic's territorial claim to Northern Ireland. It is as if the Irish were saying, 'The republic is doing well; don't let northern Protestants spoil it.' They still would like Irish reunification, but not at any price.

What sort of Ireland could accommodate northern Protestants? After reconsidering theories of nationalism, Richard Kearney (1997) suggests a post-nationalist one—a nation that respects reason and modernity and rejects irrationality and atavism. After rethinking Irish history, O'Mahoney and Delanty (2001: 188) suggest a post-national one—a nation that finds unity in diversity. 'A crucial question for the future will be whether Irish society is capable of generating a "post-national" identity, a collective identity that is no longer focused on the fiction of an "homogenous people" and their alleged common, cultural attributes but on constitutional norms and cultural identifications that emphasize the right, but associated responsibilities, of being different.' Perhaps a strictly secular constitution and a pluralizing civil society could accommodate all but the most intransigent Presbyterians.[3]

Northern Ireland

Between 1912 and 1914 Protestant unionists in the north of Ireland, led by William Carson, mobilized to defeat the home rule then under discussion at Westminster and established the Ulster Volunteer Force. The republicans' response developed into the Irish Republican Army (IRA). Following partition in 1922 Protestant unionists controlled the six counties of Northern Ireland via their majority at Stormont (the parliament in Belfast), their control of the overwhelmingly Protestant Royal Ulster Constabulary and the police reserves, their discriminatory use of public funds, their control of patronage and public appointments, and, where necessary, the gerrymandering of local government wards—all with the help of both the British constitutional convention that Westminster could not discuss the internal affairs of Northern Ireland and, until the 1950s, the indifference of the Irish government to the position and prospects of Catholics in the north. The all-male Orange Order, founded in 1795, supported the Protestant ascendancy by defending the legal provision that the monarch be a Protestant, by parading to commemorate Protestant victories in Irish history, and by facilitating Protestant connections in politics and business (Farrell 1976; Edwards 1999).

Between the wars Northern Ireland was richer than the south with a more industrialized economy. After the Second World War it needed British subventions to extend the new welfare state to the province and to deal with rising unemployment. Worried that increasing financial dependence on Britain could lead to increasing interference by British governments, Northern Irish leaders considered in the 1950s independent dominion status but concluded a poorer Northern Ireland would not be a more stable one. Instead in the 1960s Terence O'Neill's government of Northern Ireland encouraged inward investment in the belief that, inter alia, more prosperous Catholics would be less nationalist. Harold Wilson and James Callaghan, Labour prime ministers in the 1970s, both made plain their own support for Irish unity in principle even if they could not see how it could be achieved in practice (Dixon 2001: 161). Then and since British governments have indicated that they would endorse any settlement in Northern Ireland that the Protestant and Catholic communities could agree upon including a united Ireland. In 1990 Peter Brooke, the Conservative Secretary of State for Northern Ireland, said explicitly what had long been obvious to most Britons, 'The British Government has no selfish strategic or economic interest in Northern Ireland' (ibid. 225). That Conservative and Labour have continued to state that Northern Ireland would remain within the United Kingdom for as long as the majority of its people voted in favour of it has been of limited comfort to unionists who see their commitment to the union unreciprocated by British governments or British public opinion. British governments have taken care never to offer the British electorate a vote on the future of Northern Ireland.

In 1967 civil rights campaigners began marches in protest at the discrimination against Catholics in the allocation of public housing and in appointment to public and private sector jobs and at the gerrymandering of local government wards in favour of Protestants in Derry and elsewhere. The marches secured extensive media coverage in Ireland, Britain, and America and they led to violent Protestant reaction, the IRA's 'defence' of Catholic communities, the deployment of the British army, the mobilization of loyalist paramilitaries, Bloody Sunday (the killing of unarmed Catholic demonstrators by British paratroopers in 1972), the IRA's attempt to kill and bomb the British into withdrawal from Northern Ireland, and the Ulster loyalist determination to use arms to stop them. It is not practical to consider the whole dismal sequence of events from the onset of 'The Troubles' in 1968–9 to the latest, and only partially successful, attempt to resolve them with the Good Friday Agreement in 1998 (but see Rose 2000; Dixon 2001; Loughlin 2004; Ó Dochartaigh 2005). Instead a few basic points will have to suffice. First, British pressure has ensured that measures taken in Belfast and London have all but ended discrimination. If the nationalist grievance were only discrimination, the Troubles would be over. Second, Northern Ireland remains poorer than Scotland, Wales, or any English region despite having the highest per capita public expenditure. Its economy has been damaged by the Troubles and it has seen its once poorer southern neighbour overtake it. The twentieth century also saw the population of Belfast fall while that of Dublin grew; once smaller than Belfast, Dublin is now much bigger. Economic conditions are still worse west of the River Bann where Catholics are in the majority but the gap between average Protestant and Catholic household incomes has narrowed. Third, following an IRA and Protestant paramilitary ceasefire, the 1998 Good Friday Agreement between the British and Irish governments and the Northern Irish political parties set the terms of a political settlement that was then endorsed in referendums north and south of the border (71 per cent in the north on an 81 per cent turnout, 94 per cent in the south but on a turnout of only 56 per cent). Fourth, if they are to engage fully with the political and economic possibilities of any new Northern Ireland, Ulster Catholics will have to put behind them what Elliott (2000) calls their 'grievance culture' and 'extraordinary nihilism and communal fatalism'.

The three-stranded Good Friday Agreement (GFA) provides for the restoration of the parliament at Stormont elected by proportional representation and a power-sharing executive, north–south collaboration in six policy areas with the possibility of adding others in due course, and British–Irish collaboration. It confirms that Northern Ireland will remain within the United Kingdom until and unless the majority there votes otherwise and it institutionalizes Irish government involvement in the governance of Northern Ireland and protection of the interests of Catholic nationalists. That all parties to the agreement including Sinn Féin have accepted partition would seem a triumph for the unionists even if they, in their insecurity, are unable to see it as such. That all parties to the agreement—who include the loyalists, but not, significantly, Ian Paisley's Democratic Unionists (DUP)—have accepted Irish government participation in the working of the agreement is a triumph for the nationalists because it formally accommodates continuing Irish interest in the future of Northern Ireland. The GFA requires a complete and permanent cessation of violence. Disagreement about the modalities of IRA decommissioning of weapons have led to unionist withdrawals from the executive, each such withdrawal necessitating a suspension of parliament and a return to direct rule from London. The latest withdrawal continues at the time of writing (February 2005). But the ceasefire has held, the economy is improving, political violence has diminished, and on–off talks on a revised settlement within the framework of the Good Friday Agreement will, no doubt, resume in due course.

The ceasefire and the GFA have not brought with them any post-modern loosening of the communal loyalties that Cathall McCall (1999) thought possible (but Arthur Aughey (2001) thought unlikely) or any strengthening of the middle ground in Northern Irish society and politics. On the contrary 'sectarianism remains, with physical separation of the Protestant and Catholic communities in many parts of the province' (Tonge 2005: 1). The Ulster Unionist Party has lost ground to Ian Paisley's anti-GFA DUP and the nationalist Social Democratic and Labour Party has lost ground to Sinn Féin. Jonathan Tonge refers to an armed truce and a cold peace. For the British and Irish governments, these are not the most propitious of circumstances in which to get Ian Paisley, leader of the DUP, and Gerry Adams, leader of Sinn Féin to agree.

It is now apparent to almost all that the division within Northern Ireland would not somehow fade away with British withdrawal. On the contrary British withdrawal would transfer the division to the republic and could destabilize it. The old inward-looking Catholic and Celtic ethnonationalism of the republic may be in retreat but it is not obvious that the new proud but outward-looking liberal nationalism of modern Ireland could accommodate uncompromising northern Protestants (however much people in Britain might wish it could). It might also be thought that the transformation of the republic over the last three decades has made the reunification of Ireland more likely, but there is scant evidence to that effect so far. The advance of the Celtic tiger leaves northern Protestants unmoved (Shirlow 2003). As late as 2002 the Ulster Unionist leader, David Trimble, scornfully dismissed the republic as the 'pathetic, mono-cultural, sectarian state to the south' (quoted in Tonge 2005: 260). The Presbyterian hostility to Roman Catholicism that the Reverend Ian Paisley articulates so stridently still runs very deep. And the fear that the Sinn Féin/IRA conversion to democratic politics is insincere is real. It is not just the haunting possibility of a return to arms that generates the fear, it is also the suspicion that Sinn Féin obtains funds by criminal means. Other political parties in the republic, too, cannot view with equanimity the prospect of increased competition from a party they believe benefits from IRA bank robberies.

England, Scotland, and Britain have had a long engagement with Ireland but by the end of the twentieth century Britons generally had concluded that Ireland, north and south, is not part of Britain even if the unionists in Northern Ireland continue to protest their Britishness (a Britishness unfamiliar to most Britons) and even if the British government has found it hard to disengage from Northern Ireland. Two decades ago Steve Bruce (1986: 251) wrote that 'the Britain [Ulster Protestants] want to be part of seems to be a country which ceased to exist a century ago'. Often that still seems the case. Ulster loyalists are also loyal not to Britain or its parliament but to the monarch, and then only so long as the monarch remains by law a Protestant. For decades opinion polls in Britain have shown majority support for British withdrawal from Northern Ireland (Hayes and McAllister 1996; Dixon 2001; Davis 2003). As Hayes and McAllister (1996: 67) said, 'For the majority of British citizens, the problem of Northern Ireland is an unwelcome historical anachronism from which a swift political as well as military disengagement is, by far, the most preferred solution.' Only one in fifteen Gallup polls between 1974 and 1992 failed to indicate a majority in favour of British troop withdrawal either immediately or within five years; the percentages ranged from 44 in 1988 to 64 in 1976 (p. 66). All nine Gallup polls between 1979 and 1994 revealed only minority support for the continued union of Northern Ireland with Britain; the percentages ranged from 23 in 1994 to 30 in 1995 (p. 68). Support for independence for Northern Ireland was always greater than support for Irish unity. The British Election Survey of 1992 also recorded 30 per cent support for Northern Ireland remaining part of the UK but with interesting variations: 35 per cent in Scotland, 29 per cent in England, and 22 per cent in Wales (72). Fifty-two per cent of respondents favoured Irish reunification, the independence option not having been put to them. In 2001 an ICM poll in *The Guardian* (21 August) indicated that only 26 per cent of respondents in Britain thought that Northern Ireland should be part of the United Kingdom compared with 41 per cent who thought it should be part of a united Ireland. Asked who they blamed for the current problems in the Northern Ireland peace process, 3 per cent said the unionists, 5 per cent the republicans, and 64 per cent both equally. With regard to Northern Ireland, there is in Britain a strong plague-on-both-your-houses sentiment. The IRA and the Protestant paramilitaries are perceived as vile, Gerry Adams as duplicitous, and Ian Paisley as grotesque. Softer voices—those of Protestant and Catholic moderates, Catholic unionists, socialists, liberals, and women's groups—are drowned out. Were it to come to pass there is little reason to suppose most Britons would greet a united Ireland with anything other than a deep sigh of relief. In the absence of a united Ireland, meanwhile, there must be a possibility that the Republic of Ireland and Great Britain, for all their current differences, which are large, will end up more like each other than either is like Northern Ireland.

Britain and Ireland and the Irish in Britain

The British Isles may now be just the Isles for Norman Davies and those who heed him and Britain and Ireland for the rest, just as rugby's touring British Lions are now the British and Irish Lions or simply the Lions. But the pairing acknowledges a long history of interaction which has also given Britain large populations of Irish origin (Hornsby-Smith and Dale 1988; Hornsby-Smith 1999; MacRaild 1999). The population of Irish descent includes the completely assimilated at one extreme and the insistently Irish at the other, some of whom participate in Irish communities, parishes, and clubs and voluntary associations as in greater Glasgow where major Irish immigration dates from the mid-nineteenth century and Greater London where half the Irish-born live. In the 2001 census 1.3 per cent of the population of England, 1.0 per cent of the population of Scotland, and 0.6 per cent of the population of Wales gave white Irish as their ethnicity. Rather more than two-thirds of the Irish-born are from the republic, the rest from Northern Ireland (Chance 1996).

That Ireland south of the border was once part of the United Kingdom is a bit of history Britons show little interest in remembering. Northern Ireland, by contrast, has demanded attention but in its sectarianism and its violence it only confirms that it is unBritish. Ireland thus has less bearing on constructions of Britain now than it has had at any time since the union of the crowns of England and Scotland in 1603 and the first advocacy of Great Britain as a (potential) political community by James VI of Scotland and I of England.

The Commonwealth

There has already been consideration of Empire and Commonwealth in previous chapters, particularly with respect to Scotland in the Empire (Ch. 3), Anglo-British England and Cosmopolitan England (Ch. 5), and London (Ch. 6), but it is now time to draw some threads together in connection with: mission, memory, and Empire; association, cooperation, and the Commonwealth; and, later in the chapter, subjecthood, citizenship, and Britain today.

Today's is a post-imperial Britain but anyone seeking to understand it still needs to recognize how central Empire was to the formation of English, Scottish, and British identities. When writing about Anglo-Britain I accepted the argument of Krishan Kumar (2000, 2003) that empires can be vehicles for an understated national identity in which the state-bearing 'group' believes itself called to a political, cultural, or religious mission. Imperialism thereby acquires lofty motives. In the British case, at least by the nineteenth century, the mission was to civilize and liberalize. Niall Ferguson (2003) emphasizes that the reality was often horribly different but the nineteenth-century Empire did pioneer global free trade and liberal capitalism, spread the idea of parliamentary democracy around the globe, give the world English as a lingua franca, and invest heavily in a global communications network. Robin Cohen (1994: 33) took a similar line. 'The shouldering of the white man's burden may have been both a paternalistic and self-assigned task, but it provided an ideologically sustaining reason for British expansion. Establishing dominions abroad may have been an arrogant putsch against the indigenous people, but British political ideas and institutions undoubtedly spread the practice of liberty, representation and equal justice.' As recently as the coronation of Elizabeth II in 1953, the British mostly regarded the Empire as something to be proud of. Following decolonization it became something very many were ashamed of. Ferguson offers neither celebration nor condemnation but ambivalence, albeit in his case an ambivalence in which the positives outweigh the negatives. Often, Ferguson adds, the counterfactual alternatives would have been worse (our empire was less nasty than yours) and he is also no fan of today's American imperium ('an empire . . . that dare not speak its name') (p. 370). Cohen, no friend of Empire, could still see a noble side to it. Kumar, Ferguson, and Cohen articulate the more balanced view of Empire many Britons would seem to hold today. Empire building saw great feats of exploration, civil engineering, administration and justice, and education and welfare, as well as of arms, to set against the exploitation, the brutalities, and the racism. For countless families in Britain today, white, black, and Asian, past family members so often had their part in Empire and present family members so often live in what were once British colonies, protectorates, and dominions. There is still some pride in Empire, some remembrance of comradeship in arms during the Second World War, some ties that bind.

The Commonwealth, as distinct from the Empire, has a more recent provenance. Lord Rosebery first referred to the Empire as a Commonwealth of Nations in Australia in 1884. The British Commonwealth came to be associated with Britain and the king's self-governing dominions. The dominions and the dates of their foundation were as follows: Newfoundland (1855), Canada (1867), Australia (1900), New Zealand (1907), South Africa (1910), and the Irish Free State (1922). The Commonwealth thus originated as a subset of all the territories that made up the British Empire. Conferences of Britain and the dominions began in 1887. The Imperial Conference of 1926 adopted the Balfour Report which defined Britain and the dominions as autonomous communities of equal status that owed an allegiance to the crown. This principle was enshrined in the Statute of Westminster in 1931 which stipulated that the British parliament would no longer legislate for the dominions on any matter whatsoever without their prior consent. The British Empire and Commonwealth remained important, however, in terms of trade with tariff concessions, cultural and educational links, family ties, and, with the exception of the Irish Free State, a common cause in the Second World War. After the war India (1947), Pakistan (1947), Ceylon (1948), and Burma (1948) obtained their independence. All wanted to become republics whilst, with the exception of Burma, retaining an association with Britain. To accommodate this the British Empire and Commonwealth was reconstituted as the Commonwealth in 1949, an association of independent states that acknowledge their historical link with Britain and accept the position of the British monarch as Head of the Commonwealth. Irish republicans had wanted some such association in 1921 and had Britain been as accommodating then the subsequent history of Ireland could have been very different. As it was Éire declared itself a republic and left the Commonwealth in 1949.

Imperial preference in trade was reduced after the Second World War when America made its reduction a condition of aid to Britain with post-war reconstruction. Most of what remained was forfeited by Britain on entry to the European Economic Community in 1973. The Commonwealth is still active in other areas, however, and established a secretariat in London in 1965. The heads of government of today's fifty-one Commonwealth members meet in conference every four years. In 1971 in Singapore they adopted The Declaration of Commonwealth Principles which requires all members to support, inter alia, individual civil rights, democracy, racial equality, and fair trade.[4] These principles were further elaborated in the Harare Declaration of 1991 which contains references to the rule of international law, the equality of women, free trade on fair terms, sustainable development, and environmental protection. The Commonwealth has few means of dealing with breaches of its fine sentiments, but at different times disputes with South Africa, Pakistan, Fiji, Nigeria, and Zimbabwe have led to their withdrawal or suspension from the Commonwealth. Of these only Zimbabwe is not a member as of February 2005. Within the framework of the English-speaking Commonwealth a significant number of schemes promote educational and cultural exchanges, and technical, economic, and political cooperation. Every four years there is also a big multi-sport gathering, the Commonwealth Games—the next in Melbourne in 2006. Commonwealth governments also display their membership by appointing high commissioners, not ambassadors, to represent them in each other's countries. All that said, the Commonwealth is of minor political significance to Britain compared with the European Union, NATO, and the United Nations and British citizens know it. In 1969 a Gallup poll asked 'Which of these—Europe, the Commonwealth or America—is the most important to Britain?' and MORI polls have been asking the same question at intervals since.[5] In 1969 34 per cent answered 'the Commonwealth'. There has been steady decline since to 16 per cent in 2003. Those answering 'Europe' began with a low of 21 per cent in 1969, peaked at 57 per cent in 1993, and fell back to 42 per cent in 2003. Those answering 'America' began with a high of 34 per cent in 1969, bottomed at 15 per cent in 1993, and recovered to 34 per cent again in 2003.

Cohen (1994: 33) notes the visions that inspired the Empire, the European Union, and the Commonwealth and concludes that 'The notion of a world association of black, brown, yellow and white peoples, which underlay the design of the post-1947 Commonwealth was perhaps the most utopian, but sadly the most underdeveloped, vision of all,' and so it has remained.

The European Union

Within the confines of this chapter, it is only possible to make a few points about Britain, Britons, and European identity, identification with Europe, and the European Union. Winston Churchill's post-war ambivalence about Europe is a good place to start. In a famous speech in Zurich in 1946 Churchill called for a united Europe with a partnership between a France returned to greatness and a reconstructed Germany at its heart. Accordingly, he strongly supported moves towards a united Europe over the next four years; and he berated the Labour government in 1950 for not joining the European Coal and Steel Community, the first building block in what was to become the European Economic Community. But when he had the opportunity to reverse Labour's decision following the Conservative general election victory in 1951 he did not take it. Nor did he do anything to ensure Britain was on the inside of other initiatives that were to lead to the EEC. 'Churchill in government', as Roy Jenkins (2001: 856) says, 'wanted European unity to succeed with Britain benevolently on the outside.' Like many Scandinavians, Russians, and fellow Britons, before and since, Churchill regarded Europe as somewhere else—Britain was a partner of Europe, not a part of it. He greatly like holidaying in Europe but when it came to political alliances his predilections were elsewhere. He had opposed moves towards independence for India in the 1930s and had led Britain in the Second World War with an eye to saving the Empire to which he was deeply attached. He also had an admiration for America—his mother was American—which found expression in both his celebration of the achievements of the English-speaking peoples and his respect for NATO (in contrast to his scornful dismissal of proposals for a European army). The Empire's successor, the Commonwealth, inspires few Britons today but three other aspects of Churchill's worldview still have their supporters: an attachment to America ('Atlanticism'), semi-detachment with respect to Europe, and an underestimation of the prospects for European economic union and the consequent need for Britain to be a central player in determining the rules of a game it cannot avoid playing.

The European Union has long defied simple description. The changes in name from the European Economic Community to the European Community and then the European Union reflect changes in structure and practice that have been challenging in their complexity and ambiguous in their potential. The expansion from six members in 1958 to twenty-five in 2004 has also made the dynamics of the union increasingly hard to calculate. Additionally, there have been huge shifts in policy from the interventionism and protectionism of the original Common Agricultural Policy to the liberalism and regulation of the single market announced by the Single European Act of 1986 and largely put in place by 1992 (even if the CAP survives in modified form and the single market and economic and monetary union have still to be fully completed). There has also been a broadening from the economic concerns of the original foundation to the social, political, and security concerns given form by the 1992 Treaty of Maastricht (albeit a broadening that the visionary progenitors of the 'Common Market' expected). In principle, the evolution of the union is a simple story about the achievement of European integration and the 'ever closer union' anticipated by the founding Treaty of Rome in 1957. In practice, it is a convoluted story about ever more complicated collaboration between (subsets of) member states without any consensus as to what a completed union should be. It has taken an American, Jeremy Rifkin (2004: 197), to remind us that it is nevertheless a story of remarkable achievement, and even he concedes that its 'architects are unsure of exactly what the EU represents', adding 'The problem is that there has never been any governing institution like the EU.' Rifkin's description of the aspiring union as 'the "United States" of Europe' suggests a united states different from the United States, but is still a provocation to some.

The Constitution for Europe signed by the twenty-five heads of government in Rome in November 2004 will, if ratified by all twenty-five parliaments, make today's union easier to understand in so far as it rationalizes in one document what hitherto was contained in several and it supplies operating procedures which can more credibly cope with twenty-five members and more, but easier still does not mean easy.[6] Jacques Delors, when president of the European Commission, used to refer to the EC/EU as 'un objet politique non-identifié' (quoted in Schmitter 1996b: 1). *Plus ça change, plus c'est la même chose.* The union of today is still hard to describe. It has, in addition to its identity and democratic deficits, a comprehensibility deficit and this discourages citizen engagement.

In what follows I will address British ambivalence about Europe first by indicating why it is hard for all citizens of Europe to identify with Europe and the European Union, and second by suggesting some reasons why it is apparently harder than most, perhaps hardest of all, for citizens of Britain.

Foundations: where is Europe, who are the Europeans?

In Ch. 1 I made use of David Easton's (1965) three-level model of political decision-making when pointing up issues of inclusion and exclusion in connection with being British. I now want to use it again in connection with being European. At the fundamental level, the following questions arise. Where is Europe? Who are the Europeans? What makes them Europeans? At issue are territories and boundaries, values and culture, inclusion and exclusion, Europe and the Other. The boundaries question is non-trivial (Therborn 1995). The extension of the European Union in 2004 to admit indubitably European post-communist countries in a single economic community of democratic states is very widely regarded as the right and proper thing to have done. It is, however, asking a lot of citizens of the union to turn the complex political geography of Europe into a collective European political consciousness. The dilemma is easily illustrated from a British perspective. Following the Nazi invasion of Sudetenland in 1938, Neville Chamberlain, the prime minister, notoriously described Czechoslovakia in the House of Commons as a 'far-away country about which we know little'. Today many Britons know Prague as a weekend break venue. Cheap flights might now be doing the same for Riga and Tallinn, but most Britons scarcely know their Slovakia from their Slovenia and they certainly could not find Lithuania on a map. The union has gone beyond what they are able and willing to take in. If Europe stretches from the Atlantic to the Urals, could Russia be a candidate for entry even if it is Eurasian rather than European in extent? And what about Ukraine following the orange revolution and the victory of the Europe-oriented candidate for the presidency in November–December 2004? Citizens of the union are told, too, that negotiations on Turkish entry will start in the autumn of 2005 even though most of Turkey is in Asia. Europe, already challenging in its diversity, seems to know no limits.

The European Union is meant to secure European integration—which given the twentieth-century horrors of two world wars started in Europe and of the Cold War division of Europe—is a noble objective. But what does Europe, what do Europeans, stand for? The official answer has had to do with democracy, civil liberties, and market economies, but there are European countries committed to these—Norway and Switzerland—which have chosen not to enter the EU. There have also been European leaders—Roy Jenkins and Jacques Delors, for example—who have wondered aloud what the place of Muslims in Europe could be, given Europe's Judaeo-Christian heritage (Bryant 1991). Their Europe is marked off from the Muslim Other in the Middle East and North Africa (and takes no account of the Muslims in what was once the Ottoman Empire as well as immigrants from the former colonies of European imperial powers and from (Asian) Turkey). Europe is also both more secular and more liberal in its religion than America (where the expression Judaeo-Christian originated after the Holocaust), but the difference between avowedly secular states, such as France, and states that acknowledge a special status for the Roman Catholic Church, such as Poland, generated tensions when drafting the Preamble to the Constitution for Europe.

There are national media and global media but no European media as such. There is thus no way in which the people(s) of Europe can come to constitute a single public with a single public sphere (cf. Pérez-Díaz 1998; Grundmann 1999). As a consequence there is no real European public opinion, only aggregates of the public opinion in each member state. In short the European Commission may have invoked 'Citizens' Europe' and 'the People of Europe', but there has been no simple answer to the fundamental question 'What is Europe, and who are the Europeans?' For Philippe

Schmitter (1996a: 3) the basic problem has thus been 'how to make "Europe without Europeans" '. The Preamble to the Constitution for Europe tries to overcome this by invoking 'the cultural, religious and humanist inheritance of Europe, from which have developed the universal values of the inviolable and inalienable rights of the human person, freedom, democracy, equality and the rule of law'. It contains elevated statements about the transcendence of past divisions; continuation along the path of civilization, progress, and prosperity for the benefit of all; openness to culture, learning, and social progress; the deepening of democracy and transparency in public life; the pursuit of peace, justice, and solidarity throughout the world; the forging of a common destiny; and the great venture of unity in diversity. It also memorably characterizes Europe as 'a special area of human hope'.[7] In addition the Definition and Objectives of the Union refer, inter alia, to building a common future, human rights, sustainable development, a highly competitive social market economy, social inclusion, justice and protection, a rich and diverse cultural heritage, and the free movement of goods, services, labour, and capital throughout the union (the EU's 'four freedoms'). The constitution thus invokes abstract principles of universal application but claims that Europe's commitment to them is exceptionally strong for two reasons: first, because they are of European origin, and second, because Europe has had experience of both the noblest humanity and the vilest inhumanity. These principles of universal application are then combined with principles particular to the union such as the four freedoms. The result could potentially provide content for a European citizenship programme in schools throughout the union.

Constitution and institutions: what is Europe, when is Europe?

At the middle level, the European Union, and the European Community before it, have long had a confusing treaty-plus basis where the plus is deliberately undefined. The basis of the original EEC was treaty-only. Stanley Henig (1997: 83) summarizes the thinking behind it thus: 'the European entity is built solely on law or treaty. "Europe" ... lacks the inherent legitimacy and sovereignty which we assume to be endemic to nation states. The EC came into existence with the specific act of signing treaties at particular times. ... Everything which happens in the communities has to have a legal, treaty-based foundation.' The sum of the treaties and of policies adopted and decisions taken within the terms of the treaties is the *acquis communautaire*. It was originally supposed that all members, old and new, would subscribe to it in its entirety. In practice there is now a plethora of special arrangements, such as the British budget rebate, and opt-outs, such as the British, Danish, and Swedish opt-out from monetary union and the single currency, the euro, and the British and Irish opt-out from the implementation in 1995 of that part of the Schengen agreement that provides for the abolition of internal border controls.

In practice the EC/EU developed as more than a treaty-based organization in so far as the members contrived ways of working, and sought to do things, not provided for in the treaties. These required, in effect, the adoption of rules of the game supplementary to the treaties. The Council Presidency (the six-month presidency rotated between the member states); the Council Secretariat (now housed in a building separate from the European Commission); European political, defence, and security cooperation; and the European Council (of heads of state and government) were all put in place *de facto* before they were given a full *de iure* basis in the Treaty of Maastricht in 1992 (some were anticipated in part in the Single European Act of 1986).

The Maastricht Treaty of Union established a union with three 'pillars'. The first, the European Community, deals with economic and monetary union, the single market, extra-union trade, and social policy, and is the descendant of the original EEC. It is ironic that the name European Community was written into a treaty for the first time at the very moment of its supersession by the name European Union which covers all three pillars. The second pillar deals with common foreign and security policy. It is based on opt-ins in recognition that Ireland, Sweden, Finland, and Austria are neutral states and as such not members of NATO, and that Denmark, too, declined to participate with regard to defence in order to secure acceptance of the treaty in a referendum at the second attempt. The Constitution for Europe gives the common foreign policy provision more force in so far as it establishes what is in effect an EU external relations service. The third pillar covers justice and home affairs and also proceeds by way of opt-ins (in addition to Schengen with its opt-outs). The Treaty of Amsterdam in 1997 moved asylum, immigration, and civil justice from the third to the first pillar.

The Treaty of Maastricht and the Constitution for Europe extend the treaty-based activities of the union but there is nothing to stop supplementation by new rules of the game if member states find themselves constrained by the constitution. In perpetuating both the *acquis communautaire* and the special arrangements, opt-outs, and opt-ins, they complement a single Europe with a measure of Europe *à la carte*. This may be prudent but it is also confusing. They also embody two very different principles of government beyond the nation-state, the supranational or suprastate and the intergovernmental. The term supranational assumes states are nation-states, i.e. single-nation states. This is not true of some states in the union, such as Britain, and suprastate would be a more accurate term, but supranational is the more usual. The first pillar works on the supranational principle. Here member states have pooled their sovereignty, except where, as in the case of monetary union, particular states have been allowed to opt out. Thus, for example, the union has a legal personality and conducts trade negotiations within the World Trade Organization on behalf of all its members. The second and third pillars (mostly) work on the intergovernmental principle. Members meet in councils of ministers and may choose on occasions to use the union to act for them all in a matter of foreign policy in the belief that acting as one they will have more impact than acting separately and differently, or may choose to find a common position on a matter of concern to them all, such as policy towards asylum seekers and illegal economic migrants, in the belief that collaboration is necessary if any of them are to succeed. The Constitution for Europe discards all references to pillars but retains the different ways of working associated with different areas of activity.

This combination of supranationalism and intergovernmentalism makes it difficult to describe what kind of political entity the European Union is. The confusion is compounded by changes over time in the character and competences of particular institutions. Two (of many) examples concern the European Commission and the European Parliament. The European Commission was originally intended as the embryo of a European government but has seen its relative importance diminish as the Council of Ministers has grown in significance. One consequence is that a European commissioner is now a cross between a government minister and the chief civil servant in a ministry. The president of the Commission attends meetings of the G7 countries with the world's biggest economies on behalf of the union but with special reference to members other than Britain, France, Germany, and Italy which belong to G7 in their own right. If and when the new constitution comes into force there will also be a president of the Council of Ministers (to overcome the expense and inefficiency of the current rotating presidency of the union). There is also already a president of the European Parliament. One union will thus have three presidents.

If this is confusing it is as nothing compared with the powers of the European parliament. Following the Treaty of Maastricht, 'Depending on the issue to hand, Parliament is either simply informed *or* it is formally consulted *or* it may suggest amendments without having the final word *or* it shares equally in the process and its agreement is required *or* its assent is necessary and it has a veto' (Henig 1997: 88–9). It is hard to imagine an arrangement more likely to confuse and alienate citizens.

Finally, Jürgen Habermas (1998: 115) has made the principles and procedures that (should) sustain European discourse the wellspring of European integration, thereby dispensing with Easton's foundational level altogether:

the initial impetus to integration in the direction of a post-national society is not provided by the substratum of a supposed 'European people' but by the communicative network of a European-wide political public sphere embedded in a shared political culture. The latter is founded on a civil society composed of interest groups, nongovernmental organizations, and citizen initiatives and movements, and will be occupied by arenas in which the political parties can directly address the decisions of European institutions and go beyond mere tactical alliances to form a European party system.

This combines wishful thinking about the level of development of both a European public sphere and civil society with profound thinking about the discursively mediated principles that constitute democracy. The latter are, of course, not intrinsically European. 'Europe' and the EU might (come to) embody them but without some sort of substantive supplementation, there is no lasting reason for Europe to be a polity marked off from others. The objection to Habermas is thus simple. Who other than a few intellectuals is going to identify with a Europe whose sole *raison d'être* is that of stepping-stone to a rational world order?

Instead of the static political decision-making of Easton's model, the politics of the European Union are dynamic and teleological. Once this is acknowledged the intermediate level has to contend with fundamental questions too. *'What is Europe?'* is inseparable from *'What is Europe be-coming?'* The narrative that has connected past, present, and future in the EEC/EC/EU is about ever-closer union (although this expression from the 1957 founding Treaty of Rome has been omitted from the Constitution for Europe) and the widening and deepening of European integration. Is the union becoming a European superstate, or a (con)federal United States of Europe, or something genuinely novel? If the union is more than an in-tergovernmental association, what does the 'more' consist of? There have long been writers who suggest that, in its combination of supranational and intergovernmental features, the EEC/EC/EU has assumed a novel political form of a complexity which academics and politicians have struggled to ar-ticulate and which citizens can thus hardly be expected to comprehend, let alone embrace (Bryant 1991; Axford and Huggins 1999; Geddes 2004).

Gerard Delanty (2003: 486) argues that 'European integration is not for good or bad creating an integrated political community, with a unified pub-lic space and common citizenry, with shared values, principles and aspira-tions', what Philippe Schmitter (1996*b*: 150) called 'a "genuine community of fate" '. Instead, the union is rather, as Schmitter anticipated, 'a nominal "community of deeds" '. As such it has an instrumental, not an affective, ap-peal—and is justified only so long as it works. Chris Rumford (2003: 7, sum-marizing Bornschier 1997) refers to the union as 'a compromise between nationalism and liberalism, the latter being the driving force behind growth and development, the former the inherited principle of social solidarity. Based on this reading we can say that liberalism has tilted the scales at the present time, with no principle of social solidarity emerging at the European level to substitute for national attachment.' For many of those most com-mitted to the union the absence of any new principle of social solidarity is troubling. Rumford (2002: 267) also treats the union 'as a strategy for the management of emerging transnational spaces occasioned by the accelera-tion of globalization'—which might be right but is not something citizens can readily identify with.

Henig's (1997) simple European narrative—from discord to con-cord—is losing its relevance. The supersession of the twentieth-century divisions in Europe manifest in two world wars and the Cold War is a stupendous achievement and it is too easily overlooked. But quite how integral the EEC/EC/EU was to its achievement is both open to debate and no longer the issue. The question for the twenty-first century is where the

EU is, or should be, heading, and what it is to become, and about this there is not concord.

Beneficiaries: who gets what?

This is a question that citizens think of primarily in terms of what their country gets out of the union and what it puts in, and I will return to it below. Equity, however, also pertains to the distribution of sectional, regional, and local benefits and this can seem arbitrary and weaken citizen confidence in the union. Two examples will have to suffice. The first pertains to the Common Agricultural Policy which in 2004 still absorbed 46 per cent of the budget. Despite reforms the memory of absurd overproduction—beef and butter mountains and wine lakes—and of corruption still clings to it. It is also not obvious why farmers get income support when other workers do not and when the liberal Lisbon agenda adopted at the European Council in 2000 implies that none should. Attitudes to the issue will vary from state to state according to the importance of the land in national identity, the size of farms and their level of productivity, and the political strength of farmers, but in the end consumers pay more for food than world market prices require.

The second pertains to what from the perspective of citizens is the seemingly arbitrary allocation of European money to construction projects. Some projects in each member country have financial support from the European Union and are marked by site signs with the EU flag on them. Others do not. There will be reasons for the inconsistencies known to officials in Brussels and the country concerned, but to citizens it all seems a bit of a lottery. Within Britain there are fierce who-gets-what debates in parliament and the media whenever British taxpayers' money is being disbursed. By contrast EU allocations remain a mystery and are attributed to the machinations of 'Brussels'.

The newer politics of Europe

Easton's three-level model of political decision-making has exposed some of the reasons why identification with Europe is difficult, but there are three others it misses because it has a limited and dated conception of politics. First, Easton's politics are basically endogenous. There is no reference to international relations and international trade, let alone the many facets of globalization. The EU is a trading bloc and a currency zone in a global economy. It also has aspirations towards political and defence collaboration. Some of the who-gets-what politics of the EU, for example, is not about the internal distribution envisaged by Easton but Europe's share in a global distribution. For many citizens the issue here is whether or not they think the EU is better able to safeguard their interests than national governments.

Second, Easton's decision-making is all about government rather than governance. It omits any reference to modes of governing, to regimes, which connect government to other agencies of regulation and policy realization. Rectification of the omission in the EU case, however, just exposes that the workings of the EU are even more complicated and even less transparent than had hitherto been supposed. There are cross-border non-governmental organizations (NGOs) and there are mechanisms for engaging with European institutions (Meehan 1993; Dunkerley and Fudge 2004), but most citizens will not have heard of them.

Third, Easton's identity question has to do only with who we the people are—essentially the national question—not who I the individual am—the self-identity question. It is this latter that underpins what Anthony Giddens (1990) calls life politics or the politics of self-actualization, and it finds expression as much outside party politics as within it. It can involve distaste for the collectivism of 'we the people', disengagement from the structures and processes of the formal political system, and distance from the hyper-contested politics of distribution. For many so minded, the EU is an even more offputting part of the old politics and an even more distant irrelevance than national politics.

The British and the European Union

None of the above indicates why British identification and engagement with the European Union should so often be weaker than that of all or most other members, but two key sets of data repeatedly show that it is: voter turnouts for elections to the European parliament and responses to the EU's Eurobarometer polls in which the same questions are asked in all member countries. EU12 refers to the membership before the 1995 enlargement (the entry of Austria, Sweden, and Finland), and EU15 and EU24 to the membership before and after the 2004 enlargement (the entry of eight post-communist countries, Malta and Cyprus).[8]

TABLE 7.1	Turnout in elections to the European Parliament, 1979–2004 (%)	
	UK	EU15
1979	32	63
1984	33	61
1989	36	59
1994	36	57
1999	24	50
2004	39	46

Source: Mellows-Facer et al. (2004: 56).

Direct elections to the European Parliament began in 1979. In the five elections prior to 2004 the UK turnout was the lowest on four occasions and the joint lowest on the fifth. Table 7.1 gives the UK percentages compared with the EU15 averages. In 2004 the gradual decline in turnout across the EU continued and was exacerbated by some very low votes among new members in Eastern Europe. The UK turnout improved partly thanks to the strong showing of the anti-EU United Kingdom Independence Party but only Sweden had a lower vote in EU15.

Eurobarometers survey opinion in all member countries twice a year. Standard questions address support for the EU, perceived benefit from the EU, and trust in EU institutions and others. British respondents have consistently expressed greater scepticism about Europe than those of any other member. In the following discussion the UK is compared with Ireland as a supplement to discussion earlier in this chapter, France and Germany as the two key members in the union as it was originally conceived, Sweden as the next most sceptical member, and the EU average.

A Eurobarometer in 1992 (no. 37) asked 'Do you ever think of yourself as not only (Nationality), but also European? Does this happen often, sometimes or never?' The highest percentage answering 'never' was in the UK. The 'never' percentage was 69 for the UK compared with 64 in Ireland, 40 in France and 51 in Germany. The EU12 average was 48. Beginning in 1995 Eurobarometers have asked a different question: 'In the near future do you

TABLE 7.2	British and comparator attitudes to Europe, 2004 (%)				
	See self as (Nationality) only	EU membership a good thing	Benefited from EU membership	Trust European Parliament	Trust European Commission
UK	62	29	30	26	30
Ireland	49	71	80	61	64
France	29	43	46	52	57
Germany	38	45	39	39	51
Sweden	57	37	27	48	55
EU15 average	41	48	47	47	54

Source: Eurobarometer 61, April 2004.

see yourself as (Nationality) only, (Nationality) and European, European and (Nationality), European only, or don't know?' The UK has consistently had a very high percentage answering British. Table 7.2 gives the April 2004 percentages. Turning to support for membership, the picture stays much the same. Eurobarometers ask: 'Generally speaking, do you think that your country's membership is a good thing, a bad thing, or neither good nor bad?' Across the EC/EU the percentage of respondents answering 'a good thing' has fallen by a third from a peak of 72 per cent in 1990 just after the collapse of communist regimes in eastern Europe and the end of the Cold War division of Europe. The UK percentage has fallen by half from a comparatively low peak of 57 per cent in 1990. Again Table 7.2 has the April 2004 percentages. The perceived benefits question has a similar result. Eurobarometers ask; 'Taking everything into consideration, would you say that (your country) has on balance benefited or not from being a member of the European Community (Common Market)?' The EU 'benefited' figure has fallen by a fifth from a peak of 59 per cent in 1990. The UK 'benefited' response has always been comparatively low. It has fallen by two-fifths from a peak of 50 per cent in 1986. In April 2004 only Sweden's was lower.

Eurobarometers also ask questions about trust in European and national political institutions and trust in other national state institutions such as the army and civil society associations such as trade unions. The UK generally has low scores on European and national political institutions and mixed scores on other institutions and associations. For each institution or association, polls ask, 'please tell me if you tend to trust it or not trust it?' In April 2004 the UK 'tend to trust' percentages for the European Commission and the European Parliament were the lowest in EU15 (see Table 7.2). UK percentages for trust in the national government (24%) and trust in the national parliament (27%) were also the lowest in EU15.

Other Eurobarometer questions and other survey evidence tell the same story. The UK is the most Eurosceptic country in the EU15 (though the young, the better educated, and those in managerial and professional jobs are less so than their compatriots). There would seem to be a number of reasons for this. First, the EEC and its successors were established as an economic means to a political end: Franco-German reconciliation, the consolidation/recovery of democracy after the fascism of the 1930s, and unity in Europe. For this, the participants were prepared to pool sovereignty. For the British, without a modern history of war fought on its soil or experience of foreign occupation, and with a long-established and stable democracy, the political end was much less pressing. Neighbours at peace would be very welcome but 'they' had an urgent need for the EEC in a way 'we' had not. NATO, with America its most powerful member, could take care of Britain's defence. Much of the semi-detachment from Europe this stance represents still persists, as does, in some quarters, the attachment to America (Geddes 2004). It could be argued that delusions about the real possibilities of national sovereignty in a globalizing world have lingered longer in Britain.

Second, having stayed out at the start, and having had subsequent attempts to join rebuffed by General de Gaulle, Britain eventually joined on the only terms it could get which were not necessarily favourable. In particular the biggest item of EEC expenditure was the Common Agricultural Policy which had been set up in way that guaranteed prices to farmers regardless of sales, thereby encouraging overproduction, and which favoured small farmers, not the big farmers Britain had. The EEC/EC/EU has been funded by a share of the value-added tax collected in each country. The workings of the CAP ensured Britain paid in much more than it got out, which led to Margaret Thatcher's famous battle to secure the rebate agreed in 1984. Reforms, and its declining proportion of total expenditure, have made the CAP less of an issue than it once was. Britain has also fared better

from the introduction of structural funds to address industrial restructuring and regional inequalities. But if the 'who benefits?' question is applied
to countries, the benefit of membership to Britain is less obvious than it is
to many others. France obtained leadership in Europe, an opportunity to
promote the French language internationally, and funds to help transform
its agriculture; Germany obtained a framework within which to reconstruct
its economy and establish democracy, and political rehabilitation; Ireland
benefited from European funding equivalent to around 5 per cent of GDP
for many years; Spain secured funding for the modernization of its agriculture and transport infrastructure and like Portugal and Greece was better enabled to consolidate its democracy; Finland completed the severance
from Russia it began in 1917; seven post-communist countries institution-
alized their Western orientation and their release from the Soviet Union or
the status of Soviet satellite; etc.

In 1975, two years after Ted Heath's Conservative government had finally
secured British entry to the EEC, Harold Wilson's Labour government held
a referendum on continued membership of the EEC. On a 64.5 per cent
turnout, 67.2 per cent voted 'yes' and 32.8 per cent 'no'. The majority then
expected benefit from membership. The majority now think membership
has been a bad thing. The Foreign Office *White Paper on the Treaty Establishing a Constitution for Europe* (2004: 8–9) has a section addressing the
question: 'What has the EU done for us?'.[9] It claims benefits under nine
headings: wealth, jobs, peace and stability, security, fighting crime, freedom to work and travel across Europe, consumer benefits, a better deal
on holidays, and a cleaner environment. The single market of 450 million
people is bigger than that of America and Japan combined, and Britain ex-
ports three times as much to the rest of the EU as it does to the US. The
white paper estimates that three million jobs are linked to exporting to
other EU countries and that two million people are employed by foreign
investors, many attracted by Britain's EU membership. The EU has made
a repeat of the First and Second World Wars unthinkable and helped consolidate democracy in Greece, Spain, Portugal, and the post-communist
countries. The white paper also points to the value of cooperation on law
enforcement and pollution reduction, and it notes that 100,000 Britons
work, 250,000 draw their pensions, and 10,000 study in other EU countries. This would seem a formidable case even if some of the economic
benefits would probably have been obtainable by agreements with the EU

(albeit agreements that require non-members to abide by rules they have had no part in making), and some of the political benefits would also have come the way of Britain as a free-rider. But the benefits are not as obvious or dramatic as those obtained by most other members. The white paper does not mention the euro as a potential benefit, nor does it present alignment with Europe as a valuable alternative, or counterweight, to alignment with America.

My third reason for British Euroscepticism is speculative, a matter of inferences. Eurobarometer 62 (autumn 2004) ascertained that the UK had the highest percentage of respondents in EU25 who were afraid of losing their national identity and culture in an expanded Europe, 64 per cent compared with an EU25 average of 42 per cent. Given how widely English is now spoken in Europe and how accessible English culture is to many Europeans, this finding is surprising. Why are Britons so unconfident? Could it be the answer has to do with our notorious inability to speak other European languages? Are unilingual Britons uncomfortable in a Europe in which it is increasingly the norm to be bilingual or multilingual?

The last reason I have space to discuss has to do with trust in the press (cf. Anderson and Weymouth 1998; Geddes 2004: ch. 10; Lloyd 2004). Eurobarometer 60.1 (autumn 2003) provides interesting data on trust in the media. Less than half the citizens of EU15, 44 per cent, tend to trust the press. Trust in the press is highest in Spain and France at 58 per cent and lowest in Sweden at 34 per cent and the United Kingdom at a derisory 17 per cent. By comparison trust in television is greater across EU15 at 54 per cent (also the UK figure) with a high of 72 per cent in Ireland and a low of 39 per cent in Italy. Political parties aside, the UK trust figure for the press of 17 per cent was the lowest for trust in any institution anywhere in EU15. It is notable that the member states with the lowest trust in the press, Sweden and the UK, have the lowest trust in the EU, the lowest percentages saying membership of the EU has been of benefit, and the weakest support for political union. There thus does seem to be a particular problem with the British press, which also largely sets the news agenda for the broadcast media. That the press is itself distrusted does not prevent its negative reporting of the EU, coverage that sometimes amounts to woeful and wilful misrepresentation, from having a baleful effect. It would seem the distrusted breed further distrust. The EU is especially vulnerable to this treatment because its complexity, its lack of transparency, and its comprehensibility deficit leave citizens having, in large measure, to take it on trust, and trust is what much of the British press much of the time is intent on denying it.

In sum, Britain, such was its standing in the late 1940s and early 1950s, could have had a leading role in the development of the EEC but its leaders, Labour and Conservative, did not have the wit to take it and the country is still suffering the consequences. Unable to afford exclusion from a successful community it had not anticipated, Britain had then to come to terms with a community originally fashioned to meet the needs of others. British governments and (most of) the British can, in principle, engage with a community of deeds but are not disposed to commit to a community of fate or an integrated political community. The expansion from fifteen to twenty-five member states will put this union without solidarity to the practical test. Can the EU, in practice, deliver enough benefits to head off the secessions that the Constitution for Europe allows? The Foreign Office is right that Britain has benefited from membership hitherto and can expect to do so in future. I suspect, when push comes to shove, in the referendum on acceptance of the Constitution for Europe, the majority of Britons will, if grudgingly, agree with the Foreign Office view and vote for the constitution as long as they are not expected to identify with Europe or identify themselves as European and electorates elsewhere have not already voted 'no'. For Britons the practical politics of the EU are one thing, the politics of identity quite another.

British citizenship

Immigration from Ireland, the Commonwealth, and the European Union provides the cue: Who may be a citizen of Britain? I commented in Ch. 1 that Britain is in origin a territorial community with a civic conception of nation, that British has always been a composite identity, and that it has never been difficult to extend it to cover citizens of other origins from refugees from Eastern Europe, notably Poles, in the 1940s, to 'coloured' immigrants from the imperial and former imperial possessions in the 1950s and 1960s. What it means to be British, and the place of national and other identities within the union, have, however, long been something of a muddle. Take one minor example. Until the late 1970s, there used to be an annual football competition each spring between England, Scotland, Wales, and Northern Ireland.

These matches were known as the 'home internationals'. Now the notion of 'home internationals' is a very odd one if one thinks about it, but, as far as I can recall, no Britons did. It took a foreigner, the German sociologist Ralf Dahrendorf (1982: 15), to point out this 'beautiful absurdity'.

What one has in Britain is a civic nation that has proved capable of accommodating a large amount of difference. Certainly the notion of ethnic and other communities, of community relations and leaders, of different ways of being British—a notion which, albeit for very different reasons, has no equivalents in Germany and France—is to most Britons most of the time as 'natural', as unremarkable, as it is to the Dutch. Where the British differ from the Dutch is in the haphazard character of the civic nation. There is a *de facto* pluralism rather than a *de iure* one. The civic nation is the product of union and Empire without there having been any guiding principles in its formation. This can make it extraordinarily accommodating but it also means that when conflicts, tensions, and moral panics do occur there are few principles to fall back upon when responses are sought (though there may be all manner of ad hoc precedents) other than the secondary values of pragmatism, accommodation, tolerance, live-and-let-live, compromise without loss of honour, fair play, and due process which Alasdair MacIntyre (1967) identified (and whose origin he attributed to the class collaboration which evolved in the Victorian period). To give one example, the British government before 1997 resisted providing money for Muslim schools although money had long been granted to Anglican, Catholic, and Jewish schools. Objectors to this apparent discrimination sought judicial review of ministerial refusals and obtained a judgement that has part prompted policy shifts in their favour but without the state conceding the principle that public money should fund religious schools of all faiths in the same way. In the Netherlands, by contrast, the law makes exactly that provision in conformity with the principles of pillarization, and Islamic and Hindu schools have been able to secure funding on the same terms and conditions as any others without fuss.

The complex of laws governing nationality, citizenship, and political representation have for more than half a century been a quite extraordinary mess (Dummett and Nicol 1990; Dummett 1994; Cohen 1994; Hansen 2001). The basic principle of British nationality, *ius soli*, is that of the English law of feudal times. People owed allegiance to the lord of the land on which they were born, ultimately to the king, who in turn owed them protection.

It was only in 1886 that a court finally clarified that allegiance was due to the crown rather than the person of the monarch (Dummett 1994: 91). This feudal principle readily converted into an imperial one. All those born in the king's lands at home and abroad were the king's subjects (with a few exceptions—such as the children of foreign ambassadors to England, later Britain). The people of British colonies continued to be British subjects with a right of entry to Britain and the rights of citizens in Britain, even after their countries became independent, wherever the British monarch remained head of state, beginning with the dominions of Canada (and Newfoundland), Australia, New Zealand, South Africa, and the Irish Free State. Following the Statute of Westminster in 1931 the dominions acquired the absolute right to determine their own citizenship and control entry into their own territories. The Irish Free State legislated accordingly in 1935 and Canada in 1946. This left Britain in a quandary. It had now to indicate how a British subject was different from a Canadian British subject. The result was the British Nationality Act of 1948. It distinguished between British citizens who have a right of abode in Britain and British subjects in the Commonwealth. Special arrangements, described below, were made for the Irish when Ireland left the Commonwealth in 1949. In 1949 the governments of Britain and the dominions agreed that republics could be members of the Commonwealth, thereby opening the door to India and Pakistan. From then on British subjects in the dominions and Commonwealth citizens in the republics were two sides of the same coin. In both cases the governments concerned decided who their citizens were (and controlled entry to their territories) and the citizens so defined then had the additional status of British subjects or Commonwealth citizens. That status had a real significance in terms of rights of entry to Britain and the same rights as British citizens once in Britain. But whereas before 1948 the people of the world fell into two categories so far as the British government was concerned—British subjects and aliens, they now fell into three—British citizens, British subjects in the dominions and Commonwealth citizens, and aliens. The story of legislation after 1948 has two main strands to it. First, British subjects in the dominions and Commonwealth citizens lose their right of automatic entry to Britain and are subject to ever stricter immigration controls. But when they do enter Britain legally they immediately have the same rights as British citizens. For example, there are now about a quarter of a million Commonwealth citizens in Britain with the right to vote. Second, immigration rules make entry from the old white Commonwealth easier than from the new Asian and black Commonwealth.

Entry for Commonwealth citizens was unrestricted until the 1962 Commonwealth Immigrants Act, about which Randall Hansen (2001: 76) offers this wry comment: 'The scholarly literature has focused on the decision to restrict immigration as the most interesting element of the 1962 legislation. The only curious aspect of this decision is, in fact, that it was taken so late. That a nation of 50,000,000 would indefinitely keep its doors open to 600,000,000 was always incredible; it was doubly so given the manifest opposition of British public opinion.' Between 1948 and 1962 half a million non-white British subjects had entered Britain, but by the end of the 1950s the Ministry of Labour judged continued unlimited entry more than the economy could be expected to absorb (ibid.). Thereafter entrants with old and new Commonwealth passports had first to obtain labour permits whose numbers were fixed. The 1971 Immigration Act reintroduced the hitherto archaic notion of 'patriality'. Patrials were persons born in Britain or who had a parent or grandparent born in Britain. Patrials abroad, who were of course almost always white, had a right of abode in Britain; Commonwealth non-patrials, who were mostly non-white, did not and were subject to ever more stringent immigration controls. Commonwealth patrials had a right to naturalize after five years' residence in Britain. Commonwealth non-patrials, like aliens, could apply for naturalization after five years' residence but the grant was discretionary. Patriality introduced an element of *ius sanguinis* into nationality/citizenship law for the first time.

In the 1970s the Ted Heath's Conservative government had to deal with the expulsion from Uganda of Asians whose only citizenship was that of the United Kingdom and Colonies but without a right of abode in Britain. The government admitted them as refugees. This experience, and the need to remove the provision that men could pass on their citizenship to children born abroad but women could not, led to the British Nationality Act of 1981 which came into effect in 1983. It repealed the 1948 act and is still in force but has been supplemented by the Nationality, Immigration and Asylum Act of 2002.[10] The 1981 act created for the first time a British citizenship confined to the UK and it made all those with a right of abode in the UK British citizens. It left non-patrial British subjects in the colonies who had no other citizenship, such as non-patrial British citizens in Hong Kong, in an invidious position. A British passport enabled them to travel and afforded them consular protection but they could not enter Britain. As the hand-back of Hong Kong to China in 1997 neared, the government was shamed into allowing a quota of non-patrials to enter Britain. In practice the full quota was never taken up; Canada, the United States, and Australia were more welcoming.

The story of nationality and citizenship law in Britain since the Second World War is a confused and often shabby one. It is a reminder that being British has had a significance in the Empire and Commonwealth that cannot be disregarded even today. Controls on immigration were inevitable but the motives for introducing them have mixed realism and racism. The continued acquisition of the rights of British citizens, especially the vote, by Commonwealth citizens on legal entry to Britain has been of great value and contrasts with the position of aliens in Britain, and immigrants in most countries in the EU.

Ireland declared itself a republic and left the Commonwealth in 1949. Ann Dummett and Andrew Nicol (1990) have set out how Britain dealt with the consequences for British citizenship. Irish persons born in the United Kingdom before 1922 or the Irish Free State before 1949 have been able at any time to write to the Home Office declaring that they had never ceased to be British subjects. Those making the declaration can then apply for a British passport as many resident in Britain have done. The Ireland Act of 1949 provided that though it had left the Commonwealth the Republic of Ireland would be treated in some ways as if it had not, any other arrangement being deemed impractical given the numbers of Irish in Britain and the numbers of mixed families. In particular, Irish citizens can vote, stand for office, and work in the public service in Britain. If they wish to obtain British citizenship they can do so under the same terms as citizens of Commonwealth countries. Both Britain and Ireland allow dual citizenship, so there are many Irish in Britain who have acquired British citizenship without renouncing their Irishness in word or mind—but no one knows how many. British and Irish citizens have also always been exempted from passport requirements when travelling between the two countries. The Irish Republic is thus an anomaly, an ex-Commonwealth country with a closer official relationship with Britain than any Commonwealth country.

Finally, there is the issue of European citizenship. This was formalized by the Treaty of Maastricht. EU citizens are such only by virtue of being citizens of a member state, the EU having no power to confer citizenship directly.

The contributors to Hansen and Weil (2001) indicate how there is a measure of convergence in the citizenship laws of the member states of the EU as each deals with immigration, gendered laws, naturalization, mixed marriages, dual loyalties and citizenship, etc., but convergence in nationality and citizenship law does not represent the movement *Towards A European Nationality* they announce in their title. The right of European citizens to live and work in any EU country without a permit is widely valued, but there is huge debate about economic immigrants and asylum seekers from outside the EU throughout the union. What is their rightful place in (Fortress) Europe? What are their rights to residence, work, and citizenship? Do they have to sign up in some way to being European? How could they when they have first to become citizens of a member state? As yet there are no answers. In due course, however, it might be possible to make respect for the Constitution for Europe the key to being European for old citizens of member states and new.

NOTES

1 The War of the Three Kingdoms used to be known in England as the English Civil War. As the war began in Scotland and was also fought in Ireland the Anglocentric name was never appropriate.

2 All servicemen from Ireland, north and south of the border, were volunteers. There was no conscription in Northern Ireland unlike in the rest of the United Kingdom.

3 Gregory Campbell (2000: 28), a DUP member of the Northern Ireland Assembly, stresses that even if the Irish Republic were to declare itself Protestant those like him would still not want to be part of it.

4 The Singapore and Harare declarations are accessible via the Commonwealth Secretariat website: <www.thecommonwealth.org>, accessed 1 June 2005.

5 See MORI's 'State of Britain 2003' survey archived at: <www.mori.com/polls/2003>, accessed 1 June 2005.

6 The Constitution for Europe is published in the *Official Journal of the European Union*, 16 December 2004. It is accessible at <http://europa.eu.int/constitution/en/1stoc1_en.htm>, accessed 21 June 2005. The English text is written in very much clearer English than critics of the EU usually imply.

7 Two sociologists who would endorse this, albeit in very different ways, are Göran Therborn (1995) and Zygmunt Bauman (2004).

8 For the sake of simplicity polls conducted for the EEC and the EC before the EU came into being are also referred to as EU polls.

9 The white paper, Cm 6309, is accessible via the Foreign and Commonwealth Office website: <www.fco.gov.uk>, accessed 1 June 2005.

10 A description of the current law with respect to British citizenship is given in question and answer form (see BN1) on the Immigration and Nationality Directorate's website: <www.ind.homeoffice.gov.uk>.

REFERENCES

ANDERSON, PETER, and WEYMOUTH, ANTONY (1998), *Insulting the Public: The British Press and the European Union* (London: Longman).

AUGHEY, ARTHUR (2001), *Nationalism, Devolution and the Challenge to the United Kingdom State* (London: Pluto).

AXFORD, BARRIE, and HUGGINS, RICHARD (1999), 'Towards a post-national polity: the emergence of the network society in Europe', in Smith and Wright (eds.), 173–206.

BAUMAN, ZYGMUNT (2004), *Europe: An Unfinished Adventure* (Cambridge: Polity).

BORNSCHIER, VOLKER (1997), 'European processes and the state of the European Union', paper presented at the 3rd European Sociological Association Conference, University of Essex, 1997.

BOYCE, D. GEORGE (1995) *Nationalism in Ireland*, 3rd edn. (London: Routledge), 1st edn. 1982.

BRADBURY, JONATHAN, and MAWSON, JOHN (1997) (eds.), *British Regionalism and Devolution: The Challenges of State Reform and European Integration* (London: Jessica Kingsley Publications and Regional Studies Association).

BRUCE, STEVER (1986), *God Save Ulster: The Religion and Politics of Paisleyism* (Oxford: Oxford University Press).

BRYANT, CHRISTOPHER G. A. (1991), 'Europe and the European Community 1992', *Sociology*, 25: 189–207.

CAMPBELL, GREGORY (2000), 'Gregory Campbell' in Logue (ed.), 27–9.

CHANCE, JUDITH (1996), 'The Irish: invisible settlers', in C. PEACH (ed.), *Ethnicity in the 1991 Census*, ii. *The Ethnic Minority Populations of Great Britain* (London: HMSO), ch. 10.

COAKLEY, JOHN (1999), 'The foundations of statehood', in J. COAKLEY and M. GALLAGHER (eds.), *Politics in the Republic of Ireland*, 3rd edn. (London: Routledge), ch.1.

COHEN, ROBIN (1994), *Frontiers of Identity: The British and Others* (Harlow: Longman).

COLLINS, NEIL, and CRADDON, TERRY (2004) (eds.), *Political Issues in Ireland Today*, 3rd edn. (Manchester: Manchester University Press), 1st edn. 1994.

COULTER, COLIN, and COLEMAN, STEVE (2003) (eds.), *The End of History? Critical Reflections on the Celtic Tiger* (Manchester: Manchester University Press).

COX, W. HARVEY (1985), 'Who wants a united Ireland?', *Government and Opposition*, 20: 29–47.

DAHRENDORF, RALF (1982), *On Britain* (London: BBC).

DAVIS, THOMAS C. (2003), 'The Irish and their nation: a survey of recent attitudes', *Global Review of Ethnopolitics*, 2 (2): 17–36.

DAVIES, NORMAN (1999), *The Isles: A History* (London: Macmillan).

DELANTY, GERARD (2003), 'Conceptions of Europe: a review of recent trends', *European Journal of Social Theory*, 6: 471–88.

DEVEREUX, EOIN, and BREEN, MICHAEL (2003), 'No racists here? Public opinion, immigrants and the media', in Coulter and Coleman (eds., ch. 10).

DEVINE, THOMAS M. (2003), *Scotland's Empire 1600–1815* (London: Allen Lane).

DIXON, PAUL (2001), *Northern Ireland: The Politics of War and Peace* (Basingstoke: Palgrave).

DUMMETT, ANN (1994), 'The acquisition of British citizenship: from imperial traditions to national definitions', in R. BAUBÖCK (ed.), *From Aliens to Citizens: Redefining the Status of Immigrants in Europe* (Aldershot: Avebury), ch. 4.

—— and NICOL, ANDREW (1990), *Subjects, Citizens, Aliens and Others: Nationality and Immigration Law* (London: Weidenfeld & Nicolson).

DUNKERLEY, DAVID, and FUDGE, SHANE (2004), 'The role of civil society in European integration: a framework for analysis', *European Societies*, 6: 237–54.

EASTON, DAVID (1965), *A Systems Analysis of Political Life* (New York: Wiley).

EDWARDS, RUTH DUDLEY (1999), *The Faithful Tribe* (London: HarperCollins).

ELLIOTT, MARIANNE (2000), *The Catholics of Ulster* (London: Penguin—Allen Lane).

FARRELL, MICHAEL (1976), *Northern Ireland: The Orange State* (London: Pluto).

FERGUSON, NIALL (2003), *Empire: How Britain Made the Modern World* (London: Allen Lane).

Foreign and Commonwealth Office (2004), *White Paper on the Treaty Establishing a Constitution for Europe* (London: HMSO, CM 6309).

GEDDES, ANDREW (2004), *The European Union and British Politics* (Basingstoke: Palgrave).

GIDDENS, ANTHONY (1990), *The Consequences of Modernity* (Cambridge: Polity).

GOODMAN, JAMES (1998), 'The Republic of Ireland', in J. ANDERSON and J. GOODMAN (eds.), *Dis/Agreeing Ireland* (London: Pluto), ch. 5.

GRUNDMANN, REINER (1999), 'The European public sphere and the deficit of democracy', in Smith and Wright (eds.), 125–46.

HABERMAS, JÜRGEN (1998), *The Inclusion of the Other: Studies in Political Theory* (Cambridge Mass.: MIT Press).

HANSEN, RANDALL (2001), 'From subjects to citizens: immigration and nationality law in the United Kingdom', in Hansen and Weil (eds.), ch. 3.

—— and WEIL, PATRICK (2001) (eds.), *Towards a European Nationality: Citizenship, Immigration and Nationality Law in the EU* (Basingstoke: Palgrave).

HAYES, BERNADETTE, and MCALLISTER, IAN (1996), 'British and Irish public opinion towards the Northern Irish problem', *Irish Political Studies*, 11: 61–82.

HENIG, STANLEY (1997), *The Uniting of Europe: From Discord to Concord* (London: Routledge).

HORNSBY-SMITH, MICHAEL P. (1999) (ed.), *Catholics in England 1900–2000: Historical and Sociological Perspectives* (New York: Continuum).

—— and DALE, ANGELA (1988), 'The assimilation of Irish immigrants in England', *British Journal of Sociology*, 39: 519–44.

JENKINS, ROY (2001), *Churchill* (London: Macmillan).

KEARNEY, RICHARD (1997), *Postnationalist Ireland: Politics, Culture, Philosophy* (London: Routledge).

KEE, ROBERT (1972), *The Green Flag: A History of Irish Nationalism* (London: Weidenfeld & Nicolson).

KUMAR, KRISHAN (2000), 'Nation and Empire: English and British national identity in comparative perspective', *Theory and Society*, 29: 575–608.

—— (2003), *The Making of English National Identity* (Cambridge: Cambridge University Press).

LLOYD, JOHN (2004), *What the Media are Doing to Our Politics* (London: Constable).

LOGUE, PADDY (2000) (ed.), *Being Irish: Personal Reflections on Irish Identity Today* (Dublin: Oak Tree Press).

LOUGHLIN, JAMES (2004), *The Ulster Question since 1945*, 2nd edn. (Basingstoke: Palgrave), 1st edn. 1998.

LOYAL, STEVE (2003), 'Welcome to the Celtic Tiger: racism, immigration and the state', in Coulter and Coleman (eds.), ch. 4.

LUCY, GORDON, and MC CLURE, ELAINE (1997) (eds.), *The Twelfth: What It Means To Me* (Belfast: Ulster Society Publications).

MCCALL, CATHALL (1999), *Identity in Northern Ireland: Community, Politics and Change* (Basingstoke: Palgrave).

MACINTYRE, ALASDAIR (1967), *Secularisation and Moral Change* (Oxford: Oxford University Press).

MACLAUGHLIN, JIM (2001), *Reimagining the Nation-State: The Contested Terrains of Nation-Building* (London: Pluto).

MACRAILD, DONALD M. (1999), *Irish Migrants in Modern Britain 1750–1922* (Basingstoke: Palgrave).

MARKS, GARY; SCHARPF, FRITZ W.; SCHMITTER, PHILIPPE C.; and STREECK, WOLFGANG (1996) (eds.), *Governance in the European Union* (London: Sage).

MEEHAN, ELIZABETH (1993), *Citizenship in the European Community* (London: Sage).

MELLOWS-FACER, ADAM; CRACKNELL, RICHARD; and YONWIN, JESSICA (2004), 'European Parliament elections 2004', *Library Research Papers*, 04/50 (London: House of Commons). Accessed 1 June 2005 at: <http://www.parliament.uk /parliamentary_publications_and_archives /research_papers.cfm>.

Ó DOCHARTAIGH, CATHAIR (2000), 'Irish in Ireland', in G. PRICE (ed.), *Languages in Britain and Ireland* (Oxford: Blackwell), ch. 3.

Ó DOCHARTAIGH, NIALL (2005), *From Civil Rights to Armalites: Derry and the Birth of the Irish Troubles* (Basingstoke: Palgrave), 1st edn. 1997.

O'MAHONEY, PATRICK, and DELANTY, GERARD (2001), *Rethinking Irish History: Nationalism, Identity and Ideology* (Basingstoke: Palgrave).

PÉREZ-DÍAZ, VICTOR (1998), 'The public sphere and a European civil society' in J. C. ALEXANDER (ed.), *Real Civil Societies: Dilemmas of Institutionalization* (London: Sage), ch. 11.

RIFKIN, JEREMY (2004), *The European Dream: How Europe's Vision of the Future is Quietly Eclipsing the American Dream* (Cambridge: Polity).

ROSE, PETER (2000), *How the Troubles Came to Northern Ireland* (Basingstoke: Palgrave).

RUMFORD, CHRIS (2002), *The European Union: A Political Sociology* (Oxford: Blackwell).

—— (2003). 'Rethinking the state and policy-building in the European Union:

the sociology of globalization and the rise of reflexive government', University of Leeds, *European Political Communication Working Papers*, 4/03. Accessed 1 June 2005 at: <http://ics.leeds.ac.uk /eurpolcom/discussion_papers.cfm>.

SCHMITTER, PHILIPPE C. (1996a), 'Examining the present Euro-polity with the help of past theories', in Marks et al. (1996: ch. 1).

_____ (1996b), 'Imagining the future of the Euro-polity with the help of new concepts', in Marks et al. (eds.), ch. 6.

SHIRLOW, PETE (2003), 'Northern Ireland: a reminder form the present', in Coulter and Coleman (eds.), ch. 11.

SMITH, DENNIS, and WRIGHT, SUE (1999) (eds.), *Whose Europe? The Turn Towards Democracy* (Oxford: Blackwell).

THERBORN, GÖRAN (1995) *European Modernity and Beyond: The Trajectory of European Societies 1945–2000* (London: Sage).

TONGE, JONATHAN (2005), *The New Northern Irish Politics* (Basingstoke: Palgrave).

8

Conclusions: Britain and the Future

Having worked through aspects of the past, present, and future in Scotland, Wales, and England as they are seen today, it is now time to return to the question of the future of Britain. The discussion is in three parts. The first outlines three contemporary constructions of Britain and suggests that the third, Cosmopolitan Britain, is the most consistent with economic and demographic trends. The second reflects on where devolution and other constitutional changes are taking Britain, takes note of the less and more relevant precedents of Canada and Spain respectively, and asks whether asymmetrical devolution could lead to asymmetrical federalism. The third returns to the work of Linda Colley. Her *Britons: The Forging of the Nation 1707–1837* (1992) is where the argument of this book began, so let her lecture 'Britishness in the 21st century' given in 10 Downing Street in December 1999 provide the prompts for some closing comments.

Contemporary constructions of Britain

Table 8.1, Contemporary Constructions of Britain, differs from the Contemporary Constructions tables for Scotland, Wales, and England in that it is not appropriate to distinguish separate home and abroad orientations for a construction of Britain that dwells on the past. Great Britain had an outward orientation from the start. Access to the English Empire was a major part of the attraction of union to Scottish elites in 1707. Great Britain was imperial Britain. But if one considers what made Great Britain great it was more than Empire. There are three other major stories that Britons recall with pride. One has to do with the rule of law and individual liberty, the development of civil rights, the evolution of parliamentary democracy, and

| TABLE 8.1 | Contemporary constructions of Britain by time and place |

		Orientations to Place	
		Home	*Abroad*
	Past	*Great* Britain	
		(Liberty, Industry, Welfare, Empire)	
Orientations to Time			
	Present	British	Cosmopolitan
		Britain	Britain

step-by-step progress towards universal suffrage. Another is about Britain as the first industrialized nation, the workshop of the world, and *the* leading, later *a* leading, economic power. A third pertains to the rise of the labour movement and the development of the welfare state. These four stories are the great stories of a *Great* Britain and there are links between them. They are about Britain in the van of progress.

Looking to the present and the near future, there is a distinction to be made between an inward-looking Britain, a British Britain, and an outward-looking one, a Cosmopolitan Britain. It is arguable that a Britain that ceases to look outwards is the most likely to break up. Why stop at an inward-looking British Britain when Little England beckons, for example? One answer is that in addition to constructions and representations we can think of nations as the sum of personal connections and remembrances. (In Durkheimian terms this would amount to the sum of personalized perspectives on moral density and collective representations.) In other words (remembrance of) the volume of past internal migrations, intermarriages, economic and cultural exchanges, joint endeavours, and common associations has so multiplied connections between English, Scots, Welsh, and Irish that Britain could persist by a kind of inertia, and for want of conviction of anything better. Another answer supplements inertia with lingering affection for, pride in, or respect for the monarchy (even if it is of diminished majesty), the armed forces (note the Scottish opposition to the loss of famous regiments), the BBC (even in a multi-channel age),

British sporting success (for example at the Olympics), the NHS (still the most respected welfare institution), etc. Then, too, there is admiration and affection for notable achievers and celebrities in the arts, entertainment, sport, business, and public affairs regardless of the part of Britain they happen to have come from. Views can differ on whether English, Scots, and Welsh are brothers and sisters to each other or cousins, but either way they are all part of the same British family, and if there are rivalries from time to time the family still sticks together. This is a Britain that is familiar, which we are used to. It has much in it that we like and think we would not get elsewhere. This is British Britain.

British Britain is a carry-on Britain and there are two versions. Subscribers to the first suppose it is the only Britain of value, subscribers to the second do not. The first version of British Britain is exclusive. It lauds self-sufficiency and covets Little Britain. That the economy is no longer in obvious relative decline gives heart to Little Britons who cherish the notion of national economic sovereignty and an economic future outside the EU. A Little Britain that keeps clear of foreign wars and occupations has its appeal, too. But Little Britain can also so easily be sour, unimaginative, and unresourceful—a tight little island indeed, unappreciative of its own diversity, hostile to immigrants with different ways, slow to grasp new economic and cultural possibilities—in which case many of its most talented citizens would surely leave it. The radical right, once so proud of Empire, now embraces versions of a white-race Little Britain and the British National Party has won occasional ward elections in England in well-to-do white towns, such as Broxbourne, as well as multiracial towns with problems of unemployment and poor housing, such as Burnley (Sykes 2005). The second version of British Britain is non-exclusive. It is not self-sufficient and requires augmentation by another more expansive Britain. Ourselves alone is too limiting, too undynamic.

The outward-looking successor to *Great* Britain and the necessary complement to a non-exclusive British Britain is a Cosmopolitan Britain. In Ch. 5, I said of Cosmopolitan England that it acknowledges not just the diversification of the people - particularly that legacy of Empire, citizens (whose forebears are) of black or Asian origin—but also the enrichment of its economy and culture from sources abroad whether carried by immigrants or transmitted by trade or the media. It looks out not just to the former Empire but crucially to Europe, America, and the world.

Cosmopolitan Britain is like Cosmopolitan England only more so. It combines the old diversity of English, Scots, Welsh, and citizens of other origins (Irish, Jewish, etc.) with the new diversity of citizens from the Commonwealth (very often the new Commonwealth), post-war Europe (from Poland, Italy, etc.), and other parts of the world, and its economy benefits from the migrant labour of non-citizens. Cosmopolitan Britain can be hard to manage but the rewards of managing it well are great. The 1951 census established that 4.2 per cent of the population of the UK were born outside it.[1] Half a century later, the 2001 census recorded the non-UK-born at 8.2 per cent, almost double the 1951 figure, with 1.6 per cent of the increase in the last ten years. More than half the non-UK-born population in 2001, 53 per cent, were white—no doubt a surprise to some. In 2002 there was a net inflow of 69,000 from the Commonwealth, a net outflow of 36,000 to the EU, and a net inflow of 120,000 from the rest of the world. The overall net inflow of 153,000 is the stuff of tabloid scaremongering but the British economy needs to import labour. There were big net inflows in the 15–24-year-old and 25–44-year-old categories and a net outflow of older people. This pattern of migration eases a little the problems of managing an ageing population and funding its welfare. Cosmopolitan Britain needs sophisticated immigration controls—not all potential immigrants are of benefit to the British economy and society and the vitality of its culture—but it recognizes how valuable immigration has been and will continue to be.

All three contemporary constructions of Britain have some currency and, as with alternative constructions of Scotland, Wales and Ireland, citizens will vary the one they favour according to circumstance and sentiment, but it is Cosmopolitan Britain that is most consistent with economic and demographic trends. There can be no guarantee that it will be robust enough to avert the break-up of Britain—that depends largely on the Scots and whether they think they would be better off economically and culturally within Britain or outwith it—but it makes the most in today's world of what has always been a defining characteristic of Britain, its diversity, its acceptance that there is never just one way of being British. It can accommodate in principle all the versions of Scotland, Wales, and England that have been discussed except Little Scotland and Little England, and even these can be accommodated in practice provided they remain minority preferences.

Devolution, federalism, and asymmetry

Historically the Conservative Party has been the Unionist party and Thatcherites resisted devolution to Scotland and Wales in the 1980s and 1990s, believing any departure from the unitary state represented a step towards the break-up of Britain. This was consistent with a particular take on two features of British history. First the annexation of Wales by England in 1536 and the union of England and Scotland in 1707 produced an asymmetrical union. England and Scotland are kingdoms, but Wales only a principality as the absence of Welsh components in the union flag and the royal standard displays. Whereas Scotland has retained its own institutions and jurisdiction since 1707, Wales has for many purposes since 1536 been the add-on in something called England and Wales. That Scotland was from the start the junior partner in the union of England and Scotland was confirmed by government from London and the continuity of the parliament at Westminster. Second, there has long been asymmetrical administrative devolution. In particular, the Scottish Office was established in 1885 with a broad range of responsibilities, and the Welsh Office was established in 1965 originally with a limited range of responsibilities but with many more added subsequently. For many Conservatives these uneven dispositions were enough to respond to national differences; the addition of political devolution could only upset the odd balances that had enabled Britain to survive and prosper and threaten its very break-up.

I have indicated in the chapters on Scotland and Wales how and why Scottish and Welsh devolution came to pass with significantly different provisions made for Edinburgh and Cardiff. There is no doubting that the governance of Britain is now odder than ever and there will continue to be argument as to whether affording different degrees of devolution to Scotland and Wales and none to England (or the English regions) is the product of the British genius for pragmatic accommodation or the seeds of a disaster that will be Britain's undoing. Following Michael Keating (2001), it is possible to get some perspective on this by considering constitutional reform in Canada and Spain.

In his *Nations Against the State*, Keating compares the positions of Quebec, Catalonia, and Scotland *vis-à-vis* Canada, Spain, and Britain. The incorporation of French Canadians in Canada has presented problems ever since the British victory over the French in 1795, but the period that is germane to this book runs from 1960 to the present. In this period debate has shifted from French Canadians as an ethnic minority in Canada to Québécois as a national majority in their own homeland of Quebec.[2] Québécois insistence on the latter made it impossible to continue treating Quebec as one province among many in a symmetrical federation. Since the 1960s Quebec has intensified its claim that it is a 'distinct society' (with a *national* assembly) and thus unlike any of the other provinces (with their parliaments). By distinct society Québécois refer especially to the French language, but they also allude to the historic role of the Roman Catholic church in sustaining Québécois culture and society. Until the 1960s the church resisted the modern world and endorsed the protection of agriculture and the promotion of communal solidarity as a bulwark against Anglophone-owned industry and godless liberalism and materialism. In the Quiet Revolution of the 1960s the Québécois turned from anti-modernism to market capitalism and the modernization of their economy but with a continued endorsement of collective values. From then on state and civil society took over from the church as the main supports for the French language and Québécois culture, and language policy and politics came to the fore. Language policies have sought to make French the sole language of public and business life and have largely succeeded, even in Montreal where francophones are outnumbered by anglophones and allophones (people whose first language is neither French nor English) (Schmid 2001; Larivée 2003). The Quebec government has supported public enterprise and encouraged francophone business ownership in place of the old anglophone ownership of big business. Québécois nationalists now consider Quebec a 'global society', a society definable as a whole in itself and not a part of something else—Canada.

Before and after the 1960s Ottawa had agreed special arrangements for Quebec but increasingly these have not been enough to meet Québécois demands. Repeated attempts were made between 1970 and 1993 to agree constitutional reform—the Meech Lake (1987) and Charlottetown (1992) accords came nearest to success—but none proved mutually acceptable to the government and people of Quebec, the governments and peoples of all the other provinces, and the federal government, and so survive all the necessary referendums and parliamentary ratifications. For Quebec this is exasperating in so far as they consider the French and the British to be the two founding nations of Canada and they would like a single anglophone entity to negotiate with. But the Canadian government is federal, regards Quebec as part of the federation, and is committed to bilingualism, and the other provincial governments often do not speak with one voice. Quebec has had two referendums on separation from Canada with the separatists losing in the second in 1995 by just 49.4 to 50.6 per cent. Since then Keating reports that opinion polls outside Quebec have consistently revealed opposition to granting Quebec a privileged status within the federation, and the Canadian government has taken controversial steps, still untested, to make a vote in Quebec for separation harder to achieve and implement. There has also been resentment at financial transfers to an 'ungrateful' Quebec. Quebec 'receives over Canadian $3.1 billion more from the federal government than it pays in taxes' (Parekh 2000: 186). Basically there is in Canada a clash between two different nation-building projects, one Canadian with an official bilingualism and the other Québécois with an official unilingualism. There are also ironies. The proportion of proficient bilinguals is higher in Quebec with its policy of unilingualism in public and business life than in the rest of Canada with its official bilingualism, and three-quarters of federal government jobs designated bilingual are filled by Quebeckers. The Québécois also claim the right to separate from Canada but deny native peoples who are in the majority in the north of the province the right to separate from Quebec. In the end, however, there is one fundamental reality that cannot fail to make Quebec a special case. Francophone North America is a small island in a big anglophone sea and for it to survive it needs its defences. In an elegant summary of the principles at stake in the Canadian constitutional debate, Bhikhu Parekh (2000: 195–93) recommends that (anglophone) Canada stops resisting development of an asymmetrical federalism, the same conclusion Keating reached at the end of his much longer discussion of the politics of nationalism in Quebec.

It is not surprising that those concerned about the possibility of Scottish independence have looked to see what can be learnt from Quebec. The Québécois view all developments and policies through Québécois eyes first and Canadian eyes second if at all; they take for granted a right to self-determination and if Quebec does not secede it will be because Quebeckers alone have chosen not. Something similar is said of the Scots. But on inspection other parallels between Scotland and Quebec are few. In Britain nobody disputes that Scotland is a distinct society and a nation, and all attempts to accommodate this for the last three centuries have been within asymmetrical frameworks. There has also been no language issue to complicate communication and association and none of the upheavals associated with a sudden and belated embrace of modernity. Scottish nationalists could also argue that separation within the European Union would be easier to implement than anything available to the Québécois. There is, of course, a language issue in Wales but language policies there are aimed at bilingualism not at making Welsh the sole language of public and business life. Nor is proficiency in Welsh an indispensable marker of Welsh identity.

The other comparator, Spain, has not had a long democratic tradition and has been largely ignored by commentators on constitutional reform on Britain. This is a pity as it offers many parallels with Britain, especially if one considers all parts of Spain and not just Catalonia. The constitution does not refer to Spain as a federation, less than a quarter of the members of the upper house of parliament, the Senate, are elected from the regions, and mechanisms for securing the collaboration of the regions in national government are few. Instead commentators characterize Spain as a 'state of autonomies', a state composed of autonomous communities (Heywood 1995; Colomer 1999; Magone 2004). The relation of each of these communities to the government in Madrid is defined primarily by its statute of autonomy but also by subsequent agreements. The key feature of this system is that it is one of asymmetrical devolution. The autonomous communities are not all equally autonomous. The most autonomous, Catalonia (Catalunya), and the Basque Country (Euskadi), are considered as historic nations. This does not mean that most Catalans and Basques regard themselves as Catalan or Basque only. On the contrary, most also consider themselves Spanish with a loyalty not just to a Spanish state but a Spanish nation (Heywood 1995: 34), though there is also a vein of Basque nationalism that is implacably anti-Spanish. The autonomy of Catalonia and the Basque Country is lodged in a combination of institutions, (fiscal) prerogatives and practices nominally restored from pre-Franco times, and institutions, (fiscal) prerogatives and practices newly adopted. A third region, Galicia (Galiza) has almost as much autonomy in recognition of a particular identity which also had some acknowledgement in pre-Franco times. As with Catalan in Catalonia and Basque in the Basque Country this has partly to do with language. Galician is not a Celtic language even though Galicia proclaims its Celtic past (as in its famous football team Celta Vigo) but a language with affinities to Portuguese. A fourth region, Andalusia (Andalucia), has obtained almost as much autonomy as the first three without making ethnicity, language, or historical precedent the basis of a special claim. A fifth, Navarre, has also been able to recover some traditional fiscal prerogatives. The other thirteen autonomous communities have less autonomy and more in common, but there are still variations. When no national party has had a majority in the national parliament regional parties have been able to give support to a would-be governing party in return for concessions to their regions.

This extraordinary 'state of autonomies' emerged unplanned from a process of constitution building in 1977–9 following the death of Franco in which the deals political parties did to secure what each most wanted blurred any principles of devolution. Bitter memory of the Civil War also encouraged compromise. In particular, although everyone was agreed on autonomy for Catalonia, the Basque Country, and Galicia, for the rest it was a question of local and regional interests making claims for regions that may have had a historical identity (such as Andalusia and Navarre) or may not (such as La Rioja) and getting them agreed. Castille (Castilla) was split in three, Madrid, Castille and León, and Castille-La Mancha. If power and money were going to be passed from Madrid to the regions, and political and administrative jobs were going to be created, no part of the country wanted to miss out. And all could invoke some way in which they had suffered at Madrid's hands in the past. The seventeen regions which emerged from this process vary in size from Castille-La Mancha with over 87,000 square kilometres to La Rioja and the Balearic Islands (Islas Baleares) each with just over 5,000, and in population from Andalusia with nearly 6.5 million and Catalonia with over 5.6 million to the Balearic Islands and La Rioja with just 0.25 million. They even vary in the way they style themselves. Twelve go by their geographical names alone. Five do not: Principado de Asturias, Communidad de Madrid, Región de Murcia, Communidad Foral de Navarra, and Communidad Valenciana. There also significant variations in the timings of their elections.

There is a tension in the Spanish system with regard to asymmetry. Catalonia and the Basque Country claim that they are nations not regions and should be treated differently accordingly. Other regions covet their additional powers and manœuvre to obtain them for themselves. In so far as they succeed, Catalonia and the Basque Country seek additional powers to maintain their difference from other regions. In a minor way this also applies to differences between other regions in a game of 'competitive griev- ance' (Colomer 1999). The system might thus be thought to be chronically unstable and a brake on Spain's modernization. There is certainly plenty of scope for dealing and corruption. But on the whole it seems to work and, with the help of EU structural funds, Spain has developed at a rapid rate.

Compared with France or Germany, Britain's constitution is not just un- written, it is unrationalized. Spain's constitution is written but with respect to regional autonomies it is also largely unrationalized, despite the periodic efforts of would-be rationalizers (Magone 2004). In Spain pragmatism and flexibility have yielded odd outcomes which are nevertheless sufficiently at- tuned to differing sensibilities in differing parts of the country to work quite well. The main lesson Spain offers is that there is no reason to suppose that asymmetrical devolution is a sure step to break-up or breakdown. And if England were to roll out regional assemblies with varying powers for an odd assortment of regions of varying size and identity that too might be work- able, the Spanish example suggests, provided the powers were substantial enough for regional politicians and electorates to take them seriously.

Will asymmetrical devolution in Britain lead in time to asymmetrical fed- eralism? It is impossible to say. It has not yet done so in Spain, and the trav- ails of implementing constitutional change and testing its scope can sate the appetite for more, but there does not seem any reason to preclude it. John Kendle (1997: 176) concluded his book *Federal Britain* with the suggestion that an idea whose time had never come, federalism, might yet do so in the twenty-first century as it offers 'a potential solution to the national and re- gional tensions within the United Kingdom' and 'a protection for both unity and diversity rarely found in even the most pragmatic of unitary systems'. If it does, asymmetrical devolution is likely to have ensured it will be an asym- metrical federalism.

Britishness in the twenty-first century

In December 1999 Linda Colley gave a millennium lecture at 10 Downing Street in which she addressed this question: 'Since so many of the con- stituent parts of old-style Britishness have been dismantled or have ceased to function effectively, is it possible successfully to re-design and re-float a concept of Britishness for the 21st century?' Not persuaded that Britain was destined to break up, or be absorbed in a European superstate, she effectively answered 'possibly' and the possibility she supported was of Britain as a 'citizen-nation'. She invited her high-powered audience to 'leave intransigent issues of Britishness to look after themselves', let individuals choose their own identities, and focus instead on renovating British citizenship. Her stance is not so much complacent— Richard Weight's (2002: 732) complaint—as incoherent. Colley's preferred emphasis is on doing whatever is necessary to make the citizenship of all in Britain real by maximizing civil rights, equality of opportunity, political participation, and empowerment (an agenda with particular relevance to non-whites and women). She wants to convince 'all the inhabitants of these islands that they are equal and valued citizens irrespective of whatever identity they may individually select to prioritise'. There is nothing in this commitment peculiar to Britain. Colley speaks of citizenship in what are universal terms but to make such a citizenship meaningful, even inspirational, to Britons she has to connect it to British history and experience. Her citizenship project requires Britons to 'pillage the past selectively' and engage with the present, to evaluate heritage and make use of cultural and social capital.

Scotland, Wales Northern Ireland and England have in some respect different visions of the past, but not entirely so. We could all, surely, agree to commemorate the abolition of the slave trade back in 1806, something which all these islands, and black Britons as well as whites, took part in. We could all commemorate the Reform Act of 1832, the first step towards achieving universal suffrage here.

We could all, now, commemorate the Catholic Emancipation of 1829, or the end of Jewish disabilities in the 1850s, or Votes for Women in 1918. And why shouldn't we commemorate independence for India in 1947, since it is part of our history too? (Colley 1999: n.p.)

But why is Britain a better vehicle for the citizen-nation than Scotland, Wales, or England? Colley's indirect answer is that 'Britishness is a synthetic and capacious concept with no necessary ethnic or cultural overtones.' This is an overstatement—Britishness does have necessary cultural overtones, not least the paramountcy of the English language—but it reminds us that the treaty of union of 1707 guaranteed that there would always be more than one way of being British and 'synthetic and capacious', combinatory and accommodative, do describe what has been a basic feature of Britishness for centuries and must continue to be so. What Colley calls the 'multi-national, multi-cultural, infinitely diverse' reality of today's British polity confirms that the synthesizing is unending. When discussing England, I commented that English England has its historical continuities but it is also layered, variegated, and ever-changing as each generation, and each new source of people and ideas, engages with the peculiar mix of what has gone before. I added that this thought allows confidence when considering the Cosmopolitan England of today and tomorrow, as it does, too, when contemplating Cosmopolitan Britain.

Colley's advocacy of the citizen-nation also calls to mind T. H. Marshall's account of the development of British citizenship published in 1949 and discussed in Ch. 2. The third phase in the development of citizenship in Britain, according to Marshall (1949: 74), had to do with enabling citizens to realize the full range of social rights 'from the right to share to the full in the social heritage and to live the life of a civilized being according to the standards prevailing in the society'. To this end the post-war Labour government embarked on massively extending the provision of health, education, and welfare. Today the notion that the welfare state is the best way to guarantee provision of health, education, and welfare for all is contested but what is not contested is that health, education, and welfare are indispensable if citizens are to realize their civil and political rights and share to the full in their social heritage. They are also essential if citizens are to realize something Marshall did not separate out, their economic rights—especially their right to work. We are also much clearer today than Marshall was that making real the rights of women lags behind making real the rights of men. But perhaps Marshall's most fundamental limitation is that he assumed a basically unicultural social heritage albeit one with some differentiation according to class. He did not concern himself with differences of national and regional culture within Britain, nor did he anticipate the multiculturalism that was to follow from the migration to Britain of people from the Caribbean, the Indian subcontinent, Africa, and elsewhere. Given this fuller understanding of what the realization of citizenship entails, and given a more diverse population, Colley's citizen-nation project for Britain can be seen for the comprehensive challenge it is.

In her lecture Colley surmises that in a century's time Britishness might well not signify much, and this might not matter much. Citizenship would have eclipsed nationhood. This is surely a misjudgement in that the full realization of citizenship for all citizens could only be a British achievement in two ways (though it might also be a European achievement or the achievement of some polity greater still). First, it would be a prodigious achievement that could bring Britain only acclaim unless one assumes it would also be achieved universally. Second, it could be only a situated achievement. If each new generation, and each new source of people and ideas, engages with the peculiar mix of what has gone before, the full realization of civil, political, social, and cultural rights cannot but bear the marks of British history and life in Britain. Of course, what, in a century's time, those marks would be cannot be predicted now.

In Ch. 2 I indicated the position I took after first engaging with Colley's *Britons* but before exploring seriously questions of nation in Scotland, Wales, and England, namely that a post-imperial Britain might be reforgeable in terms of some distinctive configuration of common culture, the riches of multiculturalism, differences from Europe, the product of internal migration and intermarriage, and positively valued aspects of Britain's historical legacy. This is still my view but with added recognition of some of the comfortable mundanities of British Britain.[3] I also remarked at the outset that Britain seemed to be heading towards an unargued and unplanned asymmetrical federalism but that if it were to break up it would be because Scotland so decided. These are still my views except that the Spanish precedent prompts the thought that asymmetrical devolution in Britain could last a long time. There is also no evidence as yet that devolution to Scotland will lead to a demand for dissolution of the union. On the contrary it is more likely that devolution has resecured the union for a generation or more. With the nation half of Colley's citizen-nation reinstated, there is much to be said for her citizen-nation project not only in terms of justice but also in terms of giving direction to the future development of Britain. Finally, I began this chapter by claiming that Cosmopolitan Britain is the one most consistent with economic and demographic trends. There are more ways of being cosmopolitan than being a member of the European Union (Colley hints that preoccupation with Europe can crowd out engagement with the wider world), but a more constructive engagement with the EU is, I submit, preferable to the likeliest alternatives, overregard for an America careless about Britain or retreat into the sour Little Britain version of a British Britain.

NOTES

1 All the figures in this paragraph are from National Statistics. See <www.statistics.gov.uk/cci/nugget_print.asp?ID=766 and 767>, accessed 1 June 2005.

2 Although I use the Anglicized spellings of Quebec and Montreal without the acute accents, I refer to Québécois in connection with an ethnic nation (which has then to acknowledge the presence of non-francophones in its territory). By contrast Quebeckers comprise all the inhabitants of Quebec. Tension persists between the ethnic and civic dimensions of Québécois nationalism. In 1996 French was the home language of 5.771 million Quebeckers (81.9% of the total) and 589,000 people elsewhere in Canada, principally 219,000 in New Brunswick (30.1%) and 287,000 in Ontario (2.7%) (Schmid 2001: 110).

3 Had I not run out of time and space I would like to have extended discussion to history and citizenship studies in the national curriculum in England, Scotland, and Wales, and to the citizenship ceremonies the Home Office has recently introduced for those acquiring British citizenship. It does seem odd that these ceremonies are being treated as private and not public events in the districts in which I live and work.

REFERENCES

COLLEY, LINDA (1992), *Britons: Forging the Nation 1707–1837* (New Haven, Conn.: Yale University Press).

—— (1999), 'Britishness in the 21 century', Millenium lecture at 10 Downing Street, 8 December 1999, <www.number-10.gov.uk/output/page3049.asp>, accessed 1 June 2005.

COLOMER, JOSEP M. (1999), 'The Spanish "state of autonomies": non-institutional federalism', in P. HEYWOOD (ed.), *Politics and Policy in Democratic Spain* (London: Frank Cass), 40–52.

HEYWOOD, PAUL (1995), *The Government and Politics of Spain* (Basingstoke: Macmillan).

KEATING, MICHAEL (2001), *Nations Against the State: The New Politics of Nationalism in Quebec, Catalonia and Scotland*, 2nd edn. (Basingstoke: Palgrave), 1st edn. 1996.

KENDLE, JOHN (1997), *Federal Britain: A History* (London: Routledge).

MAGONE, JOSÉ M. (2004), *Contemporary Spanish Politics* (London: Routledge).

MARSHALL, THOMAS H. (1949), 'Citizenship and social class', in his *Sociology at the Crossroads and Other Essays* (London: Heinemann, 1963), ch. 4.

LARRIVÉE, PIERRE (2003) (ed.), *Linguistic Conflict and Language Laws: Understanding the Quebec Question* (Basingstoke: Palgrave).

PAREKH, BHIKHU (2000), *Rethinking Multiculturalism: Cultural Diversity and Political Theory* (Basingstoke: Macmillan).

SCHMID, CAROLE L. (2001), *The Politics of Language: Conflict, Identity and Cultural Pluralism in Comparative Perspective*

(Oxford: Oxford University Press), esp. ch. 6.

SYKES, ALAN (2005), *The Radical Right in Britain* (Basingstoke: Palgrave).

WEIGHT, RICHARD (2002), *Patriots: National Identity in Britain 1940–2000* (London: Macmillan).

INDEX

A

Aaron, J 145
Abercrombie, Nicholas 9–10
Abrahams, Harold 176
Ackroyd, Peter 173
Act of Settlement, Succession (1701) 34, 72
Adams, Gerry 252, 254
Adamson, David 135
Adrian IV, Pope 240
Aethelred 166
agriculture, and Wales 134
Aidan, Saint 164
Aitchison, John 141, 142
Alfred the Great, King of Wessex 165, 168
Alibhai-Brown, Yasmin 22, 195
Allen, Charles 74
Allen, John 74
Americanization, and England 182
Amery, Leo 183
Amsterdam, Treaty of (1997) 263
Andalusia 292
Anderson, Benedict 2, 16
  and imagined communities 16–17
anglobalization, and British Empire 185
Anglo-Irish Treaty (1921) 244
Anglo-Saxons, and England 163–7
Anne, Queen 34, 72
Arbroath, Declaration of (1320) 77
armed forces 44
Armorica 3
Arshad, Rowena 106
Ascherson, Neal 64, 91–2
Aslet, Clive 182
Asquith, Herbert 243
asylum seekers 197, 279
asymmetry:
  and devolution:
    Great Britain 288, 293
    Spain 291–3
  and federalism:
    Canada 290
    Great Britain 12, 293, 296
  and localism, England 233

Athelstan 165, 166
Attlee, Clement 42
Aughey, Arthur 38, 252
Augustine, Saint 164, 166

B

Baber, Colin 138–9
Bagehot, Walter 183
Baird, John Logie 86
Baldwin, Stanley 173
Balmoral 75
Balsom, Denis 123–4, 139, 144
Bannockburn, Battle of (1314) 77, 78
Barker, Ernest 170, 177
Barnes, Julian 175
Barnett, Joel 54–5
Barnett formula, and public expenditure
  54–6, 218
Barry, Charles 35
Basque Country 291–3
BBC 92
  and British national identity 40
  and contemporary role of 44
  and non-recognition of British nation
  11
Beck, Ulrich 66
Beddoe, Deirdre 145
Bede 162–3, 164, 166, 168
Bennett, Alan 191
Betjeman, John 174
Betts, Sandra 145
Bevan, Aneurin 40, 136
Beveridge, Craig 88
Bianchi, Tony 130
Billig, Michael 24, 198–9
Blain, Neil 105
Blair, Tony 12, 45, 136, 211
Blake, William 175–6
Blunkett, David 197, 199
Body, Richard 186
Boer War 189
Bogdanor, Vernon 211, 234
Bond, Ross 95–6, 212

Booth, Charles 224
Borland, John 146
Bowie, Fiona 146
Boyce, George 248
Boyle, Mark 102
Boyle, Raymond 100
Boyne, Battle of the 241
Bracewell, Michael 179
Bradley, Joseph 102
Breuilly, John 18
Brewer, John 103
Britanny 3
British Airways 92, 187
British Commonwealth, see
Commonwealth
British Council 187
British Empire:
  and achievements of 188, 255–6
  and attitudes towards 187–8, 256
  and citizenship 276
  and end of 43, 187
  and England:
    anglobalization 185
    anti-imperialism 188–9
    English nationalism 183–6
  and formation of British identity 36,
    39–40, 255–6
  and Scotland 37, 39–40, 89–90
British Library 187
British Museum 187
British national identity 4–7
  and changes in 4–7
  and composite nature of 24, 274
  and ethnic minorities 50–1
  and formation of 33–4
    BBC 40
    British Empire 36, 39–40, 255–6
    common parliamentary system 40
    criticisms of Colley's argument 38–9
    development of British ruling class
      36–7
    economic factors 35–6
    industrialization 39
    intermarriage 40
    internal migration 40
    monarchy 37, 40
    Protestantism 34–5, 40, 170–1
    superimposition over other identities
      37–8

war and military service 36, 40
  welfare state 40
  and future of 295–6
    Colley and citizen-nation 293–5
  and hierarchies of 28–9
  and post-Imperial Britain 42–5
  and pre-1707 Britishness 39
  and reconstruction of 58
  and sport 25, 44–5
  and Whig imperialist interpretation
    41–2
British National Party 194, 196, 286
British Nationality Act (1948) 276
British Nationality Act (1981) 277
British Olympic Committee 92
British Red Cross Society 92
Brooke, Peter 250
Brooke, Rupert 174
Brubaker, Rogers 22, 24
  and state nationalization 33
Bruce, Duncan 86
Bruce, Robert, King of Scotland 77, 168
Bruce, Steve 99, 253
Bryce, Tom 84–5
Buchan, James 86
Buchanan, Archibald 86
Buck, Nick 224
Burke, Edmund 185
Burns, Robert 77, 79, 80
Bwrdd yr Iaith Gymraeg (Welsh Language
  Board) 141

C

Caborn, Richard 211–12
Cadwaladr 119
Callaghan, James 250
Calvinism, and Scottish church 82–4
Campaign for a North East Assembly
  219–20
Canada, and Quebec 288–91
Cannadine, David 9
capitalism, and internal colonialism thesis
  46–8
Cardiff 121, 149
Carson, William 249
Carter, Harold 141, 142
Catalonia 66, 291–3
Catholic Relief Act (1778) 34
Celtic Football Club 102

Chamberlain, Neville 183, 260
Chapman, Malcolm 76
Chariots of Fire 176
Charlottetown accords (1992) 289
Charlton, Jack 25
Chaucer, Geoffrey 168
Chesterton, G K 189
Childs, Peter 210
Church of England 18, 40
  and character of 170–1
  and marginalization of 43
  and origins of 169
  and Wales 131–2
Church of Scotland 43, 82–4
  and Catholics of Irish descent 99
  and Church and Nation Committee of
    99
  and Claim of Right (1842) 64
Churchill, Winston 41
  and Europe 258–9
citizenship:
  and British Empire 276
  and citizen-nation 293–5
  and European Union 278–9
  and Great Britain 275–8
  and Marshall on 41–2, 295
  and nationality 20–1
Claim of Right (1689) 64
Claim of Right (1842) 64
Claim of Right for Scotland (1988) 64, 94
class, and Labour Wales 136
Cnut 166–7
Coakley, John 246
Cohen, Anthony 103–4
Cohen, Robin 255–6, 258
Cold War, and end of 43
Cole, Dick 227, 228
collective representations, and nations
  15–16
Colley, Linda 89
  and citizen-nation 293–5
  and criticisms of argument of 38–9
  and formation of British national identity
    33–8, 170, 186
Collins, Michael 244
Collins, Neil 248
Colls, Robert 157–8, 179, 181–2, 200, 219,
  232

Commission for Racial Equality, and
  multiculturalism 196–7
Commission for Racial Equality in Scotland
  104
Commission for Racial Equality in Wales
  149
Common Agricultural Policy 267, 271
Commonwealth 256–8
  and citizenship 276
  and immigrants from 276–7
Commonwealth Games 198, 257
Commonwealth Immigrants Act (1962)
  277
Commonwealth Principles, Declaration of
  (1971) 257
Communist Party, and Scottish
  constitutional convention 94
composers, and construction of England
  173
comprehensive schools, and Scotland 100
Connolly, James 244
Connolly, William 23
Conservative Party 57
  and decline in Scotland 94–5
  and devolution 288
  and English nationalism 186
  and Scottish constitutional convention
    94
constitutional change:
  and Labour government 4, 157
  and national identity 4–6, 7
  and possible impact of 10
  see also devolution
constitutional convention (Scotland) 94
Cook, A J 136
Cornish language 227–8, 230
Cornwall 3
  and constitutional history of 226–7
  and Cornish language 227–8, 230
  and economy of 229
  and petition for Cornish Assembly
    229–30
  and regeneration of Cornishness 228
  and symbols of 229
Council for the Protection of Rural England
  178
countryside, and England 176, 178
Countryside Alliance 173

Cowethas an Yeth Kernewek (The Cornish Language Society) 228
Cox, Harvey 248
Cradden, Terry 248
Craig, James 245
Cranmer, Thomas 169
Crick, Bernard 177–8
cricket, and England 172–3
Cromwell, Oliver 169, 241
Culloden 34, 73, 79
Cumberland, Duke of 73
Curtice, John 7, 118, 160, 192
Cymdeithas yr Iaith Gymraeg (Welsh Language Society) 124, 131

D

Dahrendorf, Ralf 45, 275
Danelaw 165
Darien colony 80
Davidson, Neil 81
Davie, George 88
Davies, Charlotte Aull 136
Davies, James 139
Davies, Janet 117
Davies, John 48
Davies, Norman 9, 167, 240, 241, 254
Davies, Rees R 70, 168
Davis, Thomas 249
Day, Graham 47, 133–4, 135, 136, 146, 150–1
de Gaulle, Charles 271
de Quincey, Thomas 223
de Valéra, Éamon 244–5
Deacon, Bernard 227, 228
Deacon, Russell M 143
decision-making, political 13–14
   and European Union 260, 261–8
decolonization 42, 187–8
Dee, John 119
Defoe, Daniel 181
Delamont, Sara 141
De-la-Noy, Michael 171
Delanty, Gerard 240, 243–4, 245, 249, 266
Delors, Jacques 260, 261
Democratic Unionist Party 252
Development Board for Rural Wales 143
Devine, T M 37, 62, 89, 98, 99, 102
   and British Empire 90, 184
   and Highlands 72

and Little Scotland 91
and Scottish church 82
and Scottish Enlightenment 86
devolution 157
   and asymmetrical:
      Great Britain 288, 293
      Spain 291–3
   and Conservative resistance to 288
   and national identity 4–6, 7
   and possible impact of 10
   and regional assemblies 209, 231–2
   and Scotland:
      referendum (1979) 93
      referendum (1997) 94
   and Wales:
      administrative 143
      referendum (1979) 118
      referendum (1997) 118, 144
   see also National Assembly for Wales; regional assemblies; Scottish Parliament
Dickson, A D R 95
Dickson, M B 104
Diniz, Fernando 106
Disruption of 1843 83
Dodd, Philip 178
Dodd, Richard 181
Donald Bane (Donald III), King of Scotland 69
Drake, Sir Francis 169
Dummett, Ann 278
Dunkerley, David 150–1
Durkheim, Emile 15

E

Easter Rising 244, 246
Easthope, Anthony 173
Easton, David, and political decision-making 13–14, 260, 267–8
economic migrants 279
economy:
   and London 222–3
   and national/regional variations 52–3
   and performance of 43–4
   and Republic of Ireland 247
   and Scotland 93
   and transformation of 45
   and Wales 117–18
      foreign direct investment 147

Labour Wales 135–6
modernization 147–8
service sector 148
Y Fro Gymraeg (Welsh-speaking
Wales) 133–4
Edinburgh 69
Edinburgh Festival 109
Edmonds, Timothy 54
Edmunds, June 191–2
education:
and England, public schools 171, 178
and religious schools 275
and Scotland 84–6, 100, 101–2
and Wales 121–2
Welsh language 141
Y Fro Gymraeg (Welsh-speaking
Wales) 132–3
Education Act (1870) 132
Education Act (1902) 132
Education Act (1918) 101
Education Act (1944) 133
Education Act (1987) 150
Education Reform Act (1988) 133, 140, 141
Edward I 77, 120, 127
Edward II 77
Edward the Confessor 166
Edwards, Owen 101
Eisteddfods 129–30
electoral politics:
and national variations in representation
56–7
and Scotland 93–4
decline of Conservative Party 94–5
divergence from England 93–4
Labour Party 95
national identity 95–6
Scottish National Party 93, 95, 107
and Wales:
divergence from England 117–18
Labour Party 137
National Assembly for Wales 144–5,
151
Eliot, T S 174
Elis-Thomas, Dafydd 146
Elizabeth I 2, 35, 117, 169, 170
Elliott, Marianne 251
England:
and Anglo-Saxon period 163–7
and asymmetrical localism 233–4

and British Empire:
anglobalization 185
English nationalism 183–6
and constructions of 159–60, 200–1
Anglo-British England 182–8
Cosmopolitan England 191–200
Early England and Old England
162–9
English England 161–82
green and pleasant land 170–82
Little England 188–91
and cricket 172–3
and cultural diversity 193, 200
and dissociation from Britain 10–11
and education, public schools 171, 178
and English nationalism, displacement of
183–6
and ethnic minorities:
British identity 195
British Muslims 195, 197–8
ethnic segregation 195–6
Parekh Report 194–5
and European Union, attitudes towards
189–90
and flag of St George 198–9
and foxhunting 173
and immigration 189, 192, 193, 194
and language:
Anglo-Saxon period 164, 165
ethnic minorities 196
Norman French 167
and multiculturalism 193–4
different experiences of 51, 193, 222
hostility to 190
need for interaction 196
questioning of 196–7
and national identity 4–7
conflation of England/Britain 183
debate over 157–8
ethnic minorities 195
identification with Britishness 158,
187
impact of crown in parliament 158,
200
multiple constructions of 159–60
political attitudes 160–1
regional loyalties 158–9, 209
and Norman England 167
and origins of name 166

England: (*Continued*)
and parliamentary representation 56–7
and population:
  ethnic composition 50–1, 106, 193
  ethnic diversity 193
and pubs 172
and racism 189, 194
and re-Englishing of 167–8
and religion:
  Anglo-Saxon period 164
  Church of England's origins 169
  nature of Church of England 170–1
and representations of 173–5
  American influence 182
  countryside 176
  diverse attitudes 181
  diverse contributors to 181
  gentlemanliness 177–8
  heritage 176–7
  Jerusalem (Blake) 175–6
  landscape 176, 178
  political motives 179–81
  suburbia 179
and rule of law 166, 180
and Tudor period 168–9
and union with Scotland 1–2, 10–11
  terms of 35
see also English regions
English Heritage 187
English language 44
and Scotland 69–71, 78–9
English National Opera 187
English regions:
and Cornwall:
  constitutional history of 226–7
  Cornish language 227–8, 230
  economy of 229
  petition for Cornish Assembly 229–30
  regeneration of Cornishness 228
  symbolism 229
and definition of:
  administrative convenience 211–12
  conformity with European Union 211–12
  disregard of popular sentiment 232–4
  problems with 212
and future of 234–5

and Government Offices in the Regions 211
  growth of 214
and government regional structures 211
and London:
  distinctiveness of 221–2
  economy of 222–3
  elected mayor 4
  ethnic composition 50–2, 106, 193
  governing difficulties 224–5
  Government Office for London 225
  government structure 223–4
  Greater London Authority 216, 223, 225–6
  housing 222
  inequality 222
  Mayor of London 226
and North-East:
  ethnic homogeneity 218
  regional identity of 217–18
  rejection of elected assembly 209, 220–1
  relative disadvantage of 218–19
and regional assemblies/government 4
  assessing demand for elected 216
  claimed advantages of 230–1
  complement to devolution 209, 231–2
  government proposal for elected 215–16
  membership of 215
  North-East's rejection of elected 209, 220–1
  role of 214
and Regional Development Agencies 4, 211
  The Northern Way 234
  role of 214
and regional identity:
  distance from London 214
  polling on strength/weakness of 212–14
  regional loyalties 158–9, 209
  weakness of 210–11, 232–3
ethnic communities, and characteristics of 19
ethnic minorities:
  and British Muslims 195, 197–8

and England:
  British identity   195
  ethnic segregation   195–6
  Parekh Report   194–5
and English language   196
and national/regional variations   50–1,
  193
and Scotland   105–7
and Wales   148–9
Eton   171
Eurobarometer, and British attitudes to
  European Union   269–71
European Coal and Steel Community   258
European Commission   261, 264–5
European Council   263
European Economic Community   247
  and Britain joins   43, 257
European Parliament   264, 265
  and turnout in elections to   269
European Union   4, 43
  and absence of European public opinion
    261–2
  and *acquis communautaire*   263, 264
  and beneficiaries of   267
  and boundaries of   260–1
  and citizenship   278–9
  and Common Agricultural Policy   267,
    271
  and complexity of   259, 268
  and confusing nature of   264–5, 266–7,
    268
  and Constitution for Europe   260, 263,
    264
    principles of   262
  and construction projects, funding of
    267
  and diversity of   261
  and England:
    attitude of   189–90
    regional definitions   211–12
  and European identity, difficulties with
    262–7
  and European integration   261, 265
  and evolution of   259
  and Great Britain   274
    attitude of   191
    Eurobarometer opinion surveys
      269–71
    European election turnout   269

Euroscepticism of   271–4
and intergovernmental principle   264
and media   261
and opt-outs   263
and origins of, British attitudes   258–9
and 'pillars' of   263
and political decision-making   260,
  261–8
and Scotland   107–9
and supranational principle   264
and treaty-based foundation of
  262–3
Euroscepticism, British:
  and doubts over membership benefits
    271–3
  and Eurobarometer opinion surveys
    269–71
  and European election turnout   269
  and linguistic abilities   273
  and national sovereignty   271
  and role of the press   273–4

F

Fainstein, Susan   224
Fawkes, Guy   241
federalism, asymmetrical:
  Canada   290
  Great Britain   12, 293, 296
Ferguson, Adam   86
Ferguson, Niall   90, 185, 255, 256
Fernández-Armesto, Felipe   210–11
Fevre, Ralph   147
Fianna Fáil   244
Findlay, Donald   101
flags:
  and Cornish   229
  and feelings towards English and Scottish
    7
  and rediscovery of English   198–9
Fleming, Alexander   86
football:
  and Home Internationals   63, 274–5
  and national identity   25, 45
  and Scotland   92
Forbes, Douglas   105
foreign direct investment, and Wales
  147–8
foxhunting, and England   173
France, as civic nation   22

Frayn, Michael 191
Free Church of Scotland 83, 84
Fry, Michael 37, 89, 90, 184

G

Gaelic language, and Celtic Scotland
    68–71
Galicia 291–2
Gamble, Andrew 43
Gellner, Ernest 18
    and invention of nations 16
General Household Survey, and national
    identity 6–7
gentleman, the, and England 177–8
Geoffrey of Monmouth 39
George, David Lloyd 136
George I 34, 72
George II 34, 73
George III 34, 37
George IV 75
Germany, as ethnic nation 22
Gervais, David 173
Giddens, Anthony 12, 18, 268
    and nation states 18–19
Giles, Judy 173
Gilroy, Paul 195
Gladstone, William Ewart 243
Glancey, Jonathan 224
Glasgow 105
    as European City of Culture 109
globalization, and England 182
Glorious Revolution 34, 63, 122, 158, 169
Glyn Dŵr, Owain 120
Good Friday Agreement 4, 249, 251–2
Goodhart, David 197
Goodman, James 248
Gordon, Ian 224
Gordon, Lord George 34
Gordon Riots 34
Gott, Richard 189
Goulbourne, Harry 188
Government of Ireland Act (1920) 244
Government of Wales Act (1998) 145
Government Offices in the Regions
    211
    and growth of 214
    and London 225
Grant, Alexander 9
Grattan, Henry 242

Great Britain:
    and accommodation of difference 275
    and citizenship 275–8
    as civic nation 23–4, 186, 274, 275
    and constitutional changes 4
    and construction of nations of 26–9
    and contemporary constructions of
        284–7
        British Britain 285–6
        Cosmopolitan Britain 286–7
        Great Britain 284–5
    and debate over future of 7–9
    and definition of 2
    and different meanings of 1–2
    and dissolution of 10–11, 58–9
    and economy, national/regional
        variations 52–3
    and establishment of 1, 3
    and European Union 274
        origins of 258–9
    and Euroscepticism:
        attitudes towards 191
        doubts over membership benefits
            271–3
        Eurobarometer opinion surveys
            269–71
        European election turnout 269
        linguistic abilities 273
        national sovereignty 271
        role of the press 273–4
    and historians' approach to 9
    and internal colonialism thesis 46–8
    and meaning of 'Great' 3
    and nationality 275–8
    and Northern Ireland 249–55
    and parliamentary representation,
        national variations in 56–7
    and political culture:
        Labour Wales 136–7
        national variations in 57
        Scotland 95–6
        Y Fro Gymraeg (Welsh-speaking
            Wales) 134–5
    and population:
        ethnic composition 50–1, 106, 193
        Irish descent 254
        national differences 48–9
    and public expenditure:
        Barnett formula 54–6, 218

national/regional variations   52–6
and social scientists' approach to   9–10
and Whig imperialist interpretation
   41–2
see also British national identity
Great Reform Act (1832)   40
Greater London Authority   216, 223, 225–6
Greater London Council   223, 225
Green Party, and Scottish constitutional
   convention   94
Greenwood, Arthur   183
Gregory, Pope   164, 166
Grundy, Sue   108
Guy, John   48
gwerin, and Welsh national identity
   122–3, 127–8
   components of   135
   economy   133–4
   education   132–3
   language and culture   128–31
   politics   134–5
   religion   131–2

H

Habermas, Jürgen   37, 265
Hague, William   57, 186
Hansen, Randall   277
Harare Declaration (1991)   257
Hardie, Keir   136
Harding, Alan   230
Harloe, Michael   224
Harper, Marjory   89
Harris, Chris   133
Harvie, Christopher   89, 159
Haseler, Stephen   37, 182
Hassan, Gerry   110
Hastings, Adrian   17
Hastings, Battle of   166
Hastings, Warren   185
Hayes, Bernadette   248, 253
Hazell, Robert   209
Hearn, Jonathan   64
Heath, Anthony   160, 192
Heath, Ted   272, 277
Hechter, Michael   37
   and internal colonialism   46–8
Heffer, Simon   8, 181, 182
Henig, Stanley   262–3, 265, 266
Henry II   167, 168, 240

Henry III   120
Henry IV   168
Henry V   168
Henry VII   39
Henry VIII   18, 39, 117, 119, 120, 127, 169,
   217, 240
Herman, Arthur   86
Hetherington, Peter   221
Highlands:
   and barbarous Highlands   72
   and Celtic Scotland   72–6
   and Highland clearances   71, 75
   and invented traditions   74–5
   and Jacobite Highlands   72–4
   and religious profile   84
   and romantic Highlands   74–5
Historic Scotland   79
Hitchens, Peter   8, 33
Hobbes, Thomas   169
Hobsbawm, Eric   18, 74
Hobson, J A   189
Hogwood, Brian   211
Hong Kong   43, 187, 277–8
Honourable Society of Cymmrodorion
   129
housing, and London   222
Howell, David   138–9
Hume, David   86
Humes, Walter   84–5
Hunt, Tristram   157, 199
Hurd, Douglas   44
Hussain, Asifa   105
Hutcheson, Francis   86
Hutton, James   86

I

Ichijo, Atsuko   107
imagined communities   16–18
immigration:
   and Commonwealth citizens   276–7
   and Cosmopolitan Britain   287
   and economic migrants   279
   and England   189, 192, 193, 194
   and nationality/citizenship law   276–8
   and Ugandan Asians   277
Immigration Act (1971)   277
India   42
industrialization:
   and formation of British identity   39
   and Wales   135–6

inequality:
  and London 222
  and national/regional variations
    52–3
Inner London Education Authority 223
intellectuals, and nation formation
  15, 17
internal colonialism thesis 46–8
International Eisteddfod 130
International Olympic Committee
  92
International Red Cross 92
invented traditions:
  and Highlands 74–5
  and Wales 129–30
Ireland 3
  and home rule 243
  and incorporation in United Kingdom
    242–3
  and Irish nationalism 243, 244
  in nineteenth century 243
  and Norman invasion of 240
  and partition of 244
  in Tudor/Stuart period 240–1
  see also Ireland, Republic of; Irish Free
    State; Northern Ireland
Ireland, Republic of 3, 245
  and British citizenship 278
  and Catholic church 247
  and economy of 247
  and European Economic Community
    247
  and Irish language 247
  and modernization of 246–7
  and national identity 246–7
  and nationalism 248
  and Northern Ireland 248–9
  and reunification 248–9
  see also Ireland; Irish Free State
Ireland Act (1949) 278
Irish Free State 3, 184, 244
  and British citizenship 278
  as Catholic state 245
  and civil war 244
  and irredentism 246
  and petit-bourgeois dominance 245
  see also Ireland; Ireland, Republic of
Irish Republican Army 244, 249, 253
Irish Republicans, and Scotland 102

J

Jackson, Colin 149
Jacobites 34, 72–3
  and Jacobite Scotland
    79–80
James, Evan 129
James, James 129
James I (James VI of Scotland) 2, 35, 39,
  72, 241
James II 34, 241
Jamieson, Lynn 108
Jenkins, Richard 28
Jenkins, Roy 258, 261
Jerusalem (Blake) 175–6
John Bull 38
John Paul II, Pope 99
Johnston, Sheila 176
Jones, Bill 10
Jones, J Barry 143–4
Jones, Peter 54, 89, 218
Jones, Richard Wyn 144

K

Kariel, Henry 13
Kearney, Hugh 9
Kearney, Richard 249
Keating, Michael 104, 288–9
Kellas, James 83, 87, 106
Kelvin, Lord (William Thomson)
  86
Kendle, John 293
Kennedy, Charles 91
Kesva an Tavas Kernewek (The Cornish
  Language Board) 228
Khan, Amir 199
Kidd, Colin 86–7
Kiely, Richard 26, 79
King, Gregory 48
Kinnock, Neil 136
Knox, John 82, 169
Krejčí, Jaroslav 66
Kumar, Krishan 158, 166, 170, 183–4, 187,
  199–200, 255
Kureishi, Hanif 188

L

Labour Party:
  and Scotland 95

and Scottish constitutional convention 94

and Wales 137

   National Assembly elections (1999) 144–5

Lamont, Stewart 86

Lancaster, Bill 232

landscape, and England 176, 178

Langland, William 168

Langlands, Rebecca 183

language:

   Cornish 227–8, 230

   English 44

      Anglo-Saxon period 164, 165

      ethnic minorities 196

      Scotland 69–71, 78–9

   French, in Quebec 289

   Gaelic 68–71

   Irish 247

   Norman French 167

   Scots 78–9

   Welsh 117, 123, 128, 150

      economic implications 148

      education 132–3

      Welsh Language Act (1993) 131, 140, 141–2

legal systems:

   and Scotland 87

   and Wales 120

Leicester 200

Lewis, Sanders 130

Lhuyd, Humphrey 119

Liberal Democrat Party, and Scottish constitutional convention 94

Liddell, Eric 176

Livingstone, David 89, 185

Livingstone, Ken 216, 225, 226

Llanover, Lady 130, 145

Llywelyn ap Gruffudd (Llywelyn II) 119–20, 126

Llywelyn ap Iorweth (Llywelyn I, the Great) 119

local government, and asymmetrical localism 233–4

Locke, John 169

Logue, Paddy 91

London:

   and distinctiveness of 221–2

   and economy of 222–3

   and elected mayor 4

   and ethnic composition 50–2, 106, 193

   and governing difficulties 224–5

   and Government Office for London 225

   and government structure 223–4

   and Greater London Authority 216, 223, 225–6

   and housing 222

   and inequality 222

   and Mayor of London 226

London County Council 223

Lowry, L S 139

Lynch, Peter 100

M

Maastricht, Treaty of (1992) 259, 263, 264, 265, 278

McCall, Cathall 252

McAllister, Ian 248, 253

Mac Alpin, Kenneth 67

McConnell, Jack 107

McCrone, David 47, 62, 64, 79, 102, 104

   and Presbyterianism 84

   and types of Scot 97

MacDiarmid, Hugh 80, 91, 200

McIntosh, Ian 105

MacIntyre, Alasdair 275

Mackay, Jane 178

Mackay of Clashfern, Lord 84

MacKenzie, John 90

MacKinnon, Kenneth 68–9, 71

MacLaughlin, Jim 243, 244

McLean, Iain 54

MacMillan, James 84, 92, 100–1, 103

McQuail, Paul 216

Madgwick, Peter 124, 139

Major, John 93, 103, 118, 180–1, 186, 211

Malcolm III Ceannmor, King 69

Manchester Metro 231

manufacturing, and Wales 147–8

Marquand, David 41

Marr, Andrew 8, 223

Marshall, T H, and citizenship 41–2, 295

Matless, David 178

Maver, Irene 98

Mebyon Kernow (Sons of Cornwall) 228, 229, 230

Medhurst, Kenneth 170

media:
  and European Union 261
  and Euroscepticism 273–4
  and Scotland 87
Mee, Arthur 173
Meech Lake accord (1987) 289
Mercia 163–4
Michael, Alun 145
Middleton, Tim 173
migration, internal, and British national
  identity 40
military service 36, 40, 44
Millar, John 86
Miller, William 105
Milton, John 169
Mitchell, Austin 210, 212
Mitchell, James 110
monarchy:
  and contemporary role of 44
  and formation of British identity 37, 40
Monmouthshire 120–1
Montgomery, Treaty of (1267) 119
Moreno, Luis 4
Morgan, Kevin 219, 232
Morgan, Prys 127–8, 129
Morgan, Rhodri 145
Morgannwg, Iolo (Edward Williams) 129
Morris, Angela 79
Morrison, John 75
Morton, Graeme 90
Morton, H V 173
Mouffe, Chantal 14
Moyser, George 170
Mrs Brown (film) 37
Muir, Edwin 80
multiculturalism:
  and different experiences of 51, 193,
    222
  and distribution of ethnic minority
    population 51, 193
  and England 193–4
    hostility to 190
    need for interaction 196
  and questioning of 196–7
  and Scotland 106, 110
  and Wales 149
Munday, Max 147
Murray, David 81
Museum of Scotland 77, 92, 187

Museum of Welsh Life 130, 136–7
Muslim Council of Britain 198

N

Nairn, Tom 1, 7, 63, 110, 158
national anthems 187
  'Flower of Scotland' 78
  'God save the King' 73
  'Land of My Fathers' 129
National Assembly for Wales 118, 140, 144
  and civil society 150–1
  and dual role of 146
  and elections to 144–5, 151
  and powers and responsibilities 145
National Covenant (1638) 64
National Eisteddfod 129–30
National Front 194
National Gallery 187
National Gallery of Scotland 92, 187
National Health Service 187
  and British national identity 40
  and Labour Wales 137
national identity:
  and markers of 26
  and multiple 157
  and political decision-making
    13–14
  see also British national identity; England;
    Scotland; Wales
National Library of Wales 130, 187
National Trust 92, 172, 176, 177, 187
National Trust for Scotland 92, 187
nationalism 25
  and displacement of English 183–6
  and Ireland 243, 244, 248
nationality:
  and citizenship 20–1
  and Great Britain 275–8
Nationality, Immigration and Asylum Act
  (2002) 277
nations:
  and appeal of 24–5
  and attributes of 19–20
  and citizenship 20–1
  as civic nations 19, 22
  and collective representations 15–16
  and constructions of 26–9
  and daily reproduction of 24
  as ethnic nations 19–22

as imagined communities 16–18
and invention of 16
and myth of common ancestry 21–2
and nation states 18–19
and nationalism 25
and people as 18
and pluralism 22–3
and political decision-making 13–14
and Weber on 14–15
Navarre 292
Nelson, Horatio 183
Netherlands 22, 275
Newman, Gerald 38
newspapers:
    and European Union 261
    and Euroscepticism 273–4
    and Scotland 87
Newton, Isaac 169
Nicol, Andrew 278
Nonconformism, and Wales 131–2
North Sea oil 93
Northampton, Treaty of (1328) 77
North-East Constitutional Convention 219
North-East England region:
    and Campaign for a North East Assembly 219–20
    and ethnic homogeneity 218
    and regional identity of 217–18
    and rejection of elected assembly 209, 220–1
    and relative disadvantage of 218–19
Northern Ireland 3
    and British attitude to 250, 253–4
    and civil rights campaign 250–1
    and economy of 251
    and end of discrimination 251
    and Good Friday Agreement 4, 249, 251–2
    and Protestant unionist control of 249–50
    and Republic of Ireland 248–9
    and sectarianism 252
    and 'The Troubles' 251
Northern Way, The 234
Northumbria 69
Northwest Regional Development Agency 231
nuclear weapons 43, 44

O

O'Connell, Daniel 243
Ó Dochartaigh, Cathair 247
Offa, King of Mercia 163–4
Offa's Dyke 126, 163–4
O'Hagan, Andrew 100–1
oil, and Scotland 93
Oldham 195–6
O'Mahoney, Patrick 240, 243–4, 245, 249
O'Neill, Terence 250
Orange Order 250
    and Scotland 102
Orwell, George 174, 177, 179–80
Osmond, John 143, 151, 182
Ossian 75
Ousby, Ian 176–7
Owen, Hugh 132

P

painters, and construction of England 173
Paisley, Ian 47, 252, 253, 254
Palmerston, Lord 37
Parekh, Bhikhu 106, 193, 290
Parekh Report (2000) on the *Future of Multi-Ethnic Britain* 194
parliamentary representation, and national variations 56–7
Parnell, Charles 243
Parry, Hubert 175
Partridge, Simon 39, 157, 210
Patchett, Keith 151
Paterson, Iain 98
Paterson, Lindsay 62, 66, 103, 106, 144
patriality, and immigration 277
Paxman, Jeremy 9, 37, 157, 176
Payton, Philip 3, 227, 228, 230
Pearse, Pádraic 244
Pentreath, Dolly 227
Peterborough chronicle 167
Pevsner, Nikolaus 173
Phillips, Mike 193
Phillips, Trevor 193, 197
Pick, Frank 224
Pilgrimage of Grace (1536) 217
Pittock, Murray 79–80, 83, 108, 109, 110
Pius IX, Pope 98
Plaid Cymru, the Party of Wales 134, 136
    and electoral performance 137

Plaid Cymru, the Party of Wales (*Continued*)
and National Assembly elections (1999) 144–5
pluralism, and nations 22–3
Poland 21
political culture:
and Labour Wales 136–7
and national variations in 57
and Scotland 95–6
and Y Fro Gymraeg (Welsh-speaking Wales) 134–5
politics, and decision-making model 13–14
and European Union 260, 261–8
population:
and ethnic composition 50–1, 106, 148–9, 193
and national differences 48–9
post-Imperialism, and British national identity 42–5
poverty, and London 222
Powell, David 39
Powell, Enoch 191
Poynings, Edward 242
Presbyterianism, and Scotland 40, 74, 76, 82–4
Prescott, John 210, 216, 220, 234
Priestley, J B 173, 182, 189
printing, and imagined communities 17, 18
Protestantism:
and British national identity 34–5, 40, 170–1
and decline in 43
public expenditure:
and Barnett formula 54–6, 218
and national/regional variations 52–6
public schools, and England 171, 178
pubs, and England 172
Pugin, Augustus 35

Q

Quebec 288–91

R

racism:
and England 189, 194
and Scotland 106–7, 109

Raleigh, Sir Walter 169
Rallings, Colin 221
Ranger, Terence 74
Rawkins, Phillip 134
Redmond, John 243
Redwood, John 8
Rees, Gareth 141
Rees, Teresa 145
regional assemblies 4
and assessing demand for elected 216
and Campaign for a North East Assembly 219–20
and claimed advantages of 230–1
as complement to devolution 209, 231–2
and government proposals for elected 215–16
and membership of 215
and North-East's rejection of elected 209, 220–1
and petition for Cornish Assembly 229–30
and role of 214
Regional Development Agencies 4, 211
and The Northern Way 234
and role of 214
regionalism, *see* English regions; regional assemblies
Reith, Lord 40
religion:
and British Muslims 198
and England:
Anglo-Saxon period 164
Church of England's origins 169
nature of Church of England 170–1
and Scottish church 82–4
and Wales, Y Fro Gymraeg (Welsh-speaking Wales) 131–2
see also Roman Catholicism
religious schools 275
Renan, Ernest 24
Renfrew, Colin 68
representation, and nations 15–16
Richard, Lord 145
Rifkin, Jeremy 259
Robbins, Keith 38, 39–40
Roberts, Brian 136
Robertson, Douglas 105
Robertson, William 86

Rogers, Byron 130–1
Roma 21
Roman Catholicism 34–5, 40, 43
  and Irish Free State 245
  and Republic of Ireland 247
  and Scotland:
    Catholics of Irish descent 98–103
    hostility in 83, 84
Rome, Treaty of 4, 190, 259
Rosebery, Lord 256
Rosie, Michael 96, 102, 103
Rosser, Phylip 133
Royal Mail 187
Royal Society 187
Royal Ulster Constabulary 249
Rule Britannia 36
rule of law, and England 166, 180
ruling class, and development of British
  36–7
Rumford, Chris 266
Russell, G W E 170–1
Ryder Cup 25

S

Saeed, Amir 105
Sandford, Mark 216
Schengen agreement 263
Schmitter, Philippe 261–2, 266
Schwarz, Bill 37–8, 159
Scotland:
  and British Empire 37, 39–40, 89–90
  and civil society:
    education system 84–6, 100, 101–2
    legal system 87
    media 87
    post-1707 development of 82
    Scottish church 82–4
  and constructions of 65–7
    Celtic Scotland 67–76
    Civic and Self-Governing Scotland
      92–107
    Civil Scotland 80–8
    Jacobite Scotland 79–80
    Little Scotland 90–2
    Scotland in Europe 107–9
    Scotland in the Empire 89–90
    Scotland the Brave 76–80
  and devolution 4
    constitutional convention 94

referendum (1979) 93
referendum (1997) 94
  and dissociation from Britain 10–11
  and economy 93
  and electoral politics:
    decline of Conservative Party 94–5
    divergence from England 93–4
    Labour Party 95
    national identity 95–6
    Scottish National Party 93, 95, 107
  and English in 103–5, 139–40
    anti-English sentiment 103–4
    as invisible minority 104–5
    number of 103
    Scottishing of 104, 105
  and European Union 107–9
  and the Highlands 72–6
    religious profile 84
  and homogenization of 110
  as independent state 76–8
  and internal colonialism thesis 46–7
  and language:
    English 69–71, 78–9
    Gaelic 68–71
    Scots 78–9
  and national identity 4–7
    ambivalence about Britain 63
    Catholics of Irish descent 100, 102
    class divisions 64–5
    covenants and claims of right tradition
      64
    impact of crown in parliament 63
    internal divisions 63
    markers of 97
    political non-alignment of 95–6
    primacy of Scottish identity 62–3
    public administration system 65
    types of Scot 97
  and non-white population of 105–7
  and origins of 67–8
  and parliamentary representation
    56–7
  and political culture 95–6
  and population:
    decline in 48–9
    ethnic composition 50–1, 106, 193
  and public expenditure 52, 53–4
    Barnett formula 54–6
  and racism 106–7, 109

Scotland: (*Continued*)
  and Roman Catholicism:
    Catholics of Irish descent   98–103
    hostility to   83, 84
  and sectarianism   103, 109
  and tartans   74–5
  and union with England   1–2, 10–11, 80
    terms of   35, 80–1
  see also Scottish Parliament
Scott, Peter   1
Scott, Sir Walter   74, 75
Scottish Convention of Women   94
Scottish Covenant of   1949 64
Scottish Development Agency   93
Scottish Enlightenment   86–7
Scottish Football Association   92
Scottish National Party   80
  and British Empire   90
  and electoral performance   93, 95, 107
  and Europe   107, 108
  and North Sea oil   93
  and Scottish constitutional convention
    94
Scottish Parliament   93, 96–7
Scottish Premier League   92
Scottish Trades Union Congress   94
Scruton, Roger   157, 173, 181, 182
Second World War, and British national
  identity   40
sectarianism:
  and Northern Ireland   252
  and Scotland   103, 109
Seeley, John   159
Shakespeare, William   163, 169
Sianel Pedwar Cymru (S4C)   131
Silicon Glen   93
Sillars, Jim   107
Sim, Duncan   105
Single European Act (1986)   259, 263
Sinn Féin   244, 252, 253
Smith, Adam   86
Smith, Anthony   21
  and characteristics of nations   19–20
  and ethnic communities   19
  and nationalism   25
Smith, Dai   122, 123, 136
Smith, Godfrey   173
Social Democratic and Labour Party   252
Solemn League and Covenant (1643)   64

Spain   66
  and asymmetrical devolution   291–3
sport:
  and national identity   25, 44–5, 63,
    274–5
  and rediscovery of English flag   198–9
  and separate Scottish identity   92
Stapleton, Julia   178
Startup, Richard   133
statehood, and nations   18–19
Staunton, Howard   171
Storry, Mike   210
Stoyle, Mark   228
Stringer, Keith   9
Stuart, Charles Edward ('Bonnie Prince
  Charlie')   34, 71, 73
Stuart, James Edward ('The Old Pretender')
  72
Stuart, Charles and John Sobięski (Charles
  and John Allen)   74
suburbia, and England   179
Suez crisis   42–3
Sutton Hoo   164

T

tartans, and Celtic Scotland   74–5
Taylor, A J P   189
Taylor, Peter   182
Tebbit, Norman   190–1, 197
Thane, Pat   178
Thatcher, Margaret   42, 45, 93, 94, 95, 103,
  118, 143, 186, 190, 225, 271
The Madness of King George (film)   37
Thomas, Dylan   139
Thomas, R S   130–1
Thompson, Andrew   150–1
Thompson, James   36
Thomson, William   86
Thrasher, Michael   221
Tilly, Charles   19
Tomaney, John   213, 214, 217, 219–20, 221,
  234
Tone, Theobald Wolfe   242
Tonge, Jonathan   252
Travers, Tony   225–6
Treaty of Union (1707)   35, 57, 64, 81
Tregidga, Garry   227, 228
Trevor-Roper, Hugh   74
Trimble, David   253

Tudor dynasty   119, 168–9
Turnbull, Richard   88
Turner, Bryan   191–2
Twigger, Robert   54

U

Ugandan Asians   277
Ulster Loyalists, and Scotland   102
Ulster Unionist Party   252
Ulster unionists   3, 11, 244
Ulster Volunteer Force   249
unemployment, and national/regional
  variations   52–3
United Free Church   83
United Kingdom, and origin of   3
  see also Great Britain
United Kingdom Independence Party   8,
  269
United Presbyterian Church   83
universities:
  and Scotland   85
  and Wales   130, 141
University of Wales   130
urbanization, and Wales   136

V

Van Mechelem, Denis   124, 139
Vaughan, William   173
Velímsky, Vitezslav   66
Versailles, Treaty of   21
Victoria, Queen   40, 75
Vikings   164–5

W

Wales   3
  and agriculture   134
  and civil society   143–4, 146, 150–1
  and constructions of   124–6, 149–50
    Anglo-British Wales   138–40
    Balsom's approach   123–4
    Cymru-Wales   140–6
    Labour Wales   135–8
    Modern Wales   146–9
    Y Fro Gymraeg (Welsh-speaking
      Wales)   126–35
  and devolution   4
    administrative   143
    referendum (1979)   118
    referendum (1997)   118, 144
  and economy:
    change   117–18
    foreign direct investment   147
    Labour Wales   135–6
    modernization   147–8
    service sector   148
    Y Fro Gymraeg (Welsh-speaking
      Wales)   133–4
  and education   121–2
    Welsh language   141
    Y Fro Gymraeg (Welsh-speaking
      Wales)   132–3
  and electoral politics:
    divergence from England   117–18
    Labour Wales   137
    National Assembly for Wales   144–5,
      151
  and English annexation of   117, 119–21,
    126–7
  and English in   139–40, 149
  and internal colonialism thesis   47
  and internal communications   121
  and invented traditions   129–30
  and legal system   120
  and national identity   4–7
    absence of history of statehood
      119–22
    ambivalence about Britain   118–19
    gwerin   122–3, 127–8, 135
    hierarchy of   28
    impact of crown in parliament   122
    language divide   123
    local production of   121
    multiple constructions of   123
  and parliamentary representation   56–7
  and political culture:
    Labour Wales   136–7
    Y Fro Gymraeg (Welsh-speaking
      Wales)   134–5
  and population, ethnic composition
    50–1, 148–9, 193
  and public expenditure   52–3
  and regional differences   121
  and religion, Y Fro Gymraeg
    (Welsh-speaking Wales)   131–2
  and urbanization   136
  and Welsh language   117, 150
    economic implications   148
    education system   132–3, 141

Wales (*Continued*)
    linguistic divide 123
    Welsh Language Act (1993) 131, 140,
      141–2
    Y Fro Gymraeg (Welsh-speaking
      Wales) 128
  and Welsh Office 142–4
  and women, in Cymru-Wales 145–6
Wales Tourist Board 139
Wallace, William 76–7, 168
Walls, Patricia 102
war, and formation of British identity 36,
  40
Ward, Neil 213, 217
Warde, Alan 9–10
Warhurst, Chris 110
Watson, Murray 104
Watt, James 86
Weber, Max 33
  and nations 14–15
Webster, Alexander 48
'wee frees' 83, 84
Weight, Richard 39, 43, 294
welfare state 295
  and British national identity 40
Wellings, Ben 186
Welsh Arts Council 143
Welsh Assembly, *see* National Assembly for
  Wales
Welsh Development Agency 143
Welsh Folk Museum 130
Welsh Intermediate Education Act (1889)
  133
Welsh language 117, 150
  and economic implications 148
  and education system 132–3
  and linguistic divide 123
  and Welsh Language Act (1993) 131, 140,
    141–2

  and Y Fro Gymraeg (Welsh-speaking
    Wales) 128
Welsh Language Act (1967) 131
Welsh Language Act (1993) 131, 140,
  141–2, 150
Welsh Language Board 141
Welsh Language Society 124, 131
Welsh Office 142–4
  and establishment of 140
Wessex 164–6
Westminster, Statute of (1931) 256, 276
Whig imperialism, and Great Britain 41–2
Whitby, Synod of 164
Wiener, Martin 176
Wilde, Oscar 173
Wilkes, John 36
William I (William of Normandy) 166,
  167
William III (of Orange) 241–2
Williams, Charlotte 149
Williams, Colin 146
Williams, Edward 129
Williams, Gwyn 2, 122, 128, 129
Williams, Hywel 142
Williams, Rory 102
Williamson, Roy 78
Wilson, Harold 250, 272
Winchester School 171, 186
Winder, Robert 174, 192
women, in Cymru-Wales 145–6
World Trade Organization 264
Wren, Christopher 169
Wyclif, John 168

Y

York, Treaty of (1237)
  76
Young, G M 170
Young Ireland 243